DEMON WITCH

Christopher Mitchell is the author of the epic fantasy series The Magelands. He studied in Edinburgh before living for several years in the Middle East and Greece, where he taught English. He returned to study classics and Greek tragedy and lives in Fife, Scotland with his wife and their four children.

By Christopher Mitchell

The Magelands Origins

Retreat of the Kell
The Trials of Daphne Holdfast
From the Ashes

The Magelands Epic

The Queen's Executioner
The Severed City
Needs of the Empire
Sacrifice
Fragile Empire
Storm Mage
Soulwitch Rises
Renegade Gods

The Magelands Eternal Siege

The Mortal Blade
The Dragon's Blade
The Prince's Blade
Falls of Iron
Paths of Fire
Gates of Ruin
City of Salve
Red City

City Ascendant
Dragon Eyre Badblood
Dragon Eyre Ashfall
Dragon Eyre Blackrose
Dreams of Kell
God Restrainer
Holdfast Imperium
World's End

THE MAGELANDS DOMINION

Serpent Dominion
Demon Witch
Death Seer

Cover by http://www.trifbookdesign.com/
Maps by Irina French

Brigdomin Books Ltd
First Edition, July 2023
ISBN 978-1-915978-14-1

To Angela

ACKNOWLEDGEMENTS

I would like to thank the following for all their support during the writing of the Magelands Dominion - my wife, Lisa Mitchell, who read every chapter as soon as it was drafted and kept me going in the right direction; my parents for their unstinting support; Marilyn Hopwood for reading the books in their early stages; James Aitken for his encouragement; and Grant and Gordon of the Film Club for their support.

Thanks also to my Advance Reader team, for all your help during the last few weeks before publication.

NOTE ON THE DOMINION CALENDAR

Due to a larger moon, Athumia's rotation is slower than that of the Earth, adding almost five minutes to each day; while the duration of Athumia's orbit around its Sun remains the same as the Earth's. This has brought the Lunar and Solar Calendars into alignment, allowing for Thirteen Months, each containing 28 days – creating a Solar Year of 364 days (with no Leap Day required). In response to this astronomical correspondence, High King Gahad devised the Dominion Calendar by shortening the existing months in the Divine Calendar to 28 days, and adding an extra month at the end of the year in his honour.

Each month (or 'inch') is named after one of the Twelve Ascendants (the old Gods); but over long millennia, the names have drifted from their originals.

In the Dominion Calendar, each year begins on the 1st day of Beldinch.

- Beldinch (January) – after Belinda, the Third Ascendant
- Summinch (February) – after Simon, the Tenth Ascendant
- Arginch (March) – after Arete, the Seventh Ascendant
- Nethinch (April) – after Nathaniel, the Fourth Ascendant
- Duninch (May) – after Edmond, the Second Ascendant
- Tradinch (June) – after Theodora, the First Ascendant
- Abrinch (July) – after Albrada, the Eleventh Ascendant
- Lexinch (August) – after Leksandr, the Sixth Ascendant
- Tuminch (September) – after Tamid, the Eighth Ascendant
- Luddinch (October) – after Lloyd, the Twelfth Ascendant
- Kolinch (November) – after Kolai, the Fifth Ascendant
- Essinch (December) – after Esher, the Ninth Ascendant
- Ghadinch (Extra Month) – after King Gahad, Praise be His Name

THE TWO EMPIRES OF ATHUMIA

The Two Empires of Athumia (in 1588, when *Demon Witch* takes place)

Two Empires dominate the continents of Athumia:

The Dragon Dominion – The Dominion originated in **Inopei** – a continent in the Eastern half of Athumia, with the arrival of the Dragon King. The calendar used in the Serpent Isle dates from the formation of the Dominion. The rule of the Dragons then spread south to encompass **Aucteran** and **Jalan**, and then the Dominion conquered the lands of the Bullan (**Klediomira Haga**). Upon completion of the conquests of Inopei, Aucteran and Jalan, the entire native population was exterminated by Dominion forces. There is no Dominion military presence on Klediomira Haga, as the Bullan are allied, rather than occupied. As tribute, the Bullan send soldiers each year to serve in the Dominion armed forces.

Much later (c.1300), when the Dominion began to cross the ocean to the Western half of Athumia, their forces also conquered **Elso** and **Irlan.** Dominion forces occupy Irlan and Elso, ruling over the native inhabitants, but they have recently withdrawn from the **Serpent Isle**. It is the stated aim and belief of the rulers of the Dragon Dominion that all of Athumia should be united under their sovereign authority.

The Gunstian Empire – Centred around the city of **Great Gunst**, the Gunstian Empire covers the northern portion of the western continent of **Kinheria**. Their Empire also includes the tributary state of **Tannum**, a heavily-forested region. Shielded by mountains and the Tvali Desert to the south, and protected by oceans on its other three flanks, the Gunstian Empire is the only inhabited place left on Athumia that has never been ruled by the Dragon Dominion. The Dominion have unsuccessfully invaded Gunst twice – in c.1050 and c.1350. Both invasions were defeated by the Gunstians, and the Dominion were forced to withdraw.

Social Hierarchy of Zamata (The Serpent Isle)

The Rulers	Dragons	Immortal Dragons	3	Igatz
		Mortal Dragons	2	
Aucterian Colonists	Upper	Aristocracy, Landowners, Bankers, Senior Officers etc	500	Mainly in Igatz
	Middle	Merchants, Smallholders, Junior Officers	4500	
	Lower	Farmers, Shopkeepers, Crafts	15000	
Foreign Soldiers	Military / Police	Bullan Soldiers	5000	Across Island
Northern Fleet		Dominion Navy (Aucterian)	5000	Handshore Naval Base
Native Police		Militia (Zamatan)	1000	Across Island
Native Zamatan Islanders	Upper	Farmers, Builders, Merchants, Militia Officers, Teachers	10000	Mainly in Kaugatz and Surrounding Villages
	Lower	Villagers, Crofters, Labourers, Servants	30000	
Descendants of former Colonists	Gunstians	Labourers etc	10000	Kaugatz
Sailors from Irlan	Irlanians	Sailors	3000	Igatz
Bottom of the Heap	Mixed Heritage	Zamatan/Aucterian	4400	Kaugatz
	Bullan Heritage	Zamatan/Bullan	600	

Dragon Royal Family

King Gahad & His Three Consorts

Snowdrift

- ♂ Tegru, 1541
- ♂ Naghad, 1497
- ♀ Macsin, 1456
- ♂ Malum, 1381
- ♀ Famula, 1319
- ♂ Saphben, 1266

Opal Min Tarsu

- ♂ Opelan, 493
- ♂ Rylan, 476
- ♀ Lykot, 401
- ♀ Natali, 352
- ♀ Marda, 331
- ♂ Tarsun, 278

Nightsheen

- ♀ Lykona, 1100
- ♀ Lenta, 1091
- ♂ Irvan, 1062
- ♀ Gilt, 1055
- ♀ Abda, 991
- ♂ Girvine, 928
- ♀ Shana, 899
- ♂ Konran, 834
- ♀ Tirna, 747

The numbers represent age in 1588

DRAMATIS PERSONAE

Zamatans

Lahnos Laimos, Horned Part-Bullan

Reyn, Part-Bullan with Horns and Tail

Friel Laimos, Leader of Zamatan Uprising

Leona, Friel's Assistant

Karl Laimos, Lahnos's Brother

Bauchlie, Zamatan Terrorist

Typan, Major in Zamatan Militia

Jancke, Villager from Fidalaimos

Smithy, Villager from Fidalaimos

Conservus, Prelate of the Serpent Faith

Aucterians

Cisca, Dragon Corps Lieutenant

Lyla, Dragon Corps Captain

Bullan

Efizel, Renegade Bullan Warrior

Gunstians

Adapnie, Gunstian Agent

Dragons

Malum Mon Gahad, Son of Gahad

Lenta Min Gahad, Daughter of Gahad

Irvan Mon Gahad, Son of Gahad

Naghad Mon Gahad, New King of the Dominion

Macsin Min Gahad, Daughter of Gahad

Rylan Mon Gahad, Younger Son of Gahad

Sigum Mon Sigel, Dragon of Inopei

Tirna Min Gahad, Former Governor of the Serpent Isle

Kheran Mon Tirna, Former Governor's Son

Gahad the Mighty, Former King of the Dominion

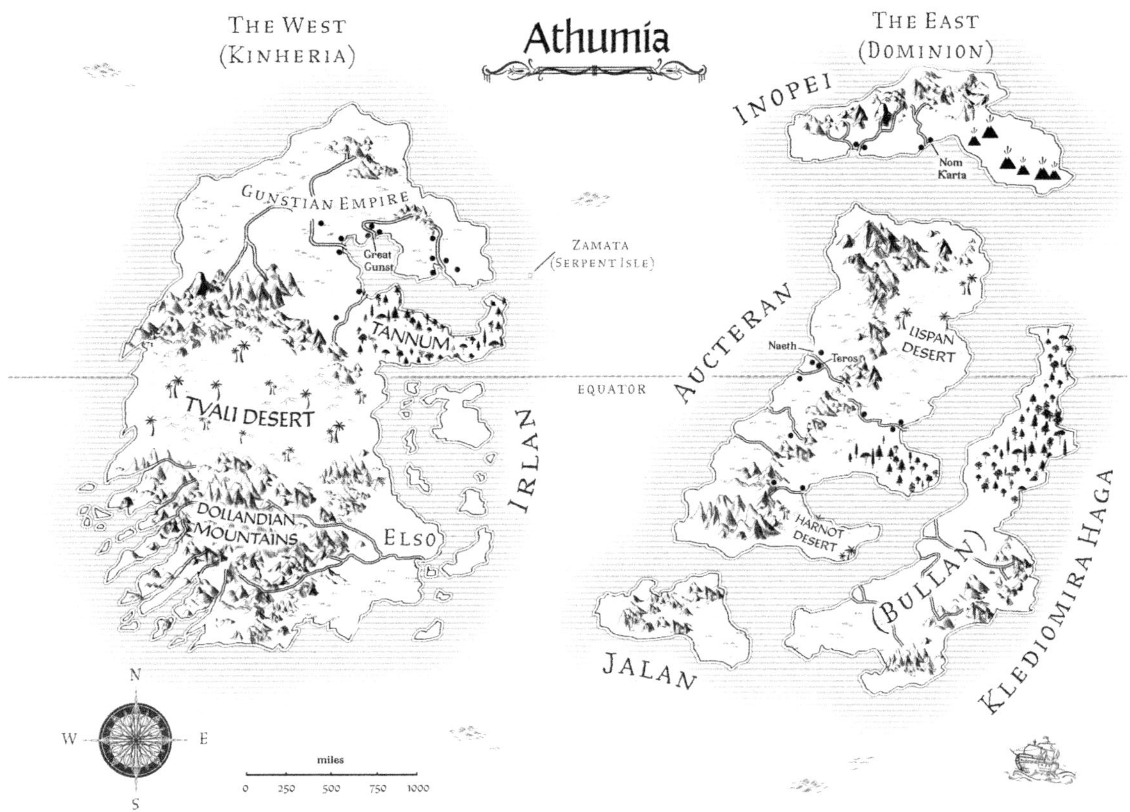
Athumia
The West
(Kinheria)
The East
(Dominion)
Gunstian Empire
Great Gunst
Zamata
(Serpent Isle)
Tannum
Tvali Desert
Dollandian Mountains
Elso
Irlan
Equator
Inopei
Nom Karta
Aucteran
Naeth
Teros
Lispan Desert
Harnot Desert
Jalan
(Bullan)
Klediomira Haga
N
W
E
S
miles
0
250
500
750
1000

Zamata – The Serpent Isle

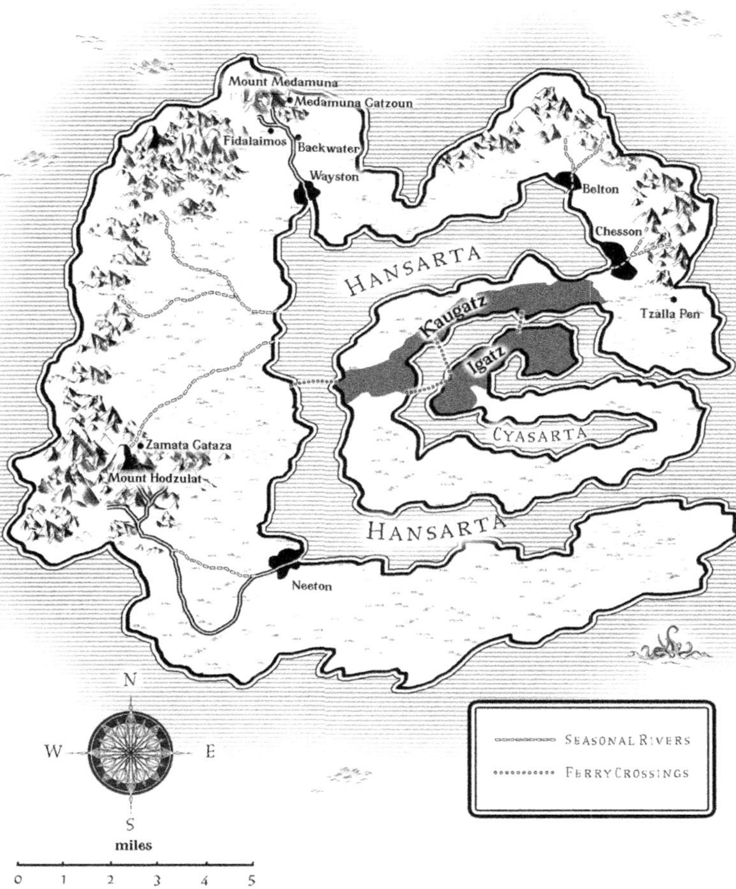

The Serpent Isle – Close-up of Kaugatz and Igatz

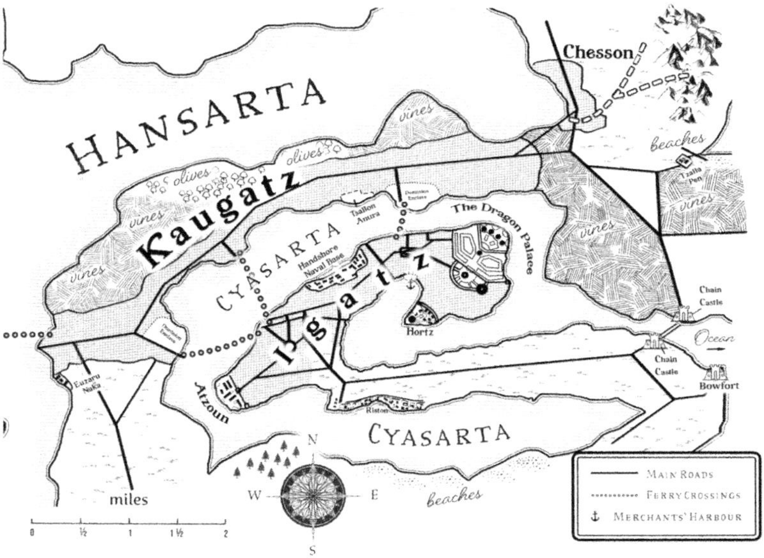

CHAPTER 1
ORANGE BLOSSOM

Igatz, Serpent Isle – 16th Duninch 1588

Reyn opened the wide wooden shutters, and the spring sunshine flooded into the high-ceilinged bedroom.

'Time to get up,' she said.

Lahnos pulled the thin blanket over his head.

Reyn walked to the side of the bed and sat. 'Should we go for a walk and then get some breakfast?'

Lahnos closed his eyes. He could hear the birds singing from the branches of the trees outside the elegant apartment block, and the warmth of the sun was already filling the large bedchamber. Reyn tugged at the blanket, uncovering his face, and he squinted at her in the bright light. She had tied her head scarf loosely round her neck, leaving her blunt horns visible. On the side of her head, the scar she had received during the burning of Lord Meer was hidden beneath her thick brown hair. It was still shorter on one side than on the other, but Lahnos quite liked it that way.

'It's a beautiful day,' said Reyn.

'It's not as beautiful as you,' he said. 'Get into bed.'

Reyn raised an eyebrow. 'We need to get up. I start work in an hour, and you're supposed to be on hand in case the Colonel needs you. Are you actually going to turn up at his office this morning?'

Lahnos laughed. 'Why bother? The Demon Witch hasn't spoken to me in weeks. What makes you think she'll speak to me today?'

'But you can't laze about in bed all day.'

'Why not?' He gazed at their opulent surroundings. 'I could stay here all day.'

'Yes? Well, I couldn't.'

'Are you uncomfortable because we stole this apartment from Aucterians?'

Reyn rolled her eyes. 'Do we have to talk about this again? We didn't steal anything, Lahnos. The owners of this apartment fled with the ships of the Northern Fleet. Should it remain empty forever, just in case they eventually turn up to reclaim it? Besides, didn't the Aucterian colonists steal this land from us in the first place?'

Lahnos sat up. 'They'll be back. The only question is – will they get here before or after the Gunstians invade?' He swung his legs out of bed, stood, and stretched his arms.

'Put some clothes on,' Reyn said. 'The window shutters are wide open.'

'And who opened them?' he said.

She reached out to where a chair sat, picked up a pair of shorts, and threw them at him. 'You have no shame,' she said.

He laughed again as he caught them. 'Anyone looking in from outside will be staring at my magnificent horns, Reyn.'

She shook her head as she watched him pull the shorts on. 'And would you laugh if it was me parading about naked in front of an open window?'

'That's different,' he said.

'Oh yes? How?'

'It just is.' He sat on a chair and pulled his boots towards him. 'I think the Demon Witch might be avoiding me. The last time I spoke to her, I asked if she would help me look for my father. She said she would think about it, and I haven't heard from her since.'

'Do you think she doesn't want to help you?'

'Perhaps she can't, but doesn't want to admit it.'

'If she could kill King Gahad, then finding your father shouldn't be impossible for her.'

'That's what I thought,' he said. He stood again, and rummaged through a pile of clothes. 'Then, what's the problem? Why would she be reluctant to help?'

'You could be reading too much into this. Perhaps she has been busy watching the dragons in the Dominion. Not much is happening on the island, so maybe she thought it more important to discover what the dragons are doing. Her absence might have nothing to do with you or your father.'

Lahnos nodded, but he wasn't sure he agreed with Reyn's assessment.

'Lord Kheran will be back in Aucteran by now,' Reyn went on. 'I wonder what the other dragons think about what he decided?'

'They will be furious,' Lahnos said, as he pulled a tunic over his broad shoulders; 'you don't need to be a tactical genius to work that out. Abandoning Zamata will have been the last thing they wanted.'

'You don't know that,' Reyn said.

'The dragons want to rule the entire world – that's a fact, and no one can deny it. How will they ever conquer Gunst if they lose Zamata? This island is the key to everything; that's what my uncle doesn't understand. He's living in a dream world, intoxicated by his fantasies of independence.'

Reyn stood, and her eyes flickered with anger. 'We have been free for exactly one month,' she said. 'Why do you always have to be right about everything? Can you not just be happy for once?'

He raised an eyebrow. 'I am happy; but I'm also a realist.'

Lahnos walked to the open window and gazed down into the streets of the island's Temple District. The Temple of the Undying Serpent was a couple of streets away to his right, while the old Settlers' Convention Hall, from where the colonists had previously run Igatz, was directly in front of the apartment he shared with Reyn. Colonel Friel had taken over the building, and was using it as the seat of his provisional government while the damaged Dragon Palace remained closed. If Lahnos peered to the right, then he could make out the ruined gardens that lay in front of the palace, just beyond the twisted metal of the old gates that had once barred entry.

Reyn joined him. 'No one knows what tomorrow will bring – should we not enjoy the present without worrying what might happen in the future? The Bullan have gone, along with the Dominion fleet, and thousands of Aucterians left with the ships. And Igatz looks so beautiful in the sunshine, so peaceful. Can you not smell the orange blossom?'

He put an arm round her waist. 'I can smell it.'

'It's the scent of hope,' she said.

Lahnos resisted the urge to tease her. Hope? The people of Zamata were deluded if they believed that either the Dominion or the Gunstian Empire would be content to leave the island in peace. What they were experiencing was a welcome respite, nothing more. The ocean was wide, and it would take time for the two powers that dominated the world to gather their forces. More than that, the respite had been earned by the direct intervention of the Demon Witch – how would the island fare if she had decided never to return?

They strode from the apartment and locked the tall door behind them. The stairwell had a large glass skylight and wrought iron banisters, and it seemed a million miles away from the cramped squalor of the tenement blocks in Kaugatz where they had previously lived. Two of their new neighbours were ascending the stairs as they were heading down, and they smiled up at Lahnos and Reyn. Almost everyone in the large block worked for the colonel, and he had requisitioned apartments in the Temple District for hundreds of Zamatans, moving them wholesale into the abandoned properties left behind by the fleeing Aucterian settlers. Reyn smiled back, but Lahnos kept his expression neutral. A few months before, every Zamatan had looked at their horns with revulsion and fear, and now they were all friendly towards the part-Bullan? It was bullshit, and he knew it.

They reached the ground floor and stepped out into the bright morning sunshine. Orange trees lined the road on one side, their branches thick with blossom, which was drifting down onto the pavement. Reyn stopped to inhale deeply, then smiled.

'Are you hungry?' she said.

Lahnos nodded, and they turned to the right and walked down a wide avenue towards one of the district's few open shops. Most commercial enterprises in Igatz had closed following the departure of thousands of the town's Aucterian settlers, and food was being rationed. Lahnos and Reyn walked past several boarded-up storefronts and joined a long queue that led to a shop that was open for business. A few Aucterians were begging on the street, not for food, but for the silver tokens that could be swapped for food. As employees of the colonel's government, Lahnos and Reyn each received five such tokens every day, and they had become more valuable than any of the old Dominion coins that had previously been in circulation. Without tokens, no food could be purchased in Igatz without recourse to the black market, and Aucterian colonists who had once been wealthy were now on the brink of poverty.

'Please, sir,' said an old Aucterian man, as he made his way down the queue. He held his hands out, revealing gold and silver necklaces and diamond rings. 'I have jewellery for sale.'

A younger Zamatan eyed him. 'I'll give you two tokens for those diamond earrings.'

'But they are worth two hundred sovereigns, sir,' said the Aucterian.

The Zamatan shrugged. 'Take it or leave it.'

'I will sell them to you for eight tokens, sir – I have a family to feed.'

'Four tokens,' said the Zamatan, 'and that's my final offer.'

The old Aucterian's eyes flickered with shame and rage, then he nodded and handed the earrings over. The young Zamatan smiled, and passed the old man four silver meal tokens. The Aucterian bowed his head, then moved to the back of the queue behind Lahnos and Reyn. Lahnos didn't turn to look at him, but he could feel the old man's presence, and it filled him with pity. He dug into a pocket, grasped hold of a couple of silver tokens, and discreetly passed them to the Aucterian.

The old man met his glance for a moment, his eyes going to the horns atop Lahnos's head, then he swallowed and slipped the tokens into a pocket of his overcoat. Reyn shook her head, but said nothing. The queue moved forward, and more Zamatans joined its end.

The shopkeeper had positioned a few long tables out in front of his store, and upon them he had arranged everything he had to exchange that day, while three Zamatan militiamen were standing close by to ensure that no thieves were able to steal anything. When Lahnos and Reyn reached the front of the queue, they handed over four tokens, and got a bottle of wine and enough food for the rest of the day in return. Reyn filled a bag with the wine and food, and they turned and walked past the long queue. They went to another stall at the end of the street and exchanged a single token for two large mugs of hot coffee. The queue for the stall was shorter than that for the shop, as coffee was deemed an unnecessary expense by most of the inhabitants of Igatz. Reyn and Lahnos took their bag and the mugs of coffee, and sat down on a bench with a view of the Temple of the Undying Serpent.

'We are rich now,' Lahnos said.

Reyn laughed. 'Hardly.'

'Food is the new currency,' he said, 'and my uncle controls the supply coming into Igatz and Kaugatz. Do you remember the old days, when there were hundreds of shops selling everything we needed? When we didn't have to queue for some bread and a few vegetables?'

'This is just temporary,' she said. 'Things will settle down again soon. And when did you start getting nostalgic about the past? You do remember how we were treated back then?'

'I remember,' he said. 'I'm just not sure if this is an improvement.'

He sipped from the mug, and grimaced. The coffee was of very poor quality, but he thought better about mentioning it in case Reyn accused him of being negative. No coffee was grown upon the island, and with all trade between Zamata and the Dominion having been cut off in the aftermath of the fleet's withdrawal, he wondered where it had come from.

Reyn opened the bag and tore off a chunk of bread. She divided it into two pieces and handed one to Lahnos.

'It's fresh,' she said, 'and it's still warm. See, Lahnos – not everything on the island is bad.' She glanced up at the high tower of the temple. 'Every Zamatan has a job now, and we're free to make our own decisions. It'll be hard work to get the island back onto its feet, but it will be worth it.'

Lahnos said nothing. It was true that Reyn worked long hard shifts sorting out and distributing possessions requisitioned from the abandoned homes of the Aucterians, but Lahnos was almost idle. His uncle kept him close by, but that was solely in case the Demon Witch decided to speak to him, and for no other reason. Technically, Lahnos was a member of the island's independent militia force, but no one ever reprimanded him if he didn't bother to show up for training or guard duty, and he had spent most of the island's first full month of freedom in indolence, with too much time to think.

He felt Reyn's elbow nudge him in the ribs, and looked up to see a militiaman running towards them.

'Lahnos Laimos, sir?' the young member of the militia said as he reached the bench. 'You are wanted in the Convention Hall.'

'Why?' said Lahnos.

'I don't know, sir.'

'Why are you calling me that? I'm the same rank as you.'

The young militiaman's eyes narrowed a little. 'Please, sir; I was told it was very urgent.'

'Give me your mug,' said Reyn, 'and I'll return it to the coffee stall.'

Lahnos handed her the mug and got to his feet. The young militiaman set off, and Lahnos strolled after him, wondering what could possibly be so urgent. He had promised his uncle that he would let him know if and when the Demon Witch contacted him, and he could see no reason why his presence would be called for. They reached the street which held both his apartment and the large Convention Hall, and passed by the guards on duty by the main entrance. Lahnos began to head for the grand stairs that led up to the Colonel's office, but the militiaman coughed, and pointed to a side door.

'What's through there?' said Lahnos.

'The stairs to the basement, sir.'

'The basement?'

'Yes, sir. Major Typan is waiting for you.'

'Who? I thought my uncle had summoned me.'

'No, sir. Please – I already had to visit your apartment to look for you, and I was told to make all haste.'

Lahnos shook his head, then followed the militiaman through the side door. They entered a dimly-lit stairwell, and descended into the gloom of the basement. Halfway down the steps, they ran into a tall, broad man who was ascending. Lahnos caught the man's glance.

'Bauchlie?' he said. 'What are you doing down here?'

The scarred rebel eyed Lahnos but said nothing; then he pushed past him on the stairs and continued upwards without a word.

'Miserable bastard,' Lahnos muttered.

They reached the level of the basement, and Lahnos squinted around. A few oil lamps had been lit, and he could see the old storage rooms that were located under the large hall. Several militia soldiers were standing by the thick wooden doors, then Lahnos heard a scream come from one of the rooms. He glanced at the young militiaman, but said nothing.

An officer approached. 'Here you are, young Laimos.'

'Who are you?' he said.

'My name is Major Typan.'

'I've never heard of you.'

The officer smiled and gave a slight shrug. 'Come this way.'

'Why?'

'Colonel Friel Laimos personally placed me in charge of this... facility,' the officer said, 'with the power to summon you if required.'

Lahnos laughed. 'Facility? This is a prison, isn't it? A secret prison, hidden away from the rest of Igatz.'

'That is correct,' the officer said. 'Zamata has many enemies. Some are out in the open, while others prefer to conceal themselves among the native population. Should we do nothing to combat their aims? Don't be so naïve, Lahnos.' He glanced at the young militiaman. 'You are dismissed. Lahnos – follow me.'

The major strode into the gloom of the hallway and stopped at an entrance. He gestured to the guards outside, and they opened the door. Lahnos walked over and glanced into the makeshift cell. It had no windows, and was bathed in darkness, but he could make out the form of a man lying on the floor.

'Who is that?' he said.

'A Gunstian agent,' said the major.

Lahnos smiled. 'And what do you want me to do? Interrogate him?'

'In a manner of speaking,' said the major. 'He's dead.'

'What?'

'You heard me, Lahnos,' said the major. 'I want you to read his thoughts; quickly, before it is too late.'

'It will already be too late,' Lahnos said. 'If he's been dead for more than a few minutes, then...'

'He has very recently expired,' said the major. 'You have time.'

'But...'

'Quickly, young Laimos. The information inside this agent's head is extremely important. Find out what he was keeping from us.'

Lahnos stared at the officer, then stepped into the cell. He crouched down by the body, and saw blood coming from the back of the man's head. An urge to vomit roiled up in his guts, and he swallowed, then placed a hand on to the Gunstian's forehead.

Darkness swept over Lahnos's mind. An image of a Zamatan militiaman swinging an iron club at his head was dominating the dead agent's thoughts, along with a sense of raw fear mixed with defiance. He had said nothing; resisting the painful interrogation until his captors had become infuriated. Lahnos tried to delve deeper, to get beneath the agent's last moments alive, but his mind was already starting to disintegrate, his brain decaying into oblivion. Lahnos surged his Gift, and was bombarded with sensory information – flashes of the agent's past life:

his youth on Zamata, his pledge of loyalty to the Gunstian Empire, his acts of treason and sabotage under the Dominion occupation. It was all draining away like water into the ground and, with an effort, Lahnos focussed on the agent's last few days before being captured. He saw a ship anchored close to the starlit northern shores of Zamata, where several black-robed figures were speaking in Gunstian.

'The Chain Castles must be rendered inoperable,' one said. 'Can you organise an assault to take them both?'

'They are too well-guarded, my lord,' said the agent. 'Friel has placed three hundred men into each, and we lack the resources to mount a full scale attack when the fleet arrives.'

'This is unacceptable,' said the agent's superior.

'There is another way, my lord,' said the agent. 'We have a dozen men infiltrated into the militia garrison posted at the Chain Castle on the southern shore of the Cyasarta. They will be ready to act as soon as the Gunstian Fleet enters the inlet, but the timing must be perfect. I can ensure that they are all on duty by the wheels that operate the chain, but I need to know when the fleet will arrive.'

The robed men glanced at each other. 'The fleet...'

The dead agent's thoughts drifted into silence, and Lahnos felt nothing but an empty corpse under his fingertips. He removed his hand from the man's forehead, and crouched in silence.

'Yes?' said Major Typan. 'What did you glean from the agent, Lahnos?'

'You can tell my uncle that I will not be doing this for you again,' said Lahnos. 'This man's blood is on my hands.'

'You're being irrational,' said Typan. 'You had nothing to do with this agent's death.'

'Would he still be alive if you didn't have a Gifted death-reader close by? You murdered him so that I could read his thoughts, and I will not be used in this manner again.'

Lahnos got to his feet.

'The information, if you please?' said the major.

'The Imperial Gunstian Fleet is coming,' said Lahnos, 'and they have a dozen agents hidden among the militia in the southernmost of the two Chain Castles. The man you killed was going to order them to sabotage the chains when the fleet arrives; or he may have already done so.'

The major's eyes widened. 'And when will the fleet get here?'

'I don't know. The man's mind gave out before I could reach that particular piece of information.'

Typan eyed Lahnos in silence for a few moments, then nodded. 'Thank you for your assistance.'

'Remember to tell my uncle what I said. I am not your personal death-reader.'

Lahnos turned, and strode towards the stairs.

Lahnos.

He hesitated, his mind filled with the voice of the Demon Witch.

I sensed you use your powers.

That was not my idea, Lahnos said in his mind. *They tricked me into doing it. I...*

I know what occurred, Lahnos.

Where have you been? A month has passed since...

That doesn't matter, Lahnos. Listen to me. Go back to the officer and demand that he opens the cell at the end of the passageway, and releases the man held inside.

Why? Who's in there?

You will see. I will ensure the officer obeys you.

Lahnos turned again, and saw that the officer and other members of the militia in the basement were all looking at him. He gave them a cold smile, and walked back to the major.

'I did you a favour,' Lahnos said, 'and now you shall do one for me. Release the prisoner in the last cell along.'

A few militiamen started to laugh, but the officer's face remained still.

'Do it now,' said Lahnos.

The major bowed his head. 'As you wish.'

The laughter fell into silence.

'Open the last cell,' said the major, gesturing to two guards, 'and release the prisoner into Lahnos's custody.'

The men saluted, then walked to the end of the long passageway. In the gloom, Lahnos watched as they unlocked the door and signalled to the occupant to leave the cell. Nothing happened for a few moments, then a large figure appeared in the shadows – a figure with horns and a tail. Lahnos frowned. Why had the Zamatans been holding a Bullan prisoner, and what was he still doing on the island?

The Bullan approached, and the major ordered his men to remove the shackles securing his wrists together. The Bullan gazed around in confusion, then his eyes met Lahnos's glance.

'Lucky Laimos?' the Bullan said. 'What are you doing here, horned lad?'

'Lahnos Laimos has ordered your release,' said the major.

The Bullan laughed, and a few of the militiamen glanced away in disgust.

'You got me out, did you, boy?' said the Bullan. 'Who told you I was in here? Why has it taken a month?'

Lahnos said nothing. He remembered the Bullan's name, but didn't want to say it in front of the other Zamatans. The Bullan shrugged at Lahnos's lack of response, and they walked for the stairs. They climbed them side by side, then strode through the ground floor of the Convention Hall. Lahnos was expecting someone to stop them, to demand to know where he was taking a Bullan prisoner, but not a single person glanced in their direction. They walked past the guards at the entrance as though they were invisible, and came out into the strong sunlight.

The Bullan stretched his arms and closed his eyes, letting the rays of the sun touch his skin, but Lahnos urged him onwards, and they crossed the road.

'I live up there,' Lahnos said, pointing to his apartment. 'Let's get off the street.'

They entered the apartment block and hurried up the stairs. Lahnos put his key in the lock of the door, and found that it was already open.

'Reyn?' he cried, as he entered. 'Are you in here?'

Reyn appeared from the kitchen, a knife in one hand and a large onion in the other. She smiled at Lahnos, then her expression fell as she noticed the huge Bullan soldier standing next to him. Lahnos led the Bullan into the apartment, and locked the door behind them.

'What…' said Reyn; 'what…?'

Lahnos glanced at the horned soldier. 'May I tell Reyn your name?'

'Do you remember it?' said the Bullan.

'Of course I do.'

'Do you trust her?'

'Yes.'

The Bullan glanced at Reyn, his eyes taking in her horns and tail. He said nothing for a while, then he nodded. 'I will tell her myself,' he said, 'for if she is your woman, horned boy, then my purpose here concerns her also. Reyn, I am Efizel, and it is a pleasure to see you again. Tell my name to no one.'

Reyn continued to stare at the Bullan. 'You've seen me before?'

'I have,' said the Bullan. 'I saw you in Tsallon Anura, just before we set sail for the Dragon Palace. I remember you saying how much you wished to fight by the side of young Laimos.'

'You mentioned you had a purpose,' said Lahnos.

Efizel turned to him. 'Before the Northern Fleet departed this island, I approached my regimental commander and requested permission to remain here.'

'Why?' said Lahnos. 'Did they grant you permission to stay?'

'Let me finish, lad,' Efizel said. 'The answer to your second question is no; I was refused permission. I tried to explain that it was a matter of honour, and my commander understood that; however, he also reminded me of the vows I swore to the Dominion. What was I to do? I threatened to abscond, and my commander told me that I would bring dishonour to the regiment if I deserted. In reply, I told him that my own soul would be shamed if I did not pledge to serve the one who had saved my life in Kaugatz. That night, my commander ensured that there were no sentries guarding the gates of the barrack block.' Efizel bowed his head. 'He let me go, but I know that I can never return to my regiment. I tried to reach you, young Laimos, but I was arrested by the militia and thrown into prison.' He raised his eyes again. 'How did you know I was there?'

Lahnos frowned. 'You want to serve me?'

'You saved my life, Lucky Laimos; and I am the only survivor of those you rescued from the Gunstians in Kaugatz. It is the least I can do. Again, I ask – how did you know I was there? I have spoken to no one in a month – my captors had nothing to ask me, and they left me in utter solitude.'

'I will tell you,' Lahnos said, 'but you must keep my secrets, just as we shall keep yours.'

'Very well,' said the Bullan. 'Am I to live here now? Perhaps you could ask your woman to lower her knife? I bear you no ill will, Reyn – on the contrary, I pledge to protect you, just as I pledge to serve and protect Lahnos Laimos.' He bowed. 'I am at your service.'

CHAPTER 2
THE CULL

Naeth, Western Aucteran – 28th Duninch 1588

The perfectly circular harbour of Naeth was one of the marvels of Aucterian construction. Large enough to fit a dozen huge dragon carriers, and with acres of shipyards, it was the greatest military port in the entire Dominion. King Gahad himself had assisted in its building, or so it was said. The mighty lord of Athumia had used his power over stone to meld the great granite blocks of the harbour wall together, creating an unbreakable barrier to stand against the waves of the ocean. It was so large, it was said that only a dragon flying overhead could perceive its true shape; from the quayside, any human saw only a vast curve stretching away to both sides, marked by regular jetties that jutted out into the calm waters of the interior basin.

As a girl, Cisca had often watched the fine warships of the Dominion's fleets come and go from the harbour – the great carriers bearing their dragon passengers across the ocean, and the squadrons of sleek frigates and destroyers that patrolled the coasts of Aucteran. Then, every year at the beginning of the month of Duninch, the Grand Convoys would be prepared. The largest two were bound for the colonised territories of Irlan and Elso, but Cisca had always noticed that a third, smaller convoy had always been included – the convoy that kept the Serpent Isle supplied. The convoy for Elso would depart first, followed by that bound for the archipelago of Irlan. Only then would the ships destined for the Serpent Isle set off upon their twenty-two day voyage to the tiny outpost, bearing Bullan soldiers, luxury goods and colonial administrators across the ocean.

That year, the ships that had evacuated Lord Kheran from the Serpent Isle had arrived in Naeth just as the convoy bound for Irlan was leaving. Since then, the ships that had been due to sail as part of the third convoy had been stuck in port, their crews awaiting fresh orders from the dragon government in Inopei. Rumours had swept through the city, rumours of a shameful defeat and an ignominious withdrawal, and the quayside taverns were full of men and women complaining bitterly about their forced removal from their homes in Igatz. Lord Kheran had been summoned by the dragons who lived in Teros City, and that had been the last Cisca had seen of the young grandson of King Gahad.

Cisca sipped the hot black coffee from her cup, her eyes on the ships of the idle convoy. Aboard the large freighters tied up by the jetties were all manner of goods, including the same variety of coffee that she was drinking, cultivated on the mountain slopes of Eastern Aucteran. A waiter at the small café caught her eye as he passed her table, and she signalled for the bill.

Could she have done more to persuade Lord Kheran to remain on the Serpent Isle? She had been as desperate to leave as he had been, but had nevertheless tried her best to remind the young dragon of his duty to the Dominion. She had told as much to her superior officers in the Dragon Corps when she had been debriefed upon arriving in Naeth; whether or not they had believed her was another matter. The officers had told her to go home and wait for further instructions; it wasn't the worst thing that could have happened, but it hardly filled her with confidence.

The waiter returned to her table and placed a slip of paper in front of her.

'Your bill, ma'am,' he said, then he leaned in a little closer. 'I should warn you that there are two men in the next café along who have been staring at you for some time. Would you like me to call you a carriage?'

Cisca frowned, resisting the temptation to turn her head to see who had been staring at her.

'Two men?' she said.

'Yes, ma'am; and neither look particularly friendly. Perhaps they have noticed that you come here at the same time every day?'

Cisca said nothing.

'They could be admirers, of course,' the waiter went on, 'or maybe they have heard about your role in the unfortunate events that befell the Serpent Isle?'

'Excuse me?' said Cisca, her eyes widening. 'How do you know about that? I mean, how do you know that I was involved?'

'Everyone who works in this café knows who you are, Lieutenant Cisca,' the waiter said, 'and some are not as discreet as I am. Perhaps it would be a good idea to find yourself a new location from which to gaze at the harbour each day.'

Cisca threw a few coins onto the table and rose to her feet. 'A carriage will not be necessary. Good day.'

She strode off between the tables and on to the side of the wide road that ran by the curving quayside. Her glance flickered to the right, where a long line of cafés sat, and she saw two men get up from their table. Her anger grew, and she came to a halt, her eyes narrow. She turned to face the two men, who frowned as they saw her waiting for them.

'Do you have something you wish to say to me?' Cisca said.

'You should go home, Lieutenant,' said one.

'Why – so you can follow me?'

'We don't need to follow you, ma'am,' said the other man; 'we know where you live.'

'How dare you?' Cisca said. 'Are you trying to intimidate me? I have done nothing wrong.'

'The investigation will discover the truth of that statement,' said the first, as they walked up next to her.

'If you touch me I will scream,' she said.

One of the men smiled and shook his head. 'We're sergeants in the Dominion Army, and we're here to prevent anyone else from touching you, Lieutenant. You've upset a lot of people in this city, and our job is to make sure no one lynches you before the investigation concludes.'

Cisca snorted. 'No one is going to lynch me.'

'We have been following you for several days now, ma'am,' said the second man, 'and in that time we have chased off more than one enraged patriot who wished to do you harm. Some are saying that the withdrawal from the Serpent Isle was your doing – that you manipulated young Lord Kheran into abandoning his position; and that you are a traitor to the Dominion. Now, let's not make a scene, ma'am. Be a good little officer and walk home. We'll trail along behind you at a discreet distance.'

'I am not a traitor,' she said, lowering her gaze. 'I tried my best to persuade Lord Kheran to stay; you must believe me.'

The two sergeants shrugged.

Cisca wanted to shout at the men, but knew no good would come of it.

'Can I ask you something before I go home?' she said.

'Of course, Lieutenant,' said one.

'The Dragon Corps have told me nothing; in fact, until you mentioned it, I had not been aware that I was being investigated. I had my suspicions, but you are the first to confirm it.'

'Was there a question in there, ma'am?'

'Yes. Do you know where the investigation is taking place?'

'We heard that Lord Kheran was escorted all the way back to Nom Karta on Inopei, Lieutenant,' the sergeant said; 'so I would assume it's happening there, in the presence of the new king. His Majesty King Naghad will likely be taking a personal interest, but that's as much as we know.'

'Thank you,' she said.

She turned from them and walked away, heading towards a side lane that led away from the harbour. She cursed her naïvety as she walked. Naeth was an enormous city, and she had assumed that no one would know who she was, and yet everyone did – from the waiters in the café to the soldiers assigned to protect her from a lynching. And to think that the new King of the Dominion would decide her innocence or guilt – it was almost too much to take in. The new monarch had been elected by a conference of the twenty-one children of the slain King Gahad, and word had reached Naeth of their decision on the seventeenth of Duninch, just five days after the ships from the Northern Fleet had returned from the Serpent Isle. It took seven days for a dragon to fly between Naeth and Nom Karta, so Lord Kheran would have arrived in the presence of King Naghad around the nineteenth or twentieth of the month. If a quick decision had been reached, then any dragons returning with news from Inopei would be due in Naeth any day. Cisca's fate may have already been decided, but there was nothing she could do but wait.

She picked up her pace as she entered a rundown quarter of the city. Ramshackle and overcrowded tenement blocks lined the narrow streets, and Cisca relaxed a little. Home. Some of her more aristocratic colleagues in the Dragon Corps probably feared to walk the streets in that part of the city, but it was where Cisca had been born and brought up, and she drank in the sights and smells of the district. She was dressed in civilian clothing, and blended into the crowds that milled through the streets, hearing the familiar rough accent that she had unsuccessfully tried to purge from her own voice in officer training. She passed a local market, where a heated argument was going on over the price of fish, and she smiled, glad in a way that she had been blissfully unaware of the danger she had been in. Her sixteen days in Naeth had seemed almost like a holiday. She climbed a flight of worn and grimy steps that rose up a hillside between rows of towering tenement blocks, and stepped over an unconscious drunk lying in the gutter. Then, for no reason that she could fathom, she wondered what Bauchlie was doing at that precise moment. He had survived the convulsions that had rippled through the Serpent Isle, and had even issued an apology to her for the way she had been treated in captivity. Why had he done that?

Was he genuinely sorrowful about his actions, or was it just a game to him? His eyes had… She stopped herself. Bauchlie was a murderer and a terrorist – a criminal with no redeeming attributes. It was true that he had featured in some of her dreams since leaving Igatz, but she always awoke annoyed with herself, angry that her subconscious had persisted in dwelling on his presence. At the same time, she was glad he was alive, even after everything he had done.

She turned down another narrow lane and entered a building. She climbed the steps of the tenement block and opened the front door of her parents' small apartment. It was too warm for a coat, but she hung up her bag on a small peg and began to walk down the hallway. She heard voices, and stopped.

A woman was talking to her mother and father about her; a woman with the cut-crystal accent of a Teros City officer.

'Is our Cisca in trouble?' her mother said.

'I would rather wait until she is here before making any pronouncements,' the upper-class voice said. 'How much longer do you think she will be?'

'She's usually getting home around now,' said her father. 'Would you like another cup of coffee?'

'No, thank you.'

'What about a sandwich? I could make you a sandwich. The wife bought in some lovely smoked fish from the market this morning – it makes a lovely sandwich.'

'Thank you, but no.'

Cisca took a long breath and entered the small kitchen, where three people were sitting. Across from her mother and father sat an elegant-looking captain dressed in the uniform of the Dragon Corps. Cisca suppressed a frown. With barely two hundred officers in the Dragon Corps, she knew most of their faces and names, but she had never seen the woman sitting in front of her before.

'Here's our girl,' said Cisca's mother, standing. 'There's a young lady here to see you, dear.'

Cisca saluted. 'Good afternoon, ma'am.'

The Dragon Corps captain smiled, though her eyes remained cold. 'You are in civilian clothes, I see, Lieutenant,' she said. 'Please, take a seat.'

Cisca said nothing, irritated that she had been invited to sit down in her own home. She sat next to her father as her mother walked up to a stove and began preparing fresh coffee.

'Nice walk?' said her father.

'Yes,' said Cisca, her eyes never leaving the captain. 'Sorry, ma'am; I didn't catch your name.'

'I am Captain Lyla,' the officer said, her accent grating on Cisca's ear more than normal; 'and I have been sent here to talk to you, Lieutenant Cisca; alone.'

'Oh,' said Cisca's father. 'I suppose we had better get out of your way then.'

Lyla smiled again, but Cisca wasn't fooled.

'We'll be in the next room if you need anything,' said Cisca's mother, then she and her father left the kitchen, closing the door behind them.

'It took me a quite a while to find your house, Lieutenant,' said Lyla, 'as every tenement block in this district looks identical. Tell me; how did you cope with the smell growing up? It's quite pungent.'

'How can I help you, ma'am?' said Cisca.

'You can pack quickly, Lieutenant; that's how. I have no desire to linger here any longer than necessary.'

'Have I been reassigned, ma'am?'

'Yes; to me. As of this moment, you are under my direct authority.' Lyla glanced around the cramped kitchen, as if she found something distasteful. 'You are aware, no doubt, Lieutenant, that the blessed children of the mighty King Gahad have selected a successor – King Naghad Mon Gahad?'

'I am aware of that, ma'am.'

'And were you aware that King Naghad has examined Lord Kheran? No, I doubt you would know that. Word arrived from Inopei this morning. A momentous decision has been reached, though it was far from unanimous. The vote that selected King Naghad was not without its difficulties. You worked in Nom Karta for several years, yes?'

'I did; yes, ma'am.'

Lyla nodded. 'And are you surprised by the identity of our new monarch? You don't look surprised.'

'I always felt that it was down to Lord Naghad or Lord Tegru, ma'am – the two oldest sons of King Gahad. I am not surprised that Lord Naghad garnered more votes; he was always the strongest of the Children of Gahad, despite Lord Tegru being the elder of the two.'

'Do you have any notion of King Naghad's policies?'

Cisca nodded. 'As far as I am aware, Lord Naghad was a proponent of a more aggressive policy as regards the Gunstian Empire, whereas Lord Tegru was more... cautious.'

'Indeed,' said Lyla. 'What I am about to tell you must remain a secret for now, although I am sure that news will reach the common citizenry of Naeth soon. Lord Tegru has taken his defeat rather badly, and has fled from Nom Karta, taking six of the other Children of Gahad with him. Their current location is unknown. However, that will not interfere with the new policy that King Naghad has ordained. As soon as he had been named king, His Majesty ordered the immediate construction and deployment of the largest invasion force this world has ever seen. He means to utterly destroy the Gunstian Empire, and so fulfil the destiny of the Dragon Dominion to control every corner of Athumia.' She smiled again. 'And then Lord Kheran arrived, bringing his tale of woe and defeat. I wasn't there when it happened, Lieutenant, but I can imagine the scene. The new king is revelling in his power, only to be told by a child that the Dominion is no longer in possession of the one place it needs in order to invade Gunst. I heard that Lord Kheran was lucky not to be torn to pieces. His mother, Lady Tirna Min Gahad, had to beg for her son's life and was humiliated in front of the entire court. Needless to say, your name also came up.' Lyla waited for a reaction from Cisca, but the lieutenant kept her features closed.

'You are fortunate that King Naghad used his truth powers on Lord Kheran,' Lyla went on, 'with the result that you have been exonerated for your role in the evacuation of the Serpent Isle. You tried to dissuade the young dragon from abandoning his post, and it was no fault of yours that your advice was ignored.'

Cisca exhaled in relief.

'Did you forget that I mentioned packing?' Lyla said. 'Your part in this is far from over, Lieutenant. You have been assigned to me as my assistant, and I have been ordered to make the voyage to the Serpent Isle with all haste.'

'I'm going back to the Serpent Isle, ma'am?'

'Yes. Does that knowledge upset you? Lord Kheran told the royal court that you had experience of dealing with the rebels who are currently in charge of the island; and I will require that you fully brief me. Of course, we shall not be travelling alone. The Grand Convoy currently sitting idle in the harbour is to be re-purposed, as the first portion of the invasion force destined for Gunst. Eight fresh regiments of Bullan shall be our co-passengers, while three Children of Gahad will be in command of the operation, with Lord Malum Mon Gahad in overall control.'

Cisca gasped. 'Three Children of Gahad?'

'That is correct; to be followed by more. Altogether, King Naghad has plans that will see over forty dragons from the royal household take part in the invasion of Gunst. As I said, this will be the most powerful invasion force this world has ever seen. Dozens of Bullan regiments are on their way to Naeth, along with countless thousands of Aucterian soldiers. We shall be setting off several days before the main force can be assembled, and our immediate mission is to wrest control of the Serpent Isle back into Dominion hands before the others reach the island. We shall have around a dozen days to fulfil our objective – a dozen days to grind the rebellion into dust. When the main force arrives, I will most likely be leaving with them, to join the invasion of Gunst.'

'Do the dragons have a plan to retake the Serpent Isle, ma'am?'

'They are leaving the tactics to us humans, Lieutenant, while they concentrate on the overall strategy. I expect you to make a full and decisive contribution to the plan to re-conquer the island.'

'There must be other officers in the Dragon Corps with more experience than me, ma'am?'

'I am sure you are right, Lieutenant. However, after hearing everything Lord Kheran had to say, King Naghad dismissed every officer from the Dragon Corps who was present on the island at the time of the rebellion. Every officer, except you. King Naghad has also dismissed every officer with any connection whatsoever to Lord Tegru and to those with whom he fled, cutting the numbers within the Dragon Corps by more than three-quarters at a single stroke.'

Cisca's mouth fell open.

'Right now,' Lyla went on, 'dozens of long-standing and highly-decorated Dragon Corps officers are being told the news that they are no longer required within the service. Out of those chosen to be a part of the advance operation, you are the only officer with any experience of the Serpent Isle. This is what King Naghad has decreed, and as His Majesty's humble servants, we are bound to obey. You may be wondering why a mere captain such as myself is here today to tell you this; well, let me enlighten you – I am the highest ranked officer in the Dragon Corps left in Aucteran. Tomorrow, I shall be promoted to major, and you shall be promoted to captain.'

'I'm being made a captain?'

Lyla nodded. 'You are. Congratulations.'

'And to you, ma'am.'

The two women sat in silence for a few moments, as Cisca tried to digest the news. Part of her was secretly pleased that so many of the condescending and smug officers under which she had served had been summarily dismissed from the Dragon Corps; but a larger part of her felt sheer terror at the new weight of responsibility that was being thrust upon her.

'The promotion ceremony begins at midday in the Corps headquarters,' Lyla said. 'Please look your best. And pack, as from there we shall be heading directly to the Grand Convoy to oversee the necessary adjustments that will have to be made. Tomorrow night, we shall be upon the dragon carrier, and I expect to hear your plan for retaking the Serpent Isle.' She stood. 'The repurposed convoy will be departing Naeth in two days. Tell me, Lieutenant – are you up to this task?'

Cisca stood to attention. 'Yes, ma'am.'

'Good. I shall see myself out.'

'Do you know the way, ma'am? Parts of this district can be a little rough.'

Lyla laughed. 'Before I entered the Dragon Corps, I fought in several campaigns against rebels and bandits in the Dollandian Mountains to the west of Elso – I think I can manage the harbour district of Neath.'

Cisca watched as Lyla strode out of the kitchen; then, a moment later, she heard the sound of the front door opening and closing. Her parents peered into the kitchen.

'Is everything all right, dear?' said her mother.

'I'm going back to the Serpent Isle,' she said. 'This will be my last night in this house.'

Her father nodded. 'I'll fetch a bottle of wine.'

Cisca smiled. 'Don't drink too much; I want you to come with me to the Dragon Corps headquarters tomorrow for noon – so you can see me being promoted to captain.'

Her mother put her hands to her face. 'My little girl – a captain?'

Her father grinned. 'Just wait until I tell all the lads in the naval club. You make us proud, Cisca; you make us very proud.'

CHAPTER 3
TAXING

Igatz, Serpent Isle – 7th Tradinch 1588

Colonel Friel Laimos leafed through the papers on his desk.

'Are you listening to us, my lord?' said one of the three brown-robed monks standing in front of him.

Friel kept his eyes on a document. 'Yes. You were complaining about the monasteries having to pay tax like everyone else.'

'But we have been exempt from taxation for almost a century, my lord,' said the monk. 'Under Dominion rule, we...'

'And are we currently under Dominion rule, brother?'

The three monks glanced at each other.

'Our work exists on a spiritual plane, my lord,' said one, 'far removed from worldly affairs; and taxation is a secular matter.'

'You receive gold from pilgrims and wealthy benefactors, do you not?'

'All donations are used to further the work of the sacred monasteries, my lord...'

'And some of that gold will now also be used to feed the poor of this island,' Friel said, his voice calm and level. 'People are going hungry, while the monks up in Zamata Gataza gorge themselves on meat and wine. My government isn't asking too much – just that the monks pay the same as everyone else.' He glanced at Leona, who was standing by his shoulder. 'I think this meeting is over. Please escort the holy brothers from the room.'

'But, my lord,' cried one of the monks, 'you are flouting a century-old tradition. The re-establishment of the monasteries came with a guarantee that the secular authorities would not interfere with our work.' He pointed a finger into Friel's face. 'I warn you now – if you continue down this path, the holy prelate will have no choice but to declare your government as profane and blasphemous.'

Friel smiled. 'The prelate should think very carefully before he decides to get involved in politics.'

'By taxing the monasteries, it is you who is dragging us into politics, my lord.'

'If the prelate feels so strongly about this, then perhaps he should come down from Mount Hodzulat and speak to me in person; instead of sending his lackeys.'

The monks looked shocked. 'But, my lord,' said one, 'the prelate is sacrosanct. He would be tainted if he stooped to speak to a... a...'

Friel chuckled. 'A what?'

The monk bowed his head. 'A god-killer, my lord. You slew Lord Meer Mon Adal, polluting the sacred precinct of Tsallon Anura with the god's holy blood. Your soul is damned.'

'Oh dear,' Friel laughed. 'My poor old soul. Perhaps you could ask the prelate to pray for me while he gathers the taxation that is owed to my government. You can leave now.'

'This is not the end of the matter, my lord,' said the monk.

'No? Well, here's a little threat you can take back to Zamata Gataza – if the prelate continues to withhold what is due, then it won't be pilgrims that he wakes up to find camped outside the door of his mountaintop monastery, it will be armed militia. And that, brother, will be the end of the matter.'

Leona walked past the monks and opened the door. The three monks glared at the colonel, then strode from the small chamber. Leona closed the door and turned to face Friel.

'I sense your disapproval,' the colonel said, his attention back on the document in his hand.

'Is it wise to alienate the religious authorities, sir? Many Zamatans still worship the serpent gods, and if the prelate orders the faithful to disobey the government, then we could face a wave of resistance.'

'The prelate would never dare,' said Friel. 'He knows that I would send troops to sack his beloved monastery. There are enough jewels and gold hidden away in Zamata Gataza to buy grain to feed the entire population for years. He will curse me, but he will pay.'

'You would sack Zamata Gataza,' Leona said, 'even after everything the monks in Tsallon Anura did to aid our cause?'

'The monks of Tsallon Anura had no choice in the matter,' he said. 'They hated our presence despoiling their beloved monastery. They're probably still cleaning away the taint of our occupation as we speak.' He picked up a quill, dabbed the tip into a pot of ink, and signed his name at the bottom of the document. 'What's next?'

'Representatives of the Aucterian community, sir,' Leona said. 'They wish to complain about some of their kin being evicted from their farms near Neeton. Apparently, a mob of Zamatans drove them off their land and left them destitute and homeless. The Aucterians want to know what your government is going to do to protect them.'

'Refer them to the militia leadership. This sounds like a policing matter.'

'They claim that they have tried, sir. They say that the militia told them that they have no resources to patrol every part of the island.'

Friel shrugged. 'Well, if the militia said that, then it must be true.'

'Could we not spare a few soldiers to help out, sir? Parts of the outer isle are descending into lawlessness.'

'And where would I find more soldiers, Leona? Do you want me to pluck them out of thin air? I have under a thousand militiamen to keep the peace throughout Igatz and Kaugatz, and another six hundred are needed to man the Chain Castles. I'm afraid that the outer towns and villages will have to look to themselves for protection at the moment.'

Leona frowned. 'You could always allow women to join the militia, sir.'

Friel chuckled. 'And I thought we were having a sensible discussion.'

'Both the Dominion and the Gunstians permit women to serve in their armed forces, sir.'

'Perhaps they do, Leona, but Zamata belongs to neither empire. Part of the reason we strived to achieve independence was so that we could decide things for ourselves.'

'By *ourselves*, do you mean the men of Zamata?'

'It was the men who fought for the island's freedom.'

'Yes, because you wouldn't allow the women to fight alongside them.'

Friel's smile faded. 'Are you angry, Leona? You seem a little angry.'

'I just think that you are wasting an opportunity, sir. The men of this island have always ignored the opinions of the women.'

'Do I ignore your opinion? You are my closest advisor, Leona.'

'Then maybe you should take my advice on this, sir. You are fond of proclaiming that every Zamatan has a job under your government, but you are really only talking about the men. There are plenty of under-employed women throughout Zamata, and we are short of labour. Would it not make economic sense to include more women, as well as being fairer?'

'I'll think about it.' He glanced out of the window at the position of the sun. 'Tell the Aucterians to come back tomorrow; I have another appointment I need to attend.'

'I checked your diary, sir; there was no appointment scheduled for this afternoon.'

He smiled. 'It isn't the kind of appointment I would add to the diary. It is of the more... intimate variety.'

'Who is it this time? Lady Mylene?'

'Oh, I tired of her some time ago,' he said. 'All she did was go on about how dreadful it was that her family lost all of its money in the rebellion. This new girl is less vocal about such matters.'

The door opened as Leona tried to think of a suitable response, and Lahnos Laimos walked in.

'Ah, nephew,' said Friel; 'I'm glad you are here. We need to talk, but first I must remind you that it is customary to knock before entering. I am the ruler of Zamata, and a ruler cannot have people barging into their private office.'

Lahnos raised an eyebrow. 'Have you finished?'

'No,' said Friel; 'I was just getting started. It has come to my attention that you are harbouring a Bullan prisoner of war within your apartment. I assume that you have received the urgent letters I sent you regarding this?'

'I threw them in the bin.'

Friel smiled, but his eyes narrowed at the same time. 'Also, Major Typan has informed me that you are refusing to use your Gift to assist us. Is that true?'

'I read the mind of a Gunstian your major had executed; I won't do it again.'

'I heard the agent died of natural causes, nephew.'

'You can believe that if you want to, uncle.'

'So, you are refusing to hand over a prisoner, and you are refusing to help Major Typan in his investigations. Tell me – why do I keep you on the payroll?'

'You know why – in case the Demon Witch speaks to me.'

'And has she spoken to you?'

Lahnos smirked. 'Yes.'

Friel rolled his eyes. 'Then why didn't you say so, nephew?'

'Because you were too busy berating me to listen.'

'I'm listening now.'

Lahnos strolled forward and took a seat in front of the colonel's desk. He glanced at Leona. 'Any chance of a coffee?'

'I am not your servant,' Leona spat.

Lahnos laughed. 'You're a little tetchy today.'

'She's feeling oppressed,' said Friel. 'Just before you barged in, she was lecturing me on how I should allow women into the militia.'

Lahnos shrugged. 'Maybe you should. It might stop Reyn complaining to me about it. She's wanted to join the militia ever since the rebellion started.'

'Can we move the conversation back to the Demon Witch?' said Friel.

'Fine. She spoke to me twenty minutes ago. The Imperial Gunstian Fleet is three hours away from the eastern coast of Zamata. Well, it was. It will now be just over two and a half hours away.'

Friel said nothing as he stared at his nephew.

'That's why I barged in,' Lahnos went on. 'Would you have preferred me to have gone through the proper channels and booked an appointment?'

The colonel jumped to his feet and ran to the door. He opened it, and stuck his head out into the corridor.

'Somebody get me Bauchlie!' he shouted. 'Now!' He turned back to Lahnos. 'How many ships?'

'A few dozen. I don't have the exact number.'

'And their plan? Did the Demon Witch discern what they intend to do?'

'The Demon Witch doesn't understand the Gunstian language,' Leona said. 'Did you forget that, sir?'

Bauchlie appeared in the doorway, a surly expression on his scarred face. 'What do you want?'

'I need your three hundred men, Bauchlie,' said Friel. 'Gather them at once and send them to the jetty by the Dragon Palace. There are enough boats there to transport them across the Cyasarta.'

'The Cyasarta?' said Bauchlie. 'Why would I send my men across the Cyasarta?'

'Because the damn Gunstians are coming,' Friel cried, 'and they have a dozen agents embedded into the garrison of the southern Chain Castle. If the Gunstians arrive before we do, their fleet could enter the inlet unopposed.'

Bauchlie said nothing for a moment, his features guarded, then he nodded. 'I will lead them in person.'

'Wait,' said Leona. 'I should come.'

The three men turned to her.

'Why?' said Friel.

'Because, sir, I have the ability to discover which of the militia soldiers are actually Gunstian agents. How else were you intending to root them out?'

Lahnos laughed. 'She has a point.'

'I agree,' said Bauchlie. 'Leona should accompany us.'

'But...' said Friel, 'it seems a little dangerous for... for a...'

'For a woman?' said Leona, her eyes tight. 'You don't need me here – haven't you got another appointment you need to keep, sir? Besides, I am sure that Bauchlie will not allow anything to happen to me.'

'She's right,' said Bauchlie. 'My men will protect her.'

The colonel slumped into his seat.

'Should we kill or arrest any agents we find?' Bauchlie went on.

'Keep one alive,' said Friel. 'Dispose of the rest.'

'And I can go?' said Leona.

Friel waved a hand at her. 'Why not? Have fun.'

Bauchlie turned, and Leona followed him out of the room.

One hour later, eight wide-hulled transport ships were ploughing through the calm waters of the Cyasarta. With only a slight wind, Bauchlie had ordered his men to row the mile and a half from the jetty by the Dragon Palace to the shore where the inlet narrowed as it led to the ocean. Leona had been told to remain by Bauchlie's side, and she stood next to him as they watched the coastline approach.

'How did you persuade the colonel to let you keep control of these men?' she asked. 'They include the survivors from the group that broke into the palace and held Lord Kheran hostage, do they not?'

Bauchlie nodded, his eyes on the horizon.

'Well?' said Leona. 'How did you persuade him? He doesn't allow anyone else to command their own private force.'

'I didn't persuade him; I just refused to hand them over after the

Dominion withdrew. Each one of the three hundred has sworn an oath of loyalty to me, and it is me they serve.'

Leona frowned. She had felt no tingle to indicate any lie coming from Bauchlie, but she still found his words hard to believe.

'But...'

'But what?' he said. 'I can use these men as an additional force to help Friel from time to time; just as I am doing right now. But he doesn't control them, and he doesn't control me.' His dark eyes flickered from the shoreline to the position of the sun, then he turned to the men rowing the boat. 'Get ready, lads. As soon as we land, we'll beach the ships and run the two miles to the southern Chain Castle. We have to get there before the Gunstians arrive; nothing else matters. Once there, we will ensure that the chains are raised. You all know what happened the last time Gunstian ships entered the Cyasarta – this time will be worse.' He gestured towards Leona. 'This woman is an asset that must be protected. If you see her identify any militia soldier as a Gunstian agent, you will believe her. Show no mercy.'

'What about the colonel's order to keep one alive?' Leona whispered.

Bauchlie shrugged. 'Do you see the colonel here? Oars up!'

The boat's hull rammed up onto the beach and they juddered to a halt. The armed men jumped down to the sand and began hauling the boat further up the beach, as the other seven vessels landed next to them. Orders were given, and the soldiers began to race eastwards along the shore in squads, their shields slung across their backs, and their crossbows over their shoulders. Leona climbed down to the soft sand and found Bauchlie, who was urging his men along.

'Why did we beach here?' she said. 'We could have rowed all the way to the Chain Castle.'

'I didn't wish us to be seen,' he said. 'This beach is out of sight of the castles, and no one will be watching the road from the west. Can you run in that skirt?'

'I can run.'

Bauchlie set off, and she hurried after him, her boots slipping on the wet sand. They crossed a few low dunes and reached a rough track, its surface rutted by countless wagon wheels. The soldiers under Bauchlie's command were already moving along the road at speed, and Leona fell in with them, her heart pounding as she kept up with the men. The road curved a little to the south, then, when it veered back to the north, the southernmost of the two Chain Castles came into sight – a tall, square tower, surrounded by high stone walls and lower outbuildings. Leona squinted up at the top of the tower, and saw several Zamatan militiamen by the parapets. All were gazing out towards the ocean, and some were pointing. The road ran above a cliff along the shore and, as Leona got closer, she glanced over the short body of water towards the other Chain Castle. It had started to raise its ends of the thick double chains, their heavy links dripping water as they were lifted into the air; but there was no similar movement happening by the southern castle.

Bauchlie raced ahead until he was at the front of his three hundred men, and Leona set off after him, her breath becoming more ragged with every step. She saw Bauchlie approach the western gates of the castle compound. He spoke to an officer from the militia for a few moments as Leona caught up, then the gates were opened and Bauchlie's forces rushed through. Bauchlie grabbed her arm and pulled her towards the main tower, as his men began to take control of the southern castle.

'What's your plan?' he said, as they reached the large arched entranceway.

'The simplest course would be for your men to take over the controls that operate the chain,' she said, 'but I assume that none of them know how the chains work?'

'You assume correctly.'

'Then take me there, and ask each militiaman in turn if they are loyal to Zamata or Gunst.'

Bauchlie nodded, then he issued some orders to a nearby squad.

'I thought you were here to reinforce us?' said the militia officer who had opened the gates.

'I lied,' said Bauchlie. 'This castle is now under my authority. Take us to the chamber from where the chain is operated.'

'Why?' said the officer. 'The Imperial Gunstian Fleet is approaching – are you trying to hinder our work?'

Bauchlie grabbed the officer by the throat. 'If the Gunstians are coming, then why hasn't your end of the chain been raised? Are you a traitor to Zamata?'

'No!' the officer gasped, his hands on his neck as he choked.

'He's lying,' said Leona.

Bauchlie drew his sword and plunged it through the officer's chest, while his left hand still gripped the man's throat. Blood seeped through the front of his clothes, then Bauchlie released him and he fell to the cobbles. A dozen other militia soldiers backed away, and Bauchlie pointed to a sergeant.

'Are you loyal to Zamata?'

'I am, sir,' said the sergeant.

Leona nodded. 'Truth.'

'Lead us to the chain-room,' said Bauchlie. 'Now.'

The sergeant raced forwards and hurried into the tower. Bauchlie signalled to his men, and several squads followed the sergeant into the gloomy interior of the old castle. The sergeant led them up a flight of worn stairs, then halted at a thick wooden door, which was being guarded by two soldiers.

'Let us in,' said the sergeant.

'Sorry, sergeant,' said one of the guards. 'No one is allowed into the control room while the chains are being operated.'

Bauchlie nodded to his men and half a dozen crossbows loosed, cutting down the two soldiers by the door. The sergeant stared at the bodies, then he crouched down and removed a set of keys from one of the dead men's clothes. His fingers grasped hold of a key, and he set it into the lock, turning it. The door swung open, and Bauchlie charged in. Lying on the floor between two great winches were more bodies, while a dozen soldiers were standing idle by the windows, watching the Gunstian Fleet draw ever nearer.

'Kill them all!' Bauchlie cried, and his men stormed the large chamber.

Bauchlie pushed Leona behind him as crossbow bolts started to fly through the air, then swords were drawn and blood was spilled over the thick wooden floorboards. One of the agents made a break for the door, and Leona picked up a crossbow and shot him in the back; and then, all at once, it was over. Bauchlie glanced at the crossbow in Leona's hands, then he turned back to the sergeant.

'Get more men in here and raise the chain. Do it now.'

'Yes, sir,' the sergeant cried.

More militia soldiers piled into the room. They cleared the bodies from the double winches, and began turning them, with six men to each winch. Leona walked to the window and watched as the mighty chains broke through the surface of the water. A cheer sounded out from the roof of the northern castle on the far side of the inlet, as the militia posted there saw the chains rise to block the entrance to the Cyasarta.

'You did well, Leona,' said Bauchlie, his eyes on the rising chains. 'How do you feel?'

'About what?' she said.

'You killed a man. These things can affect a person deeply. The first time...'

'That wasn't the first time,' she said. She pointed to her right. 'There – do you see the masts?'

'I see them. If we had been another twenty minutes, it would have been too late.'

'I want to go up onto the roof and watch from there.'

Bauchlie nodded. 'Call for me if you wish to leave and I'll have a boat brought in to take you back to Igatz. I will be staying down here for a while to clear up the mess.'

Leona handed her crossbow to Bauchlie, then she stepped over the pools of blood on the floor and left the room. Bodies were being carried down the stairs by loyal militiamen, and she waited for them to pass, then selected a spiral staircase that went up. She counted the steps until she reached a hundred, then emerged into the sunshine on the roof of the tower. An officer was there, along with several soldiers, and they glanced at her.

'Who are you?' the officer said. 'What was causing the delay with the chains? I sent two messengers downstairs to warn of the approaching fleet, but neither returned.'

'Gunstian agents had taken control of the chain winches,' Leona said. 'Did you know anything about that?'

The officer narrowed his eyes. 'There were Gunstian agents here, in the castle?'

'Yes. They were hiding among the militia. Did you know?'

'Of course not. Who are you?'

Leona felt no tingle. She walked to the edge of the parapet and gazed eastwards towards the endless ocean. In the distance, over two dozen ships of the Gunstian Fleet were visible.

'What happens now?' she said. 'What will the Gunstians do?'

'No civilians are permitted up here, ma'am,' said the officer, 'and as you are refusing to identify yourself, I am going to have to take you into custody.'

'My name is Leona, and I am Colonel Laimos's closest advisor. You can try to arrest me, but I promise that it won't turn out well for you. Now, answer my question.'

The officer swallowed, then he gazed out to sea. 'Well, ma'am, the Gunstian ships have slowed, which means that they have seen the chains being raised. There's no way through into the Cyasarta for any vessel, not without cutting the chains, and to do that they would need to land a sizable force and try to storm either of the two Chain Castles. We have ballistae and catapults to repel any attack from the sea, and they will know that, especially if they had agents in the militia.'

'Do you think they will attack?'

'It's hard to say, ma'am. It depends on how many losses they are willing to sustain to gain access to the Cyasarta. What you can see before you represents about a third of the entire Imperial Gunstian Fleet, so this could be an opportunistic raid, rather than a full scale invasion. And, they might not have enough supplies for a long siege of the Chain Castles. There are many factors.'

'They're dropping anchor, sir,' said another soldier.

The officer nodded. 'Now, we wait, Miss Leona, while the Gunstians decide what to do.'

Two hours passed. The sun was starting to set in the west over the mountains of Hodzulat and Medamuna, and still Leona and the others kept watch from the roof of the southern tower. Bauchlie joined them, and they stood in silence as every eye gazed at the two dozen ships anchored on the edge of the ocean half a mile to their east.

A loud cheer erupted from the roof of the castle on the far side of the inlet, and Leona peered into the dying light.

'The Gunstians are raising their anchors and adjusting their sails,' the officer cried.

The soldiers around him raised their arms and cheered.

'What does that mean?' said Leona.

'It means,' said Bauchlie, 'that they have decided to leave. There will be no Gunstians on Zamata – not this day.' He eyed her. 'Thank you for your help.'

'You're welcome,' Leona said. She smiled. 'I think I would like to go back to Igatz now.'

CHAPTER 4
THE HOUSE GUEST

Igatz, Serpent Isle – 8th Tradinch 1588

'Ten children were taken from my village,' Efizel said; 'ten of the strongest boys. I was proud to have been chosen, but I remember my mother was sad. She did not cry, for that would have been shameful, but I could see it in her eyes. I asked her why, and she told me that she would miss seeing me grow into a man. I told her that she still had my three younger brothers living under her roof, but she said that I was the eldest, and the most precious to her.'

Reyn watched the Bullan from the low couch. 'Have you seen your family since then?'

'No. Those selected to serve the Dominion are bound to the army from the age of fourteen to the age of twenty-eight. Beyond that, some are chosen by the Dominion to remain with the regiments as officers, but the vast majority return to Klediomira Haga to start their own families. Veterans are honoured among my people, and it does not take them long to find a wife.'

'Fourteen seems very young,' said Reyn.

'The first four years consist of training,' Efizel said. 'There is a huge encampment on the southern coast of Aucteran, close to the desert, where two thousand new boys arrive each spring.'

'Why, though?' said Lahnos. 'Why do the Klediomira Haga serve the Dominion? You make better soldiers than any human; why aren't you independent?'

Efizel smiled. 'It is true that we are stronger than humans but, alas, we are not as strong as dragons. It was the dragon gods who subdued my people, after a decades-long struggle that took place over a thousand years ago. They burned our villages and forests, and slaughtered untold numbers of my kin, until we finally submitted. My ancestors then swore an unbreakable vow – to supply two thousand young recruits every year to fight for the Dominion. Aside from this one condition, we are free to live as we please without interference. No human dwells upon Klediomira Haga; none would ever dare.'

'I have told you much,' Efizel went on, 'and now it is time for you to reveal more of your own secrets.'

Lahnos and Reyn glanced at each other.

Reyn got to her feet. 'I might just close the shutters first; it's starting to get dark.'

'Please leave them open,' said the Bullan soldier. 'I like the fresh air. Lahnos, tell me more about your Gift.'

'I've only used it twice,' said Lahnos, as Reyn returned to her seat. 'Once accidentally, and once on purpose – that day I discovered you were in prison. Did the Dominion teach you about the Gifted?'

'Yes. We were taught about all parts of the world while we were being trained. Language classes made up much of the curriculum, but there were also lessons about history. Do you know of the first major campaign that the dragons asked us to carry out? No? It was genocide. The Dominion was facing resistance from the native inhabitants of Aucteran, who outnumbered their own human colonists many times over. Among those natives were many with the Gifts that you speak of, and our mission was to exterminate them.'

'I've heard about that,' said Lahnos. 'Every single native human was wiped out in the East of this world, leaving only you and the Aucterians. Is that right?'

'Yes.'

'I don't understand,' said Reyn. 'If every human in the East was wiped out, then where did the Aucterians come from?'

'The dragon gods brought their own humans with them when they came to this world,' said the Bullan. 'They arrived in Inopei, and only later spread south to Aucteran.'

Reyn narrowed her eyes. 'The dragons came from another world?'

'They did,' said Efizel, 'or so the legends say. A great and powerful god named Nathaniel chose King Gahad to rule this world.'

'And when was this?'

The Bullan smiled. 'What year is it, Miss Reyn?'

'It's the year fifteen-eighty-eight,' she said.

'Did you not realise that the count of years is numbered from the arrival of King Gahad upon this world? The natives of Athumia had lived alone and in peace for thousands of years before this momentous event. Well, perhaps not always in peace – but there were no dragons, and no Dominion back then. Nathaniel gave this world to King Gahad, but the Dragon-King failed to conquer all of it. This is a source of great shame and humiliation to the dragons. It is why Athumia shall never be at peace until Gunst has been subdued – the dragons cannot bear the thought that any part of this world lies beyond their control. Twice the dragons have invaded Gunst in force, and twice they have been forced to retreat. King Gahad had a new plan – to occupy this island and then slowly and carefully build up his strength for a third invasion, but his death has put an end to that notion.' He sipped from his glass of water. 'It was a wise plan, but I expect the dragons will abandon all thoughts of caution and prudence regarding Gunst, now that the mighty Gahad is no more. The accursed Demon Witch has much to answer for.'

'I think I'll warm up a kettle on the stove,' said Reyn, standing again. 'I can make us all some coffee.'

She gave a pointed glance towards Lahnos as she left the living room, and he felt a twinge of guilt at the back of his mind. Despite agreeing to divulge his secrets to Efizel in exchange for hearing about the Klediomira Haga, he had yet to mention anything about the Demon Witch to the Bullan soldier. He dreaded bringing it up, not only because Efizel clearly loathed the Demon Witch, but also because he admired Lahnos for what he had done to rescue the Bullan soldiers from the Gunstians, and Lahnos knew he would think less of him if he discovered the truth.

'Your silence is making me suspicious,' said Efizel. 'What is it that your woman wants you to tell me? That is why she left the room, is it not – to give you a chance to tell me something?'

Lahnos nodded.

'Well? Say what you need to say, young Laimos. It is about your Gift?'

'No. It's about something else. The Demon Witch.'

Efizel frowned. 'And what could you possibly know about that topic that I do not?'

'I know quite a lot, as it happens. Tell me what you know first.'

'Very little,' said the Bullan; 'only that King Gahad was slain upon Inopei, and that the dragons are blaming this Demon Witch for His Majesty's death. Some think her existence is a myth, while others believe that a Gifted Gunstian agent was responsible for slaying the King. If she does exist, then she represents the greatest foe the Dominion has faced in a very long time.'

Lahnos rubbed his face with a hand. Did he really have to tell Efizel the truth? Perhaps it would be better to say nothing.

'I have shown great trust in you, young Laimos,' the Bullan said. 'I have told you things that my people are loath to reveal to humans; are you dishonouring yourself by holding something back from me?'

'What I have to say will probably enrage you,' Lahnos said.

'Even so,' said the Bullan, 'you have a duty to tell me. No matter what words come out of your mouth, I will not harm you or your woman.'

'The Demon Witch is real,' Lahnos said, 'and I know this because she speaks inside my head.'

The Bullan sat perfectly still, his eyes giving nothing away.

'It was the Demon Witch who told me that you were locked up

beneath the Convention Hall,' Lahnos went on. 'If she hadn't, you would still be there.'

'Did she kill King Gahad?'

'Yes.'

'Then she is my enemy.'

'She also assisted Zamata during the rebellion; not just against the Dominion, but against the Gunstians, too.'

'She is not a Gunstian?'

'No. I don't know where she comes from. She first spoke to me when I discovered my Gift. I think it's what drew her to me. She knows everything about me, but I know very little about her.'

'But she speaks to you? What does she say?'

'She passes on information, and then I give that information to my uncle. She told us all about the naval attack by the Northern Fleet, and that allowed us to repel it. She... she also helped me that night I rescued you from the Gunstians in Kaugatz.'

Efizel got to his feet and strode from the room without a word, leaving Lahnos sitting alone in the living room. His shoulders slumped a little, and he stared at the polished floorboards.

'You told him, then?'

Lahnos glanced up, and saw Reyn standing by the door that led to the kitchen.

'Yes. I told him.'

Reyn nodded. 'It's for the best, Lahnos.'

'For the best?' he cried. 'How can you say that? He probably hates me now; in fact, I wouldn't be surprised if he walked out of the apartment and never returned.'

'He needed to know the truth,' said Reyn. 'I know it's painful, but it was the right thing to do.'

'You want him to leave, don't you?'

Reyn shrugged. 'I was angry that you invited a Bullan soldier to live here without asking me first, but no – I don't want him to leave. I guess I've grown to like him. He seems honest, polite and honourable. He's changed the way I think about the Bullan.'

Lahnos snorted.

'He has,' said Reyn. 'He has also been very helpful around the apartment – he cooks, he cleans, and he tidies up after himself; which is more than I can say about you. He was scrubbing the floors when I got home from work yesterday. When have you ever scrubbed the floors, Lahnos?'

Lahnos simmered in silence as he watched Reyn light a couple of wall lamps, filling the living room with a soft, warm glow.

'Maybe I should be the one to leave,' he said, 'so that you and Efizel can live in domestic bliss together.'

There was a firm knock at the front door of the apartment, and Reyn smiled.

'Perhaps you could make yourself useful,' she said, 'and see who it is.'

Lahnos glared at her then got to his feet. He walked through to the hallway, but saw no sign of their Bullan house guest. He went to the front door and opened it.

'Greetings, nephew,' said Friel, a bottle of something clutched in his hand. Next to the colonel stood Leona, while half a dozen militiamen were crowding the stairs behind them.

Lahnos maintained his steady frown. 'Am I under arrest?'

Friel burst into laughter, and slapped his thigh. 'Why – what have you done now?'

'May we come in?' said Leona.

'I'm not letting six soldiers into my house,' said Lahnos, eyeing the militiamen.

'You've already got one living in there,' said Friel; 'but, no – the men will remain outside. They insisted upon escorting me across the street from the Convention Hall.' He turned to the soldiers. 'Go downstairs and wait for me there. I may be a while.'

Friel moved forwards and, for a moment, Lahnos blocked his way into the apartment. The colonel raised an eyebrow at him, then Lahnos sighed and moved to the side, allowing both Friel and Leona to enter.

'We have visitors, Reyn,' Lahnos yelled, as he closed the door behind them. 'My insufferable uncle has decided to come round.'

Reyn appeared in the hallway. 'Hello,' she said.

'Hello, Reyn,' said Leona. 'Your hair is growing back, I see.'

'What else would it do?' said Lahnos.

'Ignore him,' said Reyn. 'He's in a foul mood this evening. He has just told the Bullan soldier living here all about the Demon Witch.'

'Ah,' said Friel, glancing around. 'And where is the fugitive prisoner of war?'

'If you wanted him,' said Lahnos, 'then why didn't you come and get him?'

'And upset the one who brings me such valuable information?' said Friel. 'I am prepared to make all kinds of allowances for your behaviour, my dear nephew, as long as the Demon Witch continues to assist us.'

'Come into the living room,' said Reyn. 'I've just made a pot of coffee.'

Friel brandished the bottle in his hands. 'Thank you, but I have brandy. I mean to celebrate.'

'I would love a coffee, thank you,' said Leona.

They walked into the living room, then Reyn strode back through to the kitchen as the others sat.

'Celebrate?' said Lahnos. 'What do we have to celebrate, uncle? Our impending destruction?'

Friel chuckled. 'We are here to thank you for what you did for us yesterday, my horned nephew. Be a good fellow and fetch some glasses, and I'll open the brandy.'

'Get them yourself.'

'I will get them,' said a voice from the doorway.

Lahnos, Friel and Leona turned, and saw the Bullan soldier walk into the room. Efizel strode to a cupboard, opened it, and placed five small glasses onto a silver tray. He then walked over to where the others were sitting, and set the tray down onto a low table.

He stared at Friel, his features a mask of indifference. 'Welcome to Lahnos's home, traitor.'

'And a good evening to you,' said Friel. 'Should I be concerned about my personal safety?'

'I would never dishonour my host by sullying his home with violence,' said the Bullan, 'but make no mistake – you deserve to die in agony for what you did. Over a thousand of my kinsfolk were slain in your treacherous rebellion.'

'I think you will find that the Gunstians were responsible for most of those deaths,' said Friel, 'and it was never my intention to harm any of the noble Bullan. We are both professionals, divided only by our allegiances. Can we not leave it at that?'

Efizel sat, but his eyes never left Friel's face.

The colonel opened the bottle of brandy, and poured a measure into each glass.

'As I was saying,' the colonel went on, 'Leona and I would like to thank you, nephew, for the information you gave to us yesterday. You will be delighted, no doubt, to hear that the Imperial Gunstian Fleet was unable to force its way into the Cyasarta.'

'The Gunstian Fleet was here yesterday?' said the Bullan.

'It was,' said Friel. 'And thanks to Lahnos's timely intervention, we were able to prevent a number of Gunstian agents from carrying out an act of sabotage that would have allowed the fleet to enter the inlet. Were it not for Lahnos, the Gunstians would now be in control of this island.'

'And were it not for you, traitor,' said the Bullan, 'the Gunstians would never have dreamed of attacking in the first place. It was your actions that have left the Serpent Isle virtually undefended.'

Reyn walked into the room, and set down another silver tray onto the table.

'Fresh coffee,' she said.

'Thank you,' said Leona.

'Let's raise our glasses before any coffee is poured,' said Friel. 'I would like to make a toast.'

Lahnos and the others picked up their glasses.

Friel smiled. 'To the Demon Witch.'

Efizel set his glass down, a look of disgust on his face.

'Would you drink to the defeat of the Gunstians?' said Friel.

The Bullan scowled at him. 'I would happily drink to your death.'

The colonel shrugged, then downed the brandy in his glass.

Lahnos also set his glass down untouched. He glanced at Efizel. 'I should have told you about the Demon Witch before now,' he said. 'I was reluctant to mention her. I won't hold any grudge if you decide to forget all about the pledge you made to me.'

'Do not insult me, young Laimos,' said the Bullan. 'My people do not forget their oaths.'

'What oath is this?' said Friel.

'Your nephew saved me and thirty of my colleagues from torture and execution at the hands of the Gunstians in Kaugatz,' Efizel said. 'I am the only survivor, and I would have been dishonoured had I not remained here to serve him.'

'Ah; so that is why you stayed on Zamata. I had wondered.'

'I'm glad you're not leaving,' Reyn said to the Bullan. 'You are welcome to stay in this apartment for as long as you like.'

Efizel bowed his head to her. 'Thank you. I admit that I feel betrayed by what Lahnos told me, Miss Reyn. I am also confused. What does the Demon Witch want? Why would she slay the mighty King Gahad and assist in the defeat of the Dominion forces if she is also opposed to the Gunstians?'

'I don't know,' said Reyn. 'I don't think any of us know that.'

'It seems clear,' said Friel, 'that the Demon Witch wants Zamata to be free, but even I am ignorant of her ultimate motivations. Still, I am grateful to her all the same.'

'Have you asked her, young Laimos?' said the Bullan.

'Yes,' said Lahnos. 'She doesn't like those sorts of questions.'

'Call on her now,' the Bullan went on, 'and demand an answer.'

'It doesn't work like that. She appears whenever she feels like it, and I have no control over when she speaks to me.'

'But she spoke to you yesterday?'

Lahnos nodded. 'She told me that the Gunstian Fleet was approaching. Before that, the last time she spoke to me was in the basement of the Convention Hall. She told me that you were imprisoned there, and she helped me get you released.'

'She helped me?' said the Bullan. 'I don't understand. I am her enemy; why would she help me?'

'She does it all for Lahnos,' said Leona.

The others turned to her.

'That is what I believe,' said Leona. 'Everything the Demon Witch does seems designed to help Lahnos. For some reason, she has chosen to speak to him, and to no one else. Lahnos is the key. If we could discover why she has chosen him out of the millions of people on this world, then we would be closer to the truth.'

The Bullan eyed her. 'You may be correct, miss. I recall seeing you in Tsallon Anura, but no one has introduced you to me.'

'My apologies,' said Friel. 'This is my colleague Miss Leona of Kaugatz.'

'It is a pleasure to meet you, Miss Leona,' said the Bullan. 'By your logic, the Demon Witch fought for the Serpent Isle because young Laimos lives here. That would imply that she cares little for the politics of the situation, but it does not explain why she would slay King Gahad.'

'She didn't realise that killing him would cause such a catastrophe,' said Lahnos. 'That's what she told me. She also said that watching over me was a way to salve her conscience; but I don't see how that can be true. I think she acted to defend Zamata out of pity, not just because I live here. She saw the island suffering, and wanted to help.'

'She sounds like a fool,' said the Bullan.

Friel laughed. 'A fool?'

'Yes. She acts without considering the consequences. The rumours surrounding the death of King Gahad are legion, but one I have heard several times – that His Majesty wished to bring this Demon Witch into his service. He had discovered her presence in Eastern Inopei, and had taken her to a palace built upon the side of a volcano. There, she betrayed and killed him.'

'Perhaps she did not wish to serve him,' said Friel.

'And so she struck down the sovereign ruler of this world? The Demon Witch is a danger to us all – you are merely blinded by the fact that she has been assisting you in your treachery, Colonel Laimos.'

Friel nodded. 'Perhaps you are correct, my Bullan friend. However, I sincerely hope she continues to lend us her assistance.' He poured coffee from the pot into the five mugs on the second tray. 'One more thing – it is incumbent upon me to inform you that you will not be permitted to leave this island. If the Dominion were to discover that the Demon Witch is helping our cause, then they would send dragons and ships to destroy us.'

'Now it is you who sounds like a fool, Colonel,' said the Bullan. 'With or without that information, the Dominion will indubitably be sending a large force here to retake this island. To believe otherwise is a delusion.'

Friel smiled. 'Now you sound like my nephew.'

The Bullan frowned. 'Explain that comment.'

'Lahnos has always been a rather reluctant supporter of the cause of Zamatan independence,' Friel went on. 'Even as a part-Bullan, he seems to prefer Dominion rule.'

Efizel stared at Lahnos. 'Is that true?'

Lahnos nodded. 'It is, yes. I just don't see the point in rebelling, when neither the Dominion nor the Gunstians will ever allow us to be free. And, if I had to choose between the two, then I would choose to be ruled by the dragons.'

The Bullan soldier grinned and slapped Lahnos across the back. 'Well said, lad!'

'Yes, I thought you would like that,' said Friel. 'It is just as well that the Demon Witch has helped us despite Lahnos's feelings on the subject. Tell me, as a Bullan soldier, why wouldn't the Dominion allow us to live in peace? This island does not belong to them; it belongs to us. Isn't it dishonourable to conquer and ravage another's land? If it is wrong for the Gunstians to attack us, then why wouldn't it also be wrong for the Dominion to do the same?'

'It is not dishonourable to submit to those more powerful than you,' said the Bullan.

Friel smiled. 'So a child at school should submit to any bully who threatens him?'

The Bullan said nothing.

'I am not trying to ridicule you, my Bullan friend,' Friel went on. 'Your people were conquered by the dragons a long time ago, and you need to believe certain things in order to hold on to your sense of honour.'

'My people made an unbreakable vow…'

'…to serve those who had defeated you in combat. Yes. I know. If your ancestors hadn't submitted to King Gahad, then the Bullan might have been utterly annihilated. Ask yourself this – if you were a native of Zamata, and you saw a chance for freedom, would you not fight for it?'

'I am not a native of Zamata, Colonel; I am a soldier of the Dominion.'

Friel nodded, but said nothing more. He picked up his mug of coffee and took a sip.

Leona eyed the Bullan. 'Is that true?' she said. 'Are you still a soldier of the Dominion?'

Lahnos and Reyn glanced at each other as Efizel frowned.

'Strictly speaking,' the Bullan said, 'I am no longer part of my regiment. However, do not imagine that my loyalties have changed. I will always believe that the Dominion is the rightful authority upon Athumia. Always.'

Two hours later, Lahnos and Efizel were standing out on the apartment's narrow balcony that overlooked the Convention Hall. Leona and Friel had departed some time before, leaving half of the brandy behind, and Reyn had gone to bed. The night air was still warm, and a soft wind was blowing across Igatz. Lahnos gazed up at the cloudless sky. With shortages of oil afflicting the island, only a few streetlamps had been lit in the Temple District, and he had a clear view of the moon and stars.

'Much that has transpired today troubles me, young Laimos,' the Bullan said. 'The Demon Witch, and your uncle's words in particular have placed turmoil into my mind. Above all, however, I dread what the future will bring. The Gunstians will renew their attacks, and the forces of the Dominion might already be on their way to retake the island. I am pledged to serve and protect you – and you are the nephew of the man who led the rebellion. What will I do if thousands of Klediomira Haga disembark from ships? Will I be forced to fight them? The thought fills me with shame, and yet I can see no alternative.'

Lahnos stared up at the stars. 'Perhaps we should leave the island.'

Efizel turned to stare at him. 'And go where?'

'Aucteran.'

'Why would you wish to go to the land of your enemies?'

'To search for my father. If Leona was right, and the Demon Witch is trying to help me, then maybe she could track him down. If he's a slave, then I could free him.'

'And Reyn? Would you leave your woman here?'

'No. I'd ask her to come, too.'

The soldier shook his head. 'Two part-Bullan and a Klediomira Haga in Aucteran? We wouldn't last a day.'

'Why not?'

'There are no part-Bullan in the East, young Laimos. Your horns would attract all kinds of unwanted attention. And, more importantly, none of my people are allowed to wander the roads of Aucteran.'

'I thought you said your training camp was in Aucteran.'

'It is, but it lies in the remote and uninhabited south. A great desert and a mountain range separate it from the cities where the humans dwell. The Dominion deploys my people to the colonies in Irlan and Elso; they do not permit us to walk freely around Aucteran.'

'What about Inopei? Are there Klediomira there?'

'Yes. The royal capital is guarded by several regiments of my people.'

'All right; we'll forget Aucteran. Maybe we should go directly to

Inopei. My father is as likely to be there as on Aucteran. That way, we could escape Zamata before it is crushed by any invasion, and you wouldn't have to fight your own people.'

The Bullan folded his arms across his broad chest.

'There are smugglers' ships from Irlan that visit Igatz occasionally,' Lahnos went on. 'With enough gold we could buy passage out of here. We might have to go to Irlan first, and take another ship from there to Inopei, but it can be done, if we will it.'

'Your uncle would be greatly angered if you left.'

'Then let's not tell him. I only see him now and again; days would pass before he even realised that we had gone.'

'And the Demon Witch? What would she think about this?'

'I don't know. Would you come with me if I could arrange it all?'

'You know the answer to that, young Laimos. You know I would never abandon you.'

Lahnos nodded. 'Let me broach the subject with Reyn, and then I can keep an eye out for any Irlanian smugglers. My uncle gave me some gold; I will see if it is enough to pay for passage.'

'As you will.'

Lahnos glanced down at the peaceful town of Igatz. 'How long do we have before the Dominion gets here?'

'It is hard to say. The larger the fleet, the longer it will take to assemble. One month, perhaps?'

'A month?' Lahnos said. He smiled. 'That should be enough time. Until then, I shall be a good boy, and do whatever my uncle asks of me.'

'That would be unwise,' said Efizel. 'If you did that, then the colonel would guess that you were planning something. It would be better if you continued to defy him in a hundred small ways; that way, his suspicions would be allayed.'

Lahnos laughed. 'That sounds like good advice.'

CHAPTER 5
LANDFALL

East of the Serpent Isle – 24th Tradinch 1588

Captain Cisca of the Dragon Corps stood on the flight deck of the huge dragon carrier as the sun cleared the horizon behind her. Two miles away to the west, the faint coastline of the Serpent Isle was visible as a grey smear. If Cisca strained her eyes, she could catch the occasional glimpse of three tiny black specks circling above the landmass. The dragons were remaining at a high altitude, wary of triggering the island's defences, while the re-purposed convoy had been anchored all night, riding up and down on the waves that swept across the vast ocean.

Cisca loosened the buttons on her overcoat as the sun's rays began to warm her back. The sky was turning blue, and it was going to be another hot day. Only two months and eight days had passed since she had left the Serpent Isle with Lord Kheran, and she had spent almost two-thirds of that time on board a ship, traversing the ocean to Naeth, before returning to the place she had sworn to herself that she would never see again.

People were going to die – that was certain. If the native islanders decided to resist the forces sent to bring them back under the authority of the Dominion, then many would lose their lives. Cisca prayed that they would surrender quickly, but then she remembered the passion that Bauchlie had felt for his cause. If others shared his fanaticism, then blood would soon be flowing through the streets of Igatz.

She heard a noise next to her, and turned to see Major Lyla and a junior lieutenant standing by her side on the wide flight deck.

'Good morning, ma'am,' Cisca said.

'Good morning, Captain,' said Lyla. 'Did you rest well?'

'I awoke in the middle of the night, ma'am, and couldn't get back to sleep; so I have been up here for a few hours.'

Lyla nodded, her eyes on the western horizon. 'The Serpent Isle looks so small from here.'

'It stretches a mere dozen miles from north to south, ma'am, and only a little more than that from east to west. The two mountains you can see are in the far west of the island.'

'Mountains?'

'More like hills, I suppose, ma'am,' said Cisca, 'though the Zamatans refer to them as mountains.'

'Such a tiny place,' said Lyla. 'The islands of Irlan are far larger, and yet none of them have caused the Dominion as much trouble as this one has.'

The young lieutenant raised an arm. 'The blessed dragons are returning to the fleet, ma'am.'

Cisca glanced up, and saw the three dark specks in the sky racing back towards the ships gathered around the huge dragon carrier. A whistle sounded, and sailors began emerging from the narrow stairs that led from the decks below. Two more officers from the Dragon Corps appeared among them, and hurried to Major Lyla's side. Both were young and without experience of the Serpent Isle, and, like the other junior lieutenant on board, they looked up to Cisca as a font of knowledge regarding the island and its rebellion.

The sailors cleared away any obstructions on the wide, long flight deck, and all eyes turned upwards to watch the dragons as they approached. An enormous capstan and winch-powered lift was raised until it was level with the rest of the flight deck. It could carry only one dragon at a time, lowering and raising them between the flight deck and the cavernous holds where the dragons dwelt while on board. Above, Lord Malum Mon Gahad, third son of the slain King Gahad, and the new king's most trusted supporter, was in the lead, his pale red scales glowing in the dawn light; while behind him were Lady Lenta, Gahad's fourth daughter, and Lord Irvan, the former king's fifth son. The two siblings, both children of Gahad's second mate Nightsheen, were black with white edgings around their wings, tails and faces, and they had formed a column behind Lord Malum. The flight deck hushed as the first dragon landed, his claws digging into the thick, reinforced beams of the wide deck. Lord Malum pulled in his wings, then he raised his head and strode to the rear of the deck. Lady Lenta landed a few moments later, followed by Lord Irvan. As soon as they had moved away from the landing site, carpenters and their mates rushed forward with tools and spare wood to repair the damage inflicted upon the deck by their claws, while Major Lyla nodded to her officers, and they began walking towards the three dragons.

Major Lyla bowed low as she reached the three Children of Gahad, then Cisca and the three young lieutenants did the same. Lord Malum glanced down at them, his dark green eyes glimmering.

'Welcome back, my lords and lady,' said Lyla. 'How did the scouting expedition go? Should we retire below to discuss our plans?'

'I think not, Major,' said Malum. 'The sun is out, and the air is fresher up on deck. Let us formulate our strategy here.' The mighty dragon turned his head to gaze in the direction of the island. 'The chains at the entrance of the Cyasarta inlet have been raised, blocking passage into the interior of the Serpent Isle. Despite our great altitude, some of the rebels must have seen us flying overhead.'

'Perhaps we should have attacked during the hours of darkness, my lord,' said Lady Lenta. 'We could have stormed the Chain Castles before the humans noticed our presence. As it is, the element of surprise has been lost.'

Malum glared at his half-sibling. 'Do not underestimate our opponents, Lady Lenta. Lord Rufus and Lord Meer made that mistake, and their lives were lost as a consequence.'

'We can still attack, my lord,' said Irvan. 'We could rain fire down upon the two Chain Castles, and remove the obstruction blocking the inlet.'

'We shall be attacking, Lord Irvan, of that there is no doubt,' said Malum. 'However, it would be wise to consider any alternatives before I order a frontal assault upon the Chain Castles.' He stared at Cisca. 'What say you, Captain? You are one of the few among this fleet with direct experience of the island's defences.'

Cisca kept her features still as the dragons and officers waited for her to speak.

'The rebels used nets and ballistae to bring down Lord Meer,' she said, 'and Colonel Laimos will have ensured that the two Chain Castles have been fully-equipped with such weapons. Any dragon assault upon the fortifications would come with a heavy risk.'

'Might I suggest an alternative, my lords and lady?' said Major Lyla. 'The rebels will be expecting an assault upon the Chain Castles, but perhaps the fleet should ignore the Cyasarta for now. There is another way into the interior of the island.'

'Another way, Major?' said Lady Lenta. 'Explain yourself.'

'Captain Cisca has briefed me on the island's geography, my lady,' said Lyla. 'During the course of this voyage, the captain and I have discussed a range of plans, in case the Cyasarta was blocked. We would now like to draw your attention to the existence of the Hansarta inlet.'

'We are aware of the Hansarta, Major,' said Irvan. 'However, this inlet does not lead to Igatz, and it is Igatz that we must take.'

'You are correct, of course, my lord,' said Lyla; 'however, the Hansarta does lead towards the western edge of Kaugatz. Captain Cisca has informed me that there is a ferry terminal located there, with piers and docks large enough to handle most of the ships in the convoy.'

Lord Irvan lowered his head a little. 'Are there no Chain Castles guarding the entrance to the Hansarta?'

'There used to be, my lord,' said Cisca, 'but they date from the Third

Occupation period of the Serpent Isle, and have been in ruins for over two centuries.'

'Furthermore, my lord,' said Lyla, 'it is very unlikely that the rebels will have positioned much in the way of defences along the coastlines of the Hansarta.'

'It is true, Major,' said Malum, 'that we saw ballistae located only on the approaches to Igatz. However, to capture Igatz, we shall need ships in the Cyasarta.'

'The soldiers on board can march overland from Kaugatz to the Chain Castles guarding the Cyasarta, my lord,' said Lyla. 'Once they have disabled the chains, then the convoy can sail round the island and close with Igatz. The rebels will not be expecting this approach. If we can take the southern portion of Kaugatz, then the rebels in Igatz will have nowhere to run. At a stroke, we will have cut off their lines of supply and retreat. I commend this plan to you. The Dragon Corps feels that it offers the best chance of success, allied with the least risk.'

'Are you sure the rebels will not be expecting this?' said Lady Lenta. 'By all accounts, this Colonel Friel is a tactical genius. He successfully foresaw every move of the Dominion occupation forces during the rebellion.'

Major Lyla glanced at Cisca, her eyes narrow as she waited for the captain to support her plan. Cisca kept her features calm, and buried the doubts she held. Lyla was her commanding officer, and it was her duty to stand by the major's decisions.

'Nothing is known for certain, my lady,' said Cisca; 'but if we are to retake the Serpent Isle, then this would seem to be the soundest course of action.'

The three dragons said nothing for a moment, then Lord Malum raised his head.

'Very well, Major Lyla,' said the pale red dragon; 'we shall follow this plan of yours. Lord Irvan, I want you to patrol from the skies. Lady Lenta, you shall go below. Order the commander of the convoy to set a course for the Hansarta, and brief the army officers of our new plan. I want every human soldier on board the convoy to disembark in

Kaugatz as soon as we capture the ferry terminal. The Bullan shall remain as a reserve force, ready to push into Igatz when the time comes. You are dismissed.'

The two black and white dragons tilted their heads. Lady Lenta then began to make her way towards the huge lift set into the rear of the flight deck, as Lord Irvan extended his wings and ascended into the air. Lord Malum watched them leave, then he strode in the direction of the bow of the carrier and gazed out at the island in the distance.

'Thank you for your support, Captain Cisca,' said Lyla. 'It was a long time in coming, but you got there in the end.'

Cisca said nothing, her stomach in knots. She knew that any direct assault on the Cyasarta Chain Castles was fraught with risk, but something about Lyla's plan seemed too simple; too good to be true. What had they missed?

The convoy was underway within an hour, and the four dozen ships turned away from the Cyasarta and headed towards the south-west. The carrier's escort of destroyers led the way, with the bulk of the other vessels remaining to the rear, with the troop transports and supply vessels guarded by a squadron of frigates. Cisca remained up on the flight deck, her eyes scanning the rugged cliffs that marked the entrance to the Hansarta. On the high promontory to the east of the fleet sat the ruins of a large complex of buildings, and she remembered hearing about the ancient castle of Bowfort that had once dominated the cape. After a few miles, the convoy turned to the west, and approached the opening to the Hansarta inlet. It was over a mile wide, and Cisca wondered how it could have been sealed off by chains. In comparison, the straits guarding the Cyasarta were barely two hundred yards across. A hush descended over the fleet as the ships began to enter the inlet, with many sailors on board the carrier gazing at the cliffs to either side. The destroyers were out in front, ploughing their way through the waves as the rest of the convoy followed.

A young lieutenant joined Cisca by the bow.

'How far is it to Kaugatz, ma'am?' he said.

'Around a dozen miles, I think,' she said. 'We should be there in a couple of hours. The Hansarta widens a little once we're through the straits, and then we shall turn to the north for the last leg.'

The lieutenant nodded, his eyes peering into the distance. The channel of the Hansarta stretched away into the distance, its end lost in the heat haze from the morning sun. Above the haze, the grey peak of Mount Hodzulat was growing larger with every minute that passed.

'Do the cliffs extend all the way to Kaugatz, ma'am?' he said.

'On the northern flank, yes,' she said; 'but the ground lowers on the southern bank after a few miles before the inlet reaches the town of Neeton. The Zamatans there will see us, if we haven't already been noticed by that point. With any luck, the rebels guarding the Cyasarta will think we have decided to sail on to Irlan.'

The wind began to die away as the convoy moved west along the Hansarta. After a couple of miles, Cisca glanced to the south and saw a ruined fortress built into the side of the cliffs. She turned to look at the opposite shoreline, and could make out the faint lines of another long-abandoned fortification.

'Those must be the old Chain Castles,' she said to the lieutenant. 'Can you picture a chain stretching all the way across this inlet?'

'Imagine its weight, ma'am,' the lieutenant said. 'What a feat of engineering. It was Third Occupation-era, yes? Built in the thirteenth century?'

'So I was told,' Cisca said. 'The great fortresses of Atzoun and Hortz were built at the same time, I believe. The Serpent Isle must have been one giant castle back then.'

The destroyers ahead of them began to slow and the anxiety in the pit of Cisca's stomach increased.

'What are they doing?' she said.

One of the destroyers came to a complete stop, then it began to tilt to the side, and a low murmur of screams and shouts echoed off the sides of the cliffs.

'It's hit something!' the lieutenant cried. 'I think it's sinking, ma'am.'

'Damn it,' she muttered.

The destroyer tilted further to starboard, and Cisca saw sailors leap from its main deck into the waters of the Hansarta. The hull of the ship creaked and groaned, and, within minutes, it had disappeared beneath the waves, leaving only the three masts visible above the surface of the water. Fifty yards to the stricken ship's south, another destroyer began to go down at the bow, and the rest of the convoy slowed to a halt, the ships filling the inlet. Cisca stared at the second destroyer as its stern lifted into the air. Even at that distance, she could hear the screams of the sailors trapped in the lower decks, and she shuddered. Lord Irvan flew low overhead, his wings extended as he soared over the two lost vessels. Behind Cisca, officers were shouting out orders to bring the carrier to a halt, and sailors were scrambling over the rigging to draw down the huge sails.

'Please report, Captain,' said a voice behind her.

Cisca turned, and saw Major Lyla striding towards her, accompanied by several naval officers.

'There must be obstacles hidden under the surface of the water, ma'am,' Cisca said. 'Two destroyers have been hit.'

Lyla stared out to the west; her eyes narrow as they took in the chaotic scene ahead of the carrier.

'Serpent's breath,' Lyla muttered; 'this is a disaster. Did it slip your mind, Captain, to mention that the Hansarta might have been protected in this manner?'

'I had no knowledge of any obstacles, ma'am,' she said.

'No wonder the rebels didn't bother to place any troops here,' Lyla spat; 'there was no need. Lord Malum's displeasure will be something terrible to behold. What now, Captain? Any suggestions that might keep me from losing my head?'

Cisca glanced around at the stationary convoy. Even without much nautical experience, she could see how difficult it was to manoeuvre within the Hansarta. Several ships were lying close to each other, having only just managed to avoid a collision, and the troop transports were mixed in with the supply vessels.

'The only course of action I can suggest, ma'am,' said Cisca, 'is that we turn the fleet around and return to our original plan.'

'You mean assault the Cyasarta Chain Castles?'

Cisca lowered her gaze. 'Yes, ma'am.'

Lyla's eyes burned with anger. 'No. To advise that would be to invite the dragons' wrath upon us, and I might be ripped to shreds. Though, at least that would be quick. It would be far worse to be forbidden from joining the main invasion force when it gets here. Can you imagine a bleaker prospect than being stationed indefinitely upon a rock in the middle of the ocean?' She pointed towards the coastline, at the ruined fortifications built into the cliffs on the northern shore. 'What about landing there? Is it possible?'

'There is an ancient jetty at the base of the cliffs,' Cisca said; 'below the ruins of the old Chain Castle. A landing would certainly be possible, ma'am.'

'And can the Cyasarta be reached from there, Captain?'

'Yes, ma'am,' said Cisca. 'I would estimate that it is a four or five mile march overland to the chains protecting the Cyasarta, and then another five miles to the outskirts of Igatz itself.'

'Then we could begin transferring soldiers onto land from there,' said Lyla 'With air cover from one of the blessed dragons, it could be done.' She nodded. 'Perhaps not all is yet lost. What do you think, Captain?'

Cisca hesitated. 'I don't know, ma'am.'

'And I thought you were the expert on the Serpent Isle. Can you think of any good reason why we shouldn't make a landing here?'

'No, ma'am. It might be wise to also suggest that the convoy begins to turn back to the east while our soldiers are dealing with the Cyasarta Chain Castles.'

Major Lyla chewed her lip for a moment, then nodded. 'All right. I will take our new plan to Lord Malum. If he bites my head off then that will leave you as the Dragon Corps' most senior officer, Captain Cisca. I hope you are ready for the responsibility.'

Major Lyla strode away from Cisca, the naval officers keeping pace with her, then Cisca turned back to face the area where the two destroyers had sunk. Debris and the bodies of drowned sailors were scattered over the surface of the water, and she fought the feelings of nausea that were threatening to overwhelm her. Dozens, perhaps hundreds, had died because of the plan Major Lyla had devised, and they were yet to meet any armed resistance from the rebels in control of the island. Cisca wondered if any of the old hands on board had known about the submerged obstacles blocking the Hansarta inlet. If so, they would be cursing the Dragon Corps. The young lieutenant by her side glanced at her, but she remained silent, her gaze staring directly ahead.

A few minutes later, a great roar of anger echoed through the hull of the carrier, and every sailor on the flight deck stopped what they were doing for a moment to glance towards the rear of the ship where Lord Malum had his quarters. A handful of naval officers rushed out from a deck hatch, and organised a series of signals to the other ships in the convoy. Flags of differing colours were raised and lowered and, soon afterwards, the troop ships among the fleet began to slowly extricate themselves from the confusion to sail towards the ruined Chain Castle on the northern shore.

'It looks as though the blessed dragons have accepted the new plan, ma'am,' said the young lieutenant.

There was a sound of grinding wheels before Cisca could respond, and the enormous lift that served the flight deck was raised. Lord Malum strode off the platform. He glanced in Cisca's direction, then stepped onto the flight deck and extended his wings. He soared into the air, and joined Lord Irvan above the convoy. They circled together as the lift platform went back into action, and then Lady Lenta appeared on the flight deck. She, too, ascended into the blue sky, where the three dragons conferred. Cisca peered up at them, a hand raised to shield her eyes from the sun. She watched them circle over the convoy, then Lord Irvan peeled off, soaring away towards the ruined fortress where the ancient Chain Castle stood perched on the side of the cliff. Lord Malum and Lady Lenta then banked in the air and sped off to the west, flying low over the waters of the Hansarta.

Major Lyla came back into view on the flight deck. She lifted a hand and beckoned Cisca to join her.

'That was rather unpleasant,' the major said, 'but Lord Malum has once again decided to take our advice. I must warn you, though, Captain, that if this new plan fails, then I will be lucky to see another sunrise.' She gestured towards the dragon flying to the north. 'Lord Irvan's new role is to protect the troops landing by the jetty. He will shield them from attack as they disembark the troopships and climb the paths leading to the top of the cliff.'

'And Lord Malum and Lady Lenta, ma'am?' said Cisca. 'What is their role?'

'They have gone to raze the town of Neeton to the ground, Captain. Lord Malum's anger required some outlet, and he has chosen to make a demonstration of his power to the natives of this island. If you keep your eyes trained on the west, I am sure that we will soon see the fruits of our failure this day.'

Cisca, Lyla and the young lieutenant turned, and gazed down the inlet. The town of Neeton lay some six or seven miles from their current location, and was lost in the heat haze as the sun approached its zenith. Cisca heard the lieutenant gasp, then she saw a thin pillar of grey smoke rising into the sky.

'Those poor people,' Cisca said.

'They are rebels and traitors,' said Major Lyla.

Cisca nodded. 'Yes, ma'am.'

'One last thing, Captain,' said Lyla; 'Lord Malum has ordered you to accompany the ground troops as they make their landing at the jetty. The carrier's launch is currently being prepared to ferry you to one of the transport vessels.'

Cisca's eyes widened. 'Lord Malum wants me to fight alongside the soldiers?'

Lyla gave her a wry smile. 'His blessed lordship's actual words were "as you seem to be utterly incompetent, Major, send the captain to join the landing".'

'I am just as responsible for the plan's failure as you are, ma'am,' said Cisca. 'It was a joint decision.'

'Perhaps so,' said Lyla. 'Anyway, you are to accompany the soldiers to the Chain Castle guarding the southern shores of the Cyasarta, in order to observe the unblocking of the inlet; and then you shall remain there with the new garrison while the convoy retreats from the Hansarta. I will have a small vessel pick you up when we are ready to sail for Igatz.'

Cisca saluted. 'Yes, ma'am.'

Lyla glanced at the smoke on the horizon. 'We are very fortunate that Lord Malum decided to direct his anger towards Neeton, rather than us, Captain Cisca. Dismissed.'

Cisca found herself trudging along a steep path that wound its way up the cliffside as the sun set behind Mount Hodzulat to the west. Five thousand Aucterian soldiers had been disgorged from the lower decks of half a dozen transport vessels by the time she had reached the jetty, and thousands more were due to disembark throughout the night, as the grand convoy carried out a long series of complicated manoeuvres to turn in the narrow inlet. Most of the soldiers accompanying her on the trek up the cliffside took one look at her uniform and then promptly ignored her. She was Dragon Corps – in their eyes barely a soldier at all. At the top of the cliff, she stepped off the path and took a moment to gaze towards the west. The smoke from Neeton was hanging over the town, and the contours of the cloud it had formed were reflecting the last light from the day's sun.

She tried to imagine the terror the townsfolk had felt when they had seen the approach of the two dragons. How many families had died? How many children? She had nodded along with the major when she had called the people of Neeton traitors, but in her heart she didn't agree. Cisca had never set foot in Neeton, but she had been told that it was not a rich and prosperous settlement. What did a few hundred impoverished natives of the Serpent Isle have to do with the rebellion?

It was Colonel Laimos's fault, she told herself, though she scarcely believed it. If anyone was responsible, it was the Dragon Corps. It had been Major Lyla's plan, but Cisca had held her tongue regarding her strong reservations, and her silence had led to the destruction of an entire town.

She turned away as night fell, and saw dozens of tents being erected on the scrubby hillside beyond the summit of the cliff. Dominion soldiers were creating a perimeter around the makeshift encampment, with pickets and sentries, while campfires were burning in several places. The stars were out and the temperature was starting to drop, but she knew that her pride would prevent her from begging for a space in one of the army's tents. She had slept rough before, and she could do it again. And then, in the morning, they would march on the Chain Castle.

CHAPTER 6
A HISTORY LESSON

Igatz, Serpent Isle – 24th Tradinch 1588

Leona pressed her ear to the door, and heard a woman's voice laughing within the colonel's private study. Leona exhaled, then she firmly rapped her knuckles against the door.

'Colonel Laimos?' she said.

She listened again, and noticed that the laughter had stopped. She knocked again, a little louder.

'Colonel Laimos, sir? It's urgent.'

'Just a moment, Leona,' came Friel's voice through the door.

Leona waited outside the room, her back against the wall. She hated having to interrupt the colonel during one of his private appointments, but what else could she do? A surge of annoyance made its way up from her toes to her head. And to think that many believed that she was sleeping with the colonel; what would people say if they knew that the truth was a little more sordid?

The door opened a crack, and Friel peered out into the hallway. 'What is it? Can't it wait? I'm rather busy at the moment.'

'The Dominion Fleet has been seen a few miles east of the Cyasarta, sir,' said Leona; 'and three dragons have been spotted at high altitude scouting over Igatz.'

The colonel's face fell, and he closed the door. Leona waited and, a few moments later, a young woman emerged from the room, her clothes dishevelled. She shot a look of contempt at Leona, then smoothed down the front of her dress and strode away.

'Come in,' Friel shouted.

Leona entered the study and closed the door behind her. The colonel was looking relaxed behind his desk, his bare feet resting on a stool, and a cup of coffee in his right hand.

'Tell me everything,' he said.

'The news is a few hours old, sir,' Leona said, 'so what I say might already be out of date. At dawn this morning, what appeared to be the usual Grand Convoy from Aucteran was seen anchored a few miles east of the Chain Castles. A scout sent by Bauchlie arrived with the information in Igatz a few minutes ago – he stated that the chains were raised as soon as the ships became visible in the morning light.'

'And the three dragons?'

'They were too high to make out any distinguishing features, sir,' she said, 'but they were clearly seen by several witnesses. They flew over the Cyasarta, then circled above Igatz a few times, before returning to the fleet.'

'Then one must assume that said fleet contains a dragon carrier.' He let out a long breath. 'Damn my nephew – why did he have to be right, and why hasn't his pet Demon Witch said anything about this? Is it only Gunstian ships she keeps a look out for?'

'I have sent a militiaman over the road to Lahnos's apartment to request that he comes here immediately, sir,' Leona said. 'The scout from the Chain Castle is waiting downstairs – what message should I ask him to tell Bauchlie?'

'Let's wait until Lahnos arrives. My horned nephew has been even more difficult than usual recently. Perhaps the Demon Witch has been in contact, and he neglected to inform us.'

'I cannot believe that, sir,' she said.

'We shall see.' He placed his cup onto the desk, then leaned over and began to pull his boots on. 'If the Dominion attacks the Chain

Castles, there will be carnage,' he said. 'Hundreds of Zamatan militiamen could be incinerated, but if they can bring down even one of those dragons, then the others might think twice about the whole endeavour.'

'Possibly, sir.'

'If you were them,' he said, as he laced up his boots, 'what would you do?'

'I am not a soldier, sir. As you keep pointing out, women are unsuitable for such a position.'

'Don't give me that,' he said. 'I know fine well that you shot one of those Gunstians agents in the back with a crossbow. It stirred an almost fatherly pride in me. Well? Give me your thoughts.'

Leona pursed her lips. 'Attacking the Chain Castles would be risky, sir, but what alternative do they have? The Gunstian Fleet that arrived here two weeks ago had a far easier choice to make – as the eastern shore of Gunst is only a three day voyage from here. Retreat for them means a quick trip back to their home ports; but it's not the same for the Dominion. It would seem unlikely that they would return all the way to Aucteran at the first hurdle. Retreat for them would involve a humiliation that they would find hard to explain to the Dominion government. Therefore, they will be likely to press on, regardless of the cost.'

Friel nodded. 'Indeed. You mentioned that their fleet appears to resemble the Grand Convoy. What does that signify, do you think?'

'The ships of the Grand Convoy would have been available and easy to send, sir.'

'Although I would doubt that their holds are filled with the usual goods.'

'I agree, sir. It is more likely that those goods were exchanged for soldiers.'

The door opened and Lahnos walked in.

The colonel shook his head. 'I'm glad you didn't do that a few minutes ago, nephew. Will you ever learn how to knock?'

Lahnos shrugged. 'You summoned me. Therefore, I assumed you were expecting me. What do you want?'

'Do you remember how the Demon Witch informed you that the Gunstian Fleet was close by?'

'Of course.'

'Well, it seems that today it is the turn of the Dominion Fleet to arrive at our front door.'

Lahnos raised an eyebrow. 'Oh.'

'Did the Demon Witch tell you of this?' Friel said.

'No.'

The colonel glanced at Leona, who nodded.

Lahnos shook his head. 'Why did you look at her? Do you think I would lie about something this serious, uncle?'

'I don't know. What else do you lie to me about?'

'Nothing.'

Leona frowned and shook her head.

Lahnos glared at her. 'Would you stop doing that?'

'Why wouldn't the Demon Witch want to warn us about the Dominion?' Friel said.

'I don't know!' Lahnos cried. 'You know how it works; I've explained it to you countless times.'

An out-of-breath scout in militia uniform appeared by the open doorway. 'Colonel,' he said, 'sir; I have the latest news from Commander Bauchlie.'

Friel turned away from his nephew. 'Yes?'

'The Dominion Fleet, sir, it has raised anchor and set sail.'

'Thank you for coming, lad,' said Friel. 'Are they attacking the Chain Castles?'

'No, sir. They were seen sailing towards the Hansarta, sir.'

'The Hansarta?' said Leona.

The scout glanced at her. 'Yes, ma'am.'

'That will be all for now, lad,' said Friel. 'Please close the door, but remain outside. I'll call for you when I have a message to send to Commander Bauchlie.'

The scout saluted, then he retreated from the entrance and closed the door.

'This is bad, isn't it?' said Lahnos. 'If the fleet gets into the Hansarta, they could sail all the way to Kaugatz.'

The colonel chuckled.

'Do you think this is funny?' said Lahnos.

'Yes. I do.'

Lahnos glanced at Leona.

'The colonel isn't lying,' she said. 'Therefore, Lahnos, we must assume that he knows something about the Hansarta that we do not.'

'Who sails through the Hansarta?' said the colonel, placing his booted feet back up onto the stool.

'I don't know,' said Lahnos. 'Fishing boats?'

'Exactly,' said the colonel. 'Small fishing boats with shallow hulls. Very shallow hulls. Hulls so shallow, in fact, that they can avoid the multitude of underwater obstacles that the Dominion itself put there decades ago.'

'There are obstacles in the Hansarta?' said Leona.

'The Dominion Navy deliberately scuttled several dozen obsolete vessels,' the colonel said, 'right across the Hansarta, just beyond where the old Chain Castles stood. The inlet isn't very deep at that point, and any dragon carrier that tries to pass will rip a great big hole in its hull. It seems that whoever is making decisions for the fleet has forgotten to check their history books. Scout! Get back in here.'

The door opened again, and the scout saluted. 'Yes, sir?'

'Return to Commander Bauchlie and tell him to immediately move his three hundred men to the northern shore of the Hansarta. Have him position them along the ridge where the ruins of the ancient Chain Castle sit. And tell him to bring every catapult in his possession. I shall meet him there.'

The scout saluted again. 'Yes, sir.'

Leona watched as the young militia soldier turned and hurried away.

'Are you going in person, sir?' she said.

'I think I shall,' said the colonel, getting to his feet. 'The dragons have given us a golden opportunity that we cannot afford to miss.' He glanced out of the window. 'It's past noon, and their fleet will be stuck trying to turn for the rest of the day. They won't be foolish enough to risk trying those sorts of manoeuvres in the dark, which means that they will still be there by dawn tomorrow. That gives us tonight to sink as many of the bastards as we can.'

'What about their three dragons, sir?' said Leona.

'Summon the Master of Artillery,' said Friel. 'I want every easily-moved ballista to accompany us across the Cyasarta. We shall requisition vessels from Riston and make the crossing there. If we hurry, we could be assembled on the ridge by midnight.'

'Do you wish me to come along?' she said.

'Why not?' He turned to Lahnos and grinned. 'You can go back to your apartment, nephew. I don't think we'll be needing the Demon Witch this evening.'

The colonel opened the door to find another militia scout standing outside, his hand raised as if ready to knock.

'Sir!' the scout cried. 'Neeton is burning! You can see the smoke from Kaugatz.'

It took several hours to transport three dozen ballistae and five hundred militiamen from Igatz to the village of Riston that sat by the town's southern border. The village had a long jetty used by its large fishing fleet, and their crews were summoned from their homes and the local taverns to help ferry the colonel and his makeshift force across the calm waters of the Cyasarta. The vessels beached next to a large forest of spruce, and the men hauled the ballistae up the sand and onto the road that ran by the coast. The sun was setting by the time every artillery piece had been placed onto wagons along the road, and Leona sat next to the colonel as the convoy moved off to the east, her eyes on the sky.

'Looking for dragons?' the colonel said, as the wagons bumped along the rutted road.

'I don't like this, sir. If the dragons catch us out in the open, they will burn every wagon; and us.'

'A calculated risk,' the colonel said. 'With any luck, the dragons will be satisfied with burning Neeton to the ground.'

Leona turned. In the distance, a faint glow on the horizon marked the location of the flames that were still burning in the town of Neeton, five miles to the south-west. The smoke had been visible throughout the crossing of the Cyasarta, and Leona had caught many militiamen staring in that direction, their expressions grim.

'Why did they do it, sir? Why Neeton?'

'Who knows?' he said. 'Frustration at the situation they found themselves in, perhaps?'

'But it seems so petty, sir. Petty and cruel.'

'Dragons are not as dissimilar from humans as some think, Leona. They can be spiteful, and cruel. They just also happen to have wings, claws, and the ability to breathe fire. Did you know that, according to legend, King Gahad even had the ability to kill people with a glance?'

'That's not a legend, sir,' said Leona. 'Some of the Children of Gahad also have that ability.'

'Then why haven't I read about it in any Dominion history book?'

'Because it isn't in any Dominion history book, sir. But, it is in those written by the Gunstians.'

The colonel frowned. 'Governor Tirna Min Gahad certainly didn't possess any such... power.'

'That's right, sir; she doesn't. Only a small number of Gahad's offspring do. The eldest ones. They might not have used those powers for centuries, but they slaughtered thousands with them in the second invasion of Gunst.'

'Or so the Gunstians say.'

Leona nodded. 'Why do you think the Gunstians refer to them as demons, sir?'

'For a variety of reasons.'

'Yes, and one of those was what they did in Gunst.'

'They have never used those powers on Zamata.'

'They have never tried to annihilate the entire population, sir.'

The colonel glanced at the road. 'I have more to worry about than some scary fables concocted by the Gunstians.'

'Perhaps we should ask Lahnos's resident Bullan soldier when we return to Igatz, sir. He might be willing to share the truth on the matter.'

'Perhaps we should.'

The wagons trundled over the uneven road for a couple of miles as darkness fell around them, then they stopped at a junction, where Bauchlie and his three hundred men were taking the path that led south to the ruined Chain Castle. The colonel leapt down from the wagon and talked to his son for a few minutes, then the combined force continued on its way. Bauchlie had brought a dozen wheeled catapults, and it took several hours to move them and the ballista wagons over the rough track towards the ridge that overlooked the Hansarta. Orders had been given for complete silence, and the men worked as quietly as they were able as they hauled the vehicles up to the top of the cliffs. Above them, the night sky was clear, and the stars were shining down upon them, the moon a mere sliver. The air began to chill, and Leona wrapped her coat around her shoulders as the convoy inched towards the south. She found herself almost dozing off where she sat, then her eyes snapped open as the wagon she was on came to a halt. Ahead of them lay the dark waters of the Hansarta, and she could see dozens of tiny lamps on board the Dominion ships that had anchored there for the night. A few hundred yards away to the west, small pinpricks of light were dotted across the side of the ridge, and Leona noticed that Bauchlie was organising his men in the darkness, while the catapults were being lined up by the edge of the high cliffs overlooking the inlet. Leona clambered down to the ground, and located the colonel as he was issuing orders to the militiamen operating the artillery.

'What's happening, sir?' she whispered.

Friel glanced in her direction. 'The Dominion Fleet is exactly where we want it to be, but they have landed soldiers at the old jetty by the base of the cliffs.'

She pointed at the lights. 'Are those campfires?'

The colonel nodded. 'The fools have been considerate enough to advertise their presence to us. Bauchlie's men are going in first. Scouts have identified the positions of the camp's sentries, and squads are going to sneak past them in the dark and advance to the tents where the soldiers are sleeping.'

'To do what, sir?'

'To kill as many of the bastards as possible, Leona; what else? The catapults will do nothing for the moment, to give Bauchlie's force the element of surprise.'

'They're going to kill the soldiers as they sleep?'

'That's the general idea. They will be going from tent to tent, slitting throats. Does this offend you?'

Leona turned away. In the gloom, she could make out a few of Bauchlie's men as they prepared to attack the camp. They had removed their heavier equipment, and were carrying knives and swords. An officer gestured to them, and they padded away, moving silently through the darkness.

'Get the ballistae set up and ready,' said Friel to the militiamen by the wagons. 'And make sure they're pointing at the sky. If you see anything up there – loose.'

Leona watched as the artillery was prepared. Flammable liquid was poured over tightly-wrapped balls of linen, each the size of a large watermelon, and several were stacked up behind the catapults; while the ballista operators unpacked yard-long bolts of sharpened steel from wooden crates. Leona worried about the noise they were making, but the wind was blowing from the south, carrying the sound away from the camp. The colonel was in his element, meeting scouts and delivering orders, his eyes determined but full of confidence. Leona turned back to gaze down at the inlet. Her eyes went over the lamps of the ships until she located the huge dragon carrier, its long flight deck visible from the top of the cliff where she was standing.

The minutes passed, and Leona's nerves were stretched to breaking point as she paced up and down the track by the top of the cliff.

Several cries rang out from the direction of the enemy encampment, and the colonel raised his arm.

'Light the torches!' he cried.

A dozen men crouched down and lit the brands they had been carrying.

'Catapults,' Friel shouted; 'ignite and loose!'

The men with the lit torches touched them to the linen balls and each burst into flames. The catapults were triggered, and a dozen balls of fire arced into the night sky.

'Loose at will!' the colonel yelled.

Leona stared as the first barrage reached the ships in the inlet. Several missiles struck the surface of the water, but a few made contact with the vessels, and within seconds, four ships were ablaze. Another barrage flew over her head, then more followed, each sending flames streaking through the sky. At a signal from the colonel, four catapults were turned to face the Dominion camp and, while the others continued to pepper the fleet, the four began to send flames down onto the tents of the enemy soldiers. The first of Bauchlie's squads began to appear back by the artillery, their long knives stained with blood. They pulled their armour back on, then picked up their shields and formed a line to protect the catapults.

Bauchlie pushed his way through them to confront Friel.

'We should withdraw before the dragons and soldiers get here,' he said. 'There are thousands of Aucterians in that damn camp.'

'Nonsense,' said Friel. He turned to the artillery operators. 'Aim for the dragon carrier!' he shouted, and the hail of fire ceased for a moment as the catapults were adjusted

Leona stared down. The fires had spread to over a dozen ships, and she could see sailors on board trying to flee from the flames. A missile struck the long flight deck of the carrier, but it was quickly extinguished by the crew stationed there; then another hit one of the vessel's tall masts, and the rigging erupted into flames.

'More!' cried Friel. 'Send everything we've got into the carrier!'

A large shape soared through the sky above them, and three catapults were incinerated by a thick blast of flames, their crews rendered to ash in mere moments.

'Ballistae!' yelled Friel. 'Bring that big bastard down!'

The thirty-six bolt-throwing machines juddered into action, loosing their missiles up into the sky. Two of the remaining catapults switched to nets, and launched them upwards in the direction of the black and white dragon as it turned for another attack. A scream echoed through the night sky, and then the dragon crashed into the ridge, killing over a dozen militiamen and flattening another catapult as its net-bound body ploughed through the ground. A ballista loosed at almost point-blank range, and a bolt slammed into the right eye socket of the fallen dragon. At the same time, Dominion soldiers from the camp attacked from the west, their crossbow bolts filling the air. Bauchlie's men tried to repel them, but they were outnumbered several times over.

'Retreat!' Friel cried. 'Abandon the artillery and run!'

The militia scattered into the darkness, leaving the surviving catapults behind. The crew of one ballista loosed another bolt into the flank of the downed dragon, then they were incinerated by a blast of flames coming from another dragon above them. Amid the screams and smoke, Leona felt someone grab her arm, and she turned to see Bauchlie, his scarred face smeared in blood.

'Move!' he shouted in her face, as he began to drag her away from the chaos.

They ran from the carnage, racing down the hillside. Militia soldiers were tripping over each other in the darkness, then another blast of dragon fire set a long patch of scrubby undergrowth alight. The night seemed to turn into day for a moment, and the pale red dragon in the sky above them swooped down, his claws raking through a group of militiamen. The dragon turned his dark green eyes towards another group, and their heads exploded, coating the ground around them in bloody fragments of skull. Leona screamed, then she ran as fast as she could, Bauchlie's hand still gripping her arm, and they didn't stop until they had reached the main road that ran along the southern bank of the

Cyasarta, where a few dozen Zamatan militiamen were gasping and panting for breath.

Bauchlie released her. 'The colonel is insane,' he cried. 'I lost half my men tonight, maybe more; and for what?'

'Calm yourself,' said a voice to their left.

They turned, and saw Friel standing in the thick shadows by the side of the road, looking unflustered and wearing a smile on his lips.

'Thank you for escorting Leona back,' he said. 'Now, we should probably return to Igatz before...'

Bauchlie sprang forward and punched the colonel in the face, sending him sprawling to the ground. The militiamen around them tensed, then more emerged from the darkness, their eyes wide.

Friel rubbed his chin, then saw the blood on his hand. 'I think that was a little uncalled for, Commander Bauchlie.' He got to his feet and brushed the dirt from his uniform. 'I would say that we have had a very successful night.'

'How many men did we lose?' said Bauchlie, his eyes afire.

'No one can answer that question; not yet. It will take some time for the dust to settle. But what I do know is that at least a dozen of the enemy ships are ablaze, including their carrier; and a dragon god has lost an eye, if not his life. More importantly, we have sent the invaders a clear message, that we are willing to die to defend this island.'

'Was it worth the lives of hundreds,' said Bauchlie, 'not to mention dozens of ballistae and catapults?'

The colonel paused for a moment, then nodded. 'Yes.'

'You sadistic bastard,' said Bauchlie. 'Had I known what you were planning, I would have stayed in the Chain Castle.'

Friel laughed. 'You slit the throats of sleeping soldiers, and you call me sadistic?'

'I kill the enemy, not my own men,' said Bauchlie, 'and that's the difference between us.'

Leona stood by Friel as Bauchlie strode away. Several of his men who were by the road peeled away from the militia to follow him.

'Something happened, sir,' she said; 'on the way back.'

Friel glanced at her. 'I know. I saw it.'

'The pale red dragon…'

'Yes, Leona; I know.'

'He looked at a group of militia, and…'

'It doesn't matter.'

'How can you say that?' Leona cried. 'Those abilities we were talking about – that dragon has them. That means he must be one of Gahad's eldest children.'

'There is no need to shout, Leona,' the colonel said. He glanced at the groups of survivors on the road. 'Return to the beach,' he said. 'The fishing boats will still be there. Sail back to Riston, and make your way to Igatz. Oh, and well done. What you did this night will be talked about for generations to come.'

The men stared at him, then began to trudge down the slope towards the beach.

The colonel waited until the road was empty, then he turned to Leona again. 'You must not speak of what you saw to anyone. There could be panic in Igatz if this news spreads.'

'Dozens of survivors must have seen it, sir,' she said. 'Bauchlie saw it, too. Do you think he will keep his mouth shut?'

'No, probably not.'

They started to walk towards the beach.

'Those Gunstian history books you mentioned,' Friel said, as they passed through the edge of the spruce forest, 'do you still have them?'

'Yes, sir; I do.'

'Then you might have to let me borrow them when we get back to Igatz. It seems I have much to learn.'

CHAPTER 7
RESENTFUL

Igatz, Serpent Isle – 25th Tradinch 1588

Lahnos shook his head. 'People are so gullible.'

Efizel glanced over at him from a chair in the living-room. 'What was that, young Laimos?'

'I said people are gullible. You should come and hear what they're saying.'

'I would, but I do not think that it is a good idea for me to go out on to the balcony during the daytime.'

'The militiamen are arriving back from the shores of the Hansarta,' Lahnos said, 'and they're gathering outside the Convention Hall, after their night attack on the Dominion Fleet.'

'Who won the battle?'

'It's hard to say. It seems that a few ships were set alight, and a dragon got injured, but the militiamen look pretty angry. From what they're saying I think they took casualties – lots of casualties.'

'That does not sound gullible. If they were fighting dragons, then it sounds realistic.'

Lahnos nodded, his eyes on the growing crowd of exhausted and sullen militiamen filling the street below him.

'I agree,' he said, 'but that wasn't the gullible part. Some of them are claiming that a pale red dragon killed several soldiers with a glance. He just looked at them, and they fell down dead.'

Efizel got up and walked to the edge of the balcony door, where he remained out of sight. He tilted his head, listening to the sound of the raised voices coming from the street.

'A pale red dragon?' he said.

'Yes. Do you know any pale red dragons?'

'I have met several, young Laimos. However, I know of only one who can take life with a thought or a glance.'

Lahnos narrowed his eyes. 'Are you joking? I have never once heard you make a joke.'

'I rarely jest, but if I did, I would never jest about dragons with the power to dispense death with a glance.'

'There is no such thing.'

'Are you utterly certain about that – you who have never left the island of Zamata?'

'I used to enjoy looking up at the dragons who lived here before the rebellion. I knew all their names, and a little about each one. But I have never once heard that dragons can kill someone just by looking at them.'

'Only King Gahad and a small number of his sons and daughters possess such powers,' said the Bullan soldier. 'None of his grandchildren do, and neither do any of the mortal dragons. I was taught that the great god Nathaniel bestowed this ability, among others, on to the mighty King Gahad.'

'There you go again, talking about some god I have never heard of.'

'Perhaps you should take steps to remedy your ignorance, young Laimos. I believe there is a public library in Igatz – one of the many blessings brought here by the Dominion. In a library, there are things called books. Have you ever heard of them?'

Lahnos stared at him.

'That,' said Efizel, 'was a joke.'

'No, it wasn't – it was sarcasm, and it wasn't funny.'

'Can you read?'

'Yes. I just choose not to.'

'Your woman looks like a reader. Where are her books?'

'Don't make fun of her for this, but Reyn isn't so good at reading.'

'I would never make fun of anyone for that reason. I will ask Reyn if she would like me to teach her. Now, back to the matter at hand. If the militia are spreading stories about a pale red dragon with the power over life and death, then it might be a good idea to listen to them.'

'It was a night battle,' said Lahnos. 'From what I can gather, there were flames, and catapults, and dragons, and all kinds of chaos – all in pitch darkness. If that isn't a fertile environment for rumours to take root, I don't know what is.'

'Quiet,' said Efizel. 'Did you hear that? Someone down there is cursing your uncle's name. Perhaps his popularity is beginning to wane at last.'

'About time,' said Lahnos. 'Tell me, how long would it take to turn a large fleet around in the narrows of the Hansarta?'

'That depends. Why?'

'Do you remember my plan for going to Inopei? Yesterday, when my uncle told me that the Dominion Fleet had arrived, I thought our chance had vanished, but if the fleet is still stuck in the Hansarta, then there might be a glimmer of hope.' He stared in the direction of the harbour. 'If there is any chance, we should take it.'

Efizel said nothing.

'I thought you wanted to get off this island before your kinsfolk arrive in Igatz,' Lahnos said.

'I suppose I do,' said the Bullan soldier.

'I can run down to the merchants' harbour,' Lahnos said. 'I found out where the Irlanian sailors drink. There are bound to be a few who would prefer to leave before the Dominion takes over.'

'You will need to hurry, if you wish to find a ship before the Cyasarta is once again blocked by the dragon fleet.'

'I'll go now.'

'And Reyn? You still have not told her your plan, have you?'

'Eh, no.'

The Bullan shook his head. 'You should have told her, young Laimos.'

'I know. I will.'

Lahnos stepped off the balcony and left the apartment. He raced down the stairs and emerged into the busy street. Militiamen were clamouring to be allowed into the Convention Hall, but the doors were closed and guarded. Lahnos thought about what the Bullan had told him, but it seemed fanciful. The immortal dragons were powerful, but no one had the ability to kill with a look. He forced his way through the crowd, earning himself a few scowls, and several militiamen stared at his horns. Beyond, the wide streets of the Temple District were also busy with people trying to learn what had taken place overnight. There was an edge of panic in the air, as tales were bandied about regarding the number of casualties sustained in the fighting, and whether or not one of the dragons had been slain. The topic on most lips, Lahnos noticed, was the pale red dragon, and his seemingly impossible power to kill. A few Zamatans were anxiously discussing plans to abandon Igatz and retreat to Kaugatz or further afield, but the news about what had happened to Neeton had sent a wave of fear through most.

Lahnos listened as he walked, but took no part in any of the discussions sweeping across the citizenry. He took the road that went past the Temple of the Undying Serpent, then crossed into the Palace District. From there, it was a short walk to the merchants' harbour. The quayside was quiet, as it had been since the Dominion had evacuated the island several months before, and there was only a handful of vessels tied up alongside the long, spindly piers that jutted out into the blue waters of the bay. Lahnos walked along the harbour front. He passed the customs buildings, which had been closed and boarded up since the evacuation, and then he stopped at a tavern that sat on the site of Ar Gatz Tar, an ancient monastery destroyed centuries before by the Gunstians.

Lahnos looked over his shoulder, then he entered the tavern. At once, more than a dozen sailors glanced up from where they were sitting and stared at his horns.

'Yes,' Lahnos said to them all; 'I have horns. If anyone wishes to make something of that, then step right up and I'll be happy to break your nose. But, I didn't come here looking for a fight. I came to ask if anyone was planning to leave the island today.'

'And what business is that of yours, boy?' said a sailor, his accent placing him as from Irlan.

'I have money,' Lahnos said; 'enough to buy passage for three to Irlan.'

A few sailors laughed.

'Planning on running away, are you, boy?' said one. 'Now that the Dominion Fleet has returned, eh?'

'I notice that while all of you are sitting in a tavern,' Lahnos said, 'none of you appear to be drunk. That tells me you're planning on leaving, and soon. You all know what the Dominion do to smugglers, don't you, lads? They hang them.'

'Damn you, boy,' said an older man. 'Who says we're smugglers?'

'Are you going to tell the Bullan that you're tourists or pilgrims?' said Lahnos. 'Why else would you be here on Zamata? Irlan has been forbidden to trade with this island while it remains under the control of the rebels.' He smiled. 'And yet, here you are.' He strode to the bar and placed a handful of coins onto the counter. 'I'd like to buy them all a drink,' he said to the bartender. 'Keep the change.'

The bartender swiftly pocketed the gold, and nodded towards the sailors. 'Same again, lads?'

Lahnos strode over to a table where six sailors sat, and took a seat next to them.

'How much?' he said. 'Name your price.'

'Three passengers, did you say, boy?' said one.

'That's right.'

'Where are they, eh? The other two?'

'Close by.'

'They'd better be, boy-with-the-horns, because we're leaving in an hour. The Dominion Fleet won't be stuck in the Hansarta for too much longer, and we still need to bribe the soldiers in the Cyasarta Chain Castles to allow us to leave.'

'Then you'll take us?'

The sailor shrugged. 'It's not up to me, boy.' He nodded towards the older man. 'He's the first mate; he says whether you can come or not.'

The older man eyed Lahnos. 'Why are you running?' he said. 'Those horns get you in trouble?'

'They have, but not this time.'

'You broken the law?'

'On occasion, but the militia aren't hunting me.'

'Why Irlan?'

'Are you going anywhere else? All right, lads; here's the truth. I'm looking for my father. He was taken from this island a decade ago and sold into slavery. I intend to find him and free him. That might sound stupid, but I've only just learned that he might be a slave; for years I thought he was dead.'

The older man nodded. 'Is your father one of them Bullan?'

'No. My mother's father was the Bullan. My father was a plain old Zamatan. No horns.'

'And you believe him to be in Irlan? Irlan is a big place, boy. There are dozens of islands, and all of them are a damn sight bigger than Zamata.'

Lahnos raised his palms. 'I have to start somewhere. Look; we're wasting time. Does it matter why I want to leave? Just tell me how much gold it will take.'

The older man remained silent as the bartender came over with a loaded tray. He placed a fresh tankard of ale in front of each of the sailors, then moved on to the next table. The older man raised his drink, eyed Lahnos, then took a sip.

'One hundred Aucterian sovereigns each,' he said. 'No haggling; that's my first and final offer.'

'Deal,' said Lahnos. 'I'll bring the gold and the other two passengers to the harbour before the hour is out. Which ship do you lads crew?'

'That'll be the *Queen Parrabaia*, boy,' said the older man. 'It has a crowned figurehead at the bow; you can't miss it.'

Lahnos stood.

'And if you're not here when we're ready to sail...'

'You'll leave without us?' Lahnos said. 'I get it. Thank you.'

'There's only the one spare cabin on the old *Queen*, boy,' the older man said; 'and it's not exactly what you would call large or comfortable. I don't want to hear any complaining about it when you come aboard.'

'As long as you get us to Irlan, I couldn't give a shit,' Lahnos said. 'I'll be seeing you.'

He strode from the tavern, then increased his pace. He kept to the coastal road, and re-entered the Palace District. Ahead, the high walls of the Hortz Fortress loomed up, their ancient stones still standing after three and a half centuries. There was a large well in a plaza by the front of the fortress, and over a dozen women were collecting water, which they were using to clean a heap of clothes taken from some of the abandoned Aucterian properties in Igatz. Reyn was among them, and Lahnos smiled at the sight of her working in the shade of a row of palm trees with no head scarf covering her horns. She was leaning over a large wooden tub, and scrubbing the stains from an old jacket.

'Reyn,' he said.

She looked up at him. 'Hello, Lahnos.'

The other women stopped work and eyed him as he got closer.

'Can I talk to you for a minute?' he said.

Reyn glanced at an older woman, who nodded. Reyn wiped her hands on a rag and got to her feet.

'Be quick, lass,' said the older woman.

'It won't take long,' said Lahnos.

He walked with Reyn until they were out of earshot of the women, then Lahnos sat on a low wall that overlooked the sparkling waters of the bay.

'What is it?' she said.

'There's something I've been meaning to ask you for a while,' he said. 'Do you remember how we once talked about leaving Zamata so that I could search for my father?'

She nodded. 'I remember.'

'You said that you would come with me.'

'I did say that; yes.'

Lahnos kept his eyes on the waves splashing against the low wall. 'Our ship leaves in an hour.'

She squinted at him.

'We'll need to hurry,' he went on. 'I'll go back to the apartment and throw our things into a few bags, and then I'll collect the gold we'll need to pay for the voyage, and I can meet you by the quayside before the mid-morning bell peals. Oh, and Efizel will be coming, too, of course. It will be the three of us. You'll have to make some sort of excuse to get away early from work, but don't tell them what we're doing – I don't want my uncle to find out.'

'A ship?' she said.

He laughed. 'How else would we get off the island? Yes, Reyn – a ship.'

'Now? Today? When the Dominion Fleet is here?'

'Their boats are still trying to navigate their way out of the Hansarta, and several of them were damaged in last night's battle. But, you're right – we need to leave before they can sail north to block the Cyasarta.'

'No, Lahnos. I don't think so.'

'What?'

'I can't leave Zamata, not while we're fighting for its freedom.'

Lahnos groaned. 'The stupid cause is doomed, Reyn. The Dominion is going to obliterate any resistance once they finally break into the island's interior. Have you heard the rumours about what the pale red dragon did?'

'I have. I didn't think you would believe them.'

'I didn't, not at first, but Efizel assures me that the rumours are true. We have to get out of here, and this is the only chance we're going to get.'

'You're asking me to abandon my home?'

Lahnos's temper flared. 'You said you would come with me.'

'But I wasn't expecting to be given an hour's notice to leave. How long have you been planning this?'

'A couple of weeks, maybe.'

'A couple of weeks? Why didn't you tell me about it?'

'Is that relevant? The decision has to be made now, Reyn.'

'I'm sorry, Lahnos, but I love this island, and I want to fight for it. I know how important the idea of finding your father is to you, but do we have to leave when Zamata is in danger?'

'Are you seriously talking about fighting the Dominion?'

'You fought the Dominion, or had you forgotten? You were part of the uprising in Kaugatz.'

'And you know how I felt about that. Let's be honest – if Zamata continues to resist, the dragons will destroy us. My uncle is leading this island into disaster.'

'The Demon Witch will save us. We just have to trust her.'

'I haven't heard from the damn Demon Witch since the Gunstians arrived.'

'She must be busy, or distracted. She won't abandon us; I refuse to believe it. She cares about this island – how could she abandon it now after everything she has already done?'

Lahnos felt his temper rise. 'Do you want me to leave you here?'

Reyn folded her arms across her chest. 'Go, if that is what you want. I can't stop you. I'll be coming home from work at the usual time. If you aren't there, then I will know what you have done.'

He stared at her. 'Is that what you want?'

'No, Lahnos. I want you to stay here.'

'You don't care about finding my father, do you?'

'I care. But, if I'm honest, I care about Zamata more. Perhaps once everything has settled down again, we can properly plan a trip across the ocean, but I will not be rushed into fleeing Igatz when the Dominion is about to invade.'

He tapped his horns. 'Do you see these? You have them, too. We will never be accepted here, and you know it.'

'I disagree. Things have changed since the rebellion. The Zamatans and the part-Bullan fought side by side to win our freedom.'

Lahnos snorted. 'Freedom?' He shook his head. 'Fine. You've made your decision, and I've made mine. Goodbye, Reyn.'

He turned and walked away, his fury simmering. Why had she made it so difficult? He had given her a simple choice – the island or him, and she had chosen Zamata. A crushing sense of disappointment flooded his mind, and he hesitated, and glanced over his shoulder. Reyn was crouching by the wooden tub, in tears, while one of the older women comforted her. Lahnos stared at them for a moment, his will wavering, then he hardened his heart, turned, and strode from the plaza.

The sense of rising panic was almost tangible among the crowds outside the Convention Hall, and Lahnos had to shove his way through to get to the front door of his apartment block. Stories of what had occurred in Neeton were circulating again and, unlike the tales of dragons with the power over life and death, Lahnos had no problem believing them. Lahnos had never been to Neeton, but he had often seen its white-washed walls and houses while crossing the Hansarta. People were talking about hundreds of casualties – entire households reduced to ash and bone – and Lahnos cursed the dragon who had done it. Lady Tirna Min Gahad would never have acted in such a cruel and arbitrary manner; in fact, Lahnos couldn't think of a single human she had slain during her years as governor.

He hurried up the stairs and entered his apartment. Efizel was still in the living room, listening to the crowd outside.

'I thought you would have been packing,' Lahnos said. 'You should have been packing. We have half an hour to get on board the ship I found.'

The Bullan nodded. 'And Reyn?'

Lahnos glanced away. 'She isn't coming.'

'I see.'

Lahnos felt an ache in his chest, but ignored it. 'You pack, and I'll get the gold. This voyage is going to eat through a lot of the money my uncle gave me, but it'll be cheaper with just the two of us.'

The Bullan remained where he was.

'Did you hear me?' said Lahnos.

'I heard you, young Laimos,' said Efizel. 'Tell me – why is your woman not coming with us?'

'You can probably guess the reasons; she would rather die for this stupid island than help me look for my father. I'm done with her.'

'You intend to leave her here?'

'Obviously.'

The Bullan narrowed his eyes.

'Are you going to give me a lecture on honour?' Lahnos said.

'No, young Laimos; I was going to speak to you of courage – something you appear to lack.'

Lahnos clenched his fists. 'You cheeky bastard. I'm about to sail off into the unknown to rescue my father, and you accuse me of cowardice?'

'Your homeland is being invaded and you are fleeing, while your woman has decided to stay and fight. Yes – I am accusing you of cowardice.'

'I'll punch your teeth in,' Lahnos cried.

The Bullan folded his arms across his broad chest. 'You could try. You would not succeed.'

'I thought you were supposed to be serving me? What about all the times you've told me how much you dread having to fight your own kinsfolk? I'm doing this for you as well as me, and this is the gratitude I get?'

'Stop lying to yourself. You are not fleeing for my sake. I made a vow to serve and protect you, and I fully accept whatever consequences arise from the choice I made.'

'You can stay here. I don't need you.'

The Bullan smiled. 'No, young Laimos. If you go, then I shall follow. And then, every dawn when the sun rises over the ocean, I shall remind you that you abandoned a woman who loves you; and that you fled your home at the first sign of trouble. It will give me no pleasure, but I will do it nevertheless.'

'Have you lost your mind?' Lahnos yelled. 'You hate the rebellion as much as I do, and now it sounds as though you would prefer me to stay and fight against the Dominion.'

'It is true that I fought the rebels when your uncle revolted against the dragons,' Efizel said. 'It is also true that, were I Zamatan, I would have joined your uncle's rebellion. It would have been the honourable path to have chosen.'

Lahnos laughed through his rage. 'What? A Bullan says he would have joined the rebellion? Now I've heard everything.'

Lahnos walked from the living room and entered the bedchamber he shared with Reyn. He knelt on the wooden floor, pulled out a large canvas bag from under the bed, and picked up a pile of his clothes from the back of a chair. He tried to ignore the many reminders of Reyn in the room – the dresses hanging up by the wall, the small silvered mirror that sat on a table, the little box that contained the few items of jewellery that she possessed, her hairbrush, her head scarves.

He stopped packing. What was he doing? He loved Reyn. There was no one in the world he trusted more, no one dearer to him, no one who made him feel the way that she did. He remained on his knees as the seconds and minutes passed. If he didn't hurry, the Irlanian sailors would leave without him, and his chance to search for his father might be lost forever. He tried to remember his father's face, and the way he had spoken, but the clearest memories of him had come from the time he had read his dead grandmother's mind.

He cursed the Demon Witch. Where was she when he needed her?

'Father,' he whispered, 'I'm sorry.'

The sun was setting when Reyn returned to the apartment. Despite the dying light, Lahnos had stayed in the bedchamber, though he had heard Efizel move through the other rooms, lighting the oil lamps. The Bullan soldier had not ventured into the room where Lahnos was, and the door had remained closed. Lahnos heard Reyn and Efizel exchange a few words by the entrance to the apartment, then she entered the darkness of the bedchamber. Lahnos glanced up from where he was sitting on the bed.

'Hello,' she said.

'I couldn't do it,' he said.

Reyn smiled sadly at him.

'I wanted to,' he said, 'but I couldn't.'

She walked over and sat on the bed next to him. Lahnos turned to stare out of the open shutters at the stars in the evening sky. A warm wind was blowing off the bay, bringing the scent of the ocean into the room, along with the smell of oranges from the trees lining the street.

'The Dominion Fleet has moved up to the Cyasarta again,' Reyn said. 'The news is all over Igatz.'

He nodded.

'Do you resent me, Lahnos?'

'For what?'

'You chose me over your father.'

'I resent the island,' he said, 'and I resent my uncle for putting us all into this situation; but I will not abandon you, Reyn.'

'Even if the soldiers come?'

'Especially if the soldiers come. I didn't want this fight, but Efizel was right. It would be cowardly to flee.'

'Is that what he told you?'

'If you weren't here, then I would be on that Irlanian ship,' he said. 'I could live with Efizel calling me a coward, but I don't want to live without you. I suppose I should speak to our Bullan lodger, and let him know that he was right.'

Reyn traced her fingers down his face, then she kissed him. 'He already knows, Lahnos.'

He took her hand, and stared out at the stars.

CHAPTER 8
FAVOURS THE BRAVE

Southern Hansarta, Serpent Isle – 25th Tradinch 1588

From the path by the edge of the cliffs, Cisca could see the long line of Dominion soldiers marching along the track that led from the ancient ruins of the Hansarta Chain Castle. To her back lay the sprawling remains of Bowfort, its stone walls clinging on to the side of the cliff; and beyond that was the vast ocean. The crash of the waves against the ragged coastline filled her mind, obliterating the sound of everything else. Cisca was on the highest point of the headland, with the wide opening to the Hansarta inlet on her left, and the much more narrow entrance to the Cyasarta on her right. In front of her, past the long terraces of olive groves, she could see the sparkling blue waters of the Cyasarta where it terminated in a succession of golden beaches and quiet coves, where clusters of palm trees swayed in the warm breeze.

It was all so beautiful, she thought; and peaceful. Staring out at the view, it was hard to believe that thousands had been killed or wounded in the previous night's carnage. Bodies were still lying unburied on the ridge by the Hansarta Chain Castle, while hundreds of dead sailors were floating upon the crystalline waters of the wide inlet. A huge black and white dragon soared overhead, and Cisca recognised Lady Lenta

Min Gahad as she flew over the long column of soldiers, protecting them from any further rebel attack.

Cisca felt her eyes almost close, and she nearly stumbled. She had been awake all night, and her nerves had been stretched to breaking point. She found a low stone wall by the edge of an olive grove and sat, as exhaustion rippled through her. The heat of the sun was lulling her to sleep, so she turned to face the ocean, and allowed the wind to blow through her hair. The battered Dominion Fleet was limping out from the Hansarta, and was beginning to form up by the opening to the Cyasarta, the destroyers flanking the massive dragon carrier. Eleven ships had been left behind in the inlet – of those, six had been sunk, and five were too damaged to sail. Cisca wanted to cry; how could such a catastrophe have taken place? She had been lying awake in a low gully, her eyes fixed on the stars, when the attack had begun. Ghostly figures had moved through the Dominion camp, and one group of them had even passed by where Cisca had been trying to sleep, their long knives coated with the blood of murdered Aucterians. Then the real slaughter had begun, as the sky had been ripped apart by a hailstorm of fire balls. Cisca shuddered. In some ways, the experience had been worse than being held prisoner by Bauchlie and his men within the Dragon Palace. With Bauchlie, she had known the danger, but the fire balls had torn through the Dominion army's tents with reckless randomness, and it was pure luck that had seen her survive.

Her eyes focussed on the wide flight deck of the dragon carrier. The huge ship had taken several fire balls through the night but, apart from some damage to one of its four masts, it had come through unscathed. Lying prone on the deck was Lord Irvan Mon Gahad, being attended to by a dozen junior members of the Dragon Corps. The fifth son of the former king had nearly died during the night, and it had taken all of Lord Malum's healing skills to preserve his life. Whether or not the black and white dragon would ever see out of his right eye again was a different matter. As far as Cisca knew, none of the Children of Gahad had ever been wounded so grievously, at least not at the hands of mere humans; and if Lord Irvan had indeed been permanently blinded, then a wave of shock, anger and fear would long reverberate throughout the lands of the Dominion. Next to that, the deaths of Lord Meer and Lord Rufus were almost inconsequential – both were ordinary, mortal dragons, whereas Lord Irvan's veins ran with the blood of his divine father.

Cisca felt a hand touch her shoulder, and she turned to see a young soldier standing by her side.

'Ma'am,' he shouted over the sound of the waves hitting the cliffs, 'the army commanders are requesting your presence.'

Cisca stared at him.

'Ma'am?'

'Where are they?' she said.

The soldier pointed to his left, in the direction of the Chain Castles guarding the entrance to the Cyasarta.

Cisca nodded, and got to her feet. The soldier led her away from the edge of the cliff and down to the roadside, where the noise of the waves lessened a little. Several groups of soldiers had stopped by the side of the olive groves to drink from water skins, and Cisca noticed that most were remaining silent, their eyes grim as she passed through their ranks. She left her escort behind and began walking down the slope towards the coast of the Cyasarta. The southern Chain Castle was visible in the distance, and the Dominion army was taking up positions around it on the landward side, digging ditches into the hard dry ground, and setting up tents and supply dumps. Rebel fighters could be seen high up on the battlements of the castle's curtain wall, and more were on the roof of the tall keep. A ten-minute walk took Cisca to a guarded enclosure set within the midst of a terraced olive grove, where several Dominion officers were sitting in the shade. Cisca passed through the sentries on duty, then waited by the edge of the group as the officers listened to a report.

'A thousand casualties?' said a major. 'That must be a mistake.'

'No, sir,' said a junior officer; 'there is no mistake. Six hundred and eighty-nine fatalities, plus another three hundred wounded. As for the navy...'

'Wait,' said the major; 'are you telling me that the thousand only covers the army?'

'Yes, sir. The number of casualties suffered by the navy remains unclear, but it is estimated that at least a further thousand were drowned or burned alive in the attack.'

The officers glanced at each other.

'What about the Bullan?' said one.

'There were no Bullan casualties, sir,' said the junior officer. 'Their troopships were at the rear of the convoy, and were out of range of the rebel artillery.'

'And how many of these Zamatan bastards did our side kill?' said a captain.

'That also remains unclear, sir. Perhaps two to three hundred were slain by Lords Irvan and Malum before they were driven from the cliffs.'

'Does Lord Irvan still live?'

'I don't know, sir.'

Cisca stepped forward. 'Lord Irvan is alive,' she said, as the army officers turned towards her. 'I saw him on the flight deck of the dragon carrier a few moments ago. He appears to be wounded, and perhaps blinded; but he lives.'

'Thank you, Captain,' said the major. 'Everyone, this is Captain Cisca of the Dragon Corps; I'm sure you have all heard of her. Her presence during the rebel uprising is the reason I asked her to attend this briefing. Captain, do you have any insights as to what the rebels will do next?'

Cisca nodded. 'Thank you, sir. It is my belief that the rebels will be stung by their losses.'

A few of the officers laughed grimly. '*Their* losses?' said one. 'It appears that we lost ten men for every rebel killed.'

'That is true,' said Cisca, 'but the rebels cannot afford to lose two to three hundred fighters, especially when it is likely that they will have no information regarding the scale of our losses. They were also forced to abandon dozens of their catapults and ballistae, leaving the southern Chain Castle without any artillery cover.'

'Then what do you recommend, Captain?' said the major.

Cisca glanced past the olive trees at the soldiers surrounding the Chain Castle. 'Are we placing this side of the straits under a land siege, sir?'

'We are. Our orders are to take the castle, and then force the opening of the Cyasarta as quickly as possible.'

'Then I would recommend that we divert a few battalions to march directly on Igatz from here, sir. The siege of the Chain Castle should only require a thousand of our own soldiers, as it is likely that the rebels will only have a few hundred within the walls. An aggressive siege, allied to a frontal land assault upon Igatz should be enough to cause panic in the town. In my view, the rebels threw everything they had at us last night, in the hope that we would believe their position to be stronger than it really is.'

'And if you are wrong?' said a colonel. 'We could be walking into a trap.'

'I do not believe that to be the case, sir,' she said. 'They were trying to frighten us. If we show strength and determination, the rebels will panic and flee. We could be in Handshore within a few hours.'

The major eyed her. 'Are you quite sure that your personal feelings regarding these rebels are not interfering with your judgement, Captain? I understood that you had rather a rough time of it when you were last here.'

'The rebels had an inner core of only a few hundred dedicated fighters, sir,' she said. 'If many of those were slain in last night's attack, then their position will be far weaker than they would have us believe.'

'This sounds like a rather large risk to take,' said the colonel. 'Perhaps we should wait here until the Chain Castle has been captured, so that the fleet can enter the straits.'

'I am minded to agree with Captain Cisca,' said the major. 'The only question is – are our men up to the task? Many will be exhausted and demoralised by the events of last night. Can we scrape together a few battalions willing and able to march the eight miles to Igatz and then engage the enemy?'

'I have some eight hundred fresh men, sir,' said a captain. 'They missed last night's fighting, and have just arrived.'

The major nodded, then he glanced at a lieutenant. 'Send a signal to Lady Lenta Min Gahad, asking her to descend. If her ladyship agrees to protect the advance, then I feel it is a risk worth taking. If we can occupy Handshore before the fleet breaks through, then the Bullan will be able to land unopposed.'

The lieutenant saluted, then he disappeared through the olive grove. Water and food were passed around the officers, then Cisca looked up, and saw the huge form of Lady Lenta begin to circle overhead, drawn by a soldier raising a series of large flags. The dragon lowered herself, then alighted next to the olive grove.

The officers stood and bowed.

'Good morning, my blessed lady,' said the major. 'Might you be willing to lead an assault upon Igatz this day?'

The dragon's eyes gleamed red. 'I am most certainly willing. When do we start?'

It took an hour to organise the eight hundred fresh soldiers, and then a further two hours to march them eight miles along the dusty road towards Igatz. At the major's behest, Captain Cisca accompanied the advance forces as a liaison officer, while Lady Lenta patrolled overhead. The road was quiet, and no local Zamatans were seen anywhere until the column passed the village of Riston on their left. Long spindly piers reached out from the shoreline into the waters of the Cyasarta, while white-washed cottages and cafes sat basking in the afternoon sunshine. Elderly villagers were keeping a wary eye on the Dominion soldiers, watching them from over the low walls surrounding each property.

The column was halted, and Cisca was summoned to the front.

'What am I looking at, Captain?' said the colonel in charge of the column.

'That is Riston, sir,' she said. 'It is a small fishing village, with a few large mansions by the beach that used to belong to the settler nobility.'

'Is it a threat?'

'There is a chance that the rebels used the village harbour to cross the Cyasarta last night, sir,' she said, 'but the villagers would have had no choice about that. I recommend that we press on. The edge of Igatz is less than half a mile from here.'

The colonel nodded. 'What kind of defences can we expect?'

'The southern border of Igatz has no walls, sir,' she said, 'but there may be rebel fighters hidden among the houses. We shall be arriving at a junction soon. The way to the left goes to the old Third-Occupation-era Fortress of Atzoun; the way ahead leads to a ferry terminal; and the road to the right will take us directly to Handshore Naval Base.'

'Thank you, Captain,' he said. He issued a few orders, and the column began moving again. They reached the junction in a few minutes, and the pace of the soldiers picked up as they chose the route that led to the right. The column reformed into a thick, compact unit six abreast, and they half-ran the last quarter of a mile. They came to the brow of a low slope, and Cisca saw the southern edge of Igatz laid out before them. Wide, tree-lined avenues of well-appointed town-houses and stone villas stretched away in neat rows, their red roof tiles shimmering in the heat haze.

The first Zamatans stared at the soldiers in a stunned silence as they reached the edge of town, and then the panic began.

'Stay together!' cried the colonel. 'Straight ahead, and stop for nothing!'

The soldiers increased their speed again and raced along the wide street, as the locals scattered in every direction. Some were wailing and screaming, and many seemed to be heading westwards towards the ferry terminal. A handful of armed Zamatans stood guard at a large crossroads, but they broke and ran as soon as the Dominion soldiers came into view. The Aucterians reached another junction, and Cisca saw the walls of Handshore loom up in front of them. She pointed towards a large open gate that led into the naval base.

'The gate!' the colonel shouted. 'Secure the gate!'

The eight hundred Aucterian soldiers charged, their shields held out in front of them as they neared the iron gates. A few Zamatan fighters were there, and they pulled their crossbows from their shoulders and loosed at the approaching soldiers. Two Aucterians fell, while bolts slammed into shields or ricocheted off the worn cobbles. Cisca was shoved deep into the mass of soldiers, and they stormed through the gates and into the base. At that moment, Lady Lenta soared in low over Handshore, her claws extended. She ripped through a row of rebel fighters, then banked and sent a burst of flames into the rear of a group trying to flee. Chaos descended over the base as the Dominion soldiers moved through it towards the docks. The colonel sent squads off in every direction to close the gates and to secure the main buildings, as the great black and white dragon pursued the panicking, fleeing rebels. A solitary tower began to loose yard-long bolts from its battery of four ballistae, but the dragon flew low, her body just a few feet above the roofs of the long warehouses; then she raised her head and opened her jaws. Flames burst out, engulfing the tower in an inferno, and rendering the rebels posted there to ash in seconds.

With the tower ablaze, groups of dazed rebels began emerging from the administrative buildings clustered by the long quayside, their arms in the air. Several Dominion soldiers hurried forwards to accept their surrender, but Lady Lenta soared down before they could reach the rebels. The dragon opened her jaws again, and incinerated the rebels out in the open, her head moving from left to right until every one was dead.

'That was for my brother,' Lenta cried, her voice booming across the naval base.

Cisca stared at the smoking heaps of corpses lying on the ground in front of her, and then the dragon took to the air again, swooping low over Handshore.

The colonel joined Cisca.

'It appears the base is ours, Captain; good work.'

Three hours later, Cisca was sitting alone by the quayside of Handshore as the sun set over the mountains to the west. Part of the Dominion

Fleet was beginning to enter the great breakwaters, while the huge dragon carrier had anchored a few hundred yards out in the middle of the Cyasarta. Lord Malum had emerged from below deck, and had joined Lady Lenta in securing the entirety of the vast base. Taking their lead from the dragons, the Dominion soldiers had refused to accept the surrender of any rebels trapped within Handshore, and the cobbles were slick with blood. Some of the Aucterians looked appalled by the behaviour of their comrades, but most seemed content to take their revenge for the losses of the previous night, and the corpses of the Zamatans began to fill the lanes and roads of the base.

Cisca watched as a large troopship docked by one of the main jetties. Sailors secured the ropes and fixed a gangway into place, then the ship's cargo of Bullan soldiers began to disembark, striding down onto the solid ground as the two dragons wheeled overhead.

She heard a low cough, and turned to see Major Lyla standing with a few Dragon Corps lieutenants. Cisca got to her feet and saluted.

'Good evening, Captain,' Lyla said. 'I believe some congratulations are in order.'

Cisca frowned. 'Ma'am?'

'Come now; don't be modest,' said Lyla. 'I have heard all about your role in today's victory. While some in the army were urging caution, you advocated nothing less than a bold surprise assault on the enemy's prime asset. I heard there were only two casualties out of eight hundred? What a feat. I have spoken to Lord Malum about this. Rest assured that his lordship is more than satisfied with your performance this day.' The Dragon Corps major smiled. 'You have probably saved both of our careers. Can I buy you a drink?'

'Thank you, ma'am.'

The officers of the Dragon Corps walked through the lanes of the base. The Bullan reinforcements were taking over control from the Aucterians by every gate and building, and there was much mutual back-slapping and words of jubilation between the two contingents. Zamatan civilians were also out, clearing up the bodies of the executed rebels and mopping the blood from the cobblestones, their eyes lowered. Major Lyla led her officers to a navy mess hall, where a large group of off-duty Dominion soldiers had started drinking. They found an empty table and sat, then a couple of sergeants approached with a tray of drinks.

'This is from the lads,' said one; 'to thank Captain Cisca.' He winked. 'And who ever said the Dragon Corps were part-time soldiers, eh?'

Major Lyla laughed as she raised her glass. 'After eight years in the regular army, sergeant, I chose the Dragon Corps because I thought it would be quiet – how wrong I was.'

Cisca smiled, but her thoughts were still on the Zamatans who had been cut down as they had been trying to surrender. The sergeants saluted her then returned to their own table.

'It goes without saying,' Major Lyla went on, 'that had our latest plan been another failure, then I doubt that we would be sitting here enjoying these drinks, Captain Cisca. How did you know your little stratagem would succeed?'

'I didn't know, ma'am,' Cisca said; 'not for certain. It was always clear to me, however, that the rebels lacked any great number of fighters. What surprises me is that they would have risked everything on their night assault. They only had four ballistae left to defend the entire naval base. Four. Colonel Laimos must have hoped that we would have been so disheartened by our losses that we would have set sail back to Aucteran.'

'That filthy rebel must be cowering in his boots right now,' said a young Dragon Corps lieutenant. 'I wonder if he has fled to Kaugatz yet.'

'With any luck he will still be in Igatz,' said Lyla. She glanced at Cisca. 'What about his officers? Does Laimos have anyone capable working for him that we should know about?'

'Most of his officers were members of the old native militia, ma'am,' Cisca said.

'And that Bauchlie character?' Lyla said. 'Was he militia, too?'

'No,' said Cisca. 'Bauchlie was… I mean *is*; Bauchlie is a terrorist and a criminal. A fanatic, dedicated to his hopeless cause.'

Lyla took another drink. 'And we all know that fanatics are the worst type of people. He should be put down like a wild dog.'

'Was he the brute who held you and Lord Kheran hostage, Captain?' said a lieutenant.

'Yes,' said Cisca.

'The old militia will have to be disbanded, of course,' said Lyla, 'as we cannot allow a nest of traitors access to weapons again. Colonel Laimos will be arrested in due course and charged with treason. As for Bauchlie, we have instructions to kill him upon sight. Lord Malum has posted a reward of five hundred sovereigns for his head.'

One of the junior officers whistled. 'Five hundred, ma'am? That would make a nice contribution to my retirement fund.'

The others laughed.

'Thinking about catching him yourself, are you?' said Lyla. 'Be warned – he is reputedly a remorseless and pitiless murderer. Isn't that right, Captain Cisca?'

Cisca forced a smile on to her lips. 'So I believe, ma'am. Please excuse me for a moment; I need to visit the bathroom.'

She stood and strode away before the others could see her smile vanish. She hurried to the bathroom, and locked herself into a small dark cubicle with a pit in the floor. She grimaced at the rudimentary facilities, and leaned against the wall, her eyes welling.

She told herself to stop being so weak. Bauchlie *was* a terrorist and a criminal, and he deserved to die for all of the vile things he had done. She remembered back to the night she had stood with him watching the moon rise over Igatz, the same night that she thought she had perceived something else about him, something far removed from his reputation. She had wanted to save him, to reform him, to nurture that kernel of kindness and goodness that she had imagined to dwell within his heart.

No. It was stupid, and she should be ashamed of herself. She closed her eyes, and wondered what it would feel like to be held within his strong embrace.

CHAPTER 9
ROBED WITH DECEIT

Kaugatz, Serpent Isle – 27th Tradinch 1588

Colonel Laimos narrowed his eyes. 'Captain Cisca, you say?'

Leona nodded. 'Yes, sir – the same officer who was held prisoner by Bauchlie during the uprising.'

'And she was responsible for the loss of Handshore?'

'So it seems, sir. It appears that she is advising the Dominion forces, as one of the few in the fleet with experience of Zamata.'

'Damn that bitch!' Friel cried, his eyes burning. He glared at Bauchlie. 'And you let her live?'

Bauchlie returned the glare. 'I am not in the habit of butchering unarmed women.'

Friel snorted. 'Since when?'

'Since I stopped following your orders,' said Bauchlie. He turned to gaze out of the narrow window at the interior of the Tsallon Anura monastery. 'Cisca was an honourable officer. She did her duty and protected Lord Kheran to the best of her ability. She also flushed out a Gunstian agent who had planned to assassinate me and the young dragon. I would be dead if it wasn't for her.'

'And now Igatz has fallen because of her,' spat the colonel.

Bauchlie shook his head. 'The fleet would have broken through the chains protecting the Cyasarta even without Cisca's raid on Handshore. All she did was hasten the process a little. It is you who is responsible for the fall of the island, not a single officer in the Dragon Corps. Your ill-advised night attack left Igatz almost defenceless.'

'What nonsense,' said Friel.

'Nonsense?' said Bauchlie. 'Tell me – when the Dominion soldiers laid siege to the southern Chain Castle, where were the catapults to defend the position? And when the dragons tore through Handshore, where were the ballistae that were supposed to repel them? Lying broken and captured by the shores of the Hansarta; that's where. You brought this defeat upon yourself, and are no longer fit to lead the Zamatan resistance.'

Friel got to his feet. 'And who do you imagine should lead us – you?'

Bauchlie shrugged. 'I would have done a better job.'

'Get out of my sight,' said the colonel.

'It will be a pleasure, Colonel Laimos,' said Bauchlie. He glanced at Leona. 'If you ever feel like working for someone with a little more sense, I would be more than happy to employ you.'

Bauchlie strode from the office and slammed the door behind him.

'That truculent fool!' Friel cried.

Leona said nothing.

'Ungrateful, that's what he is,' the colonel went on, as he retook his seat behind the large desk. 'Ungrateful, and irresponsible. How dare he criticise my decisions, when he hasn't the faintest idea what it takes to run an entire island?' He put his head in his hands. 'By all the serpent gods, what have I done?'

'You took a risk, sir,' Leona said.

'Yes? And?'

'It failed, sir. But, it could be argued that we would be in the same position if we hadn't carried out the night attack. Nothing could have prevented the dragons from breaking into the Cyasarta in the end.'

'How bad is it?' he said. 'And don't try to varnish the truth.'

'Very well, sir,' she said. 'Igatz is now completely under Dominion control, as is almost all of Kaugatz. Bullan and Aucterian soldiers are also occupying Wayston, Belton and Chesson, and their forces have taken both of the Chain Castles. Troops have also reached the monastery of Zamata Gataza on the slopes of Mount Hodzulat.'

'Have they arrested the prelate?'

'No, sir. The prelate and his monks knelt before Lord Malum Mon Gahad this morning, and have been allowed to retain their positions.'

'This morning? How do we know this?'

'A monk arrived from Zamata Gataza at midday with the news, sir. The Dominion forces allowed him to enter Tsallon Anura, and then they allowed him to leave an hour later.'

'Why does that not surprise me? And I'll bet you anything that the damn prelate is currently denouncing me as a dangerous god-killer and blasphemer.'

Leona paused for a second. 'Well, sir, you *are* a dangerous god-killer, and you are also a blasphemer.'

Friel glanced up at her. 'Thank you. It's nice to know I'm still appreciated by some people. Do you have any good news to share with me?'

'Tsallon Anura is still holding out,' she said, 'though I imagine that you might have guessed that by now, seeing as that is where we are, sir.'

He gazed out of the window. 'Yes, it had occurred to me. I suppose you should leave now – the Dominion negotiators will be waiting for you.'

'But, sir,' she said, 'you haven't informed me of our negotiating position. What am I to tell them?'

'That's easy,' he said. 'First of all, you can tell them that I have decided to politely decline their kind invitation, and I have sent you on my behalf. And second, if they swear an oath to provide an amnesty for all Zamatans involved in the rebellion, then I will surrender myself into their hands without a fight.'

'It is unlikely that they will accept that condition, sir.'

He shrugged. 'I know.'

'And when they refuse?'

'Then tell them to come and get me. They must realise that I have concentrated every last ballistae here in the monastery; otherwise they would have attacked when they reached Kaugatz yesterday. I imagine that the sight of Lord Meer's skull atop the monastery walls might have given them pause.'

Leona nodded. 'Yes, sir.'

'One more thing before you go,' he said. 'Has there been any word concerning my horned nephew?'

'No, sir,' she said. 'No one has seen Lahnos since we evacuated Igatz.'

Friel nodded, his eyes remaining on the view of the Cyasarta through the window. Leona bowed her head and left the colonel's office, then she strode past the militia fighters on guard duty and out into the bright afternoon sunshine. A few wispy clouds were in the sky, but the sun had dried the rain that had fallen during the night. She nodded to a few rebels, then entered the long cloister, which was packed with more rebels, and crates of supplies. Dotted around the complex were over three dozen ballistae, all pointing up at the sky, along with net-throwing catapults that had been hidden among the monastery buildings. The sound of chanting and prayers were coming from the nearby chapel, where the monks had locked themselves in as a protest against the re-occupation of Tsallon Anura by Colonel Laimos and his remaining rebels; while a few pillars of smoke were rising from parts of Kaugatz. Leona wondered what the smoke signified. Was there still organised resistance against the Dominion forces, or was it merely piles of rubbish being burned that was causing the smoke to rise?

Leona strode to a side gate, where a squad of rebels was awaiting her. A small postern door was unbarred, while several rebels held their crossbows ready, and then Leona walked through the gate. She heard it close behind her, but didn't turn. Ahead, a platoon of Dominion soldiers was standing by the corner of the nearest building, bearing a white flag. They eyed her.

'I am here to negotiate,' she said.

The Aucterian officer narrowed his eyes. 'Where is the colonel?'

'He sent me in his stead,' said Leona. She pulled a letter from her bag. 'Here is the document to prove it. I am unarmed, as you can see.

Will you please take me wherever you have chosen as a location for the negotiations?'

The officer gave her a wry smile. 'Friel Laimos sent a girl to do his dirty work?

'He sent his chief negotiator to negotiate. I trust you will afford me all courtesy as befits my position.'

'Fine,' muttered the officer. 'This way.'

Leona walked away from the high walls of the monastery and followed the soldiers as they led her down a long alleyway. Dominion soldiers were occupying every building that bordered Tsallon Anura, and the officer took her to an old bakery, which was heavily guarded. They entered through the front door, and Leona saw that the shop area had been cleared of its produce. In its place, a large table had been assembled, around which were sitting several high-ranking officers from the Dominion army, as well as a few from the navy. Seated by the right hand of a major was Captain Cisca, but Leona kept her expression neutral when she saw her.

The Dominion major shook his head at her approach. 'What is this? Where's Laimos?'

'May I sit?' said Leona.

'Who are you?' said the major.

'I am Leona of Kaugatz,' she said, as she produced the letter. She laid it out flat on the surface of the table. 'May I sit?'

The major picked up the letter, then sighed as he read it. 'Yes. Sit.'

'Thank you,' said Leona, taking her place opposite the major. 'What terms are you offering?'

'Who is this girl?' said another officer.

'I am Leona of Kaugatz,' she repeated.

'Yes; I heard. What position of authority do you hold within the rebellion, Leona of Kaugatz?'

'I am an advisor to Colonel Friel Laimos,' she said. 'Captain Cisca can confirm that.'

All eyes turned to the Dragon Corps officer.

Cisca nodded. 'I have seen this woman in the presence of Colonel Laimos,' she said. 'He trusts her.'

'She is clearly expendable to that filthy traitor,' said another captain. He narrowed his eyes at Leona. 'We could easily have you strung up before the walls of the monastery, girl.'

'You could,' she said, 'but then you would be breaking the very conditions that you set for these negotiations. Not even the Gunstians would behave in such a manner. Have you less honour than the Gunstians?' She turned back to the major. 'I am still waiting on your terms for our capitulation.'

'Our terms are simple,' the major said: 'all rebel fighters must surrender themselves to the Dominion before sunset today. You will lay down your weapons and then open the gates of Tsallon Anura. If you do so, then there will be no summary executions – all will be charged according to the law.'

Leona smiled. 'Charged with which offence?'

'Treason, obviously.'

'For which the penalty is death?'

'I believe so.'

'Then it is not a case of surrender or die, but more like surrender and then die? And if we refuse?'

'If you refuse, then we will attack at dawn.'

Leona felt a tingle in the back of her head. 'I see. Would you care to hear an alternative suggestion?'

The major shrugged, then nodded.

'If you were to guarantee a full amnesty for all Zamatans caught up in the uprising,' Leona said, 'then we will guarantee that Colonel Laimos surrenders himself into your custody.'

'Is that it?' said the major.

'Yes.'

'You want every traitor on this island to walk away as free men?'

Leona looked puzzled. 'That is the nature of an amnesty, yes.'

'The blessed Lord Malum Mon Gahad will never allow that.'

'A pity,' she said. 'How many Zamatans do you think were involved in the uprising?'

'Is that relevant?' said the major.

'I believe it is,' she said; 'if you intend to charge and try each and every one of them. Would Lord Malum be prepared to execute the majority of the native islanders? Because that is what your condition amounts to. Do you wish to rule over a desolate and depopulated wasteland? Once again, I am reminded of the Gunstians. And to think that the people of the Dominion perceive themselves to be enlightened.'

'If we were Gunstians, then we would already be slaughtering your people, girl.'

'The way you slaughtered them in Neeton and Handshore?'

A few officers shifted uncomfortably in their seats.

'Give me a number,' Leona said.

'What number?' said a colonel.

'The number of bodies you wish to see hanging from the gallows. What quantity of corpses will satisfy the blessed Lord Malum's desire for justice? Five hundred? A thousand? Ten thousand? All of us?'

The major suppressed a grim laugh. 'You have a cheek, girl. It was your side who rebelled against the legitimate rulers of the Serpent Isle, and yet here you are, lecturing us on morality.'

'Our position is that the Dominion is not the legitimate ruler of Zamata, and that your occupation of our island was illegal and, yes, immoral. You preach to the world that you are better than the Gunstians, and that may be so, but to us Zamatans, the differences seem paper-thin. Both sides desire this island, and both sides are prepared to wade in blood to possess it. Neither seems interested in asking us what we want. If a foreign power invaded Aucteran, would you not see it as your duty to defend yourselves?'

The major stared at her for a long, silent moment, then he glanced away. 'A thousand.'

Leona nodded. 'A thousand? Thank you for your honesty.' She smiled, then stood. 'I decline your offer. Good day.'

'Do you understand what this means?' cried the major. 'This coming dawn, we will strike hard at Tsallon Anura, until every inhabitant of the monastery is lying dead in their own blood.'

Leona felt the tingle again. 'If we were frightened of you,' she said, 'we would never have rebelled in the first place. Yes, you are stronger, and yes you could annihilate every Zamatan if that is what you truly desire, but you will never cow our spirit. For centuries, you have known what it felt like to be free, and now we also know. Therefore, I tell you this – do your worst. We shall be waiting.'

She turned for the door.

'Give us Bauchlie,' said the major.

Leona glanced back at the table.

'Give us Bauchlie, and we shall consider your terms.'

'Why Bauchlie?' she said.

'Come now,' said the major; 'you seem like an intelligent young woman. You must be aware that Bauchlie was responsible for the capture and horrendous treatment of Lord Kheran. Next to Colonel Laimos, he is the most wanted criminal on the Serpent Isle.'

Leona considered for a moment. 'So, not a thousand, but two?' she said. 'You would provide an amnesty if we surrender Colonel Laimos and Commander Bauchlie? Is that what you mean? Please be clear.'

'I cannot guarantee that Lord Malum will accept this offer,' the major said, 'but I pledge to discuss it with him in good faith.'

Leona felt no tingle. 'Very well. I shall take this offer back to Colonel Laimos, and you shall have our answer by sunset.' She tilted her head a little then strode towards the door. The soldiers at the entrance moved aside, and her escort from before moved back into position around her. They led her through the streets towards the monastery, then halted just out of bow range. She nodded to them, then walked out towards the gates on her own. The rebels up on the battlements of the walls saw her approach, and the postern gate was opened to let her pass.

Waiting for her on the other side was the colonel. He nudged her into an empty guard room and closed the door.

'Well?' he said. 'What did they say?'

Leona sat. 'I managed to get them down to two people,' she said. 'You, naturally, and Bauchlie.'

Friel stared at her. 'Bauchlie? Did they threaten to attack?'

'They did, but they were bluffing. I walked away, so they said they would offer an amnesty if you and Commander Bauchlie hand yourselves over to them.'

Friel exhaled. 'They were bluffing, eh? Those damn dragons are actually afraid to attack.'

'It would appear so, sir,' she said. 'However, they don't have to attack to win; they only need to starve us out.'

'Are you suggesting that I hand over my son to the enemy?'

'No. I am suggesting that you ask him what he thinks about the offer. Perhaps Bauchlie would like to die as a martyr for the cause.'

'And what about what I think?' he said. 'I have no desire to see my son swing from a noose.'

Leona watched as the colonel paced up and down, his boots tramping over the stone floor. She took no pleasure from her suggestion, but the more ruthless part of her personality would prefer the deaths of two men to that of a thousand.

'You don't need to ask him to do it, sir,' she said; 'you need only ensure that he is aware of what the Dominion has offered, and then allow him to draw his own conclusions. Bauchlie has a keen sense of honour – why is it acceptable for you to sacrifice yourself for Zamata, but then to deny him the same opportunity?'

Friel collapsed into a chair and bowed his head.

'I am his father,' he whispered. 'I can die for him, but I could never surrender him.'

'Bauchlie will die of starvation along with the rest of us if we refuse, sir.'

'Maybe; maybe not.'

'Do you see any other way out, sir?'

'The Demon Witch. The Demon Witch might save us.'

'I believed that, too, sir,' she said; 'but we have to face reality. The Demon Witch hasn't contacted us in weeks, not since the Gunstians attempted to break into the Cyasarta. It might be bad timing, or she might have decided that our cause is no longer worth fighting for – either way, we are on our own.'

'It would have been better if she had never said anything in the first place. Would the rebellion have succeeded without her advice?' He laughed. 'I gained a reputation for being a tactical genius, but I am nothing of the kind. The first major test that comes along without her help, and I make a complete mess of it. And look at us now – even if she were to make contact with Lahnos, then how would he tell us? If only I had offered her something, but I had no idea what she wanted.'

A loud knock rapped on the door.

Friel glanced at Leona, so she stood and opened the door.

'Yes?' she said to the militia soldier standing outside.

'Is the colonel in there, ma'am?'

'He is. How can I help you?'

'There's trouble at the chapel.'

Leona nodded. 'What kind of trouble?'

'The monks have unlocked the doors, ma'am, and they are demanding to leave. They say that they have permission from the Dominion to walk out of Tsallon Anura unharmed.'

Leona glanced at the colonel.

'That wouldn't surprise me,' said Friel.

'Should we let them go, sir?' said the rebel fighter.

The colonel shrugged. 'How many?'

'All of them, sir. Forty or so.'

'Forty?' said Leona. 'I didn't think there were that many monks still in Tsallon Anura.'

The colonel waved his hand, his eyes distracted. 'Let them go. Forty fewer mouths to feed.'

The rebel fighter nodded. 'Yes, sir.'

Leona narrowed her eyes. 'I might watch this,' she said. 'I want to see if the Dominion allow them to leave in peace.'

'Suit yourself,' said Friel. 'Afterwards, come back and I'll give you my decision about what we were discussing.'

Leona nodded, then she followed the fighter out of the guard room. He led her towards a small plaza in front of the chapel, where a large number of rebels were blocking the passage of forty men in long flowing robes. Leona gazed at the monks, but their features were obscured by their hoods.

'Traitors!' one of the militia shouted at them, but none of the monks responded.

'The colonel says we should let them go,' cried the fighter who had spoken to Friel. 'Clear the way!'

Several rebels muttered, their expressions dark, but they did as they were told. One of the monks bowed his head, then he led his colleagues through the crowd of rebels towards the northern gate of the monastery. Leona and a few others followed them along the narrow lanes, until they reached a set of guarded doors set into the high curtain wall.

'Open the gates!' cried a fighter. 'Let the bastards leave.'

Leona darted down an alleyway, then climbed the steep, worn steps to the top of the battlements. She peered into the distance, and saw several squads of Dominion soldiers occupying the nearby buildings. The gates opened, and the monks began filing out from the monastery.

'They'll be massacred,' whispered one of the rebels from the walls.

'So?' said another. 'It'll be their own damn fault.'

The monks began chanting prayers to the serpent gods as they processed along the road that led from the monastery. As soon as the last one had left, the northern gates were swung closed again with a dull clang, but Leona paid no attention, her gaze fixed on the brown-robed monks as they approached the Dominion lines. A few Aucterian soldiers aimed their crossbows at the monks, awaiting the order to loose, but a squad of Bullan appeared on the street, forming a barrier between the human soldiers and the monks. The Bullan raised their shields to protect the monks as they passed the Dominion forces and, within moments, the monks were lost within the warren of Kaugatz alleyways.

'The Bullan saved them,' said one of the rebels up on the battlements. 'Why would they do that?'

'Did you not hear what happened in the monastery of Zamata Gataza this morning?' said Leona. 'The prelate knelt before Lord Malum. He must have brokered an agreement with the Dominion, and the Bullan were just making sure that it was kept.'

'Those damn traitors,' muttered the fighter. 'Curse them all.'

Leona turned from the view of Kaugatz and made her way back down the steps. She moved through the crowd of militia at the gates, then began to walk back towards the guard room where she had left the colonel. As she was passing the chapel, a scream rang through the air, followed by the sound of boots running over the paved alleyways of the monastery. Leona glanced at the chapel, and saw several rebel fighters pushing their way into the dark interior. She went to take a closer look, and slipped into the incense-filled air of the ancient sanctuary. Inside, candlelight was flickering over the worn tapestries. She looked down. The floor was covered in the naked bodies of several dozen men. Each one had been butchered, and their blood was pooling over the faded mosaics.

'Every one of them, slaughtered!' cried a rebel. 'Who would do such a thing?'

Amid the confusion, Leona knelt by one of the bodies. His throat had been cut, and he had a deep stab wound to his chest.

'If the monks are all dead,' a fighter shouted, 'then who just left the monastery?'

Leona got back to her feet, her stomach churning at the carnage. She backed out of the chapel and forced her way through the growing crowds. As soon as she was free of them, she ran towards the colonel's private apartments. She reached the hallway where Friel's room was situated, then turned and banged on a nearby door. It fell open, and she glanced inside. Empty. She put a hand to her face, almost unable to believe what had happened; then she turned, and slowly made her way to the guard room.

The colonel was outside when she arrived.

'I am hearing some disturbing reports,' Friel said, as he saw her approach. 'Are they true?

'Yes,' Leona said. 'Every monk has been killed.'

'Then, who...?' Friel paused, and Leona knew that the same thought had occurred to him as had occurred to her only moments before.

'I checked his room, sir,' she said.

'Yes? And?'

'He's not there.'

Friel's face seemed to crumple, and he staggered back a step.

'Then...' he said, 'then...'

'I'm sorry, sir,' she said, 'but Bauchlie has fled the monastery with his men. They've gone.'

CHAPTER 10
THE CHOSEN ONE

Fidalaimos, Serpent Isle – 4th Abrinch 1588

Lahnos crept through the orange grove, his eyes scanning the area ahead.

'I think it's clear,' he whispered.

Reyn joined him, keeping low, her hands and knees covered in soil.

'Where's the colonel's gardener?' she whispered. 'Can you see him?'

Lahnos turned his gaze to the large mansion. All of the shutters were closed, and there was no sign of movement.

'Maybe it's his day off,' he said. 'Come on.'

He got to his feet, then extended a hand and pulled Reyn up. They strode between the last of the orange trees and stepped onto the hard-packed dirt driveway that sat in front of Friel's mountain mansion. Without saying a word, they both turned towards the view of the island. The sun had risen an hour before, and the twin inlets were shimmering in the morning light. To their right, the high peak of Hodzulat sat dark and foreboding in the distance, while the rest of the sinewy island lay spread out before them.

'It's just as I remember it,' Reyn said. 'This must be the best view in Zamata.'

Lahnos glanced at her. After seven days on the run, Reyn was looking bedraggled, hungry and tired, but she was just as beautiful as ever. He took her hand, then he gave a low whistle. Moments later, Efizel emerged from the thick undergrowth thirty yards to the left of the orange grove. The Bullan soldier's eyes took in his surroundings, then he moved silently over to where Lahnos and Reyn were standing.

'That house is no *cottage*, young Laimos,' he said, keeping his voice low. 'It is as grand as any stately home in Igatz.'

'It's what my uncle calls it,' Lahnos said.

'The last time we were here,' said Reyn, 'it took us a single day to travel from Igatz, not seven.'

'You can blame the efficiency of my Klediomira comrades for that,' said the Bullan. 'There must be close to eight regiments now on Zamata, as well as thousands of Aucterian troops. It took all of my tracking skills to get us here undetected.' He pointed down at the island. 'I can see the dragon carrier from up here, anchored off Handshore, and there is smoke coming from Kaugatz. Do you think your uncle is still holding out in Tsallon Anura?'

'Who knows?' said Lahnos.

'So much for the rebellion,' Efizel went on. 'Crushed in two days.'

Reyn's eyes darkened, and she looked away.

'I meant no offence,' Efizel said. 'This is your home, and I respect that. However, Zamata has nothing to match the might of the Dominion.'

'I feel terrible for abandoning our apartment in Igatz,' she said.

'There was nothing else we could have done,' said Efizel. 'Young Laimos is wanted by the authorities, and you would have been arrested as his associate. As for me, well, I don't want to think about that. Your horns and my ethnicity make it exceedingly hard to blend into a crowd of Zamatans. If we had stayed, we would be in prison, or worse.'

'I wanted to fight, not run,' Reyn said.

'Against such overwhelming odds, to fight means the same thing as to die. Your uncle may have won the initial night battle, but the price of victory was high.' He turned back to face the mansion. 'I shall scout round the... cottage. It looks quiet, but silence can hide a multitude of troubles.'

Reyn squeezed Lahnos's hand as the Bullan ran towards the grand building.

'Do you wish you had taken that ship now?' she said.

'No.'

'Are you sure? You have hardly spoken in days, Lahnos.'

'I hate this stupid island,' he said, 'but I love it, too. Everything that's happened... it's exactly what I thought would happen; but it's no fun being right. I know you longed for Zamata's freedom, Reyn. I wish it could have worked out.'

Reyn said nothing, then she pointed, and Lahnos saw a tiny dark speck circling in the skies over Igatz.

'Lady Lenta is patrolling again,' she said, 'but notice how she is staying away from the vicinity of Tsallon Anura. That can only mean one thing – your uncle is holding out. One small corner of Zamata is still free.'

Lahnos resisted the temptation to point out that his uncle's capitulation was only a matter of time. He had been biting his tongue ever since they had fled Igatz on foot, determined never to say *I told you so*.

Efizel appeared behind them, his silent approach making Reyn jump. The Bullan put a finger to his lips.

'We are not alone,' he whispered. 'Follow me, and move quietly.'

The Bullan led them back into the orange grove, then they circled round to the rear of the mansion and crouched in the dense undergrowth. Efizel pointed down at a track that led off to a large grove of lemon trees, and Lahnos saw a footprint in the dirt.

'Colonel Laimos employs a gardener,' Reyn whispered.

Efizel raised his finger to point at one of the shutters. Its latch had been forced, and was hanging loose from the window frame.

'Would a gardener break into his employer's home?' he said.

'What should we do?' said Reyn.

The Bullan turned to glance at Lahnos.

'I say we go in,' Lahnos said.

'Is that wise?' said Efizel. 'You mentioned that you did not wish for anyone in Fidalaimos to know that you are here. The chances are that someone from the village has broken into this house to rob it.'

'We could sneak about and see who it is,' said Lahnos.

'Only I possess the skills to do that quietly,' said Efizel. 'Again, I mean no offence, but you two move around like lumbering cattle.'

Lahnos stood and strode out towards the window. 'Let's try the direct approach.' He reached the shutters and pulled them open. 'Hey!' he cried. 'You're trespassing! You've got two minutes to show yourself or we're coming in.'

Lahnos smiled as he heard Efizel emit a deep groan behind him, then he froze as a crossbow appeared at the window, its loaded bolt pointed at his head.

'You?' came a low voice. 'Why is it always you?'

Lahnos eyed the man holding the bow. 'Good to see you, too, Bauchlie. I didn't take you for a coward, hiding out in my uncle's mansion. I thought you wanted to go down fighting?'

Bauchlie said nothing, his grim eyes flitting over to where Reyn and Efizel were emerging from the undergrowth.

'If you don't lower that bow,' said Efizel, 'I will be forced to kill you. I say *forced*, but killing you would be a pleasure, you vile piece of dog shit.'

Bauchlie stared at the Bullan, then he laughed and pulled the shutters closed. A moment later, the back door of the mansion opened, and Bauchlie gestured for them to enter. Lahnos walked inside, followed by Reyn and the Bullan, who was glaring at Bauchlie. The scarred man said nothing, but his eyes never left Efizel. Bauchlie led them into a large living area and lit a lamp. Lahnos glanced at the blankets on the floor, and the unwashed dishes, mugs and bowls.

'How long have you been living here?' said Reyn, her nose crinkling.

'A few days,' said Bauchlie. He sat. 'What do you want?'

'This is my uncle's house, not yours,' said Lahnos. 'You have no right to be here.'

Bauchlie shrugged.

'Would you mind if we also stayed here?' said Reyn.

'Do what you like,' said Bauchlie; 'but don't get in my way.'

Lahnos narrowed his eyes. 'Why aren't you in Tsallon Anura? Has it fallen? Is my uncle still alive?'

'I don't have the answers to your last two questions,' Bauchlie said; 'but I am not in Tsallon Anura because I left.'

'Talk about stating the obvious,' said Lahnos. 'Why did you leave?'

Reyn peered at a heap of garments on the floor. 'Are those monk's robes? Is that blood?'

Bauchlie said nothing.

'We cannot trust this creature,' said Efizel.

Lahnos smiled. 'You said that about my uncle.'

'And I was right,' said the Bullan. 'But, at least with Colonel Laimos one knew where one stood. He might be a traitor, but he had honour, of a sort.' He pointed at Bauchlie. 'This murderer has no honour.'

'If you are going to attack me then do it,' said Bauchlie; 'but cease whining; you are boring me.'

The Bullan tensed, and Lahnos stepped between them.

'Let's get a few things straight,' Lahnos said. 'I'm in charge here, because this is my uncle's house.' He glanced at Bauchlie, who was staring up at him from his chair. 'Luckily, it's a big house, and there is room for all four of us.'

Bauchlie smiled. 'There might be more than four people living here.'

'What?'

'Try forty-four,' said Bauchlie. 'I didn't leave Tsallon Anura alone.'

'You have forty men in this house?' said Reyn. 'Where are they?'

'I sent them out last night,' said Bauchlie. 'They've gone to the ruins of Gatzoun Medamuna to collect a few supplies. They should be back before sunset.'

'They've gone to get food?' said Lahnos.

'Did I say food?' said Bauchlie. 'There are plenty of other useful items buried beneath the ruins of that old monastery.'

'Useful for what?' said Reyn.

Bauchlie yawned. 'You interrupted my sleep,' he said. 'Now piss off, all of you. Stay out of the rooms on this floor, and the floor above. You can have the attic.'

Lahnos's temper surged, then he felt Reyn take hold of his arm.

'Come on,' she said; 'you can show me the attic.'

'The attic?' Lahnos snapped. He clenched his fists, but Bauchlie was ignoring him, his eyes closed as he reclined in his chair. Reyn tugged at Lahnos's arm, and he strode out of the living room, his fury simmering.

'That arrogant bastard,' Lahnos muttered. 'I was trying to be reasonable; wasn't I trying to be reasonable? And he throws it back in my face.'

'Take a breath,' said Reyn. 'He has forty men to back him up; we only have Efizel.' She glanced at the Bullan. 'No offence.'

'None taken,' said Efizel. 'We should leave at once. It is clear to me that Bauchlie is intending to use this house as a base from which to organise a new uprising against the forces of the Dominion. If that is the case, then he will soon be attracting the attention of my kinsfolk.'

Lahnos cast his gaze downwards. 'We have nowhere else to go. Damn it; this island has never felt as small as it does right now.'

The Bullan glanced at Reyn. 'You are from the town of Chesson, correct?'

She nodded.

'Is there anywhere there that we could hide for a while? Any old friends or relatives that could take us in?'

'No,' she said. 'There's no one. My family would... they...'

Anger flared in Efizel's eyes. 'Your part-Bullan heritage has left you isolated and alone among those who should be caring for you. This knowledge saddens and sickens me at the same time.'

Lahnos began to walk for the stairs, his thoughts soured.

'Where are you going?' said Efizel.

'The attic,' he said; 'where else?'

'We must only stay a day or two,' the Bullan said, as he and Reyn followed him along the hallway. 'We will not be safe amid a mob of terrorists and bandits.'

'Bauchlie won't hurt us,' Lahnos said. 'Humiliate us? Maybe. Annoy us? Certainly; but he won't allow his men to touch us.'

They came to a grand set of stairs and ascended to the first floor of the mansion. Evidence of Bauchlie's men was strewn around the floor, and Lahnos saw several more discarded brown robes that looked as though they had once been worn by monks.

'I have a suspicion as to how that vile criminal was able to flee from Tsallon Anura,' Efizel said.

Lahnos knelt by a heap of sacks lying next to an ornate balustrade, and extracted some bread, wine and a ceramic jar filled with black olives. He found some goat's cheese wrapped in waxed paper, and handed it to Reyn, then they walked to the end of the landing, where another set of stairs rose. They climbed them, and came into a long, spacious attic, its sloping walls lined with old crates and boxes. Lahnos placed the food he had gathered onto one of the boxes and opened a semi-circular window, letting in the fresh air.

'This isn't too bad,' said Reyn. 'There's plenty of room for us up here. She ran a finger across the top of a crate, and it came away covered in a layer of dust. 'It could do with a clean, though.'

Lahnos sat on a box and ripped the loaf into three pieces, his pride still stinging from the treatment he had received from Bauchlie. That was all it was, he told himself – pride. Bauchlie could have threatened to throw the three of them out of the house, but he hadn't. Reyn and Efizel each took a piece of bread, and they sat eating in silence for a few minutes.

Reyn wiped her lips, and took a small sip of wine. 'What do the Bullan think of the part-Bullan, Efizel?' she said.

The soldier turned his gaze towards her. 'There are as many opinions regarding that topic as there are Bullan,' he said. 'Some feel anger when they look at people such as yourself and young Laimos – anger that any of our kinsfolk would have stooped so low as to couple with mere humans. Others feel shame, because they understand that not all such couplings were consensual. Rape is forbidden among my people, and is punishable by death; and yet the evidence of such cruel transgressions exists for all to see. Others feel pity; and some even feel a sense of kinship. It is a complicated matter.'

'Not all part-Bullan were caused by rape,' Reyn said.

'I am aware of that,' said Efizel. 'There are brothels in many parts of this island. There are strict rules which forbid my people from entering those establishments, but rules are often broken, even among the Klediomira Haga. It is hard to be without the company of women for the long years of our service.'

'That's not really what I meant,' said Reyn. 'There must be a few cases where a loving relationship developed between a Bullan soldier and a human woman.'

Efizel said nothing.

'Is that not true?' Reyn said.

'It might be,' said the Bullan soldier, 'though I have never heard of any such cases.'

'Yes, but you wouldn't, would you?' said Reyn. 'The soldiers would never admit it, and the women would also keep quiet. My mother...'

She fell silent as the two men watched her.

'Go on,' said Efizel.

Reyn glanced at the wooden floorboards. 'It sounds stupid to say it out loud. My mother – she once told me that she had loved a Bullan soldier. She was drunk when she said this to me, and then she denied it in the morning. It was the only time we ever discussed it. I want to believe it's true, though. Does that sound foolish?'

'No,' said Lahnos. 'I want to believe the same thing about my mother's mother.'

'Did she ever mention it to you?' said Efizel.

Lahnos shook his head. 'She died before I was born, and my own mother was murdered before my horns started to grow. The rest of my family refused to talk about it with me. If anyone knows the truth, it would be my uncle, but he claimed to have no knowledge of the circumstances that led to my mother's birth.'

'Your father might know.'

Lahnos nodded. 'Possibly.'

'We should have taken that ship to Irlan when we had the chance,' said Reyn. 'I'm sorry.'

Lahnos took her hand. 'Don't be sorry. I understand why you refused.'

The three of them sat in silence for a few minutes, then Efizel rose to his feet. 'I shall begin cleaning the attic,' he said. 'You two should rest for now, so that you are awake and alert when Bauchlie's men arrive.'

The Bullan soldier strode away. He forced open another window, then began to examine the crates stacked up by a wall. Lahnos and Reyn spread their travelling cloaks out onto the dusty floorboards, and lay down under the eaves of a sloping wall. He put his arms round her as she lay with her back to him, and closed his eyes.

Lahnos.

His eyes opened wide, and for a moment he expected to see a mob of rebel fighters surrounding him. He frowned. Reyn was sleeping on the floor next to him, while Efizel was busying himself with a brush at the far end of the long attic. The day's light had faded a little, but the sun had not yet set.

He closed his eyes again.

Lahnos.

He groaned silently. *You again? A little late, don't you think?*

I have been far away, Lahnos, attending to other business.

What business, Demon Witch? he said. *Business so important that you could allow the Dominion to trample us into the dirt?*

I cannot always be with you; I have a family of my own to watch over.

You have a family? Where?

Far from here, Lahnos. I cannot be with them in person, but I miss them; and so I watch over them, just as I have watched over you. I wish I could have been here when the Dominion Fleet arrived, but I longed to hear my children's voices, and to watch them laugh and play...

Lahnos hesitated. There was a deep sadness in the Demon Witch's voice. *Why can't you be with your children in person?*

Because... I'm not sure how to say this, Lahnos. I suppose that I am dead.

Lahnos felt a chill run through his bones. *Dead?*

My body was destroyed, and yet my spirit lingered on.

Do you talk to your children the way you talk to me?

I daren't, Lahnos. I fear it would scare them. My heart is torn over what to do. I long to tell them that I love them, and yet each time I try, I pull away. This is the reason I have been gone for so long. I am truly sorry that I was not here to help you.

Lahnos said nothing.

I can sense your confusion, Lahnos, she said; *and the pity you feel for me.*

Tell me more about your children.

They are twins – a boy and a girl. They will be nine years old in a little over three months from now.

Who is caring for them?

My adopted sister. She loves them keenly, and they love her in return; but I can feel the sadness in their hearts.

What happened to their father?

I don't wish to discuss that, Lahnos.

Why not?

The Demon Witch fell silent, and Lahnos wondered if she had gone again. He opened his eyes and sat up. Efizel glanced over at him, then resumed his sweeping of the attic floor. Lahnos picked up the jug of wine and took a drink. Was the Demon Witch a ghost? Lahnos had never believed in ghosts, but he felt convinced that the Witch had been telling him the truth.

I don't like the word ghost, she said.

No?

Can a ghost use her powers over others? I retain some of the powers that I had when I was still alive – the power to persuade, and the power to make others appear invisible, for example.

Do you see other... ghosts?'

Never. I have never sensed another like me.

You must be lonely.

Yes, Lahnos. I am truly alone. I tried to live a good life, but I did many terrible things. Perhaps this is my punishment.

Would you rather... I mean – would you prefer to feel nothing? To be nothing?

She paused. *I don't know. This way, I can watch my children grow, and I can still help others. What can I do to help you, Lahnos?*

He considered mentioning the occupation of Zamata, or his uncle's plight in Tsallon Anura, but there was only one question on his mind.

Would you help me find my father? he said.

Oh, Lahnos, please don't ask me that. Anything else, but not that.

Why not? If you can find me, then couldn't you please search the Dominion for my father? He might be in Inopei, serving the dragons as a slave, but I'm not completely sure. I know it might take a long time, but please, could you try?

Your father is not in Inopei, Lahnos.

His eyes widened. *Then you know where he is? Why don't you want me to find him? Is he a slave?*

Your father is not a slave.

You must tell me! This feels like torture. Please, Demon Witch, I am begging you – tell me what you know.

I... I cannot.

Then leave me alone! Get out of my head and never return.

Is that what you want?

Of course it isn't! I want you to tell me everything you know about my father. Tell me – or go.

Very well, she said, her voice choking with pain. *Prepare yourself, Lahnos. I did not want to do this, and I have no desire to hurt you, but very well. You know that I killed King Gahad.*

Yes?

I didn't mean to. I needed the dragon-god's powers to escape. Gahad tried to imprison me and my children, and I could not allow that to happen. His palace had been built on to the slopes of a great volcano, somewhere in the east of Inopei. I hadn't realised that by killing Gahad, the protections he had placed around that palace would also fade and vanish. As soon as the dragon-

king died, the volcano began to consume the palace, and it was utterly destroyed.

I don't care about Gahad! What about my father?

Your father was in the palace at the time, Lahnos.

Lahnos fell silent, as a rising tide of horror and rage began to flood his senses.

I am sorry, Lahnos, but I killed your father. I didn't mean to – I swear it. That is why I chose you; that is why I came to you, and have been trying to help you. I feel so guilty about what I did, so ashamed. Can you forgive me?

Get out of my mind! he screamed. *You vile bitch! You killed my father – get out and never come back! I hate you – I hate you...*

The Demon Witch vanished from his head, and Lahnos fell to his knees, the tears flowing from his eyes and down his cheeks. A sob racked his chest, and Efizel hurried over.

'Lahnos?' he said. 'What is wrong?'

Lahnos leapt to his feet, then nearly tripped over Reyn as he ran for the stairs. He pushed Efizel's hand aside and raced down the steps to the first floor of the mansion. He collided with a tall man at the bottom of the stairs, and lashed out, unthinking, his right fist striking the man's nose. At once, hands grabbed his shoulders, and he was wrestled to the ground as a group of men surrounded him.

'That horned bastard broke my nose!' one of them cried.

Lahnos felt a boot hit his ribs, and he curled into a ball.

'Get off him!' Bauchlie shouted, his voice filling the hallway.

'But he punched me, boss.'

'I don't give a shit,' cried Bauchlie. 'If you kick him again, I'll do worse than break your nose.'

Bauchlie pushed through the crowd of men, shoving them to the side. A few looked angry, but none dared to disobey their scarred commander. Bauchlie got down to one knee by Lahnos, and placed a firm hand onto his shoulder.

'Lahnos,' he said, his voice low and calm.

Lahnos looked up at him, grief and shock rendering him unable to speak. His father was dead, and he felt as though a large part of himself had died with him.

'Lahnos,' Bauchlie said again; 'what is it?'

Efizel and Reyn appeared by the bottom of the stairs. The rebel fighters cleared a path for them, though many were glaring at the Bullan soldier.

Bauchlie glanced up at them. 'What happened?'

Reyn knelt by Lahnos's side, and took his hand. 'I don't know. I was sleeping.'

Efizel glanced down, his eyes confused. 'Young Laimos was sitting by the wall,' the Bullan soldier said, 'and then...'

'Yes?' said Bauchlie.

Efizel narrowed his eyes at the rebel commander. 'And then he cried out and ran away. I do not know what caused it. I will say this, however – if any of your men strike him again, I will make them suffer.'

'No one will hurt him,' said Bauchlie.

'My father...' Lahnos whispered.

Reyn and Bauchlie glanced at each other.

'Go on,' said Bauchlie.

'My father is dead,' Lahnos said. 'The Demon Witch killed him.'

CHAPTER 11
MERCY

Igatz, Serpent Isle – 8th Abrinch 1588

Cisca and Lyla strode along the cool hallways of the huge Dragon Palace, the steel-rimmed heels of their boots clacking on the polished marble floor. In the eleven days since the Dominion had re-conquered Igatz, every trace of the fighting that had damaged the palace during the Gunstian invasion had been removed. Walls had been repaired and repainted, broken windows replaced, and the gardens were being painstakingly restored to their former beauty. It seemed that Colonel Friel Laimos had barely visited the palace during the rebel administration of the Serpent Isle, but as his government had barely lasted two and a half months, there would have been little to remove in any case.

Two and a half months, Cisca thought to herself – that was how long the island had been free. No, not free – that was how long the island had been ruled by criminals and terrorists. The Dominion had returned freedom to the Serpent Isle; well, that's what the dragons were saying, and who would dare to contradict the blessed Children of Gahad?

Cisca glanced at Lyla as they walked. The major's mood had been improving as the days had passed, and she was making no effort to hide the fact that she was looking forward to the arrival of the main invasion force so that she could leave the island.

'This should be interesting,' Major Lyla said, as they neared the central audience chamber. 'I believe that another attempt at securing the surrender of Colonel Laimos took place this morning. I wonder if he sent that girl to speak in his stead again? Damned coward.'

'I assume the attempt was a failure, ma'am?'

'That's what we're about to find out, Captain,' Lyla said. 'At least we didn't have to travel all the way to Kaugatz for it this time.' She shook her head. 'I cannot wait to get off this blasted island.'

They quietened as they entered the huge circular hall. Lord Malum Mon Gahad was sitting atop a great mound of embroidered cushions, while Lord Irvan Mon Gahad was reclining at a slightly lower level, his wounded head resting on soft blankets. His empty right eye socket was gaping vacantly at the humans in the hall, his blindness clear for all to perceive. In front of the two dragons stood a dozen army and naval officers – the same contingent that had negotiated with Leona nine days before, and, from their downcast expression, Cisca could guess that the most recent talks had not gone well.

'They refused our terms?' cried Lord Malum. 'Again?

'They did, my blessed lord,' said the army major. 'Leona of Kaugatz claimed that Commander Bauchlie is no longer within the compound of Tsallon Anura.'

'And you believed her?' said Malum. 'You fools. They are lying to us in an attempt to drag out these talks.'

'Their supply situation must be perilous by now, my lord,' said a colonel. 'There are several hundred rebels trapped inside the monastery. They have adequate sources of fresh water from the deep wells located there, but they will have very little food left by now.'

Lord Malum's eyes burned green. 'This is unacceptable. The fleet destined to invade the Gunstian Empire will be arriving at the Serpent Isle any day now – we must subdue this last pocket of resistance before they get here; otherwise I will be held accountable.' He paused for a moment, then a few sparks of fire leapt across his jaws. 'The time has come to attack.'

The officers bowed.

'Yes, my lord,' said the major. 'When do you plan to assault the monastery?'

'It will not be I who assaults the monastery, human,' said the huge dragon. 'Do you think I wish to be brought down by nets and ballista bolts?' He glanced at Lord Irvan. 'Do you believe I want to be blinded? No, Major – it shall be your soldiers who shall have the glory of taking Tsallon Anura.'

'But, my lord,' said the major, 'the walls of the monastery are strong and impenetrable. They were designed and built to withstand any sort of assault by land or sea. The Gunstians, when they were here in spring, did not dare to mount any attack on that place.'

The pale red dragon narrowed his eyes a fraction. 'Are you a coward, Major?'

'No, my lord, but, without air cover, a direct assault on Tsallon Anura will lead to extremely high casualties, and will probably end in failure. Starving the rebels out remains the best strategy.'

'You dare question my strategy?' roared the dragon. 'If I give the order to attack, will you refuse to carry it out?'

The major bowed even lower. 'Of course not, my lord. If you order it, we shall attack.'

'Perhaps there is another way forward, my lord,' said a vice admiral. 'I believe that the monks of this island have brokered safe passage in and out of the rebel-held area? Could we not devise a trick? Let us dress up a company of elite soldiers as monks, and have them infiltrate Tsallon Anura. Once inside, they could open the gates and...'

The rest of the vice admiral's words were drowned out in a roar of laughter from the pale red dragon. The naval officer seemed confused, his eyes tight as Lord Malum mocked him.

The major turned to the vice admiral. 'One must assume that you have not heard the news, my old friend.'

'What news?' said the vice admiral.

'It appears that the rebels have already played a similar trick on us,' said the major. 'We allowed forty so-called monks to walk out of the monastery several days ago, but none of them turned up at Zamata Gataza; in fact, no sign has been seen of them since.'

The naval officer averted his eyes. 'Ah. I see.'

'Therefore,' the major went on, 'it would seem unlikely that the rebels would fall for the same trick.' He turned back to Lord Malum. 'It is my belief, my lord, that Leona of Kaugatz is telling the truth about Commander Bauchlie. I am of the opinion that he was among the forty false monks who fled. He must have panicked when he discovered that he was about to be surrendered to us.'

The dragon lowered his gaze. 'That may be so.' He glanced at Cisca and Lyla. 'Anything to add, my Dragon Corps officers? Do you have any clever ideas that would prevent me from ordering a full scale assault by my land troops?'

Major Lyla took a step forward. 'Would the prelate of Zamata Gataza be overly upset if we obliterated the entire monastery of Tsallon Anura, my lord?'

'It certainly would not please him,' said the pale red dragon. 'However, his feelings on the subject are less important than the need to root out this last nest of rebels before the invasion fleet arrives.'

'Then, my lord,' Lyla went on, 'we should begin a vast bombardment of the monastery as soon as possible, from the landside, as well as from the destroyers and frigates stationed in the Cyasarta. Incendiary devices should be launched until the entirety of Tsallon Anura is aflame. If we do not wish to starve the rebels out, then perhaps we should burn them out.'

A brown-robed monk who had been standing in the shadows by the edge of the hall raced forwards.

'My noble and sacred lord!' he cried. 'Please do not proceed with this officer's plan; I beg you! The monastery of Tsallon Anura has stood for over fifteen hundred years. It was, as you know, the second such monastery to be built upon this isle – second only to the great Zamata Gataza. In that time it has survived being ravaged and desecrated by the vile and faithless Gunstians, and has only recently been restored to its former splendour. The last attack upon the monastery was carried out by Lord Meer Mon Adal. That noble lord burned one of Tsallon Anura's ancient towers, and the price he paid for the sacrilege was grievous indeed!'

Lord Malum regarded the monk for a few moments. 'Tsallon Anura was used as a base by the rebels during the uprising, was it not?'

'Yes, my lord – that is true.'

'Why did the monks there do nothing to resist the rebellion?'

'They did all they could, my lord – but what could a handful of peaceful and unarmed monks do against hundreds of armed bandits?'

The army colonel coughed. 'I have heard, brother, that the monks in Tsallon Anura ministered to any rebel who was wounded during the uprising.'

The monk's eyes flickered in fear. 'That is true, but the members of our sacred order have long vowed to tend the ill and wounded, regardless of their political or religious views. Surely such generosity of spirit cannot be held against us?'

'I am reluctant to order the destruction of this monastery,' said Lord Malum, 'but I see no other way. I do not wish to throw away the lives of hundreds, maybe thousands, of human soldiers – not when they will be needed for the great invasion of the Gunstian Empire.'

A soldier ran into the chamber and bowed low. 'My lords,' he said, 'Lady Lenta has landed in the palace grounds, and is making her way to this audience hall.'

Malum tilted his head. 'Let us see what my noble half-sister has to say before any further orders are issued. She may have news regarding the rebels.'

Cisca glanced at the high, wide entrance used by the dragons to access the hall. A moment later, the sound of a dragon filtered through, then Lady Lenta's black and white head appeared under the archway.

'My lord,' she said, her red eyes glowing.

'Do you bear news from the rebel stronghold?' said Malum.

'No, my lord,' said Lenta. 'I bring tidings from the east. The invasion fleet is approaching.'

Lord Malum froze for a moment. 'Already?' he said. 'The fleet is here?'

'Yes, my lord. They must have raced at full speed from Aucteran. Above the ships, I sighted a great cloud in the sky – a cloud of dragons wheeling and circling. King Naghad is among them, my lord – his form was unmistakable.'

'His Majesty has come in person?' said Lord Malum, his voice strained.

Several gasps rose up from the officers in the hall, while the monk lowered his head and began to pray.

'His Majesty must have decided to personally lead the invasion of the Gunstian Empire, my lord,' said Lenta.

Lord Irvan let out a strangled groan from where he lay. 'His Majesty will witness my shame!' he groaned. 'The King will know that I have been blinded by mere humans. Kill me now, Lord Malum – spare me the humiliation!'

'Be quiet!' Malum snapped. 'Lenta, remain here. I shall fly out to greet the fleet, and our noble King. I will inform His Majesty that the island is under our control; while you, my half-sister, will summon every servant and soldier in Igatz to prepare a welcome for our god-monarch.'

Lady Lenta bowed her head. 'It shall be so, my lord.'

Malum and Lenta switched places, then the pale red dragon disappeared through the tall archway.

Lady Lenta arranged herself onto the heap of embroidered cushions. 'Do as Lord Malum has commanded,' she said to the humans in the hall. 'Have the gardens prepared for the arrival of the King and all those dragons His Majesty has brought with the fleet. The Bullan regiments stationed in Igatz are to assemble by the palace to form a guard of honour. See to it immediately.'

The officers bowed, then the army and naval contingents broke away and began issuing orders, several hurrying out through the other entrances.

Major Lyla glanced at Cisca. 'Summon all Dragon Corps personnel, Captain. Have them meet me by the front of the palace in ten minutes.'

Cisca kept all traces of anxiety from her face. 'Yes, ma'am.'

Cisca ran out from the hall, her boots clacking off the smooth floors. She raced towards the apartments where the junior officers of the Corps were quartered, and found three lieutenants. She issued her orders swiftly and they scattered, each rushing off to gather the others. As soon as they had gone, Cisca took a moment to breathe.

The King was coming? The God-Dragon Gahad the Mighty had not left Inopei in centuries, preferring to delegate all tasks to his blessed children, and yet King Naghad was venturing out on an armed expedition within a few months of his ascension to the throne? Cisca's heart raced at the thought, then she gathered her wits, smoothed down the front of her uniform, and strode out to the front of the palace. The gardens were in chaos. Servants and soldiers were running back and forth, clearing huge patches of lawn for the arrival of the dragons, and hauling carts filled with food towards the palace. Over by the damaged perimeter wall protecting the gardens, lines of Bullan soldiers were already assembling, filing up on the lawns, and forming into ranks by the base of the wall. The town bells began to peal as Cisca made her way toward Major Lyla.

'Did you have any inkling that the King would be coming to the Serpent Isle in person, Captain?' Lyla said, as Cisca joined her on the palace steps.

'None whatsoever, ma'am,' said Cisca.

Lyla nodded. 'It seems that Lord Malum was also taken by surprise by this news. Perhaps his lordship assumed that he would be the one to lead the invasion of Gunst. Now, I wonder who will take the blame for the fact that the island has not been completely subdued.'

'Might it be us, ma'am?'

'I doubt that, Captain,' Lyla said. 'For His Majesty to blame mere humans for this failure would imply that we possessed authority over the operation. No; it will be a dragon who will have to take responsibility.'

Cisca glanced up at the sky, but the bulk of the shimmering white palace was blocking most of the view to the east. She gazed at a spot to the south-east, just beyond the edge of the marble edifice, in the direction of the Chain Castles. Her eyes widened as she saw a long line of dragons approach, and she did a quick count.

'I see a dozen dragons, ma'am,' she said.

Lyla turned, her lips closed and her eyes tight.

Cisca gasped out loud as she realised her mistake. What she had seen was merely the first wave approaching. Beyond the initial dozen dragons, three more waves of equal size were soaring through the blue sky towards Igatz. Her mouth fell open.

'More like four dozen,' whispered Lyla. 'Gods above – His Majesty has brought most of his court with him. They must have used every dragon carrier in the navy.'

The four waves of dragons drew nearer, and a deathly silence fell over the palace gardens as everyone stared at the sight. The full personnel of the Dragon Corps arrived by the palace steps, but Lyla ignored them, her gaze fixed on the sky.

'Line up,' Cisca ordered, 'and prepare to receive the royal court.'

'But, ma'am,' said a young lieutenant, 'where shall we fit so many dragons? The palace can house maybe twelve, at the most; where shall the others go?'

Cisca narrowed her eyes. 'Send messengers to the monks and soldiers occupying the monasteries of Tzalla Pen and Euzaru Naka, and tell them to expect large numbers of dragons imminently.'

The lieutenant hesitated, his eyes flickering over to Major Lyla.

'Do as the captain has commanded,' Lyla said. 'I am giving you the authority to requisition whatever supplies you need in order to ensure that the two monasteries are stocked with everything the dragons require. Go; now.'

The lieutenant saluted, then he gestured to two members of the lower ranks, and the three of them raced off through the gardens.

Cisca turned her gaze back to the sky. In the centre of the first wave, one dragon in particular was prominent, his length and bulk greater than all of the others. The King. It was true; King Naghad was coming.

'I wonder if anyone has informed Colonel Friel Laimos yet,' said Lyla. 'The rebels on the walls of Tsallon Anura must surely be able to see this by now.'

'I hope the colonel is watching, ma'am,' said a lieutenant. 'I would like to see his face.'

The first wave of dragons crossed the edge of the Cyasarta and began to circle over the Palace District of Igatz. Next to the King, the size of Lord Malum stood out, but even he seemed small compared to Naghad. The dragons descended, and a hushed awe fell over the humans waiting in the gardens. King Naghad alighted in the central part of the lawn, his golden brown scales shimmering like bronze in the sunlight. Hundreds of humans dropped to their knees, their heads bowed, as the King surveyed them. Lord Malum landed by the King's right-hand side, then the other dragons from the first wave found places to settle across the width of the gardens, their claws digging into the newly-laid grass.

'Welcome to the Serpent Isle, Your Immortal Majesty!' Malum exclaimed, his gaze lowered.

King Naghad gazed around. 'What a tiny, insignificant speck in the ocean is this Serpent Isle,' he said, his voice booming out over the gardens; 'and yet. what a strategic treasure – a precious jewel on hand to serve our need to bring down the Gunstian Empire.' He glanced at the white marble palace. 'I have brought forty-six dragons with me from Inopei – tell me, brother; where am I to place them all while we prepare the greatest invasion this world has ever witnessed? This palace seems hardly adequate.'

Lord Malum bowed low. 'Such details are within the remit of the Dragon Corps, Your Majesty. They will find suitable accommodation, or they will be punished.'

Major Lyla raised an arm from where she was kneeling on the steps next to the other officers. 'If I may be permitted to speak, Your Sacred Majesty?'

The King glanced down, his silver eyes gleaming. 'Yes, human?'

'The monasteries of... of...'

'Tzalla Pen and Euzaru Naka,' Cisca whispered.

'...of Tzalla Pen and Euzaru Naka are currently being prepared to receive all members of your blessed court that cannot be accommodated within the palace, Your Majesty. Captain Cisca will be delighted to provide directions to your entourage on how to find these locations.'

'That will suffice,' said the King. 'Pass on the directions to all members of the Dragon Corps, and direct the following three waves to these two monasteries. I am sure the monks will be pleased to serve so many gods at once.'

'The monks will be honoured and privileged to do so, Your most gracious Majesty,' said Lyla.

'I am sure they will,' said the King. He glanced at Lord Malum. 'Where are my half-sister and half-brother – Lenta and Irvan?'

'They are awaiting your presence inside the palace, Your Majesty,' said the pale red dragon.

'Then let us greet them,' said Naghad. 'Have the senior officers among the humans attend to us.'

Lord Malum began to lead the King up the broad steps of the palace, while every officer among the army, navy and Dragon Corps lined up in their wake to follow them inside. Cisca ordered a few junior officers to remain out in the gardens, and passed on directions to the two monasteries she had mentioned; then she hurried after Major Lyla. Ahead of them, she could hear the King speaking to Lord Malum, and it became clear to her that his lordship had omitted to mention the lingering rebel presence in Tsallon Anura. She and Lyla glanced at each other, then they entered the huge, circular audience chamber in the centre of the palace, where Lady Lenta and Lord Irvan were waiting.

Two other dragons squeezed into the audience chamber, and Cisca recognised them as Lady Macsin Min Gahad, the new King's full sister, and Lord Rylan Mon Gahad, His Majesty's half-brother. They took up position by the King's shoulders as Naghad glanced at Lenta and Irvan.

The King opened his mouth to speak, then he noticed the gaping eye socket on Irvan's face.

'What is this?' the King said. 'What happened to your right eye, Lord Irvan?'

'My brother was struck by a ballista bolt at point blank range, Your Blessed Majesty,' said Lenta.

'Did I ask you?' said Naghad. 'Has your brother also lost his tongue?'

Irvan cowered before the King. 'I lost my eye in battle, Your Majesty; fighting the damned rebels. Curse them! Lord Malum used his healing powers to preserve my life, but I fear I shall never see from that eye again.'

King Naghad said nothing for a long moment, as the human officers continued to file into the audience chamber.

'Blinded, eh?' said the King, his tone soft.

'Yes, Your Majesty,' said Irvan, his head lowered.

'A Child of Gahad the Mighty,' the King went on, 'blinded by a sub-created human?'

Irvan remained silent, his shame almost tangible.

The long claws on King Naghad's forelimbs gouged their way through the marble floor. 'And what happened to the unworthy rebel who took your eye, half-brother? Was his body fed to the crows?'

'The rebels who did this remain within the walls of Tsallon Anura, Your Majesty!' Irvan wailed. 'It is Lord Malum's fault! He was unable to subdue the last rebel stronghold – he is to blame, not I!'

'What did you say?' said the King, his rumbling voice making the chandeliers rattle. 'There are rebels still holding out upon this island? Is this true, Lord Malum?'

'A tiny pocket is still resisting, Your Majesty,' said Malum. 'They are occupying a monastery in the town of Kaugatz. We have the location completely surrounded. In fact, I was in the midst of ordering the final assault when you arrived, Your Majesty.'

'I see,' said the King. 'You had but one command, my brother – to extinguish the fires of rebellion upon this tiny rock before the great invasion fleet arrived.'

'Yes, Your Majesty,' said Malum, keeping his eyes lowered. 'My humble apologies, Your Majesty.'

King Naghad's gaze roamed over the audience chamber. 'Someone will have to pay for this failure.'

The large hall fell into silence at the King's words. Cisca held her breath, praying that Naghad's gaze would pass over her. The King turned his long, thick neck to glance at Lady Macsin and Lord Rylan, whose heads had remained bowed.

The King narrowed his eyes. 'Remove Lord Irvan's head.'

Lady Lenta gasped, but did nothing. Irvan tried to cower away, wailing, but Macsin and Rylan were on him in seconds. Lyla grabbed Cisca's arm and pulled her back as Rylan's long tail swept past the humans in his haste to push the blinded dragon to the ground. As Rylan drove Irvan down with his forelimbs, Macsin's head lunged forward, and her jaws closed round Irvan's neck. Dragon blood sprayed across the floor and walls as Macsin clamped her jaws shut. She pulled, ripping out Irvan's throat, then Rylan used his claws to shear through what remained of the black and white dragon's neck. Macsin turned towards the King, the severed head of Irvan dangling from her bloody jaws.

'This is what you should have done, my brother,' the King said, his eyes on Malum. 'It was a mercy killing; you should never have allowed a blinded dragon to live in such shame. I have done the decent and honourable thing, and spared Lord Irvan any further humiliation.'

Lady Lenta let out a heart-rending sob as Lady Macsin dropped the head of Irvan onto the floor, and the King turned to her.

'Do you disagree with my command, Lady Lenta? Do you think I should have permitted your brother to live in such shame and degradation?'

Lenta prostrated herself before the King, her wings folded in and her neck lowered. 'No, Your Sacred Majesty.'

'And whose fault was it that the rebels were allowed to man their stronghold of Tsallon Anura?' King Naghad said. 'Think carefully before you answer, half-sister.'

'It was Lord Irvan's fault, Your Majesty,' Lenta said.

'That is right, Lady Lenta,' said the King. 'It was Lord Irvan's fault. Now, clear up this mess, while Lord Malum directs me to the location of this Tsallon Anura. We shall attack at once, I think. It will be a useful exercise for my dragons – it will help them prepare for the invasion of Gunst. Lead on, my brother.'

'Yes, Your Majesty,' said Lord Malum. He turned, his eyes avoiding the sight of his decapitated half-brother, and then he led the King, Lady Macsin and Lord Rylan from the audience chamber. The humans stood in stunned silence as Lady Lenta wept over the body of Irvan.

'Prepare a pyre in the palace gardens,' Lenta sobbed. 'We shall burn my brother.'

'Yes, my lady,' said Major Lyla. 'The Dragon Corps shall see to it at once.'

Lenta met the major's glance, then she turned and retreated from the hall in silence.

'Everyone out,' said Lyla to the assembled officers; 'everyone except members of the Dragon Corps.'

The army and navy officers hurried away, each appearing glad to be gone from the scene of blood and carnage. When only those from the Dragon Corps remained, Major Lyla lined them up in front of the gigantic corpse. She took a breath, then gazed at them.

'Fetch ropes, nets, mops, and plenty of soap and water. I want the body of Lord Irvan taken out via the rear entrance of the palace and a pyre set up by the shoreline of the Cyasarta, and then I want this chamber scrubbed and cleaned. We shall also need masons to repair the claw damage to the floor tiles. I will deal with the pyre, while Captain Cisca oversees the cleaning. In two hours from now, there will be no trace left in here of what occurred – is that understood? Get to work.'

Cisca stared at the head of Irvan as the others scattered. Lyla walked to her side, her eyes dark.

'Have you ever seen anything like that in your life?' said the major.

'Never, ma'am,' said Cisca. 'I can't quite believe it. I have seen dragons punished in Nom Karta when they angered King Gahad – they were bitten and clawed, and some even had their wings chained for a while, but they were never killed.'

'It was as I said, Captain; someone needed to take the blame, and Lord's Irvan's blindness made him the ideal candidate. A mercy-killing, as His Majesty put it. Lord Irvan would have been useless in the invasion of Gunst, and His Majesty did not want to be associated with a blinded Child of Gahad. Is this the third dragon you have seen slain this year?'

'Yes, ma'am,' said Cisca, 'but Lords Meer and Rufus were ordinary dragons, unrelated to the Royal Family. Lord Irvan was immortal.'

'He doesn't appear to be very immortal from where I'm standing.'

Cisca said nothing.

Lyla shook her head. 'So, this is the new regime ruling the Dominion? We had better harden our hearts, Cisca, for we shall have to adjust to it quickly; otherwise...' The major's voice trailed away into silence, then she strode towards the entrance that led to the rear of the palace.

Cisca watched her leave, then swallowed, and got to work.

CHAPTER 12
AN EYE FOR JUSTICE

Kaugatz, Serpent Isle – 8th Abrinch 1588

Leona raced down the worn sandstone steps of the curtain wall, her heart pounding. At the bottom, she ran into a tall rebel fighter, who cursed as they collided, his hands dropping a crate, which fell and broke on the cobbles.

'Watch where you're going, girl,' he cried.

'Get out of my way!' Leona shouted.

'And who's going to clean up this mess?' he said, pointing at the broken crate, its contents spilling out over the ground.

'Who gives a shit?' Leona cried. 'Look up, you idiot – look at the sky!'

She swerved past him and sprinted through the ancient cloister, dodging a dozen more fighters who were peering at her.

'Dragons!' yelled a rebel up on the walls. 'Dozens of the bastards!'

The fighters in the cloister stopped staring at Leona, and turned their gazes to the blue sky. Leona rushed past them, and entered the building from where the colonel organised the last vestiges of the rebellion. She ran straight into the meeting room without knocking, and saw a dozen rebel officers arguing with Colonel Friel Laimos over rationing.

'The men will protest if their wine allowance is cut...' one was saying.

'Shut up!' Leona cried. 'None of that matters any more.'

The officer turned to her, and the colonel raised an eyebrow from behind his desk.

'The dragons are here,' she said.

'Who – Malum and Lenta?' said the colonel, swinging his boots off the stool in front of him. 'We need to ready the damn ballistae.'

'Not Malum and Lenta,' Leona said.

'Then who?'

Leona took a breath. 'The invasion fleet has arrived.'

'You're not making any sense,' said an officer. 'The invasion fleet arrived weeks ago, if you hadn't noticed. Zamata has been thoroughly invaded.'

'Not that invasion fleet, you stupid imbecile,' Leona shouted. 'The fleet the Dominion are going to use to invade Gunst.' She pointed at the window. 'Over forty dragons are flying towards Tsallon Anura.'

The colonel jumped to his feet, his mouth falling open.

'She must be exaggerating, sir,' said another officer. 'The Dominion would never send that many dragons just to crush a rebellion on Zamata.'

Leona felt like screaming. Instead, she calmed herself. 'Perhaps I need to spell it out for you as though you were children,' she said in an even tone. 'The Dominion has gathered a great force to invade the Gunstian Empire, and Zamata just happens to be on the way. If you don't believe me, gentlemen, please feel free to walk a few steps over to the window and take a look for yourselves.' She glanced at the colonel as several officers frowned and strode over to the window. 'If you have any spare monk's robes, sir, then I suggest that now would be a good time to put them on.'

'Gods above!' cried an officer from the window. 'The sky is full of dragons!'

The colonel gestured to Leona then he rushed from the room. She followed him, leaving the officers staring out of the window, and they ran into the cloister. Dozens of rebel fighters were frozen to the ground, their mouths open in horror as they gazed up at the sky. A great line of dragons had spread out, filling the horizon from the east to the south in a long arc. Up on the monastery battlements, a soldier screamed in terror and ran from his post, abandoning a ballista. The others manning the same machine stared at the fleeing fighter, then, as if they had all shared the same thought at once, others began running from the walls in a headlong panic, and the monastery descended into chaos. As the dragons flew nearer, the confusion deepened. Some fighters were trying to force open the gates that led out into the rest of Kaugatz, but others there were attempting to keep them back; while separate groups of fighters were racing towards the cellars that ran under the compound.

'Get back to your posts!' cried an officer, but he was shoved out of the way by his fleeing men.

'It's over,' the colonel whispered. 'We're finished.'

'Raise a white flag,' said Leona, 'or the dragons will attack.'

Friel's shoulders slumped, and he bowed his head.

Leona clenched a fist and punched his arm. 'Sir! We must surrender, or everyone in Tsallon Anura will be dead in minutes!'

'Yes,' he said in a low voice. 'That is what we must do. Raise a flag. Yes.'

She stared at him. He seemed to be in a daze, as though despair had robbed him of the ability to move. Leona cursed under her breath and ran back into the building. She went straight to her own room, burst through the door, and pulled the white sheet from her bed. She gathered it up in her arms and ran back outside. She found the colonel where she had left him, just as the dragons closed the arc above the monastery, forming a circle overhead. Leona loosened the sheet and began to wave it about.

'We surrender! We surrender!' she cried. 'Please!'

Several rebels saw what she was doing, and threw down their weapons, falling to their knees at the same time. Above them, six dragons peeled off from the main formation, and soared downwards in a coordinated movement. They aimed for the deserted battlements of the curtain wall, extended their forelimbs, and ripped through the abandoned ballistae, their claws tearing the machines to pieces. Two of the dragons banked, then descended lower. Both picked up net-throwing catapults in their talons, then dropped them into the Cyasarta, as the rebels screamed and fled in all directions.

'Lay down your weapons!' came a booming voice from above. 'Prostrate yourselves before your lord and sovereign – the glorious, blessed high monarch His Majesty King Naghad.'

The screaming ceased, and every rebel threw themselves to the cobbles, their crossbows and swords cast away. Leona fell to her knees, her breath coming in ragged gasps, then she reached up and pulled the colonel down to kneel next to her.

The six dragons who had already descended took up position on the curtain walls, and then a further ten dragons lowered themselves from the sky. In the centre was the largest dragon Leona had ever seen, his bronze-coloured scales glimmering as though they were on fire, while, on his right was the pale red dragon Lord Malum.

Malum landed in the centre of the cloister, then the huge bronze dragon alighted next to him. As the bronze dragon gazed at the prostrate rebels, the other eight dragons landed throughout the monastery – some perching atop the buildings, while a few moved to block the gates.

'Where is the rebel commander?' said the bronze dragon. 'Where is the human named Laimos?'

Leona glanced at the colonel, while keeping her head bowed at the same time. Friel was staring into space as he knelt on the ground, as though he hadn't heard the words of the bronze dragon.

'Where is Colonel Laimos!' cried Lord Malum. 'His Majesty King Naghad has requested that he show himself, and if he does not, then we shall kill every human inside this monastery!'

One of the rebel fighters raised a finger and pointed at the colonel. 'There he is!' he cried. 'That man is Colonel Friel Laimos.'

The colonel glanced up, as if awakening. 'What?'

Malum lowered his head until his jaws were a foot from the

colonel's face. 'Are you the leader of this treacherous insurrection, human?'

Friel stared back at the pale red dragon. 'Yes.'

King Naghad glanced at Friel, then he raised his eyes. 'Open the gates, my kin, but ensure that none of the rebels escape. My beloved army shall take these rebels into custody.'

The dragons by the gates began to remove the stout beams that were keeping them closed, as the rebel fighters remained still, their hands in the air. As soon as the gates were unbarred, the dragons pushed them open, and Dominion soldiers began rushing into the monastery grounds.

The King glanced at Lord Malum. 'See, my brother – that is how you deal with a rebellion. The insurrection is over! The Dominion is whole again!'

'What shall we do with these traitors, Your Majesty?' said Lord Malum.

'Place them all into custody, brother,' said the King.

'The jails of the island are already full of rebels, Your Majesty,' said Malum. 'Several hundred were killed when we suppressed the uprising, but hundreds more are awaiting trial.'

'This monastery can serve as their prison for now,' said the King; 'and as their place of execution. They are to be given no food, as all supplies are to be diverted to feed the invasion force; but I want you to ensure that each is charged according to the law.'

'You wish me to do this, Your Majesty?'

'Yes, brother,' said Naghad. 'I have decided to lead the invasion of Gunst in person, while you shall remain here as the new Governor of the Serpent Isle. Does this displease you?'

Lord Malum bowed low. 'It is an honour to serve, Your Majesty.'

'Then it shall be so,' said the bronze King. He watched as Dominion soldiers poured into the cloister from several directions at once. 'Arrest Colonel Laimos,' he said to an army officer. 'We shall be taking him back to Igatz with us.'

'Yes, Your Majesty,' said the officer, his gaze lowered. He pointed at Leona. 'What should we do with the girl?'

Leona cursed as the King and Lord Malum turned their fierce gazes towards her.

'And why should I concern myself with a mere mortal girl?' said the King.

'This is Leona of Kaugatz, Your Majesty,' the officer said. 'She served as Colonel Laimos's chief advisor and negotiator.'

'This is Leona of Kaugatz?' said Lord Malum, his eyes tight. 'I was expecting someone older, and less... fragile.'

'This is she, my lord,' said the officer, as soldiers surrounded Friel and Leona. 'After Colonel Laimos and Commander Bauchlie, she is the third most wanted rebel on our list.'

The bronze King laughed softly. 'Then bring her along with the colonel,' he said. 'We shall try them both in Igatz.'

'Yes, Your Majesty,' said the officer.

'And what of Commander Bauchlie?' said Lord Malum. 'If he is hiding somewhere in Tsallon Anura, we must find him.'

'We shall search every corner of the monastery, my lord,' said the officer. He gestured to Friel and Leona. 'Bind their hands and place them on a launch. We'll ship them over to Igatz at once.'

Leona felt strong hands grab hold of her shoulders, and she was hauled to her feet. Next to her, the colonel was keeping his head bowed, and his mouth closed. Their arms were pulled behind their backs and their wrists were bound by soldiers. Leona and Friel were then led through the crowd of soldiers and surrendered rebels, but while Friel avoided eye contact with anyone, Leona kept her chin high and returned the stares that were sent her way. They were halfway towards the gate that led to the jetty when the bronze dragon King noticed the skull of Lord Meer atop a wooden post.

'Who is responsible for this blasphemy?' King Naghad cried, his voice echoing off the monastery walls.

The cloister fell into silence.

'I am waiting for an answer,' the King said.

'The skull belonged to Lord Meer Mon Adal, Your Majesty,' said Lord Malum. 'The rebels slew him some months ago when he tried to quash the uprising. His death was mentioned in Lord Kheran's report, I believe.'

'I know that!' the King cried. 'What I did not know was that his bones had been desecrated in such a manner.' He turned his head, and his eyes pierced Friel and Leona. 'Was this your doing?'

For a moment, Leona didn't think Friel was going to answer, but the colonel began to lift his head, until his eyes met the wild stare of the King.

'It was I who ordered the death of Meer,' the colonel said; 'and it was I who ordered that his skull be mounted on a pole, as a warning to those trying to oppress my people.'

'*Your* people?' bellowed the King. 'You vile maggot; you godless blasphemer! I should utterly destroy this island for such a sacrilege.' He glared at an army officer. 'Take out this creature's right eye, just as he blinded Lord Irvan.'

'Yes, Your Majesty,' said the officer. He pulled a knife from his belt and nodded to the soldiers holding Friel's arms. They pushed the colonel down onto his knees, then a sergeant gripped Friel's neck with an arm. The colonel stared calmly up at the blue sky, where dozens of dragons were still circling; and the officer approached, his knife held out.

'No,' said Leona.

'Silence,' said Lord Malum, 'unless you wish to share in his just punishment.'

The cloister stilled as every soldier, rebel and dragon watched the officer reach Friel.

'Get it over with, you damn coward,' said Friel.

The Aucterian officer stared at him, then he leaned forward, and the tip of the knife blade entered Friel's right eye. The colonel grunted as the blood trickled down his face, then the officer twisted the knife and ripped out Friel's eyeball. The sergeant released the colonel's neck, and Friel cried out in agony. The officer stepped back, a nauseous look on his face, then he wiped the blade on Friel's militia jacket. Blood was streaming down Friel's face from the gaping wound, but he clamped his mouth closed, his head hanging forward.

'Justice for Lord Irvan has been satisfied,' said the bronze King, his eyes gleaming. 'Later, when we return to Igatz, we shall seek justice for all of the other crimes this traitor has committed against the Dominion. Take them to the boat.'

Leona watched as Friel was dragged by the soldiers towards the gate facing the Cyasarta. He seemed to have lost consciousness, and his legs were trailing along the cobbles as she walked by his side. She turned away from the sight of his ragged face, unable to bear it any longer.

She glanced at the soldier gripping on to her right arm. 'His wound needs dressing. If you don't stop the bleeding, he will die before we reach Igatz.'

'Shut up, girl,' the soldier muttered.

The gate leading to the jetty was opened, and Leona was shoved through. Behind her, Friel was half-carried out on to the jetty, then his limp body was dropped next to her. One of the soldiers pulled a cotton bandage from his pack, ripped off a section, then he knelt and pressed it against Friel's bloody eye socket.

'Keep him alive until we get them on to the launch,' the officer said.

'Yes, sir,' said the soldier.

Leona pulled her gaze away, and stared out over the sparkling blue waters of the Cyasarta. A launch from one of the destroyers was approaching, filled with rowing sailors, and she tried not to think about what was going to happen to her. When she had been arrested by the Gunstians, she had presumed that both she and the colonel would be executed, and she remembered her surprise when she had been released. All she had needed to do was promise to attend religious classes and pretend to have been Friel's prostitute, and they had let her go. There would be no such escape this time, she knew.

The launch bumped against the jetty, and four sailors stepped across from the deck. Ropes were secured to the ancient cleats, and a naval lieutenant joined them on the jetty. He nodded to the army officer, then glanced at Leona and Friel.

'These two are to go directly to the palace,' said the army officer. 'His Majesty wants them both kept alive to stand trial.'

The lieutenant glanced down at the body of Friel. 'This one looks as though he might expire at any moment.'

'I am handing him over into your custody while still alive,' said the army officer. 'He's your problem now.' He gestured to the other soldiers. 'Let's get back to the monastery.'

The naval lieutenant watched as the soldiers withdrew from the jetty, then he nodded to the sailors. 'Get these two on board; we're taking them to the destroyer.'

'But, sir,' said one, 'I thought the prisoners were to go straight to the palace?'

'He'll be dead by the time we get him there,' said the lieutenant. 'We'll save his life first, and then we'll transport him to the palace. Move.'

Two hours later, Leona sat alone in a guarded cell deep within the bowels of one of the destroyers anchored out in the Cyasarta. The colonel had been rushed to the ship's infirmary as soon as they had stepped on board, while Leona had been led below deck and secured within the tiny, windowless brig. Her hands were still bound behind her back, and her arms and wrists were aching; but far worse than that was the thirst. The cell was stuffy and hot, and her thoughts had strayed from Friel, until all she could think about was getting a sip of cool water. She tried to move on the narrow wooden ledge where she was sitting, and she felt the sweat trickle down her back.

Leona.

She glanced up at the door, but it remained closed.

Leona, can you hear me?

She began to laugh. Her mind was starting to go if she was hearing voices in her head.

You are not going mad, Leona. I am in your mind, speaking to you.

'Who...? What?'

I am the Demon Witch, Leona.

'I thought you only talked to Lahnos.'

You don't need to speak out loud, Leona; I can hear your thoughts. As for Lahnos... he hates me now. He told me to leave and never return, but how can I stand by and watch what is happening to your island? I tried to get into the minds of the new dragons who have arrived, the same way that I entered Lord Rufus's mind, but these ones are much stronger.

Leona bowed her head. *You killed King Gahad, yet his children are too strong for you?*

I was still... alive when I destroyed King Gahad. I am not as powerful as I was in those days. But never mind that – listen to me. Sailors are on their way to give you food and water. The doctors on board have stopped the bleeding in Friel's right eye, and he is going to live. I came here to give you this news, and to let you know that I haven't abandoned you. Be strong, Leona. You will get through this.

The voice disappeared, but some of her words had struck home. Leona lifted her gaze, feeling more hopeful than she had any right to be. She needed to be strong; no – she *was* strong, stronger than even Friel might have guessed.

The door to the cell opened, and two sailors glanced down at her. One was holding a knife, and he moved forward and cut the cords round Leona's wrists with a deft flick of the blade; then the other sailor placed a jug and a small bag on the deck of the cell. The sailors then retreated, and the door was locked as if nothing had happened.

Leona lunged forward and grabbed the jug. She ripped out the stopper and lifted it to her lips. Fresh, cool water spilled out, and she gasped in relief, almost gagging as she drank. She panted. Had the Demon Witch ordered the sailors to come to her aid? Regardless, she had never been so grateful to feel the taste of water on her tongue. With her thirst quenched, she began to go over what the Demon Witch had told her. She had said that Lahnos hated her – why would that be? She had also told her that the colonel was going to survive the loss of his right eye. Had she been hallucinating? It was possible, she told herself, but if so, it had been a strange coincidence that the sailors had arrived when the voice had said they would.

She picked up the bag and found half a loaf, two apples and a strip of dried and salted fish. She sprinkled some of the flakes of fish onto a piece of bread, and began eating. Within seconds she was thirsty again, so she drank more water from the jug. She smiled, as the out-of-place feelings of hopefulness returned. She had been through much in her life, and had experienced more than she had ever told anyone. The Demon Witch would have seen it all if she had been in her mind, but Leona didn't care. If anything, she was glad that another person now knew the trauma and pain she had suffered. She paused, remembering what the Witch had said about her powers being stronger when she had been alive.

Was the Demon Witch dead? No, that was impossible. Dead people spoke only to death-readers like Lahnos, and Leona was certainly not Gifted in that way. She knew that for a fact, as she had tried to read corpses more than once before in her life, and nothing had ever happened. The Demon Witch must have meant something else by her words, something cryptic.

She ate her fill, and pocketed the leftover apple just as the door opened again. Leona glanced up and saw the same two sailors from before, alongside the naval lieutenant from the jetty.

The lieutenant peered in, and frowned. He turned to the two sailors.

'Who brought the prisoner food and water,' he said; 'and who untied her hands?'

The two sailors glanced at each other.

'It wasn't us, sir,' said one.

Leona felt no tingle, which meant that the sailor believed himself to be telling the truth. She kept her expression neutral, but there was only one conclusion to be drawn – the Demon Witch had altered the sailors' memories.

'Who removed your binds, girl?' said the lieutenant.

'I don't know,' she said. 'I was sleeping, and awoke to find my hands free. The water and food had been left on the floor for me.'

The lieutenant rolled his eyes. 'Get up; we're taking you to the palace.'

Leona stood and walked from the cell. She placed her hands behind her back, but the officer gestured towards the hatch.

'Through there, girl,' he said. 'You'll need your hands to climb down into the launch.'

The officer and sailors escorted her to a door in the side of the destroyer. Leona gazed out, and saw the launch bobbing up and down in the water ten feet below her. She scrambled down the net, and jumped the last few feet, landing on the deck of the small vessel. The officer and two sailors came down after her, then they led her to the bow, where Colonel Friel was lying on a stretcher, the side of his head wrapped in thick, fresh bandages.

'His wound has been cauterised to stop the bleeding,' the officer said, as Leona knelt down by Friel; 'but I expect he will be unconscious for a while yet.' He nodded to the crew. 'Take us to the palace.'

The crew got to work, and the launch moved away from the side of the destroyer, its oars slicing through the water as they turned towards the east. The lieutenant wandered off to keep an eye on proceedings, and the two sailors sat Leona down next to the stretcher.

'Are you my guards?' she said to them.

'Only until we get to the palace, miss,' said one. 'Are you really a rebel leader? You don't look much like one.'

'I did what I thought was best,' she said. 'Are you part of the fleet Lord Malum brought, or did you arrive more recently?'

'We came with Lord Malum,' the sailor said. He pointed over Leona's shoulder. 'That, miss, is the new fleet.'

She turned her head, and stared. Dozens of Dominion ships were sailing up the Cyasarta, so many that the entire waterway was clogged with vessels, their masts like a dense forest on the horizon. Huge dragon carriers were towering over the other ships as they inched along in the direction of Handshore Naval Base, while countless other vessels were anchoring along the coast to the west of Tsallon Anura, their white sails gleaming in the sunshine.

'Eight dragon carriers,' the sailor said, 'over sixty destroyers, two hundred troop transports, and who knows how many supply ships? Some sight, eh, miss? Still, they'll only be here a day or two – just long enough to restock with food and water – and then they'll be off to Gunst.'

Leona stared at the vast fleet filling the Cyasarta. 'I didn't know the Dominion had so many ships,' she said. 'Are they all going to Gunst?'

The sailor laughed. 'Yes, miss.'

'The Gunstian Empire has no idea what's coming,' said the other sailor; 'I almost feel sorry for the bastards.'

CHAPTER 13
ROUNDED UP

Fidalaimos, Serpent Isle – 9th Abrinch 1588

Lahnos lay on the thin pile of blankets that he and Reyn used as a mattress, his eyes open. The fading light of evening was coming in through the two semi-circular windows in the attic, and Lahnos could hear the birds singing from the trees outside the large mansion. Downstairs, Bauchlie's rebel fighters would be eating dinner but, despite an invitation to join them, Lahnos, Reyn and Efizel had preferred to stay away. The Bullan was sitting in the far corner of the attic with his back to a wall, reading. He had discovered a small library within a room used by Colonel Friel as a study whenever he visited, and had carried several volumes up to the attic. Reyn was sitting next to the soldier, as Efizel used a finger to point out words on the page for her. They had asked Lahnos to sit with them, but he had refused, his anger at the Demon Witch still simmering five days after she had told him that she had killed his father.

Lahnos dreamed of what might have been. In the period of time between his grandmother's death and the Demon Witch revealing the truth to him, he had often fantasised about freeing his father from slavery. He had pictured himself slaying his father's captors, and releasing him from the chains he had imagined around his ankles. His father, of course, had wept tears of gratitude and pride whenever Lahnos had rescued him in his mind.

It was bullshit. All of it was bullshit. His father had indeed been a slave for many long years, but he had died on the same day that the Demon Witch had murdered King Gahad. Lahnos found himself wishing that his grandmother had died years before, so that he could have read her memories while his father had still been alive; what a cruel irony it was, to have discovered that his father had been taken into slavery only after his death. Worse, the Demon Witch had known about it the entire time, and had said nothing to him. She had helped Lahnos and aided the rebellion, while keeping the information he most desired a secret from him.

He hated her. He was glad she was dead, and glad that she would never be able to see her children again.

The sound of laughter echoed up from the dining room where the rebels were eating. Lahnos hated them, too. How could they laugh and drink when the island was being ground underfoot by the Dominion? On the previous day, Lahnos and the others had been called outside to look down at the Cyasarta, only to see that the greatest collection of warships imaginable had assembled, filling the inlet from the Dragon Palace to Handshore and beyond. Efizel had pointed out the long row of dragon carriers anchored in a line down the middle of the Cyasarta, and they had all seen the dozens of tiny specks wheeling over Igatz.

Bauchlie had laughed at the sight. While the others had started to panic, the rebel leader had calmly pointed out the obvious – that the monstrous fleet was not in Zamata to hunt down a few freedom fighters, but to invade the Gunstian Empire. He had soothed his men's nerves by assuring them that the fleet would soon be gone and, when it left, it would be time for the rebels to start attacking the Dominion outposts again. After that, the rebels had gone back into the mansion, leaving Lahnos, Reyn and Efizel staring down at the crowded waters of the Cyasarta.

'Now you try,' said Efizel. 'Just follow my finger.'

'All right,' said Reyn, as she peered at the pages of the book. 'The

Gan... Gun... Gunstian Empire... was foo... foonided... what's that word?'

'Founded,' said Efizel. 'The Gunstian Empire was founded. Wait; do you hear that?'

'Hear what?' said Reyn.

Efizel got to his feet and walked to one of the open windows. Lahnos turned his head to watch him, then he noticed that the sounds of the rebels in the dining room had faded to nothing. There was a thud-thud-thud from the stairs, and Bauchlie appeared in the attic.

'Out!' he cried. 'Leave your things and follow me; now!'

Reyn's eyes widened, but Lahnos continued to lie on the blankets.

'Get up, horned boy,' Bauchlie yelled at him. 'We have only a few minutes to spare.'

The noise from downstairs increased again – a mixture of shouts and the clatter of boots running along the hallways.

'What's happening?' said Reyn.

'They've found us,' said Bauchlie. 'Don't ask me how, but they've found the mansion.'

'He is right,' said Efizel. 'Bullan soldiers are advancing up the hill-side towards us.' He ran to Reyn and pulled her upright, then Bauchlie leaned over, grabbed Lahnos's arm, and hauled him to his feet.

'Get off me,' Lahnos spat.

'Do you want to die, you stupid boy?' said Bauchlie. 'Move.'

Bauchlie set off back down the stairs, and Efizel shoved Lahnos along after him.

'I don't understand,' said Reyn, as they followed Bauchlie down to the first floor. 'The rebels here haven't done anything so far – not a single attack. How would the soldiers know where we were?'

No one answered her as they reached the fighters on the landing. Some were picking up weapons and packs, but most were already descending to the ground floor, as the red glow of sunset filtered in through the gaps in the shutters. Bauchlie directed them to a side door, and Lahnos, Reyn and Efizel tagged along at the rear as the rebels began to leave the mansion.

'Straight through the lemon groves,' Bauchlie said from the doorway. 'Follow the goat track to the ruins of Gatzoun Medamuna. Go.'

'Stay where you are!' roared a voice from the orange groves.

Lahnos peered out from the side entrance of the mansion, and saw movement amid the trees and undergrowth. Two rebel fighters pulled their crossbows down from their shoulders and aimed them into the groves, as the others looked around in confusion.

'Drop your weapons or we will loose,' came the voice from the groves.

'Bullan,' whispered Efizel. 'We are surrounded.'

The two rebels aiming at the orange groves squinted into the gathering gloom, then a low thrumming began. Bolts ripped through the twilight, and the two fighters fell, each pierced by three bolts to their chest.

'Raise your hands!' came the voice.

Lahnos glanced around to look for Bauchlie, as the other fighters began shoving their way back into the mansion. At the same time, several squads of armoured Bullan emerged from the orange groves and advanced. One of the rebels pushed Lahnos to the side and slammed the door shut, leaving four rebels stranded outside. The fighter barred the door, and gripped his crossbow.

'We fight to the death,' the rebel cried to the others. 'Block every entrance. No surrender!'

Efizel pulled Lahnos and Reyn away from the door, and they went to a shuttered window and looked through the slats. Outside, the four rebels who had been left behind were on their knees with their hands on their heads, their weapons lying discarded on the hard-packed dirt. Lahnos held his breath as he watched the Bullan soldiers move forward, sure that the four fighters would be cut down where they knelt. Instead, the soldiers bound the wrists of each of the four, and led them off into the orange grove.

'Where is Commander Bauchlie?' shouted one of the rebels inside the dark mansion. 'Was he outside?'

'There are Bullan at every door!' another cried. 'We are surrounded.'

Lahnos kept his eyes on the soldiers outside. Four of them brought forwards a short battering ram with iron grips attached to the sides and, while others covered them with their shields, they rushed towards the side door. On the other side of the door a dozen rebel fighters took up position with their crossbows, ready to loose.

'We should surrender, young Laimos,' said Efizel. 'If we resist, my kinsfolk will kill us all.'

'They will kill us all anyway!' cried a rebel.

'Not so,' said the Bullan. 'They did not kill the four who were trapped outside. Commander Bauchlie is the only one they will kill on sight – and where is he?'

The Bullan soldiers outside swung the ram, and its iron-clad tip battered off the side door. The rebels lined up in the hallway jumped a little, their eyes wild. The ram swung again, and the side door bulged inwards, but did not break.

'Lahnos,' Reyn whispered; 'what should we do?'

He turned his gaze from the soldiers outside and gazed into her face. Her blunt horns were glinting in the dim light as the sun disappeared over the side of the mountain to the west. He touched her cheek, and knew what he needed to do.

He walked towards the side door, and found Efizel by his side. The rebel fighters cursed them both as they moved between them and the door. Lahnos got to his knees and raised his hands in the air, and Efizel did the same.

'Get out of the way, you freaks!' shouted a rebel, as the ram battered off the door a third time.

'No,' said Lahnos. 'You can die if you wish, but if I can save Reyn by surrendering, then that is what I shall do.'

The door was struck again, and it flew open, sending fragments of splintered wood into the hallway. The Bullan charged into the mansion, their crossbows raised, then they pulled up as they saw Lahnos and Efizel kneeling in front of them.

Efizel said something in the language of the Klediomira Haga, his voice clear and strong, and a Bullan officer replied. Over to their left, more Bullan soldiers appeared from the direction of the mansion's front door, and the rebels threw down their crossbows. Two Bullan approached Efizel, pulled his arms behind his back, and bound his wrists, then another pair came for Lahnos.

'Name?' said one.

'Lahnos Laimos,' he said, keeping his head held high despite the despair coursing through him.

The Bullan glanced at each other, then one spoke to an officer in their own tongue. The Bullan officer narrowed his eyes, then shrugged and said something.

'You are to be treated the same as the rest of us, young Laimos,' Efizel said.

'The girl is innocent,' said Lahnos to the soldiers, as his wrists were bound behind his back. 'Let her go.'

'We have no interest in her, Laimos,' said one of the soldiers. 'Where is Commander Bauchlie?'

'I don't know,' he said.

The officer gestured to a squad, and they moved off into the rest of the mansion, as more soldiers entered the hallway. The rebels were lined up and then their wrists were bound.

'We should have gone down fighting,' said one, weeping. 'Now the bastards will hang us all in Igatz.'

The Bullan officer smiled at the rebel. 'You may well die, traitor,' he said, 'but it will not be on Zamata. Take them away.'

Lahnos and Efizel were hauled to their feet, and shoved into line with the other rebels. Reyn ran forwards, her hands outstretched to embrace Lahnos, but a soldier pushed her back.

'Behave yourself, girl,' the soldier said, his eyes glancing over her horns and tail.

'Where are you taking them?' Reyn cried.

The soldiers ignored her.

'Go to the village and hide there,' Lahnos said, as the soldiers shoved them towards the side door.

'Lahnos, I love you,' Reyn shouted, as he was pushed outside.

'Escort them to the wagons,' the officer said, 'and then we'll raid Fidalaimos and the other villages in the vicinity.'

The soldiers saluted. Twenty moved in to surround the captive rebels, and they set off down the hillside.

Dawn was breaking over the eastern horizon when the ships docked at the western point of Kaugatz. The vessels were packed full of Zamatan men, each with their wrists tightly bound, and the Bullan soldiers forced them down the gangway, where more soldiers were waiting to receive them. Lahnos staggered as his feet touched solid land. He hadn't slept all night as he and the others had been moved across the island. They had been placed into guarded wagons, and then taken down the slopes of Mount Medamuna to Wayston, and then they had waited while more wagons had been filled with the native men of the area. As far as he could tell, he was the only part-Bullan among the captives, and Efizel was the sole non-Zamatan. They had been forbidden to speak throughout the long night, and Lahnos took the opportunity to glance at the others who had been arrested. Most seemed to be farmers or villagers rather than rebels, and their ages ranged from late teens to perhaps their mid-forties, with no young boys or old men among their numbers. Several hundred were taken from the ferries, and then they were led by armed Bullan towards a road that led to the south. The way was lined by palm trees, with a beach on their right as the captives trudged through the outskirts of Kaugatz in silence. Ahead of them, a dozen dragons were circling in the air over the monastery of Euzaru Naka, and the streets of Kaugatz were deserted apart from the long procession of soldiers and captives.

The renovated monastery of Euzaru Naka was small compared to Tsallon Anura, and its two-storey white-washed buildings were glowing pink in the light of the sunrise as they approached. Above them, the dragons were monitoring the progress of the captives. The monastery gates were open, and the hundreds of prisoners were led into a large open courtyard, where they joined an equal number of other Zamatans who were sitting on the dusty ground. The new arrivals were crammed in, and the gates of Euzaru Naka were closed. Bullan soldiers had taken up position on the roofs of the compound buildings surrounding the Zamatan men, and Lahnos sat down next to Efizel.

'If they try to execute us,' Lahnos said, his eyes lowered; 'we go down fighting.'

'I do not think that is their intention, young Laimos,' Efizel whispered.

'Then what do they want with us?' Lahnos said. 'It looks as though they're rounding up every man on Zamata.'

Efizel's eyes scanned the huge crowd sitting in the dusty courtyard. 'There are perhaps a thousand here,' he said in a low voice, 'and there might be other camps elsewhere on the island.'

Lahnos's chest tightened. 'Are they taking us into slavery?'

'I do not know the answer to that,' the Bullan said.

Lahnos noticed that several of the other captives were staring at him and the Bullan by his side, then his eyes settled on a face he recognised.

'Karl?' he whispered. 'Shit; my brother is here.'

Lahnos got to his feet, and Efizel rose beside him. They walked through the thick, tight press of men, ignoring stares and a few hostile comments, then Lahnos stopped in front of where his older brother was crouching next to a few other men from Fidalaimos. The last time he had seen his brother had been in their grandmother's home, just before she had died of a heart attack; and Karl would know nothing about all that Lahnos had discovered regarding the fate of their father. For a moment, Lahnos considered telling him, then he noticed that Karl was refusing to glance up, and anger drove out any desire to confide in his brother.

'Karl,' he said. 'Will you not look at me?'

His brother frowned, then turned his gaze upwards. 'Lahnos.'

'What are you doing here?' said Lahnos.

'The same as everyone else,' Karl said. 'The Bullan bastards raided the village and took every able-bodied man.' He narrowed his eyes at Efizel. 'You know, brother, somehow I'm not surprised that you have befriended one of the Bullan. Like attracts like.'

Lahnos felt a suitable response linger on his tongue, but he could sense the enmity towards Efizel simmering through the crowd.

'This Bullan is on our side, brother,' he said.

'Lahnos saved my life,' said Efizel. 'I am pledged to protect him.'

'You might want to think about protecting yourself first, Bullan,' said Karl. 'You think you're stronger and better than the rest of us, but here, in this courtyard, you are outnumbered a thousand to one.'

'My kinsfolk bound my wrists, just as they bound yours,' said Efizel. 'To them, I have switched sides. My old regiment has disowned me.'

Karl shook his head. The other villagers from Fidalaimos looked nervous, as if they didn't wish to be seen or associated with Lahnos and his Bullan companion.

'How are the girls?' said Lahnos.

'Our sisters are well,' Karl said; 'or at least they were until last night when the Bullan kicked down our front door. Auntie Fenna is looking after them now.'

'And Uncle Frickel?'

Karl shrugged. 'They left him alone. The Bullan said he was of no use to them.'

'Why?' said Efizel. 'Is he sick or ill?'

Karl narrowed his eyes. 'He has a bad knee.'

The Bullan soldier nodded. 'I think I know the reason why we have all been gathered here.'

'Yes?' said Lahnos. 'Don't keep it to yourself.'

A loud whistle blast pierced the air, and the assembled Zamatans turned. A collection of Aucterian army officers in Dominion uniforms had gathered on the flat roof of one of the monastery buildings, flanked by armoured Bullan.

'Men of Zamata!' one of the officers shouted. 'The divine King Naghad has decided to show you mercy. His Majesty has ordained that your past transgressions against the Dominion shall be forgiven.'

None of the captive men spoke, their full attention on the Aucterian officers.

'Only the leadership of the uprising shall be punished,' the officer went on. 'Colonel Friel Laimos is in our custody, and he shall stand trial for his crimes against the Dominion, but the gracious King Naghad has decreed that none of you shall be held responsible for the actions of that vile traitor. Instead, you are to join with your brothers in the Dominion upon our noble mission to unite this world. As of this moment, you men are now part of the Third Zamatan Regiment. In a few days from now, you and the other newly-formed native regiments will embark upon the transport ships anchored in the Cyasarta, and from there you will sail to the Gunstian Empire – where each of you will do your duty and fight for the Dominion.'

A loud groan echoed across the courtyard, and several of the men cursed or wept.

'You are honoured indeed,' the officer shouted, his voice raised over the chorus of despairing complaints; 'for you have a chance to prove your loyalty and allegiance to the Dominion, and to restore the reputation of this island in the eyes of His Blessed Majesty.'

'We're not soldiers!' shouted a Zamatan man. 'We're farmers! We have families depending on us.'

'You are servants and subjects of the Blessed King,' said the officer, 'and you will do your duty.' He pointed up at the circling dragons. 'The gods are watching you,' he said. 'Any outbreaks of cowardice shall be met with swift and terrible retribution.'

The eyes of the Zamatans lifted upwards to gaze at the dragons, and the complaints ceased. A silent pall of fear descended over the men in the courtyard, and the officer smiled.

'The registration process shall now commence,' he said. 'You will form into lines and give your details to the officers who are assembling by the monastery gates. There, you will be assigned to your new companies, and then you will be escorted through Kaugatz to the Cyasarta, where you will embark upon the transport ships awaiting you.'

Another whistle pierced the air, and Bullan soldiers moved into the crowd of Zamatans, urging everyone to their feet and shoving them into long queues. Several of the Zamatan men had managed to loosen or cut the bonds securing their wrists, but none resisted, and an air of sullen, desperate resignation moved over the crowd.

Lahnos stuck close to his brother, and Efizel remained by his side as they were pushed into a line that shuffled forward every few minutes. Above them, the dragons wheeled and soared, their gleaming eyes watching for any signs of disobedience. The sun climbed the eastern sky, its rays beating down without pity upon the thirsty and exhausted men. Lahnos's thoughts went to Reyn. If he allowed himself to be placed on to a transport ship bound for Gunst, then he knew he would likely never see her again. The Zamatans would be used as fodder in the coming invasion, that much seemed clear to him; if they went into battle, few would be returning home.

An hour passed before the villagers from Fidalaimos reached the front of their queue. A line of tables had been arranged close to the gates, and each queue terminated at one, where Aucterian sergeants and officers were sitting flanked by armoured Bullan. Other teams of Bullan were working their way along the queues, removing the bonds from each captive before they reached the tables.

'Name and place of residence?' said an officer, glancing up at Lahnos's brother.

'Karl Laimos of Fidalaimos,' he said. 'I tend olive groves; I have never held a sword or a crossbow. I...'

'You are now in the Seventh Company,' said the officer, as the sergeant next to him wrote on a large scroll. 'Next.'

A Bullan shoved Karl to the side as Lahnos and Efizel stepped forward, their hands freed.

'Name and place of residence?' said the officer, his eyes still lowered.

'Lahnos Laimos of Igatz,' he said.

'Ninth Company.'

'Karl Laimos is my brother,' said Lahnos. 'I want to serve beside him in the Seventh.'

The officer frowned and looked up, his eyes widening at the sight of Efizel standing next to Lahnos.

'Ah. So this is the horned Laimos boy and his Bullan bodyguard, eh? I've heard about you two. You were arrested in the company of Commander Bauchlie, were you not?'

'I was staying in my uncle's mansion,' said Lahnos. 'Bauchlie's presence there had nothing to do with us; and no – I have no idea where he is. Have you caught him?'

The officer said nothing for a moment, then he glanced at the sergeant by his side.

'Seventh Company, sir?' said the sergeant. 'We have permission to place siblings together if they request it.'

'And the Bullan renegade?' said the officer.

The sergeant shrugged. 'Our orders said nothing about that, sir.'

'With all respect, Major,' said Efizel, 'I am not a renegade. Honour demanded that I pledge my service to Lahnos Laimos, in return for him saving my life from the Gunstians. Place me with him, and I will do my duty to the Dominion.'

The officer turned back to Lahnos. 'I hear that you have some experience of fighting the Gunstians. Is that true, boy?'

'Yes,' said Lahnos.

'Give him some corporal's stripes, sergeant, and place them both in the Seventh Company.'

The sergeant nodded, then he wrote something on the scroll and dipped a hand into a pocket. He produced a corporal's insignia, and handed it to Lahnos.

'A corporal?' said Lahnos. 'But...'

The officer frowned. 'That's what I said. The Zamatan regiments are a little short of men with any combat experience. Next.'

Lahnos and Efizel were pushed out of the queue, and they returned to where they had been sitting.

Karl glanced at them.

'We're in the same company,' Lahnos said.

Karl said nothing, but several of the Fidalaimos villagers muttered curses under their breath.

'You should be grateful,' Lahnos said, his eyes narrowing. 'None of you fools know the first thing about fighting, and now we'll have a trained Bullan soldier to help us. Oh, and I'm your corporal now, so you'll have to do as I say.'

'They made you a corporal?' said Karl, his features contorting with contempt.

'They did,' said Lahnos. 'I was in the rebel militia and I fought the Gunstians in Kaugatz. What did you lot do when the Gunstians invaded?'

'You're out of your tiny mind, brother,' said Karl. 'We're being sent to Gunst to die. Your pet Bullan will make no difference – none of us will be coming home.'

'No one can tell the future,' said Efizel. 'If we keep together, maintain our discipline, and fight bravely, then we might survive. Have any of you had any military training?'

The villagers glanced at each other.

'What do you think?' said Karl. 'Do we look like soldiers?'

'No,' said Efizel, 'you do not. In twenty days or so, we shall be landing upon the shores of Gunst. I say to you now, that if you follow my advice, you will have a chance of seeing your families again.'

'Why do you care about us?' said Karl. 'I thought all Bullan despised humans.'

Efizel smiled. 'You are right – I care about none of you except Lahnos. However, in order to keep him alive, I am prepared to help you all.'

'Leave us alone,' said one of the villagers. 'You are going to be lynched as soon as we're on board the ships, and I don't want to be near you when that happens.'

'That's where you're wrong,' said Lahnos. He stood, and glared at the vast crowd of Zamatans surrounding the villagers from Fidalaimos.

'My name is Corporal Lahnos Laimos,' he cried, 'and I'm warning you all – if any of you bastards thinks about harming one of the lads from the Fidalaimos squad, then we will kick your skulls in. We have a Bullan on our side, and if you touch one of us, you touch us all. If any of you have a problem with that, step right up, and we will settle it here and now.'

A wave of hostility washed over the crowd, and Lahnos clenched his fists, ready to attack the first Zamatan who tried anything.

'Settle down!' cried a Bullan soldier, as an armoured column moved through the crowd. 'Save your anger for the Gunstians.'

Lahnos sat back down, as the Fidalaimos villagers glared at him.

'You reckless idiot,' cried one. 'I want no part of this.'

'Too late,' said Lahnos. 'We stick together, or we die together.'

Efizel raised an eyebrow at Lahnos, but he said nothing.

Karl shook his head. 'We're doomed.'

Lahnos glanced at his brother. Perhaps, one day, he would tell him the truth about their father, for all the good it would do. He lay back on the dusty ground, folded his arms behind his head and closed his eyes, feeling the warmth of the sun on his skin.

CHAPTER 14
DISGRUNTLED

Igatz, Serpent Isle – 14th Abrinch 1588

A squadron of sleek destroyers was the first to leave, their tall sails filling with the wind as they sailed past the Dragon Palace on their way to the Cyasarta straits. Following them were a dozen heavily-laden troopships, and then a further two destroyers. After that came the first of the eight dragon carriers bound for Gunst, its flight deck crowded with six huge dragons, their scales glinting in the bright sunshine. It had rained incessantly overnight, but the dawn had seen the clouds swept away to the south-west, leaving the skies clear and blue.

'This is bullshit,' muttered Major Lyla. 'I should be on one of those ships, not stranded on this damn rock.'

Captain Cisca remained silent next to the other Dragon Corps officers as they watched the departure of the invasion fleet. She had expected to be among those chosen to remain behind on the island, as Lord Malum seemed to think that she was an expert on the affairs of the Serpent Isle; but Major Lyla had been devastated by the news that she had not been selected to join the invasion fleet. Next to them stood three young lieutenants, also from the Dragon Corps, and then the senior officers of the Dominion Army, Navy and Bullan regiments were arrayed along the jetty. Only a small garrison was staying on the island to govern it while the King led the fleet to Gunst, but as almost every able-bodied male adult from Zamata had been crammed aboard the troopships, it was felt that another uprising was far from likely. At a single stroke, the population of the island had been reduced by a fifth, leaving only the women, children, and those men too old or sick to be pressed into the army. The Aucterian settlers and all islanders descended from Gunstian stock had been exempted from the raids that had corralled so many Zamatan men, but their numbers were too few to make much of a difference.

A dozen dragons flew low overhead, then they banked and wheeled over the palace jetty where the officers had assembled. Seven began to circle above the promontory, while the other five descended, and they landed along the strip of gardens between the palace and the shining waters of the Cyasarta.

The officers turned and saluted, then bowed their heads as King Naghad strode forwards, with Lady Macsin and Lord Malum by his shoulders. The illustrious King glanced at the men and women lined up along the jetty, then he turned to Lord Malum.

'I trust you will take good care of this isle in my absence, brother?' he said.

Malum bowed low. 'You can be assured, my Blessed King, that I will govern to the best of my ability.'

'Our sister Lady Macsin will make a capable deputy,' the King said, 'and you will also have Lady Lenta and Lord Rylan to assist you in your work.'

'Yes, Your Majesty,' said Malum; 'together, we will await the day when we shall welcome your victorious return to the Serpent Isle, after you have crushed the Gunstian Empire.'

The King gazed out at the massive fleet wending its way past Igatz towards the straits.

'I long to reach the city of Great Gunst,' Naghad said, 'as I long to bring the wretched Gunstians to their knees. Their cities shall burn, and their people shall be slaughtered like animals; and then, at last, this world shall be united under the Dominion.'

'Yes, Your Majesty,' said Malum. 'How soon should I expect the first supply fleet to reach us from Aucteran?'

'It should be here in under a month,' said the King. 'Do not allow the ships to tarry on the isle – send them on to me in Gunst without delay. A second supply fleet should then arrive a month after that, although I hope that it will not be needed by then. I intend my invasion of Gunst to be swift and overwhelming – a great, savage burning that will consume their defences in days, rather than months.'

'I am sure that will be the case, Your Majesty,' said Malum.

The bronze-scaled King tilted his head. 'One last thing before I leave you, my brother – if you hear any word about the treacherous activities of the failed claimant to the throne, send a message to me by fast ship. If that coward Lord Tegru tries anything in my absence, I wish to know about it; is that understood?'

'Yes, Your Majesty. If that traitor's emissaries arrive here, they shall not leave the island alive.'

'I am placing much trust in you, brother – do not let me down.' He glanced at Lady Lenta, Lady Macsin and Lord Rylan. 'Farewell, my kindred. The next time I see you, I shall have conquered Gunst.'

King Naghad extended his wings, and he took to the skies. He joined the circling dragons overhead, then they flew off towards a pair of dragon carriers that were rounding the promontory. Lord Malum turned his gaze to Macsin, Lenta and Rylan, his eyes burning with suppressed fury.

'Lady Macsin, patrol the inner isle – Lord Rylan, the outer. Lenta, remain here to bid farewell to the fleet.'

Two of the dragons bowed their heads and ascended into the air, then Malum began striding towards the white marble palace.

Major Lyla raised an eyebrow. 'The Blessed King didn't even acknowledge our presence,' she muttered under her breath.

Cisca said nothing.

Lyla snapped her fingers at the three Dragon Corps lieutenants. 'Come on; let's join the new Governor in the palace; we may be required.'

The five members of the Dragon Corps moved away from Lady Lenta and the army, navy and Bullan officers who remained on the jetty watching the fleet as it departed. Lyla led the way, and Cisca and the three young lieutenants followed. Cisca kept her gaze lowered, unsure who out of Malum and Lyla was the more angry at having been left behind.

They entered the cool interior of the palace and walked to the main audience chamber, but it was empty. Lyla narrowed her eyes.

'You three,' she said to a lieutenant; 'split up and look for Lord Malum. When you find his lordship, tell him that we are at his service.'

The young lieutenants saluted and hurried off, then Lyla strode to a table by a far wall, and poured herself a glass of white wine from a silver decanter.

Cisca joined her, but remained quiet.

'Am I over-reacting, Captain?' Lyla said. 'Tell me the truth.'

'I don't know, ma'am,' said Cisca. 'It is clear that you are disappointed about…'

'Disappointed?' said Lyla. She laughed, but it was a bitter sound. 'I am furious, Cisca. I am the most senior member of the Dragon Corps, and yet I am not to accompany the King on the largest invasion in history? In the old days, the dragons would have had dozens of Dragon Corps officers around them for an operation like this – and who does King Naghad take with him? A mere handful of junior lieutenants. I can understand why you were left here – the Serpent Isle needs a dependable senior officer to look after things, but me? What am I supposed to do on this barren rock? I know nothing about the island. It's a punishment, that's what it is. I am getting the blame for the losses we incurred in the Hansarta. I am being humiliated.'

'Perhaps, ma'am,' Cisca said, 'it doesn't help that you are new to the Dragon Corps. King Naghad barely knows you.'

'That is the sole reason I survived the cull of officers,' Lyla said. 'Every long-serving Dragon Corps major, colonel, general – all of them; they all had some sort of link to Lord Tegru, and so King Naghad dismissed them all.'

'When we spoke about Lord Tegru before, ma'am, I got the impression that you might have agreed with his views on the invasion of Gunst. If that is so, then why were you so eager to go?'

Lyla gave her a wry smile. 'For my career, what else? Do I think the invasion is a good idea? Not necessarily; but with so many other Dragon Corps officers having been dismissed, I thought that this would be my chance to rise to the top.' She shook her head. 'I should never have left the damn army.'

'Why did you, ma'am, if that is not too personal a question?'

'I was sick of policing the natives of Irlan and Elso,' Lyla said, 'and I wanted to see more of Inopei. After eight years of service, I reckoned that I deserved a rest. What a joke. I was in Inopei for a total of five days, and now I am stuck here.'

'I think I know how you feel, ma'am,' Cisca said. 'I, too, was angry when I was told to remain here instead of accompanying Lady Tirna to Inopei for the dragon conference. Lord Konran had taken a fierce dislike to me, and so he left me behind.'

Lyla stared at the floor. 'Why do we serve such arrogant masters?' she said, then her features flushed a little. 'Forgive me, Cisca, and please forget that I said that. I spoke in anger.'

'It is already forgotten, ma'am.'

Lyla smiled. 'Look at us both – we are still in our mid-twenties, and yet we each have the weight of the world on our shoulders. I should never have been promoted to major at such an age. I was so thrilled at the time, but now I can see that I wasn't ready for such a responsibility. To think that we two were entrusted with the entire strategy to retake the Serpent Isle; it's ridiculous – no wonder we made mistakes. Had I remained in the army, I would still be a lieutenant, and I would probably be on board one of those troopships, commanding a mere company.' She bowed her head. 'Enough about me – you haven't mentioned anything about being ordered to remain on the island.'

'I was expecting it, ma'am,' said Cisca. 'Frankly, I would have been shocked if I had been chosen to go along with the invasion fleet. Lord Malum has an inflated opinion of my expertise on all things Zamatan.'

'Well, at least the uprising is finally over,' said Lyla. 'With any luck, we can relax for a while.'

'Yes, ma'am; although the island will feel quiet and empty with so many men gone. I wonder how many will return.'

Lyla's eyes darkened. 'Too few, I imagine. For the life of me, I cannot see the strategic value of impressing thousands of farmers and peasants into the Dominion army. Despite the flowery words about duty and honour, I suspect it is a collective punishment for the island as a whole. Without training, and with sub-standard equipment, the new Zamatan regiments will be torn apart by the regular Gunstian armed forces. Even if the invasion proves to be a great success, I fear that there will be many left widowed and orphaned upon this island.'

An army scout ran into the audience chamber. His eyes went to the empty piles of cushions in the centre of the hall, then he noticed Lyla and Cisca by the wall.

He saluted. 'I am looking for Lord Malum, ma'am.'

'I have three lieutenants out trying to track him down,' said Lyla. 'Is it urgent?'

'A report has come in from the town of Wayston, ma'am,' the scout said. 'Three Aucterian soldiers have been killed.'

'By whom?' said Lyla.

'It happened only hours after the fleet began to depart, ma'am; their mutilated bodies were found...'

'I said, by whom?'

The scout's face paled. 'According to unsubstantiated reports, ma'am, Commander Bauchlie was seen leaving Wayston just before the bodies were discovered.'

Cisca stared at the scout, not trusting herself to speak.

'Bauchlie?' said Lyla. 'I thought he was slain in a Bullan raid.'

'His body was never formally identified, ma'am,' said the scout.

'Give me the full report,' said Lyla.

'Yes, ma'am. The new garrison of Wayston consists of twenty Aucterian soldiers, though the town was temporarily hosting well over a thousand from the invasion force. As soon as they had left the town at dawn this morning to embark upon the troopships, locals reported seeing Commander Bauchlie enter the town in the presence of a part-Bullan woman. An hour later, an Aucterian farmer notified the authorities that Bauchlie and the woman had left the town on horseback. Three soldiers were then reported missing, and a search was carried out. The new garrison found their comrades hanging from nooses in a barn. Their throats had been cut, and there was evidence of torture on all three bodies.'

'Did none of the locals try to apprehend Bauchlie or the woman?' said Lyla.

'His reputation in those parts is sizable, ma'am. The Aucterian farmers were too scared to do anything, while the local Zamatans see him as a hero.'

Cisca grimaced. What Bauchlie and the part-Bullan woman had done was despicable and horrible, but her heart seemed restored by the knowledge that Bauchlie was alive. Mixed with the relief, however, was a twinge of jealousy. Who was the part-Bullan woman who had helped him, and what was Bauchlie doing with her?'

'The woman,' said Cisca; 'has she been identified?'

'No, ma'am,' said the scout; 'but she had horns and a tail, so, in theory, she shouldn't be too hard for the garrison to track down. There aren't many part-Bullan in the outlying areas of the island.'

'You may return to your post,' said Lyla. 'We shall inform the new Governor of the Serpent Isle of these developments.'

The scout saluted, then he about-turned and hurried from the audience chamber.

'Well, well,' said Lyla. 'No sooner does the fleet leave, than that vile little terrorist crawls out from the hole in which he had been hiding. He is sending us a message, of course – the timing makes that clear.'

'Is a garrison of only twenty sufficient to guard a town as large as Wayston, ma'am?' said Cisca. 'Prior to the uprising, I believe that eighty Bullan were stationed there.'

'Come now, Captain,' said Lyla; 'you know as well as I do that this island has been stripped to the bone to bolster the grand invasion force.

Everything that wasn't nailed down has been taken – this year's harvest, most of the Zamatan men, all of the stockpiled weapons and munitions, and every last Dominion soldier that our blessed monarch believed could be spared.'

'We still have the Bullan to protect us, ma'am.'

'No, Cisca – we have a single regiment of Bullan – one thousand soldiers. How many were here before the uprising?'

'Five thousand, ma'am.'

'Lord Malum is not going to be happy to hear this latest news. With so few soldiers on the island, Bauchlie could run riot. Come; let us inform the new Governor.'

'But, ma'am, I thought we were waiting for the lieutenants to return? We don't know Lord Malum's current location.'

Lyla smiled. 'I have a pretty good idea where his lordship will be. I sent the lieutenants away because I wished for a moment's peace.'

Major Lyla set off, and Cisca hurried along after her. They left the circular audience hall through a wide archway, and then descended a dragon-sized flight of stairs into the palace basement.

'Tell me about Bauchlie, Cisca,' said Lyla. 'What are his motivations?'

'To free the island, ma'am; nothing else matters to him. He is prepared to sacrifice the lives of his own men if necessary, and, clearly, he is prepared to employ torture and murder to achieve his ends. He once slit the throat of an Aucterian businesswoman while she slept in her own bed.'

'He must know that he cannot win,' said Lyla.

'He believes that he can make the occupation of the island so painful for the Dominion that they will eventually leave.'

'He is deluded,' said Lyla. 'Let's just say for a moment that the Dominion gave up the island entirely, then what would stop the Gunstians from taking over? Does Bauchlie favour the Gunstians?'

'No, ma'am. He hates them as much if not more than the Dominion.'

'Is he religious?'

'I don't think so. He doesn't believe in the serpent gods, nor in the Gunstian's one god.'

'What will he do next, if you had to make a guess?'

Cisca narrowed her eyes. 'He was hiding out with thirty or forty men on Mount Medamuna, or so the Bullan reported. When they raided the location, the Bullan took most of the rebels prisoner, so Bauchlie will not have any fighters around him at the moment. That is presumably why he had a part-Bullan woman working with him – because he has run out of men, at least for now. That will limit his options. He will probably carry out attacks on a similar scale to the one he did this morning – striking small numbers of Dominion soldiers at a time, rather than taking on anything too ambitious. At the same time, I believe he will be trying to recruit a new following.'

'From where? Every able-bodied man is currently crammed on board a troopship, bound for Gunst.' The major smiled. 'Unless he plans to recruit from among the women of the island, though I find that a little hard to believe.'

'Why, ma'am?'

'Zamatan women seem awfully subservient to their menfolk; don't you think? At least, compared to Aucterian women. You never see any Zamatan women in the militia, or in any positions of authority. Housewives, farmer's wives – yes, there are plenty of those, but bold rebels?'

They reached the end of a long, dragon-sized corridor, and Lyla halted in front of an enormous door.

'Have you been in the baths before, Captain?' she said.

'Once, ma'am, with Lord Kheran.'

Lyla nodded, then she pushed open a smaller door that had been cut into the large entrance. A gust of steam escaped through the doorway, then Lyla and Cisca entered a huge underground hall. A narrow tiled walkway went around the walls, while, in the centre of the room, a vast hot pool was issuing clouds of steam into the air.

'Lord Malum?' Lyla called out. 'Are you in here, my lord?'

A pale red head appeared through the fog of steam. 'What do you want?' Malum snapped. 'Can you not leave me in peace?'

Lyla and Cisca bowed their heads.

'My humble apologies, my lord,' said the major. 'A scout arrived with news from the outer island that I felt I should bring to your attention. We can speak at a later time, if that is your desire.'

'Well?' said the dragon. 'What news?'

'It seems, my lord, that the death of Commander Bauchlie was announced prematurely. Witnesses in Wayston state that he captured and killed three Aucterian soldiers this morning.'

Lord Malum stared at Lyla, his eyes piercing her. 'Why is there a smirk upon your lips, Major? Do you take some measure of satisfaction in delivering this bad news?'

Lyla's face fell. 'No, my lord; not at all.'

'Do not lie to me,' said Malum. 'You have a high opinion of yourself, don't you; yet you have consistently offered me nothing but bad advice. Who was it who suggested that we attack via the Hansarta? And who advised that we land our soldiers at night, allowing them to be mauled by the rebels?'

'It was I, my lord,' said Lyla. 'I have made mistakes, for which I apologise once again.'

Malum's dark green eyes regarded her with disdain. 'Perhaps it is time to discover what you really think, Major Lyla.'

'No,' Lyla said, her voice filled with fear; 'please, my lord. I am your loyal servant.'

'We shall see about that,' the dragon said, fixing her with a heavy stare. 'I compel you to speak nothing but the truth, Major Lyla.'

Lyla fell to her knees on the wet tiles, unable to tear her glance away from the dragon.

'Let us begin,' said Malum. 'What are your thoughts about being left on the Serpent Isle?'

'It makes me so angry I could scream,' said Lyla.

Malum laughed. 'I thought as much. Now, tell me what you think of the Blessed King Naghad. It was His Majesty, after all, who made the decision that you remain here.'

'I hate him,' Lyla said, her eyes wide with terror. 'He is stupid and arrogant. He thinks he is as good as King Gahad, but he will never match up to the old King.'

'Oh dear,' said Malum, his eyes bright; 'that all sounds a little like treachery. Tell me – who would make a better monarch – King Naghad or the coward Lord Tegru?'

Lyla began to weep, but her gaze remained fixed on the dragon. 'Lord Tegru would be a far better king,' she sobbed.

Lord Malum glanced away, and Lyla fell to the floor, panting and weeping.

'Your words betray you,' said the pale red dragon. 'Captain Cisca, escort this vile traitor to the prison cells within the palace and place her into the custody of the Bullan soldiers. I shall decide what to do with her later. Once she has been incarcerated, I would like you to order the Bullan to conduct an immediate search for Bauchlie. Failure will not be acceptable.'

Cisca swallowed. 'Yes, my lord.'

The dragon stared at her. 'You are now the senior Dragon Corps officer upon this island, Captain Cisca. Your advice has, so far, been wise and considered. Let us pray that it continues to be such. And, if you ever interrupt my bath again, I will see if you also enjoy playing the truth game. Dismissed.'

Cisca bowed low, and when she looked up, the pale red dragon had vanished into the thick clouds of steam. She crouched down, and took Lyla's hand.

'Get off me!' Lyla cried. 'I can walk on my own; I don't need you to help me.'

Cisca stood back as Lyla pulled herself to her feet. The major wiped the tears from her cheeks, but then started crying again as she stumbled towards the door. Cisca followed her out into the corridor, then she closed the door behind her.

'Damn them!' Lyla cried. 'Damn them all!'

Cisca said nothing.

'Don't think you're safe,' Lyla said. 'That could just as easily have been you on your knees in front of that bastard. Everyone has doubts; don't you understand? Everyone has secrets; even you, Cisca.'

Lyla hurried off down the corridor, and Cisca followed on behind her, her heart torn by what she had witnessed. Lyla was right in every respect. Cisca often had doubts about the wisdom and divinity of the dragons, and what would they make of her suppressed feelings for Bauchlie? She shuddered at the thought.

As they walked, Cisca wondered if Lyla would try to make a break for it, but the major strode with purpose towards a guarded wing of the basement and approached the soldiers posted there.

'I am under arrest,' she announced to the Bullan. 'Please take me into custody.'

'Ma'am?' said the Bullan sergeant on duty.

'You heard me!' Lyla cried. 'Find me a nice dark cell where I won't have to pretend to like our beloved overlords.'

The Bullan glanced at each other.

'What is the charge, ma'am?' the sergeant said.

Lyla lowered her glance. 'Treason.'

She held out her hands, and a Bullan soldier secured her wrists with cords. One opened a wooden door, and two soldiers escorted Lyla into the darkness that lay beyond.

'And you, ma'am?' said the sergeant, his gaze on Cisca. 'Are you also under arrest?'

'No,' said Cisca. 'I am now in command of the Dragon Corps on the Serpent Isle, as ordered by Lord Malum.'

The Bullan sergeant nodded. 'Then I guess it's your lucky day, ma'am.'

CHAPTER 15
THE FINAL INTERROGATION

Igatz, Serpent Isle – 16th Abrinch 1588

'Curse them all!' the woman cried from the next cell along, her upper-class Aucterian roots betrayed by her accent. 'I hate them!'

Leona groaned on the hard mattress, her hands half-covering her ears. The first six days of imprisonment had been bad enough, but the Aucterian woman's constant ranting and complaining in the neighbouring cell had made the last two days even worse.

'Damn lizards!' the Aucterian yelled. 'I hope the Gunstians slaughter them all!'

Leona rolled over onto her back and stared up into the pitch darkness. She had pledged to herself never to react or reply to the woman in the next cell along, but her impatience and irritation with her was wearing thin.

'They can't hear you,' Leona shouted, 'and I'm trying to sleep.'

The voice fell silent, and Leona gasped in relief. She pulled the blanket over her, moved on to her side, and closed her eyes. Eight days. In that time, she had heard no news about the colonel; in fact, the Bullan jailors hadn't deigned to speak to her at all, let alone bring her any news of the outside world. She wondered if the colonel had been executed. If he had then that would explain the Dominion's apparent lack of interest in her. The Bullan had taken her name when she had arrived at the Dragon Palace, and then led her to the cell; and then... nothing. No interrogation, no accusations. Nothing.

'Who are you?' the woman in the next cell shouted. 'I didn't think anyone could hear me down here; I thought I was alone.'

'You're not alone,' Leona said. 'Let me sleep – we can talk in the morning.'

'It might be morning now,' the woman said. 'How do you know it isn't?'

'Because the Bullan bring us breakfast at dawn, then dinner at sunset.'

'Yes, but maybe you have the two mixed up – did you think of that? Maybe the last meal we ate was breakfast, not dinner.'

Leona tried not to scream.

'Well?' the woman said. 'I asked you a question. You are Zamatan, aren't you? What's your name?'

'Miss none-of-your-damn-business,' said Leona.

The woman laughed. 'They're going to execute me; did you know that? I am a little surprised that they haven't done it yet. That lizard bastard tricked me.'

'Shut up!' cried Leona.

'Why? I'm just being civil.'

'Are you? How do I know you haven't been sent down here to get information out of me?'

'I have absolutely no idea who you are,' said the woman; 'so why would I care what information you might be hiding?'

Leona felt no tingle, but that didn't mean she wanted to strike up a conversation with a condemned Aucterian.

'Two days ago,' the woman went on, 'I was the senior Dragon Corps officer upon the Serpent Isle, and now I am destined to swing from a noose – if I'm lucky. The flying lizards might devise a more gruesome end for me; after all, I did say some rather unpleasant things about our new monarch.'

Leona frowned. 'Why would you do that?'

'Ah, so you are interested?'

'No.'

The woman laughed again. 'Are you also condemned to die?'

'I don't know.'

'Are you awaiting trial?'

'Maybe. My captors weren't entirely clear about that.'

'What did you do?'

Leona bit her tongue. She had already said far too much to a complete stranger.

'Was it awful?' said the woman. 'It must have been, if you cannot bring yourself to tell me. Let's see – who would be imprisoned within the Dragon Palace, as opposed to one of the island's ordinary jails? Now, there's a puzzle. Colonel Friel Laimos is somewhere down here, or so I imagine – I haven't laid eyes on the man, so I am speculating a little. Our lizard overlords might have ripped his head off for all I know.'

'Tell me your name,' said Leona.

'And then you will tell me yours?'

'Maybe.'

'You know, I hate to sound like a typical Aucterian, but Zamatans all sound the same to me. If I didn't know any better, then I would say that I have heard your voice before. But that... oh. Wait a moment. If I guess your name correctly, then will you confirm it?'

'I doubt it,' said Leona.

'Are you Leona of Kaugatz? If you are, then we have actually met, although I didn't speak at the meeting. Well, are you? If so, then your imprisonment down here would make sense, as you were negotiating on behalf of Colonel Laimos. Am I in the presence of a notorious traitor? And I thought I was bad. My crimes pale in comparison to yours.'

'I want to go to sleep.'

'I'm afraid that is now out of the question,' the woman said. 'I am far too intrigued. I will tell you my name – I am Major Lyla of Teros City. Do you know where Teros City is?'

Leona rolled her eyes.

'It's in Aucteran,' Lyla said; 'well, it's the capital of Aucteran, to be precise. I am in here for treason.'

'What did you do?'

'I have already mentioned that; weren't you listening? I said some treasonous things about that bronze oaf on the throne of the Dominion. I didn't want to say them, but Lord Malum used the damn truth spell on me. And so ends my career, and soon, my life.'

Again, there was no tingle. Leona narrowed her eyes.

'That seems harsh,' she said.

'You didn't hear what I said. It wasn't very complimentary. I told Lord Malum that I thought Lord Tegru would make a better king.'

'So?'

'Are you not aware of the schism that took place in Nom Karta, my ignorant little Leona? Lord Naghad and Lord Tegru both claimed the throne. Tegru was older, but Naghad, alas, was stronger. Ten of Gahad's children voted for Naghad, while only six voted for Tegru.'

'What about the other three?'

'What?'

There are twenty-one Children of Gahad,' said Leona. 'Ten plus six is sixteen, plus two for Tegru and Naghad themselves, as I presume they didn't vote. That makes eighteen. Who did the other three vote for?'

'Perhaps I underestimated your intelligence,' said Lyla. 'The other three did not vote. Two put forward the idea of a grand council made up of King Gahad's children, where every decision would be voted upon. Their idea was laughed at by the others. And, finally, Lady Tirna arrived too late to vote.'

'What happened next?'

'Lord... no, *King* Naghad demanded that Lord Tegru and his six followers prostrate themselves before him and pledge their allegiance. They refused, and fled from Inopei. I think they were last spotted close to the Lispan Desert in Eastern Aucteran.'

'And would Tegru have made a better king than Naghad?'

'Indubitably. For a start, Tegru had no desire to launch a massive invasion of the Gunstian Empire. His thinking ran along the same lines as that of King Gahad himself – a more patient, cautious approach. Zamata would be in a far better state if Tegru was king. Did you know that Naghad ordered the removal of every able-bodied Zamatan male on the island?'

Leona sat up. 'He did what?'

Lyla laughed. 'That got your attention, did it? Over ten thousand Zamatan men were rounded up – the Bullan cleared Igatz and Kaugatz first, then they swept through the smaller towns and villages.'

'Where are they taking them?'

'Try to guess.'

Leona's mind whirled with the possibilities. She had heard that there were slave colonies in the eastern half of Inopei, working in the mines dotted around the volcanic landscape; but then she groaned.

'Gunst?'

'Well done,' said Lyla. 'Yes – they were shoved on to troopships, and are on their way to be slaughtered by the Gunstian army.'

Leona fell into silence, and a tear trickled down her cheek. She sobbed aloud, then cursed her weakness.

'Oh,' said Lyla. 'Did I upset you? Sorry. I should have thought about how this news would affect you.'

'All the men?' Leona said.

'No. Not all. The Bullan spared all boys under eighteen, and any men aged over forty-five. They also left behind those plagued with illness or injury. What's more, their search could not possibly have found every man on the island. A large number must have managed to remain hidden during the round ups. Well, at least I think so. I don't have the figures so I cannot be sure. What I am sure of, however, is that this act of cruelty and wanton disregard for life is a prime example of Naghad's unsuitability as king. Damn that stupid lizard.'

The two women fell into silence. Leona lay back down on the hard mattress and closed her eyes. The rational part of her mind tried to analyse the situation, but her thoughts kept returning to an image of the men of Zamata crammed into troopships and being sent to their deaths on a foreign battlefield. The Gunstians wouldn't need Gifted to defeat them; any well-trained force of soldiers would be able to destroy a disorganised rabble of peasants, farmers and labourers. The Dominion would not glean any benefit from having them, except perhaps to delay or distract the Gunstians while the regular army attacked. It was a punishment – a collective punishment; and it was an insurance policy, to guarantee that the island could not stage another rebellion while the fleet was busy.

Lyla whispered something.

Leona opened her eyes. 'What did you say?'

'I said Bauchlie still lives.'

'Bauchlie?'

'Yes. Do you know him? What am I saying; of course you must have known him. He killed three Dominion soldiers a couple of days ago, just as the invasion fleet was departing. The dragons and Bullan will be out hunting for him. Did he escape from Tsallon Anura dressed as a monk?'

'I think I remember you now,' Leona said. 'Were you sitting next to an officer named Cisca during the negotiations over the surrender of Tsallon Anura?'

'Yes. Cisca and I were the only women in the room; well, apart from you, obviously.'

'You were wearing a Dragon Corps uniform.'

'I still am. I haven't been allowed to change my clothing since I was arrested.'

'Do you think Cisca holds the same beliefs about Naghad as you?'

'If she does, then she keeps her thoughts to herself; as did I, until I was compelled to open my heart to Lord Malum. It is possible that many officers in the Dominion dislike our new King, but don't let that thought give you any hope. The Aucterian officers will obey any orders given to them, regardless of their personal feelings. The same is doubly true for the Bullan; they may despise us mere humans, but they are utterly loyal to the Dominion. No; if there is any hope for the overthrow of Naghad, it will come from either Lord Tegru or at the hands of the Gunstians. There will be no mutiny. Alas.'

Lyla drifted into silence again, and Leona rolled on to her side. Her thoughts went to Bauchlie. Could the colonel's son make a difference? He was ruthless and strong, but he was only one man.

The hours went by slowly, the darkness never wavering within the underground cells; and Leona blinked when the door at the end of the hallway opened. Was it breakfast-time already? She felt as though she had hardly slept all night. She listened to the sound of the soldiers' boots on the stone floor, but they didn't halt outside Lyla's cell as they normally did when bringing their meals. Instead, they carried on until they were outside the door to where Leona was confined. A key turned, and the door swung open. For a moment, Leona was blinded by the light of a lamp shining through the entrance, and she shielded her eyes.

'On your feet,' came a voice.

She glanced up, and saw the soldiers' horns silhouetted in the lamplight.

'What are you going to do to her?' Lyla called out.

The soldiers ignored the Dragon Corps officer. Leona swung her legs off the mattress and pulled herself into an upright position, her back sore.

'This way,' said one of the Bullan.

'Don't you beasts hurt her,' cried Lyla.

'Shut your mouth, prisoner,' said a soldier.

'Or what?' said Lyla. 'I am awaiting execution – do you think your threats frighten me?'

Two Bullan entered Leona's cell, gripped her arms, and then led her out into the hallway. They escorted her past Lyla's cell, and Leona peered through the narrow barred slat in the door. Lyla was on her feet inside the cell, her face pressed up by the slat, and her eyes on Leona.

'Be brave,' said Lyla. 'Give the bastards nothing.'

The two soldiers led Leona out through the door at the end of the hallway, and they entered the main part of the basement under the Dragon Palace, where regular wall lamps provided a dull glow to the passageways. They left the human-sized corridors and passed into an area where the ceilings were high enough and the entrances wide enough for dragons to come and go. Leona was taken into a cavernous hall, where three more Bullan were waiting. Next to the soldiers, Colonel Laimos was lying shackled on the stone floor, his face beaten and bloody.

'Bring the prisoner over here,' said a Bullan officer, gesturing to a chair positioned by a damp wall. 'Secure her arms and legs.'

Leona was taken to the chair, then she was pushed down into it, and her wrists and ankles were tied to the wooden frame. She eyed the soldiers, but kept her mouth closed. The soldiers waited in silence, then the colonel groaned from the floor. Leona glanced down at him. She hadn't wanted to look too closely at his face, but his cry of agony drew her gaze. His empty right eye socket was staring vacantly up at her, while his left eye was closed. His nose had been broken, and his chin was bruised and bleeding. Leona suppressed her feelings of sympathy and disgust, but allowed her anger to simmer through her body.

A sixth Bullan soldier entered the hall. 'Her ladyship is on her way.'

The other soldiers stood to attention, and then the head of a huge black and white dragon appeared through an archway.

The soldiers bowed.

'We have brought the two prisoners as ordered, Lady Lenta,' said the officer.

'I can see that,' said the dragon, as she entered the large hall. 'Remove the man's shackles and place him into a chair next to the girl.'

The soldiers got to work. Two leaned over Friel, and used a hammer and pliers to remove the chains and shackles from his body, then two others hoisted him up, while another brought over a chair. The soldiers lowered Friel onto the seat, and his head slumped forward. Lady Lenta stared at him, and a few sparks flickered over her jaws.

'Lord Malum has decreed that you both be executed,' Lenta said, 'and he has sent me to carry out his orders. This day will be your last, but I cannot promise that your end will be swift. You, Colonel, are responsible for the blinding of my brother, and the loathing I feel for you will never be assuaged. However, before you both die, Lord Malum requested that I conduct a final interrogation. It seems that Bauchlie remains on the loose, and we require more information from you.' She glanced at the soldiers. 'Open his left eye.'

A soldier reached forward, and pinched Friel's eyelid. The dragon locked gazes with Friel, then the colonel shuddered. He raised his arms as if to defend himself, and two soldiers pulled them down and bound his wrists behind the chair.

'I have already told you everything I know about Bauchlie,' Friel slurred.

'Indeed,' said the dragon; 'including the fact that the scarred terrorist is your son. The information you provided led the Bullan to your mansion upon the slopes of Mount Medamuna, but Bauchlie managed to evade capture.'

'Good,' spat Friel, then he noticed Leona sitting a few feet to his right, and he swallowed.

'Once again, Colonel,' said Lenta, 'I compel you to say nothing but the truth; no lie may pass your lips.'

Friel sagged in the chair.

'Now,' the dragon went on, 'Bauchlie was recently seen in the presence of a part-Bullan woman with horns and a tail. Do you know her identity?'

'There are hundreds of part-Bullan women on Zamata,' said Friel.

The dragon tilted her head. 'You are proficient at playing the truth game. You tell me no lies, but you rarely provide me with the answers I seek. So, let us change the rules a little. You will tell me the identity of this woman, or I will order the soldiers here to torture the girl sitting next to you. Do you understand?'

Friel glanced at Leona again, his face contorted with pain and regret. 'Yes.'

'Who is the part-Bullan woman, Colonel?'

'I do not know for certain.'

'Give me your best guess. A part-Bullan woman was seen in the mansion when the Bullan carried out their raid. Who was she?'

'I do not know for certain.'

Lenta's eyes glowed bright. 'Soldiers – remove one of the girl's ears.'

A Bullan pulled a long knife from his belt and stepped forward.

'No!' cried Friel. 'Fine; I'll give you a name, but it is only a guess. I was in Tsallon Anura when Bauchlie went up to the mansion.'

'The name?' said the dragon.

Friel looked at the floor. 'She is probably Reyn of Chesson.'

'And why do you think that?'

'She is my nephew's girlfriend. She has horns and a tail. If Lahnos was in the mansion, then she might have been there, too.'

'Is this Reyn of Chesson a rebel?'

'All Zamatans are rebels in their hearts.'

The dragon glanced at the Bullan officer. 'Take this new information to the squads searching for Bauchlie. I want this Reyn of Chesson found and arrested as soon as possible.'

'Yes, ma'am,' said the officer. He gestured to one of his men, who saluted and hurried off.

'That will be all,' said the dragon, then she paused and glanced at Leona, who had kept her mouth closed for the entire time. 'The way you reacted when I threatened to harm this girl... interesting. I wonder what she means to you. Up until now, all of our interrogation sessions have centred on capturing those rebels still on the run, but this girl has been in our custody.' She turned to the Bullan again. 'Has she been questioned?'

'No, ma'am,' said the officer. 'Our orders concerned only Colonel Laimos, not the girl.'

'She is probably insignificant, but Lord Malum asked that I be thorough before the executions take place. Colonel Laimos, let me ask you – what role did this girl play in the rebellion?'

Friel kept his gaze on the floor. 'She was my advisor.'

'What else – your lover?'

'No.'

'There must be more to it than that,' said Lenta. 'Tell me why you selected her as your advisor. Let the truth free your soul, Colonel.'

Friel swallowed again, then his mouth opened. He was clearly trying to stop himself from speaking, but the power of the dragon held him in its grasp.

'She... she is...'

'Yes?' said Lenta.

Friel clenched his left eye closed. 'She has the Gift of Truth.'

The cavernous room fell into complete silence. The five Bullan soldiers stared at Leona, and then the dragon turned her enormous head to gaze at her.

'The Gift of Truth?' the dragon whispered. 'And to think that I came here this morning to enquire about the identity of a mere part-Bullan. I must inform Lord Malum of this at once. Soldiers, keep the prisoners here and permit no one to leave or enter.'

The dragon turned, and left the hall through the archway. Friel gasped in pain, and glanced up at Leona.

'I'm sorry,' he said.

'It's not your fault, sir,' she said.

One of the Bullan soldiers shook his head. 'Why are you sorry, Laimos? What you said has probably just saved this girl's life.'

'And what kind of life will she have?' said Friel. 'She will be enslaved by the dragons and forced to work for them.'

'How is that any different from what she did for you?' said the Bullan. 'You admitted it yourself – she was your advisor because of her Gift. You're just angry that the dragons will now be in control of her powers.'

'Quiet,' said the officer, and the soldiers snapped back to attention as Lady Lenta re-entered the hall, with Lord Malum next to her.

The pale red dragon lowered his head to gaze at Leona. 'This... girl?' he said.

'Yes, my lord,' said Lenta. 'Colonel Laimos confirmed it while under the truth spell.'

'I feel no powers emanating from her,' Malum said.

'I believe that dragons are blind to the powers of the Gifted, my lord,' said Lenta.

'Is that so? I recall King Gahad telling me the same thing, a very long time ago. The Gift of Truth? How does it work? Is it similar to the truth spell? Girl – answer me.'

Leona gazed into the dragon's eyes. 'Do you want me to help you? Is that it? Do you think I could be useful to you? You have a choice to make, Lord Malum. If you treat me with respect, then I will willingly serve you. If you shackle and torture me, then I will refuse, and you will have to kill me. I have other conditions. Firstly, you must cancel the execution order for Colonel Laimos. You may keep him confined to a cell, but he is not to be beaten or mistreated in any way. Secondly, I must be free to move around the palace, or wherever you decide to take me. You may guard me, but I will not be chained or held in a cell. If you agree to these conditions, then I will tell you about my Gift, and I will use it to assist you.'

The pale red dragon said nothing for a long moment, then he laughed out loud, the sound filling the chamber.

'This girl has some mettle about her,' he said. 'I like her. I agree to your conditions, Leona of Kaugatz, but with one caveat – if you ever betray me or try to feed me falsehoods, then both you and the colonel will be slowly torn limb from limb. Do you accept?'

Leona nodded. 'I do. My Gift works like this – if anyone utters a lie in my presence, I feel a slight tingle in the back of my head. If no lie is spoken, then I feel nothing.'

'I require proof before this agreement can be ratified,' said Malum.

'Were I in your position, I would demand the same,' said Leona. 'Please order the Bullan to release me from this chair, and we can commence with your test.'

'Her arrogance irks me, my lord,' said Lenta.

'Does it?' said Malum. 'I find it rather refreshing. I am too used to humans bowing and kneeling in front of me, their fear in our presence making them seem weak and pathetic. If a human is to speak unpalatable truths to me, then I require her to be bold rather than cowering. Bullan, cut her bonds and allow her to stand.'

Two soldiers moved forwards and removed the cords from her

wrists and ankles. Leona got to her feet, then slightly inclined her head towards the two dragons. Part of her mind was close to panic, but she drew on everything she had learned throughout her short life. Every time her life had been in danger had been another lesson; every time she had been beaten and abused, or left for dead in a filthy alleyway – they had been nothing but a preparation for this moment. She hardened her heart and kept her features still.

'I am ready, my lord,' she said.

'I will utter a few statements,' said Malum, 'and you shall tell me if what I say is the truth or a lie. Understood?'

Leona tilted her head again.

'I have fathered five dragons,' he said.

'Truth.'

'My second-born son died thirty-two years ago.'

'His death is true, but the date was a lie.'

Malum stared at her. 'I killed him myself.'

'Truth.'

'He stole from me.'

'A lie.'

'He dishonoured my name.'

'The truth.'

'We were alone when I slew him.'

'Truth.'

'His last words were, "Forgive me, father".'

'A lie.'

Malum closed his mouth, his eyes burning.

'May I try?' said Lenta.

Malum moved to the side, and Lenta swung her long neck down until her face was a foot in front of Leona.

'Humans are weak and stupid creatures,' the black and white dragon said.

Leona smiled. 'I sensed no lie, my lady. My Gift detects whether or not the speaker believes something to be true or false. In this case, your belief is false, Lady Lenta, but you clearly believe it to be true.' She glanced at Lord Malum. 'Do we have an agreement?'

'Will you willingly serve me?' Malum said. 'Will you stand by my side, pretending to be a humble servant, and point out whenever anyone lies to me?'

'If that is how you wish matters to be arranged,' she said. 'You have my word.'

'Can we trust her?' said Lenta.

Malum said nothing, then he lunged forward, his claws extended, and attacked the five Bullan soldiers inside the hall. His talons sliced through their flesh in seconds, decapitating three, and showering the floor in blood. The colonel flinched in his seat, but Leona did not react, her gaze level, and her features impassive as she watched the slaughter unfold in front of her. The last two Bullan tried to run for the doors, but Malum went after them. He opened his jaws and tore the soldiers in half with his teeth. Lady Lenta began to edge away.

'Do not move, half-sister,' said Malum, his jaws dripping with blood and gore. 'The elimination of these soldiers was a necessary action. This is a secret that we shall not be sharing with anyone – is that understood? If you utter a single word regarding this girl's powers, then I will not hesitate to slay you also.'

'I will not say a thing, my lord,' whimpered Lenta. 'I swear it.'

'Then fetch more soldiers,' Malum said. 'Have them escort Colonel Laimos to a clean cell, where he will be treated with more tenderness than we have shown him in the past.' He glanced at Leona. 'The order to execute you both is hereby rescinded, as we agreed, my Gifted Witch.'

'Thank you, my lord,' said Leona.

'Now,' said the pale red dragon, 'you shall come with me. We will think of a new name for you, and then I shall put you to work. Follow me.'

Leona glanced down at the colonel, who was staring up at her as if seeing her for the first time. A slight smile traced across her lips, then she turned, and followed Lord Malum out of the hall.

CHAPTER 16
GUNST

Off the Gunstian Coast – 7th Lexinch 1588

Lahnos felt someone nudge his shoulder and his fists clenched, ready to lash out.

'It is I who woke you,' whispered Efizel.

Lahnos opened his eyes to the gloom of the ship's hold. His hammock was gently swaying alongside hundreds of others in the cramped space, and the sound of men snoring filled his ears.

'What is it?' he said. 'Are you running another training session tonight?'

'Feel the movement of the ship,' Efizel said, keeping his voice low as the other Zamatan recruits slept around them. 'We have stopped.'

Lahnos focussed his thoughts. The ship was still riding up and down on the waves, but all forward motion had ceased.

'Wake the others,' he said.

Efizel nodded, then he began to shake the shoulders of the men from Fidalaimos who had organised themselves into the same squad as Lahnos and the Bullan. Karl groaned in his hammock, and Efizel placed a hand over his mouth to quieten him.

'What's going on?' muttered another villager, a blacksmith in his late thirties with a swollen eye and bruises across his knuckles.

'We're going up onto the deck,' Lahnos said, as he climbed off the hammock. He helped Efizel to wake up the others in their squad, and cajoled them to their feet. 'The ship has stopped.'

'You go,' said the blacksmith. 'I need more sleep.'

'You know the rules,' said Lahnos. 'We stick together.'

The eight villagers from Fidalaimos that made up the squad joined Lahnos and Efizel on the deck of the hold, then they filed quietly between the long rows of hammocks. A few Zamatans glanced at them as they passed, but no one tried to stop them. Every one of the squad had bruises and cuts from the many fights that had broken out on the packed troopship, but few men were willing to tackle the squad from Fidalaimos when they were all together. Efizel led the way towards the deck. No sergeant had been assigned to their squad, and the Bullan had developed into their unofficial leader, his intelligence matched by his fighting abilities. The Bullan had been involved in more fights than the others, and had once laid out four Zamatan farmers on his own before the rest of the Fidalaimos squad could get to him.

Lahnos felt sweat trickle down his back from the oppressive humidity below deck. Like the odour emanating from so many unwashed men, the heat was a constant presence, along with the pervasive seasickness that had afflicted almost everyone apart from Efizel. The Bullan shoved his way past two men standing by the base of a narrow flight of wooden stairs, and the squad ascended into the open air of the main deck, Lahnos savouring the westerly breeze as he glanced up at the stars in the night sky. The main deck was almost as crowded as the hold, with Zamatan recruits sleeping in any spare space they could find, but several were on their feet, peering over the ship's starboard side towards the north. Efizel led the way to a clear area by the railing, and the squad gathered to either side of him. Most were keeping a wary eye on the other Zamatans, but Lahnos stared out to the north. In the distance, beyond the dozens of other Dominion vessels, a long string of lights was visible on the horizon.

'Is that Gunst?' said Lahnos.

Efizel nodded.

'We're here?' said Karl. 'We've reached Great Gunst?'

'No,' said Efizel. 'The city of Great Gunst lies forty miles north of the coastline, in the loop of a wide river. I do not know where we are, but if the fleet is going to attack Great Gunst, then the place ahead of us might be Toraq – the port city that serves the Gunstian capital.'

'Toraq?' said Lahnos. 'I've never heard of it.'

'That does not surprise me,' said Efizel. 'The Gunstian Empire contains dozens of large cities, but their names are almost unknown in the Dominion. Everyone has heard of Great Gunst, but that is as far as their knowledge goes.'

Karl narrowed his eyes. 'Then how do you know?'

'The men in my regiment attended many lessons on the history and geography of Gunst, my friend,' said the Bullan; 'just as we learned about Irlan and Elso; and yes – even the Serpent Isle.'

'We've spent over twenty days on this damned boat,' said Karl, 'and you haven't told us a thing about Gunst.'

'You are correct, my friend,' said Efizel. 'We have had little time together, and I wished to concentrate on how to keep us all alive in combat. Adhering as a team was of more value than wasting time on geography; and learning how to handle a crossbow correctly was of more benefit than worrying about what lay before us.'

'Well, now that we're here,' said the blacksmith, 'what can you tell us?'

Efizel glanced into the north. A faint light in the eastern sky presaged the dawn, and the coastline was becoming visible as a faint line on the horizon.

'There are large mountain chains to the north-east and south-west of here, but this part of Gunst is flat and fertile. Several great rivers flow down from the mountains, and the Gunstian cities cluster around their banks. Great Gunst, though, is no ordinary city – it is the largest settlement on Athumia, bigger than any city in Aucteran. Like the rest of the Empire, Great Gunst is ruled by the Gifted – who govern as a powerful, close-knit aristocracy, united by their faith in Chadura, whom they believe to be the one true god of the universe. No other religions are permitted, and it is for humans only. The Gunstians perceive dragons and my own kinsfolk to be demons, and believe that we have no immortal soul to take us into the hereafter.'

'Do the Gunstians believe in an afterlife?' said Karl.

'They do but, as the Bullan said, it's only for humans,' Lahnos muttered. 'Well, some humans – the ones who believe in their god. My horns exclude me from their divine plan. Just like the serpent-worshipping monks on Zamata, they see the part-Bullan as demonic. Neither of the religions of this world has a place for people like me.'

'There is only one Gunstian family living in Fidalaimos,' said a villager; 'and they keep quiet about their beliefs.'

Efizel eyed the squad. 'Raise your hand if you can speak any Gunstian.'

Lahnos and three of the villagers lifted their right hands.

'Can any of you read it, too?'

Lahnos kept his hand raised, but the other villagers lowered their arms.

Karl stared at him. 'You can read Gunstian?'

'Not as well as I can read the Divine Tongue,' Lahnos said, 'but yes, a bit. I lived in Kaugatz for four years, brother, and that's where the majority of those with Gunstian heritage dwell. You had to understand some of what they were saying and writing; otherwise their merchants would take advantage of you. I also needed to know what they were calling me behind my back.'

'Make no mistake,' said Efizel; 'if the Gunstians capture me or Corporal Lahnos, they will kill us immediately.'

'What about the rest of us?' said a villager.

'That depends,' said Efizel. 'They are committed to converting every human on Athumia to their religion, so if you were prepared to kneel before their god and join their faith, then they might allow you to live.'

'This Chadura,' said the blacksmith; 'is he a good god?'

'She is the source of all goodness, according to the Gunstians,' said Efizel; 'and they believe that she bestowed the Gifts upon the people of

Athumia. They also believe that she created this world.' He smiled. 'And they are correct.'

'What?' said Karl. 'Do you believe in their religion?'

'No,' said Efizel, 'but it has been clear to Dominion scholars for many years that *Chadura* is an ancient corruption of *Theodora* – the same god worshipped by the dragons.'

'I've heard of Theodora, but only because of the Gifts,' said Lahnos. 'I thought the dragons also believed in someone called Nathaniel. That's what you told me.'

'Nathaniel and Theodora are but two of the old pantheon of ancient gods worshipped by the dragons. Theodora created Athumia, but it was Nathaniel who brought King Gahad to this world.'

'It's complicated enough having to worship the damn dragons,' muttered a villager. 'Now you're saying that the dragons worship their own gods?'

'It's all a hoax,' said Lahnos; 'all of it. The dragons aren't gods, and these so-called ancient gods are just bullshit legends.'

'Now you can see why I did not waste time on this during the voyage,' said Efizel. 'What use will any of this knowledge be when we are face to face with the Gunstian army?'

Karl pointed towards another troopship a hundred yards off their starboard flank. 'Look. Signal lights.'

The others turned, and Lahnos gazed out over the dark waters, his eyes watching as a large lamp flickered on and off in a steady rhythm.

'The fleet is preparing to move,' said Efizel. 'Our ship is being ordered to get into line.'

'We're... attacking?' said a young villager.

'It appears so,' said the Bullan. 'We should go below, and ensure that we have all the equipment we need before the others awaken and steal it. Boots are the priority, followed by rations and water. Load up with everything you can get your hands on.'

'What about the crossbows we hid under the deck slats?' said Lahnos.

'Take half the squad with you and collect them, too, corporal,' said

Efizel; 'while I lead the other half to get our equipment. Once we have everything, assemble on the main deck by the starboard bow.'

Lahnos watched as the squad obeyed Efizel without question. They had loathed the Bullan when they had first met him, but after five days together in the camp outside Kaugatz, followed by twenty-one days at sea, they had grown to understand that he was their best chance of surviving what was to come. The villagers still disliked him, but that didn't matter; they trusted him. In all that time, the Dominion had made no attempt to train their new recruits, and had been miserly when it had come to distributing uniforms, weapons and everything else needed for the campaign. While the Aucterian soldiers had the best equipment, the Zamatans had been left with the scraps, and several were still dressed in the same civilian clothes they had been wearing when rounded up by the Bullan regiments.

Lahnos led four men towards the bow of the ship, as the Aucterian sailors on board began following the orders relayed by the signal lamp. The sailors ignored the five Zamatans, as they had for the entire voyage. One of the sails was raised, and the large capstan was turned, lifting the forward anchor from the depths, its chain clanking and grinding. Lahnos and the four villagers reached the bow hatch, and they descended into the stuffy darkness of the hold. They squeezed past the closed galley, and came to a part of the ship where the sloping planks of the bow curved, leaving a narrow space that had been filled with empty water barrels. Lahnos nodded to the blacksmith, who grunted. The blacksmith had no military experience but, other than Efizel, he was the strongest man in the squad. He crouched down and shifted two of the massive barrels, then Lahnos stooped and began to prise up a few loose deck slats, while the three other men formed a line behind him to block anyone from seeing what he was doing. When the hole was large enough, Lahnos reached in and removed a large bundle that had been wrapped in waterproof leathers. He untied a cord, laid the bundle out in front of his knees, and gazed at the three crossbows, and several packets of bolts. He passed two bows to the blacksmith, who took the straps and swung them over his broad shoulders, then he leaned the third against the bulkhead as he quickly replaced the deck slats. He then stood, the top of his horns almost snagging on the low ceiling, and handed the last crossbow to another villager, a tall quiet man called Jancke, who had shown the most promise in the crossbow drills that Efizel had put them through.

Lahnos pointed towards the bow hatch, and they began to move off.

'Where did you find those, horned freak?' came a low voice.

The five men turned, and saw a group of Zamatans watching them from the thick shadows of the hold. The man who had spoken was the leader of a group from Wayston, and they had frequently clashed with the villagers from Fidalaimos.

'You stole them, I'd guess,' the man went on.

'What's it to you?' said Lahnos. 'Is it my fault you're too stupid to get any weapons for yourselves?'

'The Dominion will give us weapons when we land,' said another man from Wayston. 'They won't throw us into a battle with no weapons.'

'I hope you're right,' said Lahnos, 'but judging by the way they've treated us so far, I wouldn't count on it.'

'We're moving again,' said another man, his eyes darting around. 'Why are we moving again?'

'Give us those crossbows,' said the Wayston group's leader. 'I'm a sergeant, and you're a corporal. You have to do as I say.'

Lahnos smiled. 'If you want them, sergeant, come and get them.'

'This is your last chance,' said the Wayston sergeant. 'Hand them over.'

'Piss off, you wankers,' the blacksmith grunted, as he stepped forward to stand next to Lahnos. He pulled one of the crossbows from over his shoulder and held it like a club.

The sergeant narrowed his eyes, then he laughed as if unconcerned. 'I bet none of you even know how to use one of those things.'

Lahnos shrugged, then he began to lead his squad to the stairs. The Wayston group eyed them, but none tried to stop them.

'Remember whose side you're on when we land, boy,' the sergeant shouted.

Lahnos climbed the stairs to the deck, then he watched as the four villagers came up after him.

'That lad from Wayston is scared,' said the blacksmith. 'You could see it in his eyes.'

Lahnos said nothing.

'And I'm not talking about us,' the blacksmith went on. 'It's not us that's frightening him; it's what we're about to be walking into.' He shook his head. 'If the Dominion was going to arm us, they would have trained us first.'

One of the younger villagers swallowed. 'We're going to be slaughtered, aren't we?'

'Not if we stick together,' said Lahnos. 'Remember everything that our Bullan has told us. Listen; from now on, we'll refer to the Bullan as *sergeant*, got it?'

'But he hasn't been made into a sergeant,' said the villager.

'So? What difference does it make? We had to organise ourselves into our own squad; the Dominion doesn't give a shit about the chain of command, not in the Zamatan regiments.'

They turned as Efizel and the other four members of the squad approached along the port railing.

'We got the crossbows, sergeant,' said Lahnos.

The Bullan raised an eyebrow. 'Thank you, corporal, but I... I am not...'

'Tough shit, sergeant,' said Lahnos. 'You are now.' He gazed out at the brightening sky. Dozens of destroyers and troopships were on the move, sailing north towards the coastline.

'Corporal Lahnos is right, sergeant,' said the blacksmith. 'Will you lead us?'

Efizel lowered his gaze.

'You have to say yes,' said Jancke. 'If you don't tell us what to do, we won't last an hour when we... when we...'

'I will do it,' said Efizel; 'but you must agree to follow my orders without question. If I tell you to run, we run; if I tell you to fight, we fight.'

Lahnos glanced at the squad. 'You are the best chance we have, sergeant.'

Efizel's stern expression almost cracked for a moment. 'I will do what I can to get us all through this. But if I fall in battle, then Corporal Lahnos is the next in command. You must also agree to follow him as you followed me.'

Karl emitted a grim laugh. 'Fine, but make sure you don't get killed, sergeant.'

The blacksmith offered Efizel one of his crossbows and a packet of bolts.

'Thank you,' said the Bullan, 'but give it to Karl – he will need it more than I.'

Karl took the weapon and shouldered the strap, then the Fidalaimos squad stared at the approaching coastline. A huge dragon carrier was sailing to the right of the troopships, and three dragons were in the air above it, circling over that portion of the great fleet.

'Where is the Imperial Gunstian navy?' said the blacksmith. 'Why aren't they defending their coast?'

'I suspect that their main fleet is behind us to the east,' said Efizel. 'I think that we slipped into the Great Bay of Gunst before they could catch us, and that now they will be blocking our escape, should we be defeated here. As for their other vessels, I imagine that they will have retreated out of range of the dragon carriers.'

The buildings of the city in front of them grew visible in the growing light, and then large twin breakwaters of a harbour emerged from the gloom.

'This is Toraq,' said Efizel. 'I am sure of that now. Do you see the tall spire flanked by domes? That is a temple of Chadura. But I see no masts in the harbour.'

'Are they expecting us?' said a villager.

'Yes. The Gunstians will have been aware of our presence since we entered the Great Bay – their outposts there will have seen the fleet and sent messengers to the capital.'

The main deck of the troopship became more crowded as the coastline got nearer, and hundreds of Zamatans were watching in silence. Most were unshaven, unwashed, and looked as far from a disciplined army as Lahnos could imagine.

'Will Zamata ever recover from this?' he said. 'If we are slaughtered, then what will happen to the women and children left on the island?'

Efizel said nothing.

'This was the Dominion's plan all along,' muttered the blacksmith. 'At one stroke, the menfolk of Zamata will be destroyed.'

Karl shook his head. 'The Dominion wouldn't do that to us. You're exaggerating.'

'Concentrate on staying alive,' said Efizel.

One of the younger villagers threw up over the side of the troopship, and Lahnos began to wish that he had a weapon in his hands. Above them, more dragons appeared in the sky, ascending from the eight huge carriers scattered among the fleet. The bow of the troopship dipped into a wave, and the Zamatans on deck were sprayed by seawater. On their port side, another troopship was edging closer to them, and Lahnos glanced over at its deck, which was also crowded with men. Among them, Lahnos could make out several with horns.

'Part-Bullan,' he said, pointing.

'They must be from the Kaugatz round-ups,' said Efizel.

'Do you wish you were with your own kind, brother?' said Karl.

'I am from Fidalaimos,' Lahnos said. 'This squad is my own kind.'

Karl shook his head and snorted. 'You abandoned Fidalaimos years ago.'

'I didn't abandon it,' snapped Lahnos; 'it drove me out. You drove me out. You made me unwelcome in my own village.'

A few of the squad looked away.

'Forget the past,' said Efizel. 'None of that matters now. All that matters is the present. We will fight for each other, and we will die for each other.'

With the coastline less than a mile away, the destroyers and dragon carriers in the fleet began to slow and turn, while the troopships kept on in a straight line, heading directly for the harbour of Toraq. The dragons in the cloudy sky above them wheeled and banked, then over two dozen split away from the others and soared towards the north.

'There they go,' said Efizel. 'The invasion is about to begin. Whether you love or hate the dragons, for our sakes let us hope that they prevail.'

The dragons climbed to a high altitude, until they had diminished to tiny specks in the sky, then, when they were above the city of Toraq, they plummeted downwards, their great wings folded in as they dived. Every eye on the troopship followed them, and the Zamatans on the deck hushed as they watched. When the dragons were a hundred yards over the city, a great sweep of flames erupted from their jaws, and the harbour front exploded in an inferno. The dragons peeled off into two columns, one to the east and the other to the west, but their flames were unceasing, and the conflagration spread over the high buildings of the city. The tall temple was engulfed, its domes cracking and its spire collapsing into the smoke and flames.

'I see no people,' said Efizel, his eyes squinting into the distance. 'There are no Gunstians on the ground. The harbour is deserted.'

'Maybe they evacuated the civilians,' said Lahnos.

'Or they fled in terror,' said Karl. 'The dragons are unstoppable.'

The sky darkened as smoke rose from the burning city. The dragons banked again, sending more flames down into the districts to the north of the harbour. An old castle stood upon a low ridge on the western flank of the city, and six dragons bathed the stone battlements in fire. The ancient keep crumbled, its massive blocks falling amid the intense heat with a crash of noise that reached the troopships. The entrance to the harbour was wide, but the troopships began to bunch together as each tried to manoeuvre past the long breakwaters. The lead troopship sailed on, then it slowed to a halt in a grinding of metal against wood.

'The harbour entrance has a chain,' said Efizel.

The other troopships tried to slow, the sailors pulling down the sails, but over a dozen of them were soon caught up against the huge, thick chain that stretched underwater between the two breakwaters, while the others clustered close behind them. Several collided with each other in the confusion and one capsized, the men on board spilling into the bay. Gunstian soldiers emerged from behind the walls of a series of low towers built along the breakwaters, and crossbow bolts spat out from their bows, peppering the men on the closest troopships. A huge ballista was hauled out from where it had been hidden, and was aimed at the bow of a troopship. The yard-long steel bolt was barbed at the end, and it was attached to a long chain. It loosed, smashing through the wooden bow of the troopship, then the chain began to be hauled back. The barbs ripped a large hole in the bow as the bolt was dragged out, and the troopship sank within seconds, the men trapped within screaming as it disappeared beneath the waves.

Two dragons soared towards the chaos at the mouth of the harbour, but as they swooped down, both howled in agony, and dropped like stones from the sky. One fell into the calm waters of the harbour basin, but the other crashed into the cluster of bobbing troopships, sending another two to the bottom of the bay in an explosion of water.

The Zamatans on Lahnos's troopship stared, their mouths falling open at the sight. Their troopship was in the centre of the others, and was unable to move in any direction. More dragons soared overhead, while another skimmed low over the bay, then swooped up at the last moment, sending a great plume of fire over the left-hand breakwater. Dozens of Gunstians were incinerated, and the huge ballista was reduced to ash and glowing-hot fragments of metal. A green dragon soared down from the sky. Its forelimbs ducked under the surface of the water, clutched hold of the chain, then the dragon ascended. One of the entangled troopships rose up with it, then it fell, crashing back down into the water as the dragon ripped the chain in two. At once, the troopships began to advance again, and the first few broke into the harbour basin, their sails raised. On the right-hand breakwater, Gunstians were still loosing their crossbows, striking every troopship that passed, but Lahnos's vessel was shielded by another boat close to its starboard flank, and they passed into the basin unscathed. The green dragon turned its attention to the right breakwater, and sprayed it with flames until every Gunstian soldier there was dead or had fled in disarray.

Lahnos and the others turned their gazes back towards the city. The harbour front buildings were burning, and the rising sun was obscured by the sheets of thick smoke. After the bottleneck at the entrance, the troopships spread out again, each heading for a different part of the huge harbour. Amid the gusting, billowing smoke, Lahnos lost sight of the dragons overhead, and he focussed on the long pier looming in front of his troopship.

A Dominion naval officer appeared on deck, flanked by armed sailors.

'Prepare to disembark!' the officer cried.

The Zamatans on the deck stared at him in anger and disbelief.

'We have no weapons!' one cried.

'You will collect weapons discarded by the dead and fleeing Gunstians,' the officer said. 'You shall have the honour of being among the first soldiers of the invasion to step onto Gunstian soil. Advance into the city and eliminate all opposition. No quarter is to be shown.' He signalled to a sailor. 'Bring us in.'

The sails were lowered again, and the bow of the troopship swung round as its starboard flank bumped up against the long pier. Gangways were fixed in place, but none of the Zamatans on the main deck moved.

'Disembark!' cried the naval officer.

Efizel began shoving the squad towards the gangway. 'Follow me!' he roared.

Lahnos grabbed Karl by the arm and half-dragged his brother along as the squad started to run after the Bullan soldier. Efizel raced over the gangway and onto the wooden pier, the squad right behind him. Seeing their example, the other Zamatans on board hurried to join them. The Fidalaimos squad charged down the long pier with Efizel at their head. At the end of the pier was a wide stone quayside, and then the row of burning buildings. A huge warehouse was among the few structures not aflame, and Efizel led the squad towards it. They reached a tall wooden door, and Efizel pushed it open. Inside, the huge warehouse was empty, its contents stripped, leaving only a few broken crates and fragments of pottery scattered across the vast floor-space. Efizel ushered the squad inside, then they turned and gazed out over the harbour. Dozens of troopships were disgorging the Zamatan regiments into the city, while any that had been emptied were already sailing back towards the main fleet. Hundreds of disorientated Zamatans were moving through the harbour, while thousands more were awaiting their turn to disembark.

'We are the first wave,' said the Bullan soldier. 'Our purpose is clear – if this is a trap, then we are to draw out the city's defenders, so that the dragons can deal with them before the regular army makes its landing.'

The blacksmith grunted. 'I knew it. We are the bait.'

'What now, sergeant?' said Jancke.

'We made it off the boat alive,' said Efizel, 'and we shall now carry out the orders given to us. We shall advance through the city, and secure as much of it as we can before the rest of the army lands. Our priority is to find water, food and then weapons, in that order. If we encounter armed resistance, we shall hold our position but not attack – is that clear?'

The squad nodded.

'Corporal Lahnos,' Efizel said, 'take your half-squad to the left. I shall proceed to the right with the others, and we shall meet at the far end of the warehouse.'

'Yes, sergeant,' said Lahnos. He signalled to his four men, and they hurried off, following the wall of the dark warehouse to their left. They came to the corner of the building, and Lahnos glanced back at the four men following him.

'Smithy,' he said.

'Yes, corporal?' grunted the blacksmith.

Lahnos gave him a wry smile. 'Load your damned crossbow, and shoot anyone who speaks Gunstian.'

CHAPTER 17
LADY TAKRI

Igatz, Serpent Isle – 8th Lexinch 1588

'Ensure that you have packed everything you need,' Captain Cisca said. 'If you are late, the carriages won't wait for you.'

The three young lieutenants saluted, then they rushed off to their quarters to collect their bags. Cisca glanced at two servants, who picked up her luggage.

'Load that onto the rear wagon with the other baggage,' Cisca said; 'and be careful.'

'Yes, ma'am,' said one, then the two servants began to make their way to the side door of the Dragon Palace.

Cisca glanced at the white marble walls and ceiling. She was glad to be going, and wouldn't miss the palace; the memories of her captivity with Lord Kheran within its walls were still strong, and she was looking forward to breathing in the cool mountain air. The summer heat in Igatz had become oppressive, and she was tired of having to change her clothes every few hours. She wiped the sweat from her forehead, and strode along the passageway. She passed a few Bullan on guard duty and entered the huge, circular audience hall, where she bowed low before Lord Malum.

'My lord,' she said, 'the Dragon Corps officers are almost ready to depart. Shall we leave before you set off, so that we are in our new location to greet you?'

'No,' said Malum. 'I shall fly to the monastery within the hour, taking Ladies Lenta and Macsin, and Lord Rylan with me. It will be sunset before you and the other humans arrive, and I do not wish to fly in the dark.'

Cisca bowed again, being careful not to look at the young woman standing close to Lord Malum's forelimbs.

'As you will, my lord,' Cisca said. 'Might I enquire what is to be done with the two prisoners who remain in the dungeons?'

'Colonel Laimos shall be accompanying us,' said Lord Malum. 'I am sure the monks will find him appropriate accommodation.'

'And Major Lyla, my lord?'

'Is she still alive?' said the pale red dragon. 'I admit, I had almost forgotten about her.'

'She is alive, my lord,' said Cisca.

Lord Malum shifted a little, as though he was uncomfortable. 'I am minded to bring her along. I feel a touch of regret at how I manipulated her into betraying herself. I was exceedingly angry when she interrupted my bath, and perhaps I was unkind. What do you advise, Takri?'

The young woman standing by his forelimbs smiled. 'Is Major Lyla a threat to your rule, my lord?'

'Hardly,' said the dragon. 'She merely possesses a few unsavoury views.'

'Then perhaps she might still be of some use to you, my lord.'

'Thank you, Takri,' said the dragon; 'I shall accept your advice. Captain Cisca, you shall organise the transport of both Colonel Laimos and Major Lyla to Zamata Gataza. My servant Takri shall also be coming with us, and I want you to ensure that she is well guarded on the journey. If anything happens to her, I shall hold you responsible. Oh, and while I am on the subject, say nothing to either prisoner about Takri. Is that understood?'

'Yes, my lord,' said Cisca, bowing again.

'You shall depart in one hour from now,' said Malum, 'and I shall see you in the monastery when you arrive. Dismissed.'

Cisca backed away, then left the audience hall. She wondered what Lord Malum would do if he discovered that she recognised his new servant, the one who had never left his side since she had suddenly appeared in the palace a few weeks previously. The first time Cisca had witnessed her in the presence of the pale red dragon, she had almost called her Leona, and was about to ask why a rebel was now seemingly a trusted advisor to the Governor of the Serpent Isle; but then Lord Malum had introduced her as Takri, and had insisted that no questions be asked about her past.

Cisca frowned as she made her way to the dungeons. Had Leona been a Dominion spy throughout the entire uprising? Was she really an agent called Takri? Cisca had seen her three times before – at a dance in the palace, where they had briefly chatted, and then when Colonel Laimos had attended an audience with Lord Kheran; and once when the young woman had been acting as the colonel's negotiator outside Tsallon Anura. Each time, she had behaved as though she was loyal to the Zamatan cause. Had it all been an act? If not, if she really was a dangerous rebel, then how had she insinuated herself into a position as Lord Malum's advisor? Cisca had kept all such thoughts to herself, and had been careful not to let her expression waver in the presence of the pale red dragon, lest he decide to play the game of truth with her.

She passed by more Bullan soldiers, and descended the stairs to the palace basement. She made her way to the isolated dungeon wing, and ordered the soldiers on duty to bring the two prisoners before her. The Bullan saluted, then they disappeared through a series of doors at the end of the hallway. Major Lyla was brought out first, her chains clanking as she trudged along the stone floor. Cisca bit back her sympathy at Lyla's condition. The young major had been incarcerated within her cell for twenty-two days, and she had lost weight in that time, and her clothes and hair stank.

Lyla narrowed her tired eyes. 'Cisca?' she said, her tone flat. 'What a lovely surprise. Am I to die this day?'

'No, ma'am,' said Cisca. 'Lord Malum has decided to move his court up to the monastery of Zamata Gataza to escape the summer heat, and you are to come along with us.'

Lyla snorted. 'That stupid lizard. Why should I care what...?'

'Please stop, ma'am,' said Cisca. 'The Governor has voiced his regret at your treatment. He thinks it was unkind. If you... if you were to show some remorse...'

'Then what?'

'He might release you.'

Lyla's back straightened a little. 'Oh.'

'As a friend,' said Cisca, 'I beg that you try not to antagonise Lord Malum.'

'You want me to behave myself?' said Lyla. 'To save my life, I suppose I could do that. Do I owe you my thanks for this turn of events?'

'The Governor refused to speak to me about you. Well, until today, when I reminded him that you were still languishing in the dungeons.'

She paused as Bullan soldiers led Colonel Laimos out of another door. Unlike the major, Colonel Laimos seemed rested and well-fed, and he was wearing simple but clean clothes, with a patch covering his right eye socket. Major Lyla frowned at him.

'It seems that rebels are better treated than Dragon Corps officers in these parts,' she said.

Friel stared at her with his one good eye, then he turned to Cisca. 'Where is Leona?'

'Good question,' said Lyla. 'Has the poor girl been executed?'

'How do you know Leona?' said Friel.

'She was in the cell next to mine, and I...'

'Silence,' said Cisca. 'You are not to utter another word about Leona of Kaugatz. If you do, then I will instruct the Bullan to place you back into your cells, and you can sweat out the summer here.'

Friel closed his mouth at once, as if he realised what had occurred, but Lyla crinkled her brow in confusion.

'We are going to Zamata Gataza for the fresh mountain air,' Cisca went on. She nodded to the Bullan soldiers. 'Take them to the carriages in front of the palace, but ensure they travel separately. They must speak to no one on the way.'

The Bullan saluted then they began to escort the two prisoners out of the dungeon wing. Cisca hesitated, then strode after them.

'I require a quiet word with Major Lyla first,' she said. 'Alone.'

The Bullan nodded, and led Colonel Laimos to the end of the passageway, where they waited out of earshot.

'Why all the subterfuge?' said Lyla.

Cisca leaned in close. 'I meant what I said before. Please, Lyla, you must listen to me. Never mention Leona's name again. If you see a woman in Lord Malum's presence who looks like her, pretend that you do not recognise her.'

'What?'

'I can't explain what's happening,' said Cisca, 'because I don't understand it; but you have to trust me.'

'And what if... this woman greets me as an old friend?'

'She won't,' said Cisca. 'Let's go.'

Lyla eyed Cisca for a moment, then she trudged away, her chains clanking off the stone floor.

Half an hour later, Cisca was standing outside the front of the Dragon Palace. Her three lieutenants had loaded their luggage onto the baggage wagon, and were occupying one of the dozen carriages that were lined up on the gravel driveway. Lyla and Friel Laimos had also boarded their own carriages, each with two Bullan soldiers to guard them, while a collection of army officer and servants were taking up the others. Only one carriage remained empty, and Cisca felt her anxiety increase as she waited for Takri to emerge from the palace. She had been ordered to protect the young woman, and had decided that the best way to do that was to sit with her for the journey to Mount Hodzulat. Over two hundred Bullan were standing by the carriages, waiting for the command to leave, and Cisca sweated in the glaring sunshine on the palace steps, her stomach in knots.

'Were you waiting for me, Captain?'

Cisca turned, and saw Takri step out from the palace. She was wearing loose white clothes that flowed to just above the sandals on her feet, and a golden necklace embedded with diamonds was around her slender neck.

Cisca saluted. 'Yes, ma'am. This way, if you please.'

'Thank you,' said Takri.

Cisca led her to the empty carriage, and assisted the young woman as she climbed up into her seat.

'Ensure that this carriage is well-protected,' Cisca said to the Bullan officer on duty. 'If there is any trouble on the journey, the safety of the young woman in this carriage shall be your priority.'

'Yes, ma'am,' said the Bullan officer.

Cisca clambered into the carriage and sat down opposite Takri. The Bullan closed the carriage door, then a whistle sounded, and the convoy moved off. The carriages and wagons were pulled through the gardens in front of the palace, while the Bullan marched on either flank.

'I am looking forward to the mountain air,' said Takri, as she gazed out of the window. 'How about you, Captain?'

'Yes, ma'am,' said Cisca, feeling the tension in her stomach increase. She should have placed Bullan in the carriage, she realised. How was she going to keep up the charade for the entire journey?

'I must say,' said Takri, 'that you have been very discreet.'

'Ma'am?'

'Neither of us are stupid, Captain. Might I call you Cisca?'

'If you wish, ma'am.'

'Where is Colonel Laimos?'

'He is in the third carriage from the front, ma'am; and Major Lyla is in the one behind that.'

'Have you been to Zamata Gataza before?'

'No, ma'am.'

'Neither have I, although I have always wanted to see it. This was actually my idea. The humidity was clearly bothering Lord Malum, and as soon as the first supply convoy from Aucteran had come and gone, I suggested that we move the entire court to Mount Hodzulat for the rest of the summer.'

Cisca glanced out of the window. 'Yes, ma'am.'

Takri sighed. 'Is the whole journey going to be like this? Are you going to continue to pretend that you don't know who I am?'

'I... uh... You are called Takri, and you work for Lord Malum. That is all I know, ma'am.'

The young woman laughed, then she leaned forward. 'I won't tell if you don't. Lord Malum has no idea that we have met before. If he realised that you knew me, then he would kill you, just as he killed five Bullan soldiers who happened to be in the wrong place at the wrong time. He is a little protective of me, as you might have gathered.'

Cisca stared at her. 'I thought I knew who you were, ma'am, but it seems I was mistaken.'

Takri said nothing, then she sat back in her seat, her expression guarded. 'How is Major Lyla?'

'Alive, ma'am,' said Cisca. 'I informed her of Lord Malum's change of mind. Thank you for speaking up for her.'

'She hardly deserves to die for saying a few silly things under the influence of the truth spell.'

Cisca gazed out of the window as the streets of Igatz rolled past, unsure of what to say. Was she being tested?

Takri eyed her. 'What did you say to Lyla about me when you released the major from her cell?'

'Nothing, ma'am.'

Takri laughed. 'Come on; do you expect me to believe that?'

'I... uh... I warned her to say nothing about you. Was that wrong of me, ma'am?'

'Not necessarily. Tell me, Cisca – do you agree with any of the things that Lyla said about the dragons?'

Cisca swallowed. 'No, ma'am.'

Takri shook her head. 'Are you sure? Tell me that you think the dragons are wise and noble; that you believe them to be infallible gods.'

'I do believe that; I believe all of it, ma'am.'

'Why are you lying to me?'

Cisca brushed the sweat from her forehead. 'I am not lying, ma'am.'

'I think Bauchlie has a crush on you – did you know that?'

Cisca almost opened the door and jumped out of the carriage. Her hands started to shake.

'Are those feelings mutual, Cisca?' Takri said.

'No! I hate Bauchlie. He is a vile criminal.'

Takri's mouth opened, her eyes alive with a mischievous joy. 'Oh dear. You're not in love with him, are you?'

'No. I swear it. Please, ma'am, I am completely loyal to the Dominion.'

Takri rubbed the back of her neck. 'I am getting a headache from all of the lies you have just told me. Perhaps it would be better if you stopped talking for a while. You have given me much to think about.'

'Are... are you going to mention this to Lord Malum?'

Takri smiled. 'Of course not. If I did that, he would rip your head off. Try to avoid any situations where he or any of the other dragons might decide to use the truth spell on you. You wouldn't last two minutes. Now, I think I might have a little nap.'

Takri leaned back and closed her eyes. Cisca trembled with fear, her heart racing as she stared at the young woman opposite her. Her life was in Takri's hands, of that there was no doubt. And how had she known about Bauchlie? Cisca choked back the tears that threatened to overwhelm her, and tried to breathe.

The journey to the western ferry terminal south of Handshore seemed to take an age to Cisca. Takri, or Leona, or whoever she was, fell asleep as if she had no worries in the world, while Cisca felt as though she was on the verge of a complete breakdown. No one disembarked from the carriages as they were pulled onto the flat-bottomed ferry, and the voyage across the Cyasarta did nothing to calm her nerves. And then they were off again, crossing the southern portion of Kaugatz. It was strange to see no men out in the streets, and the local women were staring at the fine carriages with venom in their eyes, as if they would like to do nothing better than tear the occupants to pieces with their bare hands. The ferry from Kaugatz was interrupted by the sight of the four dragons from the Dragon Palace flying low overhead. Lord Malum was in the lead, followed by Lady Macsin, while Lady Lenta and Lord Rylan were at the rear. The Bullan soldiers gazed up at the sight from the deck of the ferry, and Cisca leaned out of the window to look up as the gods soared past. They banked a little to the south-west, heading for the tall mountain peak that loomed on the horizon.

As a dragon flew, it was five miles from the ferry terminal to the monastery of Zamata Gataza, but the way by road was much longer, and the horses toiled as they pulled the line of carriages up the steep slope of Mount Hodzulat. The road switched back and forth, leaving the flat wheat fields behind as it climbed up to the ancient monastery.

Zamata Gataza faced east, so that the monks could gaze in the direction of Inopei, the home of the serpent gods. The structure was over a dozen storeys high, and seemed to cling on to the mountainside as if held there by the power of prayer alone. At its base was a large courtyard surrounded by a collection of squat buildings, while a temple was perched on the top floor, its three towers almost hidden by the evening shadows cast by the mountain. The air cooled as they climbed, and Cisca was just starting to relax when Takri opened her eyes.

'Are we there?' she said.

'Yes, ma'am,' said Cisca. 'We shall be arriving in a few minutes.'

'I assume that the dragons got here hours ago?'

'I believe so, ma'am, although I have yet to see them in the vicinity of the monastery.'

Takri stretched her arms out and yawned. 'I may have a few jobs for you to do, Cisca,' she said. 'I trust that you have no objections?'

'I am happy to serve, ma'am.'

'I'm glad to hear it.'

They glanced out of the window as the carriages pulled into the courtyard. Over a dozen monks were arranged outside to greet them, along with several groups of servants. The Bullan soldiers formed up in front of their officers, who then assigned them to guard the various entrances and high points of the monastery, while the monks studiously ignored them. The convoy came to a halt, and a soldier opened the door of the carriage where Cisca and Takri were sitting.

'Lord Malum is awaiting you both, ma'am, Captain,' he said.

'Thank you for getting us here safely,' said Takri.

The soldier bowed his head, then helped Takri step down from the carriage. Cisca made her own way down to the cobbled ground of the courtyard, and then a group of soldiers surrounded them and escorted them towards the waiting monks.

'Introduce me,' Takri whispered, as they approached the steps.

Cisca forced a smile on to her lips. 'Good evening, brothers of Zamata Gataza. May I please introduce Lady Takri, a close adviser to the blessed Governor Lord Malum?'

The monks bowed.

'We are delighted to welcome you to our humble monastery, Lady Takri,' said one. 'Lord Malum has requested that we treat you with all respect. Would you like us to show you to your new quarters? They have a balcony with an excellent view of the sunrise. Or perhaps you are hungry after your long journey?'

'Thank you,' said Takri, 'but first I think I will personally inform Lord Malum that I have arrived. Before that, however, I wish you to know that the convoy is carrying two prisoners – Colonel Laimos of the uprising, and Major Lyla of the Dragon Corps. The Bullan will be escorting them out of their carriages shortly. They are to be kept isolated from the other occupants of Zamata Gataza, but please ensure that they are well-treated. Is that understood?'

'Yes, my lady,' said the monk.

Takri gestured to Cisca. 'And this is Captain Cisca, acting commander of the Dragon Corps upon the Serpent Isle. I would be grateful if you could find her and her three young lieutenants comfortable quarters within the monastery. Captain Cisca has proved herself to be of great service to the Dominion.'

'We would be delighted to provide hospitality to all officers from the Dragon Corps, my lady.'

Takri smiled. 'Please show me to where Lord Malum and the other dragons have gathered. Cisca, you shall accompany me.'

The monks bowed again, then four of them led Takri and Cisca into the ground floor of the monastery. Lamps had been lit to illuminate the musty old chambers, and the four monks gestured towards a set of stairs that descended into the gloom.

'There are ancient mines and tunnels excavated under the monastery complex, my lady,' said one, 'and they are large enough to accommodate a dozen dragons. This, of course, is the entrance used by us mere humans – the dragons can enter and exit via a large cavern that faces the south. We have tried our best to make the caverns as comfortable as possible for our blessed visitors.'

Takri nodded. 'I am sure you have, noble brothers.'

They came to the bottom of the stairs and walked along a narrow tunnel to a thick wooden door. One of the monks eased it open, and they strode into a huge open space burrowed out of the rock of the mountain. Lamps hung from chains attached to the ceiling, while rugs and flowers had been strewn across the floor. On the left of the chamber, close to a massive archway, the four dragons who had left Igatz earlier that day were standing in a line, while dozens of monks were kneeling before them. One of them was clad in purple robes rather than the usual brown, and he was the only one who was not down on his knees. Around his neck hung a thick gold chain, at the bottom of which was a broad gilt medallion, encrusted with jewels that seemed to shimmer with their own light.

The dragons turned their heads as the monks led Cisca and Takri into the cavern.

'Ah, there you are, Takri,' said Malum. 'I was wondering when you would arrive. How was the journey?'

'I found it quite relaxing, my lord,' said Takri, bowing. 'Captain Cisca was a gracious and helpful companion.'

'Good, good,' said the pale red dragon. 'Come and stand by my side. Captain Cisca, you may also join us.'

'Thank you, my lord,' said Cisca, as her heart began to pound again. One word from Takri was all it would take, and her head would be torn from her shoulders. She swallowed, then followed the young woman to stand by the giant forelimbs of Lord Malum. Lady Lenta gazed down at Takri for a moment, then averted her eyes.

'Prelate Conservus was just telling us about the work the monks do here in the monastery,' Lord Malum went on. 'Carry on, prelate.'

'Yes, my blessed lord,' said the old man in purple robes. 'As I was saying, the surviving monasteries of the Serpent Isle all have differing functions. Tsallon Anura, for example, ministers to the faithful Zamatans who dwell in Kaugatz, while Tzalla Pen functions primarily as a farm, cultivating produce to be distributed to the poor of the island. Unlike the others, Zamata Gataza is located far from any human settlement, and this frees us to concentrate on the more spiritual aspects of the faith. It is here that the ancient scrolls and texts are studied. This is the first and oldest monastery, established by Irlanian seafarers eighteen years before the mighty and blessed King Gahad arrived on Athumia, and it is from here that the worship of the serpent gods is regulated.'

'The monastery is a little rustic,' said Lady Macsin, as she glanced at the roughly-hewn walls of the cavern; 'at least for dragons. I assume that you, prelate, live in great comfort?'

'I humbly apologise for the basic facilities, my lady,' said the prelate. 'In truth, it has been many long years since we were honoured by such blessed visitors.'

Lord Rylan tilted his scaled head. 'The cool mountain air goes some way to compensate for the simplicity of our accommodation.'

'You are too kind, my noble lord,' said the prelate. 'Rest assured that wagon-loads of supplies intended to make your stay more comfortable have been ordered, and are on their way up to the monastery as we speak.'

'That is good,' said Malum. 'Now, I think it is time to hear your pledges of allegiance, prelate.'

'My lord?' said the prelate. 'The monks of the Serpent Isle have always been your faithful servants.'

'Is that so?' said Malum. 'Is there no chance whatsoever that they haven't been infiltrated by Gunstian agents? If that is the case, then there should be no problem in swearing your oaths openly in front of me and my kin. Ensure that your monks swear their oaths one at a time. You may begin now.'

The prelate looked almost insulted by the suggestion, but he bowed his head, the gold chain jangling.

'Of course, my lord. I shall go first. I swear that I am loyal to the serpent gods and to the Dominion. I am a faithful servant of the true faith.'

Lord Malum tilted his head. 'Thank you, prelate. Next.'

The monks formed into a line, and began to recite the same oath one by one, each prostrating themselves before the dragons as they spoke. Cisca frowned as the process dragged on. What was the purpose of such an exercise? In the unlikely event that any of the monks were working for the enemy, then that would not prevent them from falsely taking the oath.

After two dozen or so monks had sworn allegiance, a man with fair hair prostrated himself before Lord Malum.

'My sacred lords,' he said, his gaze lowered. 'I swear that I am loyal to the serpent gods and to the Dominion. I am a faithful servant of the true faith.'

The man rose to his feet, and began to make his way back to where the other monks were waiting.

'Halt,' said Lord Malum.

The fair-haired monk turned. 'My lord?'

The pale red dragon stared down at him. 'Confess, traitor, and I will make your end a quick one.'

The monk began to tremble. 'But... no, I...'

'Brother Hajim has been a loyal member of this monastery for over a decade, my lord,' cried the prelate, his eyes wide.

'And yet you did not perceive him to be faithless, prelate?' said Lord Malum. 'That says much about your lack of judgement.' He narrowed his glowing eyes at the fair-haired monk. 'Hajim, I compel you to tell only the truth.'

The monk cried out and fell back to his knees, his hands clutching the sides of his head, as the other monks stared in silence.

'Hajim,' said Malum, 'whom do you serve? Who is your true master?'

'I work for the Gunstians!' Hajim cried. 'I am loyal to the only true god – Chadura!'

The other monks gasped in horror, some crying out in anguish while others began to weep.

'And what are your true thoughts regarding the dragons, Hajim?' Malum went on.

The monk's face twisted with fear, but his mouth opened again. 'You are demons!'

Malum glanced at Lady Macsin, and she lunged out with a taloned forelimb. The claws ripped through Hajim's body, slicing him in half and spraying the other monks with his blood. A sound of weeping and wailing arose as the monks fell to their knees.

'My merciful lord,' said the prelate, 'Brother Hajim was believed to be loyal by every one of us here in Zamata Gataza. How did you know?'

Lord Malum smiled. 'The gods know everything, prelate,' he said. 'Now, let us continue with the oaths. I shall rest only when every monk within these walls has proved their loyalty to me.'

'Yes, my lord,' the prelate cried, his voice wavering.

Cisca stared at the butchered body of the Gunstian agent lying on the stone floor of the cavern, then she turned to glance at Takri. The young woman's face was unmoved, her expression serene, and Cisca forced her gaze back to the monks.

She had to survive, she told herself. That was all that mattered.

CHAPTER 18
A DEEP DECEPTION

Zamata Gataza, Serpent Isle – 9th Lexinch 1588

Leona sat alone on her balcony, watching the sun rise. The monks had brought her a silver platter filled with meat, cheese, bread, fish and olives along with fresh cool water and a flagon of sweet wine. It sat on the table to her right, as her eyes took in the glorious spectacle before her. She had seen the sun rise from the colonel's mansion on the slopes of Mount Medamuna, but the monastery on Mount Hodzulat was at a much higher altitude, and the view over the island was unparalleled. It was so beautiful that she almost wept at the sight of the sun's rays spilling over the sinewy land and sparkling waters of Zamata. The white marble of the Dragon Palace in Igatz was shimmering in hues of pink, and she could see the bottom of the Hansarta through its crystal clear waters.

It was her island, and she loved it. She would die for it; in fact, if Lord Malum discovered the depths of her deception, then she would most certainly lose her life. The thought frightened her, but she knew she had no choice but to see it through, whatever the cost. Alone on the balcony, she allowed her hands to tremble, saving her strength for when she needed to become Lady Takri again.

She listed her worries. Captain Cisca was at the top of her major concerns. Perhaps she had been a little too forward with the Dragon Corps officer during their journey the previous day from Igatz, but the information she had gleaned from Cisca's lies might prove to be invaluable. Cisca held the dragons in contempt, and was bound to the Dominion by fear rather than fidelity. And what was she to make of the officer's feelings towards Bauchlie? Leona hadn't been expecting that. She had suspected for a while that Bauchlie liked Cisca, but she hadn't been prepared for the officer to have practically confessed that she was in love with the colonel's son. How could Leona use that to her advantage? Blackmail sprung to mind. Cisca was clearly terrified of her; what would she do to prevent her secrets from being revealed to the dragons? Could she be turned to the cause of Zamata's freedom?

Next on Leona's list of worries was the colonel himself. Friel would no doubt be confused by her apparent conversion to the Dominion – was he clever enough to perceive that it had all been an act? He could cause her untold amounts of trouble if he had misunderstood the situation. He knew about the Demon Witch, for a start. Perhaps she should have him quietly killed before he could divulge his secrets to the dragons. If she did it discreetly, she could place the blame for his death on the monks of the monastery. They loathed the colonel, and many would probably rejoice in his death.

And what about Major Lyla? Her unpredictability could easily cause Leona's downfall. Or, perhaps like Cisca, there was an opportunity to be found in the officer's hatred of the dragons.

Leona sipped the cool water from her silver goblet. She would leave the wine untouched; she needed to keep all of her wits about her, despite longing for drunken oblivion to ease her concerns. One mistake, that was all it would take.

She glanced at the sun. If the Demon Witch was true to her word, then it was time.

Good morning, Leona; or should I call you Takri now?

Leona smiled.

When I came to you yesterday, I told you that I would speak to you at this hour, the Demon Witch went on; *did you doubt me?*

No, but my mind is almost paralysed by fear. You must be able to sense it.

I can. You have risked much, Leona, but I am very proud of what you have achieved. Lord Malum trusts you, and you have earned the fear and respect of every human in the monastery. Are you ready for the next step?

I don't know if I can do it.

You can. I believe in you.

Have you seen Lahnos? Does he live?

He lives. I watched him from afar yesterday, while you were travelling from Igatz. I wanted to speak to him, but... well, he hates me, as you know. The Dominion invasion of Gunst is underway, and they have landed thousands of soldiers along the coastline. Casualties among the Zamatans have been high.

I feared they would. Have you seen Reyn or Bauchlie?

Yes. They are still working together, although the Bullan are closing in on their hideout in the ruins of Gatzoun Medamuna.

Please don't tell me where they are. I worry that Lord Malum will use the truth spell on me.

That is no longer a concern, Leona.

She frowned. *Why?*

I have shielded your mind. The truth spell of the dragons will not work on you.

But what if they try? They will realise that something...

Tell them that it is a consequence of your Gift. Tell them that those with the Gift of Truth are immune. You will be safe.

Leona panted with relief. 'Thank you,' she whispered.

I will do what I can to protect you. Today, however, I want you to denounce me.

I don't understand.

I want the dragons to focus on me; I want them to waste their hours searching for the infamous Demon Witch. Today, I will reveal my presence to them, and then you will volunteer to help them find me.

How will you reveal yourself to them?

One of the four dragons is weaker than the others. The loss of her brother has sapped Lady Lenta's spirit. Secretly, she loathes Lord Rylan and Lady

Macsin for the death of Lord Irvan, and her confusion over what to do about you has further weakened her will. She is vulnerable, and I shall strike. If you can, provoke her to anger – that will make it easier for me to invade her mind. It will take all of my limited powers to do what I have to do; and therefore you might not hear from me again for a while. It will be your job to sow discord and fear within the hearts of the dragons. Will you do this?

Yes.

You know, Lahnos used to constantly ask me to explain my motives, the Demon Witch said; *whereas you never mention such things.*

I don't care why you are helping us, said Leona. *I want Zamata to be free.*

Farewell, then. I shall come to you again when I am able.

The presence vanished from Leona's mind. She rubbed the back of her neck and took another sip of water, her gaze on the island of her birth. She steeled her nerves; there was much to be done.

Half an hour later, Leona strode towards the tiny apartment on the fourth floor of the monastery where Colonel Friel Laimos had been incarcerated.

'Open the door,' she said to the Bullan on guard outside.

'Yes, my lady,' said one, as the other withdrew a key from a pocket.

The door was unlocked and opened, and Leona entered the small living chamber. The door closed behind her, and Friel glanced up from where he was sitting, a fresh eye patch covering his wound. He stared up at her, but said nothing.

'I require you to be silent about everything you know about me,' she said to him.

He shrugged. 'Am I likely to get many visitors? Take a seat. There's wine.'

'No, thank you, Colonel. I shall remain standing, as this will not be a long discussion.'

'You astound me,' he said, smiling and shaking his head. 'How quickly you were able to switch sides, I mean. Truly remarkable.'

'Your beliefs are of no concern to me,' she said. 'The dragons might choose to use the truth spell upon you at any moment. It would be wise not to lead them in certain directions.'

'Oh yes? And which directions would those be?'

'Do you still believe in the cause?'

'What a stupid question. The cause is over, in case you hadn't noticed. How can Zamata ever be free if most of the men have been removed from the island? Anyway, I thought you didn't care about my beliefs.'

'Do you want to live?'

He glanced out of the narrow window. 'I don't know. I don't want to die in horrendous agony, but I'm not altogether sure that life is worth living any more.'

'I could make your end a pleasant one; a peaceful one, if that is what you desire.'

'How thoughtful. Why are you here, Leona?'

She smiled. 'For the mountain air.'

'Have they found Bauchlie?'

'No.'

'Good. I hope he kills you.'

'You still retain your anger, I see. That is good. It will keep you going if all else fails. I know that you are not a stupid man, Colonel. I want you to reflect deeply on everything that I have left unsaid. And then you can draw your own conclusions.' She pulled a short, sheathed blade from her robes and set it down onto the floor a few yards in front of the Colonel. 'You can use this,' she said, 'if you decide to end it all.'

Leona knocked on the door, and the Bullan soldiers let her pass back into the corridor. Sorrow tinged with despair seeped through her as she walked away. She wished that she had been able to open up to the colonel, to tell him the truth about what she was trying to achieve, but she couldn't take the risk that one of the dragons might decide to use their truth powers on him. When he had said that he hoped Bauchlie would kill her there had been no tingle in the back of her mind. He believed that she had betrayed him, and there was nothing she could do about it. She wondered if he would kill himself with the knife she had left him. In many ways, his death would simplify matters. She owed much to the colonel, not only for being rescued from the streets of Kaugatz, but for all that she had learned from him during her years as his assistant. In that time, she had kept quiet and listened, absorbing everything he had to teach her until she was ready to make her own mark on the island. That time had come, but she still hoped that he would understand her true motives.

She made her way up to the temple on the top floor of the monastery. The structures on the upper levels were built from wood, and the ungainly building seemed likely to topple from the mountain-side at any moment. The monks within the temple fell into silence as she entered the gloomy interior. Incense was burning, and a few candles were lit amid the statues of serpents and faded tapestries. Leona found an empty pew, knelt, bowed her head, and pretended to pray.

Three times. The Demon Witch had been in her head three times, including that morning at dawn. With Lahnos refusing to communicate with her, she had chosen Leona instead, and Leona was more than willing to allow herself to be used as the vessel of her powers. She smiled a secret smile as she remembered what the Demon Witch had said about the truth spell. Her greatest fear had been that a dragon would force her to admit to the truth, but that fear had dissolved into nothing.

She kept up the pretence at prayer for an hour, ensuring that the monks could all see her kneeling before the serpent shrine. She didn't care if they thought she was devout, all that mattered was that word of her attendance in the temple would make its way back to Lord Malum. She got to her feet, and walked up to a thick row of candles. She dropped a coin in the box, took a fresh one and lit it off the flickering flame of another. She placed the candle onto a low spike, then bowed her head and left the temple.

She made her way down a dozen flights of stairs to the caverns that lay beneath the monastery, and found Captain Cisca waiting by the huge opening in the southward flank of the mountain, from where the dragons could access their quarters. The sun was halfway up the eastern sky, and the waves of the ocean were visible in the distance, while, to the south-east, the blackened ruins of Neeton were scarring the landscape.

'Good morning, Captain,' Leona said, as she approached.

Cisca jumped from fright, and Leona suppressed a wry smile.

'Did you sleep well, Captain?'

'Yes, ma'am,' Cisca said, lying.

'How are your rooms?'

'They are... beautiful, ma'am,' said Cisca, telling the truth. 'I have a balcony, and the view is breathtaking.'

'I agree,' said Leona. 'I watched the sunrise this morning and nearly wept at the sight of it. After that, I went to the temple for morning prayers, but I didn't see you there, Cisca.'

A look of fear passed over Cisca's expression.

'Visitors are permitted to attend prayers after dawn each day,' Leona went on; 'and it pleases the dragons to hear that we humans are pious in our devotion to them.'

'I see, ma'am,' said Cisca. 'I will try to attend tomorrow.'

Leona nodded, her gaze on the skies. In the distance, a solitary black speck was approaching.

'How long have the dragons been out flying, Captain?'

'A little over an hour, ma'am,' Cisca said. 'I think that might be Lady Macsin returning now.'

Leona kept her expression serene. Lady Macsin loathed her, although she had been careful never to show it in Lord Malum's presence. The large dragon soared towards the mountain, circled over the high peak, then descended to the cavern entrance. Leona and Cisca bowed their heads as she strode through the high archway.

The dragon glanced down. 'Greetings, Dragon Corps officer. Is there fresh water for me?'

'Yes, ma'am,' said Cisca. 'I ensured that cool water from the mountain stream was brought here in time for your return.'

'Excellent.' She turned to Leona, and her eyes narrowed. 'And greetings to you, sub-created servant. Tell me again; how did you come to attain such a position of trust with the Governor of this territory?'

'I am a humble advisor, ma'am,' said Leona, bowing.

'You know, Takri,' Macsin said, 'one day I might feel the need to extract the truth from you.'

'Lord Malum knows that I always tell him the truth, ma'am.'

'I would like to have some proof of that claim,' the dragon said, as she strode into the cavern.

Cisca directed her to a long stone trough filled with fresh water, and the dragon began to drink.

'Is Lord Malum aware,' said Leona, 'that you harbour doubts about my veracity, Lady Macsin? If not, then perhaps I should mention it to him.'

Macsin spluttered and coughed, then raised her head.

'Do not anger me, human,' the dragon said. 'Was that a threat?'

'No, my lady,' said Leona. 'It was a warning.'

'You dare speak to me in such a tone?' Macsin cried. 'I am a daughter of the mighty King Gahad, and the sister of King Naghad. I do not fear you.'

Leona felt a tingle in the back of her mind, and it caught her by surprise. Could it be true? Did a dragon fear her?

'How can I prove my loyalty to you and to the Dominion, my lady?' she said, changing tack.

'You can start by voluntarily submitting yourself to the truth spell,' Macsin said. 'If you do this then, depending upon the outcome, I might be more likely to trust you.'

'I will suggest it to Lord Malum,' Leona said. 'Until then, it might be prudent if you kept your unfounded doubts to yourself, my lady.'

Macsin stared at her with venom. Leona wondered if she had gone too far, and then a sound of claws against stone behind her announced the arrival of the other three dragons.

'My beautiful Takri,' said Lord Malum, striding forwards.

Leona smiled. 'My lord, did you enjoy your flight?'

'I did,' he said, as he folded in his pale red wings.

'Captain Cisca has brought fresh water for you all,' she said, gesturing towards the long trough.

'Thank you, Captain,' said Lord Rylan, tilting his head slightly.

Lady Macsin's eyes flashed with rage. 'Do not thank a mere human, half-brother, you weak fool,' she cried. 'They are our servants!'

'Control yourself, Lady Macsin,' snapped Malum. 'Lord Rylan was merely being polite. Even a god can show gratitude to those who serve them out of loyalty and devotion.'

Macsin glared at her full brother, but said nothing.

'It is an honour to serve you, my lords and ladies,' said Cisca, bowing low.

'Pay no attention to Lady Macsin's outburst, Captain,' said Malum. 'Clearly, something has irritated her this morning.'

He dipped his head into the trough to drink, and Leona sidled over to Lady Lenta, who eyed her warily.

'Good morning, my lady,' Leona said.

Lenta said nothing.

Leona narrowed her eyes at the dragon. 'It would be wise,' she whispered, 'if you at least pretended to like me; otherwise, who knows what Lord Malum might decide to do to you? At a glance from him, Lady Macsin and Lord Rylan might rip out your throat, just as they did to your poor, unfortunate, blinded brother.'

Lady Lenta roared in anger, and her claws flashed out, their razor-sharp edges glinting in the morning light.

Lord Malum swung a forelimb and battered Lenta aside.

'How dare you?' Malum cried. 'You raise your claws against my favoured human?'

Lenta's eyes rolled up into her head, and she spasmed on the floor of the cavern as the other dragons stared.

'I did not strike her that hard,' Malum said. 'Lenta – can you hear me?'

Leona grabbed Cisca's arm and pulled her back, as Lenta's tail coiled out like a whip. The black and white dragon howled in torment, then her head lifted from the ground, and she stared out at the others.

'You will die!' Lenta cried, but her voice seemed different. 'You will all die, and I will be the one to strike you down.'

'Lenta!' Malum cried. 'What madness has overtaken you?'

'Lenta is no longer in possession of her own mind,' said the voice coming from the black and white dragon. 'I now control it; I, who slew the mighty King Gahad. It is the voice of vengeance that you are hearing – the voice of the Demon Witch.'

The other three dragons stared at Lenta, their eyes wide, then Malum risked a quick glance at Leona, who gave him a brief nod.

'The Demon Witch?' said Malum, his voice almost cracking.

'For too long your kind has oppressed the peoples of this world,' the voice from Lenta went on; 'but your reign of cruelty and fear will soon be over. Witness my power. If I will it, I could make Lenta rip out her own throat.' Lenta raised a forelimb, and her talons traced lines of blood across the scales on her neck.

'No!' cried Lord Rylan. 'Leave her alone, you beast!'

Lenta laughed. 'I sense your cowardice, little Rylan. Does Lord Malum know that you loathe him, that you fantasise about killing him? And you, Lady Macsin – perhaps Lord Malum should be aware that you threatened to butcher his pathetic little human just moments before he returned to this cavern? Maybe I should kill this Takri myself, to hurt you, Lord Malum.'

'What do you want?' Malum cried.

'Your destruction,' said the Demon Witch. 'I shall begin with Lady Lenta; I shall utterly obliterate her mind, leaving her as helpless as a newborn, removing her memories, her powers, her identity, and her very self; and then, perhaps, you will taste the same fear that you have instilled into the hearts of the people of this world.'

Lenta roared in agony, and her body convulsed, striking the side of the cavern. She let out a last whimper, then lay still, her eyes closed.

Lord Malum took a step forward. 'Lady Lenta, can you hear me?' He lifted a forelimb, and shook the black and white dragon's shoulder.

Lenta opened her eyes, but they were glazed over.

'Is she alive, my lord?' said Rylan.

Malum cast his younger half-brother a look of contempt. 'She lives.'

'What the Demon Witch said about me, my lord,' Rylan went on. 'It isn't true; I swear it.'

Malum glanced at Leona, who touched her ear to denote that Rylan was lying.

'Everyone out,' said Malum, his gaze cast down. 'Now.'

Leona kept a grip of Cisca's arm, and pulled her towards a human-sized doorway, as Macsin and Rylan bowed their heads and walked through to their cavernous living quarters.

'What just happened?' said Cisca, as Leona closed the door behind them.

Leona glanced at the Dragon Corps officer. She was shaking with fear, her eyes wild.

'It seems the Demon Witch has paid us a visit, Captain,' Leona said.

Cisca sat down on the floor of the corridor and sobbed. 'The Demon Witch? How could that be possible? I thought she was a myth.'

'No, Captain; the Demon Witch is very real. She slew King Gahad, and now she has turned her attention to the Serpent Isle.'

'I thought she was going to kill you,' Cisca sobbed. 'And now, Lady Lenta... How can you remain so calm? Who are you?'

Leona said nothing.

'I'm sorry, ma'am,' Cisca cried. 'Please... I'm sorry. Don't tell Lord Malum that I shouted at you.'

Leona crouched down next to the weeping officer and placed a comforting hand upon her shoulder.

'I won't,' she said, 'if you do something for me.'

'Name it, ma'am.'

'Send a message to the Bullan companies hunting Commander Bauchlie,' she said. 'Tell them that they are looking in the wrong place. Order them to turn their attention back to Kaugatz immediately.'

Cisca stared at Leona. 'But... but Bauchlie was seen close to Gatzoun Medamuna, and that's where the Bullan are looking.'

Leona smiled. 'You want Bauchlie to live, don't you? And don't lie to me. Never lie to me again. Order the Bullan to move their search to Kaugatz; is that clear, Captain?'

'Yes, ma'am.'

'Go. Do it now.'

Cisca got to her feet, then she wiped her eyes and hurried away.

An hour later, Leona was summoned from her apartment by a monk to appear before Lord Malum. She calmed her features, then strode back down to the subterranean basement, where the pale red dragon was alone, waiting for her.

'The events of this morning have grieved me deeply, my Takri,' he said.

'And I, my lord,' she said, keeping her gaze downcast.

'I have... relieved Lady Lenta of her misery,' the dragon said. 'The monks shall mourn her loss, as will every Child of Gahad.'

'Lady Lenta will be greatly missed, my lord. She was a noble and honourable dragon.'

'Let me ask you – are you completely sure that the voice we heard belonged to the Demon Witch?'

'The voice uttered no lie, my lord. Whoever spoke believed themselves to be the Demon Witch, but I cannot say any clearer than that.'

'And now my mistrust turns to Lady Macsin and Lord Rylan,' he said. 'My sister does not like you. Of course, she has no knowledge of your Gift, and she wonders why I have placed so much power into your hands. She believes that I should use the truth spell upon you. What do you say to that?'

'It does not surprise me, my lord.'

'And should I do such a thing? Would you continue to willingly work for me if I were to subject you to such an ordeal? I fear to lose you, as you have proved your worth countless times since you became my advisor. To have you by my side gives me an unassailable advantage, but I need to know – would you treat this as an abuse of my trust in you?'

'There is no need to worry on that account, my lord, as the spell does not work upon those with the Gift of Truth.'

Malum eyed her. 'Impossible. No one can resist.'

'I invite you to try, my lord, and I will not hold such an attempt against you; you have my word.'

He stared into her eyes. 'Then, with reluctance, I shall do so. Leona of Kaugatz, I compel you to speak nothing but the truth. No lie can escape your tongue.'

Leona felt nothing. She smiled. 'Ask me a question, and I will tell you an obvious lie.'

Malum continued to gaze at her. 'Very well. What colour are my scales?'

'They are green, my lord, with pink dots.'

Malum gasped. 'No! How can this be?'

'It is as I said, my lord. The Gift I possess renders me immune to any other form of truth. The way I prove myself to you is through my actions. I made an agreement with you, my lord, and I always keep to my promises. If you do not believe me, then please strike me down, for I cannot live under a cloud of suspicion.'

He lowered his gaze. 'That will not be necessary. As you say, you have proved yourself by your actions.' He took a slow breath. 'And now I must decide what to do about the Demon Witch.'

'Use me to assist you, my lord. The Demon Witch also threatened my life, and if she knew about the Gift in my possession then she would surely kill me. Let me help you track her down; there must be a way we can defeat her.'

'There might be,' he said, 'though it will be perilous. It is strange, but I felt something while poor Lady Lenta's body was under that foul witch's control – a faint sensation of powers being used. As you know, dragons cannot sense the powers of the Gifted, and so I must presume that the powers used by the Demon Witch are related in some way to the powers used by the dragons. If this is so, then there could be a way to defeat her. Regardless, now that I have felt her presence once, I think I will be able to sense if her powers are used again.'

Leona bowed her head. 'What do you need me to do, my lord?'

He glanced at her. 'Did you sense anything?'

'I sensed nothing other than the truth or falsehood of the words that came from her mouth, my lord.'

'Then I fear that you cannot help me in this endeavour. It will be for the dragons to bring this Witch to justice. Carry on with your current role, and remember that you have become dear to my heart, Leona of Kaugatz, my Lady Takri. I shall not let the Demon Witch harm you; this I solemnly swear. Now go. There is much I need to discuss with Lady Macsin and Lord Rylan.'

Leona bowed again, then she walked from the dragon's presence. She cursed to herself as she left the cavern. Whatever plan Lord Malum was concocting to defeat the Demon Witch, it was one that he seemed unwilling to share with any human, even his beloved Lady Takri.

CHAPTER 19
KING OF TORAQ

Toraq, Gunstian Empire – 13th Lexinch 1588

Lahnos stared into space, his eyes bleary from lack of sleep. He rubbed his face and tried to concentrate on what he was seeing through the hole in the side of the burned-out housing block. Ahead of him was a road that ran between high rows of blocks identical to the one where he and the squad were positioned. All had been damaged by the dragons, their roofs gone, and their brickwork exposed and blackened. Someone had painted something in the Gunstian language on the block opposite. *Toraq – the grave of the Dominion* it read in red paint. Lahnos rubbed his face again, trying to remain alert. Gunstian soldiers were occupying the other side of the street, and he had to be ready in case they mounted another counter-attack. He moved his crossbow from his left to his right hand, feeling the wooden stock resting in his palm, while his knees were aching from crouching in the same position for so long.

Was that movement? He narrowed his eyes at the gutted-out window thirty yards ahead of him, but saw nothing. Perhaps his mind was deceiving him again. The day before, he had been so tired that he had started to imagine that the Gunstians were entering the building, and Efizel had been forced to order him to get some sleep. He had managed four hours – the longest sleep he had enjoyed since their troopship had berthed at the pier six days before. Had it only been six days? In that time, he had loosed his stolen Gunstian crossbow four times, but had struck nothing but brick walls. The Gunstians moved around like ghosts, emerging from the basements and cellars where they had sheltered during the initial dragon attack that had ravaged half of Toraq. And they had been reinforced, their supply lines to the north clear and open. Whenever they counter-attacked, the forces moving against the Dominion soldiers always seemed to be fresh and well-supplied, while the Zamatan regiments had been slowly ground down, their makeshift uniforms bedraggled and filthy, and their lack of training all too apparent in the face of disciplined opposition. If it hadn't been for Sergeant Efizel... Well, they would all be dead, that seemed certain. As it was, through a combination of Efizel's leadership and blind luck, every one of the squad was still alive, and only two had been sent back to the harbour with injuries.

Lahnos longed to lie down, or even stretch his arms and legs, but he had been told to watch the other side of the road, and so that was what he did. If he closed his eyes, even for a moment, he might drift off to sleep, and then, if the Gunstians advanced, the squad would have no warning of their approach.

'Report, corporal,' came a low voice with a Bullan accent.

'Nothing, sergeant,' Lahnos said, keeping his eyes on the ruined block in front of him.

'An entire day has passed without a counter-attack,' Efizel muttered. 'The bastards are planning something. Stay alert, and let me know if you see anything.'

Lahnos nodded, then he heard the Bullan creep away through the wrecked living room where a Gunstian family had once dwelt. Lahnos lifted his crossbow and balanced the end on the edge of the hole in the wall. He gazed along the sights, the index finger of his right hand hovering an inch away from the trigger mechanism, just as Efizel had shown them. He closed one eye and scanned the broken windows opposite him. Far off to his right, he heard screams, but he paid them no attention, and then he saw the glow of a new fire begin to rage, followed moments later by two black specks soaring overhead. The dragons were out again, but they were being cautious. Five had been brought down on the first day, of which three had died. It was the Gifted who had struck them, or so the rumours said. The Dominion leadership had made no official comment. Reduced to hit and run raids, the dragons had allowed the initiative to pass to the Gunstians, who had dug in along the northern half of the embattled city, and were forcing the Dominion infantry to fight for every street, and every housing block.

Lahnos moved the crossbow a little to his left, and focussed on another window. The room beyond was thick with shadows, and the contrast between the bright sunshine outside with the dark interior made it almost impossible to make out anything that might be within. The shadows flickered, but it was only a cloud passing next to the sun overhead. Lahnos frowned, pulled his head back from the crossbow, and stared out with both eyes. He was wrong. Something was on the move in the building opposite. Without thinking, he raised the crossbow again, aimed into the room, and loosed, feeling the stock of the large bow juddering into his shoulder.

A bolt spat out, crossed the street, and passed through the broken window frame. A scream of pain followed moments later, then another bolt was loosed, this time aimed at Lahnos. It flew two inches past his left ear, then ricocheted off the wall behind him.

He ducked his unprotected head down. 'Sergeant!'

More bolts thrummed through the air. One deflected off the edge of the hole in the wall, then skittered across the floorboards by his right leg, while others struck the outside of the building. Efizel crawled into the room, followed by Smithy and Karl.

'The bastards are shooting at me,' Lahnos said.

Efizel reached the wall next to him. 'Did you give your position away?'

'I loosed at someone in the room opposite,' Lahnos said. 'I got him, too.'

'You hit someone?' said Karl.

Lahnos nodded, then he set about reloading his crossbow.

Efizel peered out of the hole. 'Karl, run downstairs and tell the lieutenant from the Sixth that we have sighted multiple enemies moving in the building opposite. I think our position is about to be assaulted.'

Karl crawled away, then the blacksmith joined Lahnos and Efizel at the hole in the wall, his own crossbow raised to his shoulder. Apart from the Bullan, Smithy was the only member of the squad who had killed a Gunstian since the battle had begun.

'I see the man you shot, corporal,' he grunted. 'You got him in the throat.'

Lahnos lifted his loaded crossbow. 'Is he dead?'

'Well, he certainly isn't alive. You've stirred up a wasps' nest across the street, and no mistake. I see Gunstians in five, six, seven windows.'

'Keep your head down,' muttered Efizel. 'We need to move next door. Go.'

The three men crawled through the room as another crossbow bolt sped through the hole. They reached the neighbouring room, where the rest of the squad had been resting, and Efizel pressed his eye against a tiny gap in the floorboards that they had nailed over the window frame.

'Get your equipment and load your weapons,' he called out to the squad. 'Be ready to move at my command.'

Karl hurried back into the room. 'We've been ordered to remain here, sergeant. Movement has been noticed along the entire street, and the lieutenant said that Bullan reinforcements are being sent up to strengthen our position. We are not to retreat, no matter what.'

A few of the squad looked panicked, their fear overriding the exhaustion felt by all, but the sergeant's face remained impassive.

'Thank you, Karl. Squad, start removing the boards from the windows – just enough to provide space for the crossbows. Corporal, take Smithy and Karl and head back next door. Keep watch on the street, but do not loose until the Gunstians have left the buildings. Go.'

Lahnos ran back into the room from where he had shot the Gunstian, and then he, his brother, and the blacksmith crouched by the hole in the wall.

'Look what you've started, brother,' muttered Karl.

Lahnos raised his crossbow to the gap in the brickwork. 'As much as I'd like to take the credit for it, I'm not sure the Gunstians would launch a full scale attack just because I shot one of the bastards.'

'Shut up, the pair of you,' said Smithy. 'Sorry, corporal.'

Lahnos laughed as a tired wave of exhilaration gripped him. As exhausted as he was, his desire to survive was keeping his mind racing. He rolled his shoulders, and flexed the fingers of each hand as he gripped the large bow.

'Here they come!' cried Karl.

More shouts echoed out from the Dominion side of the street as over a dozen doors opened on the opposite side. Raised shields emerged first, the Gunstians behind them crouching low as more spilled out onto the paved road.

'Don't waste your bolts,' said Smithy. 'Loose only when you have a clear shot.'

Bolts were loosed from the floor above where another squad was situated, and Lahnos laughed again.

'I don't think the other Zamatans are paying heed to your sage advice, Smithy.'

A few bolts struck the Gunstians' shields, while others hit the ground in front of them. A Gunstian was hit on the head, the bolt striking his steel helmet, as more continued to pour out from the opposite building. The soldiers charged across the thirty-yard gap, and as they did so, more gaps in their shield wall appeared.

'Now,' said Smithy.

The three soldiers loosed, as did dozens of others on the Dominion side, and a hail of bolts rained down onto the Gunstians. A ballista positioned forty yards to their right loosed, and a long steel bolt ripped through two Gunstians, pinning their bodies together as they fell. The screams and shouts echoed upwards as more soldiers fell in the street, and time seemed to slow down for Lahnos. He aimed, loosed, then crouched down to reload, and then he repeated the cycle. Each time he looked down at the street, more bodies were lying on the cobbles, but the Gunstians were closer to the Dominion side. He hit another soldier, striking him in the shoulder and causing him to spin round. The man dropped his shield, and then another bolt slammed into his chest, and he sank to his knees. The cries of the injured seared their way through Lahnos's mind as he loosed again.

'It's impossible to miss the bastards at this range,' the blacksmith grunted.

'Look out!' cried Karl, his eyes wide.

Lahnos glanced around for the danger, then a glass bottle flew through the hole in the wall and landed a few yards from the three men. It spun on the floorboards, then rolled to a halt. Lahnos stared at the clear liquid inside it, and the long piece of cotton that had been rammed into its neck. The edge of the cotton was singed, but the flames had gone out.

At that moment, explosions roared through the building, and flames erupted from several windows to their left and right. Lahnos scrambled forward and picked up the intact bottle.

'By all the serpents,' Karl gasped. 'How are we not dead?'

'Shut up and give me a light,' said Lahnos.

The blacksmith struck a match, and held it to the end of the cotton dangling out of the bottle. Lahnos waited until the cotton was burning, and then he dropped the bottle out through the hole in the wall. The three men crouched down as another explosion roared through the air from below them, followed by screams.

Lahnos laughed manically.

'Stop laughing, you demented freak!' Karl shouted.

Smithy peered out of the hole.

'How many did I get?' said Lahnos.

'A few, but it doesn't matter. The Gunstians have broken through several doors; they're inside the damn building.'

Lahnos placed his crossbow onto the floor, and pulled the short-handled Gunstian battle-axe from over his shoulder.

'Stay here, boys,' he said, then he ran to the door.

He raced through to the other room, where Efizel was directing the rest of the squad to keep loosing into the Gunstians in the street.

'Sergeant,' he yelled. 'The Gunstians are in the building.'

Efizel turned, then raised an eyebrow.

Lahnos hefted the axe in his right hand. 'I'm much better with this than I am with a crossbow. How about I watch the stairs while you lot keep loosing?'

Efizel nodded. 'Take Jancke with you to watch your back, and do not stray too far, young Laimos. Stick to the stairs, and guard the apartment door.'

Lahnos nodded, then he grabbed Jancke by the arm and hauled him to his feet. Jancke picked up the only shield that the squad had managed to procure, then the two men ran to the front door of the apartment. The door was hanging off its hinges, and Lahnos glanced out into the stairwell. There was no movement coming from the levels above them, but he could hear the sounds of fighting echoing up from the ground floor.

'Set your shield in front of us and point your bow down the stairs,' he said to Jancke, and the young man followed him out on to the landing. He wedged the shield into the iron bars of the balustrade, and then they crouched down, waiting.

'When will the Bullan get here?' Jancke whispered.

'Who knows? Probably never.'

'I don't want to die in this place.'

Lahnos shrugged. 'Then don't.'

'That's easy for you to say – you don't seem to give a shit about whether you live or die. You brush all this off as if it was nothing. You were the same in the damn village; strutting down the main street with your horns on display.'

'You were there that day, were you?'

'Yes; I was there. You were lucky you weren't lynched.'

'Luck had nothing to do with it.' He squinted into the gloom as several Gunstians appeared on the landing on the next floor down. 'Loose, you dozy bastard!'

Jancke aimed his crossbow and the bolt spat out, striking one of the Gunstians above the left knee. Lahnos raised his axe and roared. He charged down the stairs, jumping the last few, his boots kicking a Gunstian's shield as he landed. He lashed out with the axe and scalped a man two feet from him, then he stamped a boot down onto the neck of the soldier who had been hit in the knee. A shield barged into him, then a crossbow was raised, and Lahnos felt his instincts take over. He jabbed the spiked end of the axe into the soldier's chin, and ripped upwards, and the bow fell to the floor. A fourth Gunstian crashed into him and they both fell. Lahnos lunged out in a frenzy, and rammed the handle of the axe into the man's eye. He pulled it out, then brought it down again, driving it through his other eye. The axe made a sucking sound as he ripped it back out, then he got to his feet, swayed, and glanced around for more Gunstians. There were none left on the landing, but more were fighting the Zamatans on the floor below them, and Lahnos began to head for the stairs.

'Get back up here, corporal!' Efizel shouted from above him.

Lahnos cursed, then he bounded back up the stairs to where Jancke was staring open-mouth at him. Efizel grabbed Lahnos by the collar and hauled him back a few steps.

'What did I say about not straying too far?' the Bullan yelled.

'Sorry, sergeant,' said Lahnos. 'I got a little carried away.'

Efizel turned to Jancke. 'And you were supposed to be watching his back!'

'He charged off before I could do anything,' Jancke said.

'What does it matter?' said Lahnos. 'I killed them all, didn't I?

Efizel glanced down at the blood-soaked landing below them. 'Yes, young Laimos; you did.' He rubbed his forehead, his tail swishing in anger. 'The attack is over; the Gunstians have pulled back to their side of the road.'

He pointed to the apartment, and watched as Jancke and Lahnos went through the door.

Jancke frowned at the men in the room. 'Lahnos went berserk and killed four Gunstians.'

Lahnos smiled, and raised his bloody axe. 'I am the horned king of Toraq City.'

'Put that thing down and get some rest,' said Efizel. 'Karl, you are on duty by the hole in the wall. Stay alert; the Gunstians might return.'

Lahnos sat down and leaned against a wall, his heart pounding. He pulled a rag from his boot and wiped the blade of the axe, and then the spike and the handle, as the others in the squad eyed him.

'You're some fighter, lad,' said Smithy, 'but that doesn't mean you're a good soldier.'

'And what would you know?' said Lahnos. 'You're a blacksmith.'

'He is right, young Laimos,' said Efizel. 'You have courage, and a good awareness of what is happening around you, but you are reckless and lack discipline. Perhaps if you were to endure four years of training as the Bullan do, then they might be able to turn you into a decent soldier.'

Lahnos narrowed his eyes. 'I killed more Gunstians than anyone else in the squad today.'

'You killed more than the rest of us put together,' said the blacksmith; 'but you shouldn't be a damn corporal.'

Lahnos shrugged, then closed his eyes. 'Wake me up if something interesting happens.'

Lahnos felt a presence in his mind as he awoke.

He frowned. *Is that you in my head again, Witch, after I told you to leave me alone?*

Silence.

Do you think I'm stupid? he went on. *I can feel you in my mind.*

Yes, Lahnos; I am here.

Why? Do you not understand what 'leave me alone' means?

I'm sorry. I needed to know if you were all right.

Lahnos opened his eyes. The light of the day had dimmed, and most of the squad around him were resting.

You sound tired, Witch, he said in his mind. *You sound almost as tired as I feel.*

I am tired. I did something a few days ago that almost completely drained my powers. And yet, I could not stop myself from coming here to make sure that you were alive. I am sorry for what I did to your father, and I'm sorry that I didn't tell you about it sooner.

Lahnos said nothing.

I know you hate me, she said.

Lahnos cursed under his breath.

Reyn is safe, she went on. *She's been helping Bauchlie, and he's been protecting her.*

He narrowed his eyes. *Reyn is with Bauchlie?*

Yes. They have become friends.

If that asshole touches her, I'll break his damn neck.

Bauchlie would never do that, Lahnos; I have seen inside his mind. And Reyn still loves you. She thinks about you all the time.

Is this what you came here to say, Witch? Nothing useful to tell me? No advice?

Would you listen to my advice if I offered it?

Probably not.

The voice fell silent for a few moments.

The dragons are planning a massive attack this evening, she said. *They are going to burn the rest of this city to the ground, and then abandon the ruins and strike out towards Great Gunst. By dawn, the northern half of Toraq will be nothing but ash. Stay where you are. If you cross the street, you will be caught up in the conflagration.*

The voice vanished from his mind. Lahnos sat and did nothing for a few moments. His loathing for the Demon Witch had abated in her absence, but her return had set the flames of his hatred blazing anew. He glanced at the resting members of the squad, then his thoughts turned to the thousands of Zamatans dug in along the front lines.

'Sergeant,' he said; 'can we speak alone for a moment?'

. . .

The squad lay still in the apartment as the sun set over the buildings to their left. The cobbles below them were still littered with the bodies of the Gunstians who had fallen in their latest counter-attack. Soldiers from both sides usually emerged from the housing blocks during the night to retrieve their casualties, but Lahnos knew it would not be happening that night. He had told Efizel what the Demon Witch had said, and the sergeant had sent Karl and Jancke into the neighbouring apartment blocks to spread the rumour of the attack, and to warn the Zamatans not to leave their side of the street.

'Why are you so sure that there's going to be a dragon attack, sergeant?' Smithy muttered, as they peered through the gaps in the boarded-up windows.

'I have a feeling, nothing more,' said the Bullan. 'It makes strategic sense.'

'And what if the Gifted start bringing them down?'

'If we do not get out of Toraq soon,' the sergeant said, 'then the invasion is over before it has even begun. I think the King will take the risk.'

The blacksmith crinkled his brow.

'I see movement in the building opposite,' said Karl.

The others quietened as they stared through the small gaps. Lahnos saw a shadow flicker within the depths of a room in the apartment across the street from them, then it stopped.

'The Gunstians are settling down for the night,' said the blacksmith. 'I don't think they're expecting any attack.'

The squad lay on the floor and waited. An hour passed without incident, and Lahnos was starting to wonder if the Demon Witch had been mistaken, when Efizel glanced up at the sky.

'Here they come; stay down!'

The flames seemed to come out of nowhere. In the darkness, Lahnos had seen no sign of any approaching dragons, but their presence in great numbers became clear as the buildings opposite them erupted in flames. The inferno stretched from one end of the street to the other, then spread northwards, carving fiery paths through the Gunstian-occupied areas of Toraq. Lahnos shielded his eyes from the fierce light, the roar of the flames thundering in his ears. A few black shapes were silhouetted against the raging fires for a brief second, then they disappeared from sight as more buildings exploded ahead of them. The heat from the blaze reached Lahnos's face, and he covered it with a rag, leaving only his eyes free as he watched.

On and on it went without respite, as wave after wave of dragons soared over the city, but none of the flames came close to touching the front lines where the Dominion soldiers were located.

'The Children of Gahad are using their power over fire to shield us,' said Efizel, 'and to push the flames only to the north.'

Karl grimaced. 'What do we do, sergeant? I'm being cooked from the heat.'

'We do nothing,' said the Bullan; 'nothing but stay here and wait for it to be over.'

Another hour passed, then two, and still the dragons rained fire down upon the northern half of the city. The apartment blocks opposite the squad collapsed into red-hot, smoking rubble, and as soon as they had fallen, Lahnos and the rest of the squad could see the devastation afflicting the streets beyond. The sky was thick with smoke, but the flames were illuminating Toraq with a red and orange glow.

At some point during the destruction, Lahnos's exhausted body drifted off into a light and uncomfortable sleep, and he awoke to a grey and miserable dawn. Ash was swirling through the sky, and towering pillars of smoke were rising over the city like a thick dark funeral shroud. Rain started to fall over Toraq, the wind from the south gusting through the ash of the broken ruins. The squad got up from the floor and ate a silent breakfast together, no one speaking about what they had witnessed throughout the long night of flames.

The orders to advance reached them an hour later, and the squad filed down the stairs, passing the bodies of the four Gunstians that

Lahnos had killed in the stairwell. Out on the street, Zamatan soldiers were staring at the city with wide eyes. On the southern side of the street, every building was still standing, but to the north was nothing but mile after mile of smoking rubble.

'I take it all back, sergeant,' muttered the blacksmith. 'You said there would be an attack, and there was. You're a bloody genius.'

A squad of Bullan soldiers appeared from a side road behind them, and began directing the Zamatans forward.

Karl pointed towards the rubble. 'Are they expecting us to march through that?'

'No,' said Efizel, his gaze on his kinsfolk. 'We are being told to go around it. The northern half of Toraq no longer exists.'

Lahnos stared into the distance at the ruins. He had always known that the dragons were powerful, but his mind found it hard to believe what they had done. Unable to occupy the city, they had decided to wipe it off the map instead.

The Bullan company passed the squad on the street, but the professional soldiers averted their eyes from Efizel, as though even a brief glance at him would besmirch their honour. Efizel stared at them, his eyes dark, then he turned back to the squad.

'Let us go,' he said. 'There is nothing for us here.'

CHAPTER 20
LAID WASTE

Zamata Gataza, Serpent Isle – 14th Lexinch 1588

'Captain Cisca, if you please?' cried the Bullan officer.

Cisca halted on the stairs. She composed herself, and then she turned and smiled.

'Yes, Lieutenant? How can I help you?'

The Bullan walked down the steps until he was level with her. His eyes narrowed a little.

'I thought I would inform you, Captain,' he said, 'that after five wasted days searching Kaugatz for Commander Bauchlie, the criminal has again been seen in the vicinity of the ruins of Medamuna Gatzoun. It seems that your orders to hunt for him in Kaugatz were... ill-advised.'

'Thank you for letting me know, Lieutenant,' she said.

'Despite the delay,' the Bullan went on, 'we should round him up soon. Two hundred of my kinsfolk are currently closing in on his position within the ruined monastery. I am confident that his head will shortly be brought to Lord Malum.'

'That is good to know.'

'Might I ask, ma'am, where you received the information that he was in Kaugatz? I am concerned that someone might have been misleading you with malicious intent.'

'I regret that I am unable to supply you with that information, Lieutenant,' she said. 'Rest assured that I will look into it personally.'

The Bullan officer stared into her eyes for a moment, then he saluted and walked back up the stairs. Cisca glanced down, wondering if he had sensed her fear. For five long days she had been trying to avoid the Bullan stationed within the monastery of Zamata Gataza, terrified that she would be arrested or dragged before the dragons and forced to reveal everything to them. And now she had Bauchlie to worry about again. At least while the Bullan had been in Kaugatz she had known that he was safe. She tried to push him from her mind. She had to stop pretending that she knew him – she didn't, and, besides, it had been months since she had last laid eyes on the fugitive criminal. All the same, Takri's words to her had been swirling around her thoughts incessantly. Could they be true? Did Bauchlie like her? And why would Takri say such a thing unless she was trying to entrap her?

She took a breath, and began to descend the stairs. She trusted no one in the monastery – not the dragons, not the Bullan or the monks, and certainly not Takri. There was always Lyla, but Cisca was too afraid to visit her, as the Bullan guards on duty outside the major's small room could easily inform Takri that she had been there.

Cisca made her way to the ground floor of the monastery where the stores were kept, and busied herself by filling out forms requisitioning more supplies for the three dragons. The monks were still mourning the death of Lady Lenta, and none spoke to her as she walked to a quiet desk in the corner of the storeroom and began to work. She had been attending prayers in the temple each morning, as Takri had advised, and had heard the lamentations of the monks as they grieved for Lenta – the second Child of Gahad to die on the island in little over a month. The death of Lord Irvan was being blamed on Colonel Laimos and the rebels, but it was the Demon Witch who was being held responsible for Lenta's demise, and the monks had been fulsome in their visceral hatred for the evil Witch, calling upon the serpent gods to strike her down. Takri had also been present at the morning prayer sessions, but she had never once glanced at Cisca or even acknowledged her presence within the temple. Aware that Lord Malum was devoted to her, the monks had been treating Takri with exaggerated deference and respect, bowing low before her as if she were almost godlike.

Cisca scowled to herself. She was tired of living in fear of the young woman, and it seemed to Cisca that if some terrible accident were to befall Takri then all of her problems would be solved. Could she get close enough to her to kill her? Possibly, but how would she evade being caught, and, regardless, Cisca was no murderer.

'Am I interrupting you, Captain?'

Cisca flinched in her seat, and Takri laughed.

'Perhaps I should stop creeping up on you like that,' Takri said.

Cisca swallowed, but said nothing.

The young woman leaned in closer. 'I need you to speak to the Bullan again, Captain. It appears that they are diverting soldiers back to the ruins of Medamuna Gatzoun, and...'

'I know, ma'am,' Cisca said. 'One of their officers informed me of this a short time ago. The Bullan have made it clear that they think I am being misled. I doubt they will obey any of my orders again without checking with their superiors first. They also told me that two hundred soldiers are moving up to the ruins of the monastery on Mount Medamuna.'

'I see,' said Takri.

'I am sorry, ma'am,' Cisca went on, 'but I think that if I try to speak to them again about this, it will only arouse their suspicions.'

'Perhaps you are right,' Takri said, 'but this is an unfortunate turn of events.'

Cisca glanced away.

'There is another thing you could do for me, Captain,' Takri said.

'Ma'am?'

'I want you to tell me if you hear any of the dragons discussing how they intend to capture or kill the Demon Witch. You enjoy more access to Lady Macsin and Lord Rylan than I, and if they mention anything about it in your hearing, you must tell me at once.'

Cisca narrowed her eyes.

'I can sense the question you wish to ask me,' said Takri. 'The truth is that Lord Malum has decided that his scheme to ensnare the Demon Witch is a secret matter, and he has told me nothing about what they intend to do.'

'You wish me to eavesdrop on private conversations held among the dragons, ma'am?'

'Yes. Is that a problem?'

'It will be if they catch me doing it, ma'am.'

'Then make sure you are discreet, Captain. If you are caught in the act, it will probably be the end for you.'

'And what about you, ma'am? If I am caught, the dragons will likely use the truth spell on me, and I will be forced to inform them that you ordered me to feed the Bullan false information regarding the whereabouts of Commander Bauchlie.'

'Then I shall rephrase it – if you are caught, it will probably be the end for both of us. Nevertheless, it is vital that I discover the means by which they intend to deal with the Demon Witch.'

Cisca pondered her choices. 'And if I refuse? What will you do, ma'am? You are asking me to break one of the strictest regulations in the Dragon Corps code of conduct. Private words uttered by the dragons are not to be mentioned to anyone – that is one of the rules I swore to obey.'

'I have no wish to threaten you,' said Takri, 'but since you asked – if you refuse to do as I say, then I will have Lord Malum kill you. Is that clear enough? There will be no need for him to use the truth spell, as he believes everything I say. One word from me, Captain, and your head would be forcibly removed from your shoulders. It would be a pity, as then I would need to find another useful person to carry out little jobs for me, but I suppose there is always Major Lyla.'

Cisca bowed her head, her eyes closing for a moment as fear swamped her. She was trapped, and Takri knew it. She glanced up to tell her that she would obey her orders, only to find that the young woman had already gone. Cisca tidied away the papers and ink from the desk and got to her feet.

She frowned. The initial shock from hearing Takri's threat was starting to wear off, and she wondered if she had perceived a slight change in the young woman's demeanour. Up until that moment, Takri had strode around as if she were the most important human on the island, but if that were the case, then why would Lord Malum have decided not to confide in her? The pale red dragon doted on her, and yet he was unwilling to reveal his plan to capture the Demon Witch. Did he suspect that Takri was unreliable in some way? Lady Macsin loathed her; had she warned Lord Malum not to be too trusting of his new advisor? Whatever the reason, Takri had seemed different – almost as though she was worried, or even scared.

Cisca left the storage chambers and descended a flight of stairs. She had a choice to make – she could either continue to follow Takri's orders, embroiling herself deeper into a conspiracy that might end in her execution; or she could confess everything to the dragons and beg for forgiveness. She doubted that Lord Malum would be prepared to listen to any wild accusations against his favourite human, but perhaps Lady Macsin would be more receptive.

She reached the underground caverns and strode into the central chamber. It was large enough to fit all of the dragons, but only Lady Macsin and Lord Rylan were there. Cisca checked the water trough and the food supplies, and the two dragons ignored her. It was a situation Cisca was used to; in the palaces of Nom Karta, days could sometimes go by without a dragon directly addressing their Dragon Corps assistants. Cisca noted down the number of rugs and blankets that needed laundering. The dragons had been trailing in mud and leaves from the outside, and the bones from a devoured goat were lying in a heap by a wall.

'You are weak,' Macsin growled. 'Weak, cowardly and devious.'

Cisca froze. Her glance darted over to the huge dragon, then she realised that Macsin had been talking to Lord Rylan, who was sitting with his head lowered, his features displaying his unhappiness.

'You are only here to make up the numbers,' Macsin went on; 'do you know that? You are fortunate to be alive after the way you and your sister behaved during the conference that elected Naghad to be our new King. If it had been up to me, then both of you would have been torn to pieces.'

Lord Rylan said nothing, and Cisca went about her duties, keeping as quiet as possible.

'I have more respect for Lord Tegru than I do for you,' Macsin said. 'Lord Tegru might be a traitor, but at least he had the courage to stand up for himself, and for those who voted for him; whereas you and your sister displayed nothing but low cunning followed by abject cowardice. I laughed when you knelt before King Naghad.'

'I know,' said Lord Rylan; 'I heard you.'

'Does that not anger you?' Macsin said. 'Do you not wish to strike me, Lord Rylan? If you had laughed at me, you would already be dead.'

'You are my elder, Lady Macsin,' Rylan said.

'That's right!' she cried. 'I am a thousand years older than you: the eldest daughter of King Gahad; while you are merely the child of our father's third mate. Your mother was frail and delicate, barely worthy to become the mighty Gahad's partner. She was like a child compared to me! I was with my father when we subdued the Klediomira Haga; tell me – where were you? What great feats of strength, what deeds of renown have you ever accomplished?' Her eyes burned as she glared at him. 'If you had voted for King Naghad, then I would perhaps be more willing to be sympathetic to your weakness and youth, but your... suggestion, your proposal... it disgusted me.'

'But, my lady,' Rylan said, 'if we could vote for King Gahad's successor, then why could we not vote on other matters? Don't you think the decision to invade Gunst should have been made by all of the Children of Gahad?'

Sparks flew across Macsin's jaws, and she raised a forelimb, her claws extended.

'After everything,' she roared, 'and you are still advocating this nonsense? The Dominion needs a firm hand – a monarch, not a foolish debating chamber. Do you think we are like the humans?'

'No, my lady,' said Rylan. 'I submitted to the will of the other Children of Gahad. I am faithful and loyal to King Naghad.'

Macsin laughed. 'Weak, so weak.'

Two Bullan soldiers entered the chamber, and the dragons turned to gaze at them.

The soldiers bowed. 'My lady and lord,' said one; 'we bring news from the lowlands of the island.'

'Then speak,' said Macsin, lowering her claws.

'A terrible affliction has been reported by our kin in the farms and fields between Wayston and the ruins of Neeton, my lady.'

Cisca glanced over, her eyes narrowing.

'What kind of affliction, soldier?' said Macsin.

'Whole fields of wheat are rotting, my lady. The scourge has devastated hundreds of acres of crops, and the vines on the slopes of Mount Medamuna have also been affected. The destruction has obliterated this season's harvest.'

The dragons said nothing for a moment, then Rylan raised his eyes.

'Disease?' he said.

'No, my lord,' said the Bullan. 'We suspect that Gunstian agents are responsible. We believe that there is at least one agent upon the island with the Gift of Famine.'

'Are you sure about this?' said Macsin.

'We are, my lady,' said the Bullan. 'There is no other logical explanation.'

'And what will this mean for the island?' said Rylan.

'Food stocks were already at a very low level, my lord, following the requisition of so much for the invasion force. The loss of this season's harvest on top of that will result in the deaths of many from starvation. And, if the agent or agents are allowed to do the same to the other parts of the island, the effects could be catastrophic.'

'I will need to speak to Lord Malum about this,' said Macsin, 'but in the meantime, I want the Bullan to start guarding the olive groves and other farmlands that have so far been unaffected. We must find and eliminate the Gunstian agents before they turn the Serpent Isle into a barren desert.'

'Yes, my lady. Should I order the forces encircling the ruins of Medamuna Gatzoun to be re-deployed?'

'Yes. The capture of Bauchlie is secondary to preventing the accursed Gunstians from completing this vile act of sabotage.' She turned to Rylan. 'Half-brother – fly out and survey the damage. I shall awaken Lord Malum and tell him the news.'

Rylan tilted his head. 'Yes, my lady.'

'Captain Cisca,' said Macsin.

'My lady?'

'Fetch Takri from wherever she is lurking. No doubt the esteemed Governor will wish to consult with his pet before making any decisions.'

Cisca bowed. 'At once, my lady.'

She and the Bullan soldiers hurried from the chamber, and ascended the stairs to the ground floor of the monastery.

'That bastard Bauchlie is going to get away, again,' muttered one of the soldiers.

'I know, corporal,' said the other, his eyes on Cisca. 'We could have caught him days ago, had we not been diverted to Kaugatz.'

Cisca said nothing, then she left the two soldiers in a hall on the ground floor, and climbed the stairs to Takri's apartment. She suppressed a smile. Bauchlie was alive and free. A surge of guilt followed her relief – the people of the island could be starving over the next few months, and she was pleased that one man – and a vile criminal at that – had not been arrested? Her parents would be ashamed if they knew the thoughts that raced through their daughter's mind. She reached the fourth floor and quickened her pace. Two Bullan soldiers were on guard outside the front door of Takri's apartment, and they eyed her as she approached.

'I need to see Lady Takri,' she said.

'Sorry, ma'am,' said one, 'but her ladyship is currently entertaining a guest.'

'A guest?' Cisca said. 'Who?'

The soldier shrugged. 'An Aucterian soldier, ma'am. They are not to be disturbed.'

'Oh. Unfortunately, I have express orders from Lady Macsin to summon Lady Takri downstairs. It's urgent.'

One of the soldiers nodded, then he rapped a large fist against the door.

'Lady Takri?' he called out. 'Apologies, but there is an urgent summons from Lady Macsin.'

'One minute, please,' said a voice from through the door.

Cisca tried not to picture the scene within Takri's rooms. What the young woman did with Aucterian soldiers was none of her business.

The door opened a little and Lady Takri peered through the gap. She appeared to have all of her clothes on, and her features were expressionless.

'I will be out in a moment,' she said to the soldiers, then her gaze caught Cisca. 'Perhaps you should come in, Captain.' Takri opened the door a little further, and gestured to Cisca. 'Inside; now.'

Cisca entered the apartment, and Takri closed the door behind her. Standing by the balcony doors was a tall man in an Aucterian army uniform. Cisca tried to avert her eyes, but then she noticed a scar on the man's face, and her mouth opened.

Takri smiled. 'I presume no introductions are needed?'

Bauchlie folded his arms across his chest. 'I thought you were trying to be discreet, Leona?'

Cisca stared at him.

Takri laughed. 'What is so urgent, Captain?'

Cisca's face flushed. 'The dragons... I, uh... How did you...?'

'Quickly, please,' said Takri.

'The crops are dead,' she said.

Takri and Bauchlie glanced at each other.

'The crops?' said Bauchlie.

'Yes,' she said, her eyes never leaving him. 'The Gift of Famine.'

Takri's expression altered. 'Wait here, both of you,' she said. 'I shall find out what's going on.'

'I can't stay here much longer,' said Bauchlie. 'My boat is waiting for me at the bottom of the cliffs.'

'Then I shall be quick,' she said.

Takri strode to the door and left her quarters, leaving Cisca and Bauchlie alone in the large living room.

Cisca tried to speak, but her mind had gone blank.

'How have you been, Cisca?' he said.

'I... Takri...'

'You mean Leona?' he said. 'She told me that she had recruited you. Well, that's not exactly what she said.'

'She's blackmailing me.'

Bauchlie eyed her.

'Why are you here?' she said. 'If you are caught, then...'

'I needed to speak to her, to coordinate our efforts. Thank you for sending the Bullan to Kaugatz.'

Cisca nodded.

'How bad is it?' he said.

'How bad is what?'

He narrowed his eyes. 'The Gift of Famine? I sailed around the west coast of Zamata to get here, so I didn't see any destruction. What areas have been affected?'

'The Bullan said that all of the wheat fields and vineyards between Wayston and Neeton have been devastated.'

Bauchlie's gaze fell, and he sat down on a long couch.

'I remember you mentioning the Gift of Famine in Igatz,' she said. 'What do you know about it?'

'The name is fairly self-explanatory,' he said. 'Those who possess this Gift can kill plants with a thought or a glance. I should go.'

'The Bullan are being withdrawn from the ruins of Medamuna Gatzoun to protect the surviving farms,' she said.

He nodded, then got to his feet.

His eyes met hers. 'Be careful,' he said. 'Leona is committed to the cause and she can be ruthless. Do not be afraid to stand up to her.'

'Bauchlie, I...'

'Another time,' he said, then he walked past her to the door. She turned, and watched him leave the apartment.

Cisca remained where she was, her gaze falling on the closed door, then she walked out on to the wide balcony and felt the warmth of the sun on her face. She had just seen Bauchlie, had been alone with him for a few minutes, and she had acted like a fool. Worse, Bauchlie had been inside Zamata Gataza, the headquarters of his enemies, but not to see her. If Cisca hadn't gone to Takri's rooms, then he would have come and gone without her even knowing about it. It was clear – he wasn't interested in her, and she had been deceiving herself. She thought about going to her own rooms, so that she could lie down in the darkness with the shutters closed, but someone needed to tell Takri that Bauchlie had gone. She shook her head. The woman's name was Leona, and she was a rebel. The courage of Leona and Bauchlie gave her pause – the risks they were running for their beloved island were beyond anything Cisca could imagine. To have had the guts to walk into Zamata Gataza dressed as an Aucterian soldier; and what Leona was doing put even that into the shade. Still, they were traitors to the Dominion, and now Cisca was complicit.

She stared out at the view of the island. The monastery was too high for her to be able to see any damage to the fields that stretched out below the slopes of Mount Hodzulat, but she caught a glimpse of Lord Rylan as he soared over the low lands north of Neeton.

She heard the door open and close behind her, then Leona walked out on to the balcony.

'Has he gone?' she said.

Cisca nodded.

'You should leave,' Leona said. 'I need to get ready.'

'Ready for what?'

'Lord Malum and Lady Macsin have decided how to proceed,' said Leona, 'and they want me to assist them.'

'Proceed?'

'Yes, Captain. The dragons are going to have the Bullan round up everyone on Zamata of Gunstian heritage. There are around five or six thousand of them, mostly in Kaugatz. Once they have been arrested, the dragons are going to interrogate them in an attempt to discover the identities and locations of the agents with the Gift of Famine. And then, they will all be executed.'

Cisca blinked. 'Executed? But, they can't.'

'Why not? Lord Malum has the authority to act as he pleases. It was Lady Macsin's suggestion. She said that the deaths of several thousand Gunstians will relieve the threat of famine for everyone else.'

'But the Gunstians on the island can't all be traitors,' Cisca said. 'And they have families – children.'

'I know.'

'Are you going to help the dragons kill them?'

'I have no choice.'

Cisca snorted and shook her head. 'Don't pretend you care about the fate of the Gunstians. You are a fanatic. You have probably dreamt about destroying everyone on the Serpent Isle who is not of pure Zamatan stock.'

'You are wrong,' Leona said. 'The Gunstians have been here for hundreds of years. I have no desire to see them exterminated.'

'Would you help the dragons if it were Zamatans who were about to be rounded up and slaughtered?'

'The Zamatan men have already been rounded up, Cisca; and at this very moment they are being slaughtered in Gunst.'

'You didn't answer my question. Why did you tell Bauchlie that you had recruited me? I am not a rebel.'

'I think you will find that you are, Cisca,' Leona said. 'You have aided and abetted Commander Bauchlie – he is free because of you. And I know what you think about the dragons currently ruling the Dominion – you hate them. Do you recall what I said to you this morning? If one of us is caught, then we shall both die.'

'Then that is what will happen,' Cisca said. 'We cannot win. Your cause is hopeless, and the Serpent Isle will never be free.'

'If I believed that, then I would have given up a long time ago,' said Leona. 'You are forgetting something – we have the Demon Witch on our side. I have seen what she can do.'

'We all saw what she did to Lenta.'

Leona lowered her voice. 'The Demon Witch has done more for this island than merely incapacitating one dragon, Cisca; much, much more. Did you seriously believe that Colonel Laimos was the strategic genius who masterminded the success of the uprising?'

'I don't understand. Are you saying that the Demon Witch has been helping the rebels all this time?'

'Precisely, Cisca. That is why it is vital that we discover how the dragons are intending to confront her. Do you understand? The Demon Witch is our only hope. We must carry on, even when everything seems bleak and hopeless. Look deep into yourself, and find the strength you need.'

'Your cause is not my cause.'

'Then do it in order to survive. Now, go. The dragons are expecting me.'

Cisca strode back into the apartment, her mind spinning. She paused at the front door and glanced over her shoulder. Leona was still standing by the balcony railings, looking small and vulnerable as she gazed out over the Serpent Isle. How could someone like that have manoeuvred Cisca into a position where her only chance of survival was to aid the rebels? Cisca cursed under her breath. She hated Leona but, at the same time, she could not help but respect her.

She left the apartment, and went back to work.

CHAPTER 21
THE GUNSTIANS OF THE SERPENT ISLE

Kaugatz, Serpent Isle – 16th Lexinch 1588

Leona stared into the blotchy and tarnished mirror, as flies buzzed around the dank toilet trough behind her. She felt tired and sick, disgusted and ashamed. A few dozen yards away, in a public square in the eastern district of Kaugatz, the bodies of over eighty islanders of Gunstian ancestry were lying dead. Almost one thousand had been slain already that day, and the ground of the square was thick with blood.

Leona hadn't killed any of them, but nor had she tried to prevent Lady Macsin from tearing their bodies to pieces. Cisca's words reverberated around her mind. Would she have assisted the dragons if it had been Zamatans who were being slaughtered? Leona knew the answer to that, and it made her want to curl up in a dark corner and die.

She wiped her eyes with a handkerchief, then dipped into a pocket and re-applied some mascara. Under no circumstances should the dragons know that she had been crying; it was far better that they thought her cold and callous rather than betray her inner feelings. She gazed at her reflection for a moment, then she slipped the make-up into her pocket, unbarred the door and stepped back out into the bright afternoon sunshine.

The Bullan were unloading more Gunstians from the backs of wagons, and were herding them into the square, while others were removing the corpses. Their bodies were being taken to join the others on a vast site on the eastern edge of town, where a funeral pyre was being laid out, and the soldiers were throwing the body parts up onto tarpaulin-covered carts. A few screams arose from the live Gunstians as the Bullan shoved them towards where Lord Malum and Lady Macsin were waiting. The dragons eyed them, then they turned to watch as Leona approached.

'Stand by my side, my beloved Takri,' Malum said.

Macsin looked away, her anger clear. 'Why must she be here, my lord? What possible use does she have?'

Malum turned to his sister. 'Perhaps today is the day when I shall reveal that to you. For now, though, please start interrogating our latest batch of traitors.'

Leona strode over until she was standing next to Malum's right forelimb, then she watched impassively as the Gunstians were pushed forward. One of them, a teenage boy, tried to flee, and a Bullan soldier clubbed him over the back of his head with the butt of his crossbow. The boy fell into a pool of blood and lay still.

'One of you,' Macsin said, 'knows something about the Gunstian agents who have infiltrated this island. Perhaps you have provided them with food and shelter, or perhaps you have been told of their location. If you step forward and admit to your crimes, then you and your family might survive this day. If no one confesses, you will all die.'

The sound of shouts and more screaming rose up from a few streets away, and Lord Malum glanced at a Bullan officer.

'The Gunstian civilians have spread word of what is taking place here, my lord,' the officer said, 'and they are attempting to resist arrest.'

'Kill all who resist,' said Malum. 'Show no mercy, for the Gunstians have forever been our enemies.' He turned to the crowd as the officer saluted and hurried away. 'This carnage will only stop when we have found the agents responsible for destroying the harvest.'

'We know nothing!' cried an old man. 'The Gunstian agents, if there are any, would never tell us what they were doing.'

Leona felt a tingle and touched her right ear.

'You are lying!' roared Malum. 'Sister – kill that man.'

Macsin lunged forwards, and her claws gripped the old Gunstian. She raised him to her jaws and tore his head off, then she threw the decapitated corpse to the ground.

'Who here knows where the agents are hiding?' said Malum, his voice calm again. 'Do you want to see your children slaughtered?'

'Damn you, demons!' cursed a woman in the Gunstian language.

Macsin brought a forelimb up, then she slammed it down onto the woman, crushing her into the bloody ground. The other Gunstians in the square trembled and huddled together, the children among them wailing and crying. Leona struggled to keep her composure, as she tried to remember what she was fighting for. She had always mistrusted the Gunstians who lived on the island, and recalled that many had assisted the Gunstian army when they had invaded in the spring. Had she secretly longed for their destruction, as Cisca had implied? The colonel had often talked about how everyone on Zamata would have to learn how to live with each other – the Zamatans, the part-Bullan, the Gunstians, and even the Aucterian settlers, but Leona had never felt that to be a realistic prospect.

'All it will take is for one brave soul standing here to step forward,' said Malum, 'and the slaughter will cease. Confess! Where are the agents?'

'I don't know; I swear it!' cried a man.

Leona felt no tingle, so she kept her arm by her side.

'If you did know, would you lie to protect the agents?' said Malum.

'No!' the man shouted.

Leona touched her ear.

'I grow tired of this charade!' roared Malum. 'Sister – kill them all. Bullan – bring in the next batch.'

Leona looked away as Macsin tore through the crowd of screaming Gunstians, her jaws and talons ripping their bodies apart. Beyond the lines of armoured Bullan at the edge of the square, Leona could see a crowd of Zamatan women and old folk who had gathered to watch. A few were cheering the dragons on, but many looked shocked and revolted.

Lady Macsin lowered her claws, and the Bullan began loading the dismembered corpses onto the carts. Lord Malum gazed up at the position of the sun.

'The day wears on,' he said, 'and we are no closer to discovering the truth.'

'Might I suggest the truth spell, my lord?' said Leona.

'You fool,' spat Macsin. 'Are we supposed to use our powers on thousands of mortals? We would be here for months.'

'Refrain from insulting my beloved, sister,' growled Malum. 'Takri, go on with your suggestion.'

'If I could be allowed to pick out one or two from the next batch,' Leona said, 'then you could employ your powers on them and them alone.'

'And how would you know whom to choose?' said Macsin. 'Are you one of them? Are you working for the Gunstians, girl?'

'Let us try Lady Takri's approach, my sister,' said Malum. 'Ensure you have a squad of Bullan to protect you, my beloved.'

Leona bowed her head, then she gestured to a Bullan officer as more Gunstian civilians were herded into the square.

'Come with me,' she said, 'and bring a few men.'

'Yes, ma'am.'

The officer assembled six soldiers, and they moved into position around Leona as she set off towards the new batch of Gunstians. Leona eyed their faces, looking for any signs that they might be hiding something.

She pointed at a middle-aged woman. 'You – do you know anything about the agents?'

'No,' cried the woman.

No tingle. Leona pointed again. 'And you? Do you know where the agents are?'

'I have no idea, Dominion bitch,' the man said, 'and if I did I wouldn't tell you.'

No tingle.

Leona strode closer to the crowd, who eyed her with a mixture of hatred and fear.

She pointed at another man. 'Do you have any information that might lead us to the agents?'

The man spat on the bloody ground. 'No.'

Leona's head tingled, and she nodded to the Bullan officer. 'Pull that man from the crowd and bring him before Lord Malum and Lady Macsin.'

The Bullan charged into the civilians, and grabbed hold of the man. Macsin raised a clawed forelimb as the Gunstians cried out in anger, and the Bullan dragged the man towards her.

'This one knows something, my lord and lady,' said Leona, bowing.

Macsin stared at her. 'There had better be a good explanation for what I just witnessed.'

'There is, my sister,' said Lord Malum. 'Please be patient while I examine this man.'

'But...'

'Not now, sister.' Malum brought his head down and stared into the eyes of the Gunstian lying on the ground in front of them. 'I compel you to only speak the truth; no lie can leave your lips. Tell us all that you know regarding the agents with the Gift of Famine.'

'Tell the bastards nothing!' cried a woman from the crowd.

The man stared up at Malum from the bloodied earth. 'I... I...' His face contorted with helpless rage, and he clenched his fists. 'I helped two Gunstian agents three nights ago,' he gasped. 'I did not know that they were Gifted. The man who brought them to my house told me to ask no questions. I fed them, and allowed them to sleep in my home, and in the morning they were gone.'

'At last,' said Malum; 'now we are getting somewhere. The man who brought the agents to your home – do you know his name, and where he lives?'

'Yes.'

'Then tell us.'

'His name is Adapnie, and he lives in Chesson, in a cottage in the Gunstian quarter by the harbour, the fourth house along from the fishing pier. A white cottage.'

'And is Adapnie also a Gunstian agent?'

'Yes,' said the man, his eyes revealing his inner torment.

'You filthy traitor,' said Macsin.

'The great Chadura will strike you all down, you spawn of the demon Gahad. Long live Gunst! Death to...'

Macsin crushed him with a forelimb, grinding his head into the gravel.

Malum turned to the Bullan. 'Send a detachment to the area mentioned by this man, and round up every Gunstian who lives close to the harbour. Bring them all here.'

'Yes, my lord,' said the officer.

'Sister,' Malum went on, 'kill the others.'

Two hours later, Leona sat alone under the shade of an orange tree, her back to the square. While waiting for the Bullan to return from Chesson, Lord Malum had allowed his sister to slaughter the other Gunstians who had been arrested that morning. His stated reason was to alleviate the famine for the other inhabitants of the island, but Leona had sensed the falsehood in his words. He didn't care how many Zamatans starved; he just wanted to destroy every Gunstian on the island.

There were Bullan present whose role it was to record the numbers killed, and when the carnage came to an end, Leona summoned them to her side.

'Well?' she said. 'How many?'

'Three thousand, nine hundred and twenty, ma'am,' said the Bullan soldier, reading from a document.

'And how many remain?'

'That is unclear, ma'am. We estimate that another thousand are still to be rounded up within the town of Kaugatz, while there are other Gunstians dwelling in the outlying areas. Three hundred or so live in Chesson, for example.'

Leona glanced over to the east and saw a plume of smoke rising into the cloudy sky.

'The pyres have been lit,' she said.

'Yes, ma'am. They will be burning well into tomorrow, I would imagine.'

Leona gazed down, and saw a trickle of blood from the square gather by her sandals.

'Thank you,' she said. 'That will be all.'

The Bullan saluted and went back to their posts.

Leona lowered her head. 'What have I done?' she whispered.

None of this is your fault.

Leona closed her eyes. *Demon Witch? Please leave me; I cannot bear for you to see what I have become.*

I know what lies within your heart, Leona, the Demon Witch said. *The dragons would have slaughtered the Gunstians of Zamata with or without your assistance; you know this to be true. I have news from Gunst – do you want to hear it?*

I don't know. If you have come to tell me that the menfolk have all been killed, then I don't think I could stand it.

Most are still alive, said the Demon Witch, *though their numbers fall day by day. I spoke to Lahnos. I tried to apologise, but he still hates me.*

Apologise for what? Why does he hate you? What did you do?

I thought you didn't care.

Maybe I don't. I feel... sick. Sick and exhausted.

Do you want to know why he hates me?

Leona thought in silence for a few moments, though she was aware that the Demon Witch could see everything that was in her mind. Did she care what the Witch had done to Lahnos? Leona liked Lahnos, but he was only one man among the thousands who had been forced into the Dominion army and sent off to Gunst. But perhaps it was relevant. Perhaps she should know.

Tell me, she said.

I killed his father.

Leona narrowed her eyes. *Why?*

It was unintentional. Lahnos's father happened to be in the volcano palace on Inopei when I destroyed it. There were hundreds of slaves living there, and Lahnos's father was one of them.

You killed hundreds of slaves?

Yes. It was a mistake. I did not know that the palace would be consumed by the volcano when I slew King Gahad.

If you killed hundreds, then why did you choose to help Lahnos? Why not the families of the other slaves? Why did you choose him?

Because Lahnos's father was the only one there who spoke the same language as I do, she said. *The minds of the others were closed to me. I have since learned that they were speaking Gunstian. Every slave in the palace, and all of the slaves working in the mines in the valleys below, were Gunstian – all but Lahnos's father. From him I learned his name, and that he had a family. I knew nothing about the others, so I decided to help Lahnos. I think the Gunstians in Inopei have been there for generations. They worshipped Gahad as a god, and their dialect was not quite the same as that spoken by their kinsfolk in Gunst. Do you know what they were mining?*

No, though I have heard the colonel mention to me that the Dominion took thousands of Gunstians back to Inopei as slaves. That was a long time ago. Their descendants must still dwell there.

So, now you know why Lahnos despises me. Do you also hate me, Leona?

Of course not. Lahnos is clearly a fool. You killed his father, yes; but it was an accident, and since then you have done nothing but try to make amends. You could have walked away, but you didn't.

I couldn't. The guilt I feel over what I did eats at me. But I disagree with you; Lahnos is not a fool – he is hurting. He knows that I kept the truth from him for a long time.

The voice fell silent, and Leona frowned. *Are you still there?*

Someone has sensed my presence, Leona; I must go before you are discovered. And thank you; thank you for not hating me.

The Demon Witch vanished from her mind, and Leona opened her eyes to the sunshine. The thought occurred to her that if Lahnos had been more understanding, then the Demon Witch might never have contacted her, and for that she was grateful. She got to her feet, and turned to see two Bullan soldiers running towards her.

'Lord Malum orders that you attend to him immediately, ma'am,' said one.

Leona made sure that her face was betraying no emotion, then she followed the soldiers back into the blood-soaked square, where a double line of open-topped wagons were being loaded with body parts.

'There you are!' cried Malum. 'I was concerned for your safety, my beloved Takri.'

'Thank you, my lord; but why?' she said. 'I was perfectly safe.'

'You poor child,' he said; 'you do not realise what has just happened. The Demon Witch was here! Both Lady Macsin and I felt her powers being used in this vicinity, just a few moments ago. Did you sense anything?'

Leona tried to look shocked. 'No, my lord; I felt nothing.'

'Why would this girl feel anything, brother?' said Macsin. 'She is a feeble human.'

'What was the Demon Witch doing here, my lord?' said Leona.

'We do not know,' said Malum. 'Her powers are strange to us, though not as strange as the Gifted. It may be that she was merely watching us for a few moments, or perhaps she was trying to corrupt our minds, as she did to Lady Lenta.'

'We are far stronger than Lady Lenta, brother,' said Macsin. 'We shall not be humbled in the same manner.'

'Were the powers also directed towards Zamata Gataza, my lord?' said Leona.

'Why do you ask?'

'Because, with all due respect, Lord Rylan is not as powerful as you or Lady Macsin.'

The two dragons glanced at each other.

'Wise words,' said Malum. 'Sister, fly back to the monastery with all speed, and ensure that our young half-brother remains in one piece.'

'And if he does not?' said Macsin. 'Should I do to him what you did to Lenta, brother?'

Malum said nothing for a moment, then he tilted his head. 'Yes.'

Macsin extended her enormous wings and ascended into the air. She circled once over the square, then hurtled off towards the west.

'I intend to tell my sister the truth about you,' Malum said, as they watched Macsin fade into the distance. 'I did not wish to, but her animosity towards you grows ever stronger. If she understands how you have been assisting me, then perhaps her heart will soften a little.'

Leona bowed her head. 'As you will, my lord.'

'However, I shall not be telling Lord Rylan. You are correct about him – he is not as strong as my full sister, and if the Demon Witch strikes him down, then I do not want her to learn about your Gift.'

'Might I ask, my lord, if you are any closer to formulating your plan against the foul Witch?'

'Today has helped,' Malum said. 'Her use of powers has given my sister and me more to work with. The Witch's skills are similar in some ways to those possessed by the mighty Gahad himself, though they differ in some key regards. It is almost as though... as though she were not from this world. My father often told us stories about the worlds he visited before he came to Athumia. He knew King Nathaniel, and lived for long ages in the form of a human. Did you know that?'

'No, my lord.'

'An immortal human, of course,' Malum went on; 'not like the weak specimens to be found here. Lady Macsin also remembers many of the tales Gahad taught us, and our plan to ensnare the Demon Witch has been pieced together from our father's own words. It will be fitting, I feel, that the wisdom of Gahad be used to destroy the one who slew him. Wouldn't you agree?'

'Yes, my lord. I don't want you to think me a coward, but the Demon

Witch scares me. Might I ask when you will be able to move forward with your plan?'

Malum gazed down at her. 'We will strike at the first opportunity, my beloved Takri, but I cannot give you a precise date. Our attack can only take place while the Demon Witch is using her powers; otherwise, she will be impossible to trace.'

'Thank you, my lord.'

There was a commotion at the eastern end of the bloodied square, and an entire company of Bullan appeared, escorting several wagons. An officer ran all the way across the square to Lord Malum and bowed.

'My lord,' he said, 'we have brought every Gunstian who was found within the harbour district of Chesson; and we believe that the two agents and their handler are among their number – they tried to flee by boat as we surrounded the area.'

'Excellent work, Lieutenant,' said Lord Malum. 'Have the civilians brought into the square, but leave them in the wagons for now. As for the three suspects, bring them directly to me.'

'Yes, my lord.'

The Bullan officer hurried back to his comrades, and then the wagons were pulled into the square. Each was packed with Gunstian civilians who began to stare at the blood-soaked gravel on the ground. A few panicked and tried to jump down from the wagons, but they were clubbed by the Bullan soldiers. Two officers got down from the lead wagon, and more soldiers formed up by their sides, flanking three hooded men whose wrists had been bound behind their backs. The soldiers led the three men over the gravel, and the officers bowed their heads.

'These are the three suspects, my lord,' said the lieutenant. He gestured to the first. 'We believe this one to be Adapnie, the local handler. The cottage was registered in his name, and witnesses have claimed that he has lived in Chesson all his life. The other two appear to be strangers. The Zamatans we questioned in Chesson claim to have never seen them before.'

Lord Malum tilted his head a fraction. 'Remove their hoods.'

The soldiers bowed, and then the hoods were ripped from the three men. The handler had grey hair, and seemed older than the other two men, who were glancing at the dragon with defiance in their eyes.

'You will answer my questions one at a time,' said the pale red dragon, 'starting with the suspected handler. Old man, do the accusations lodged against you have any truth to them? Are you working for the Gunstian government?'

'No, my lord,' the man said. 'There has been a terrible mistake. These two men are my cousins – they used to live in Neeton before it was destroyed; that's why no one recognised them.'

Leona touched her right ear.

'I see,' said Malum. 'You are a terrible liar, old man. Had you confessed to your crimes, then I would have given you a quick death.' He shifted his gaze to the first suspected agent. 'And you? Do you also work for the Gunstians?'

The man looked away, his lips closed.

'I will take your silence as evidence of your guilt,' said Malum. He turned to the third man. 'What about you? Do you possess the Gift of Famine? Did you and your colleague destroy the wheat harvest and devastate the vineyards south of Wayston?'

The man gave Lord Malum a cold smile. 'Yes. The treacherous, Dominion-loving Zamatans will starve, as will the godless Aucterian settlers; praise be to Chadura!'

Lord Malum kept his expression serene. 'Well, at least one of you is honest.'

'Your unprovoked invasion of Gunst has been a disaster for the Dominion, demon,' the third man went on, his eyes lit with a savage joy. 'Your soldiers are being slaughtered, and your new King will be brought low, humbled by the Gifted! Thrice you have come to our shores, and thrice you will be defeated! The fields between Toraq City and Great Gunst are carpeted with your dead, and...'

Lord Malum lifted a talon, and the man's head exploded in a shower of blood, brains and fragments of skull.

'As I was saying,' said Malum, 'those who confess shall be given a quick death. However, it is too late for you two. Your deaths will be a torment of agony, as your own flesh rots from within; for such is how the enemies of the Dominion are treated.'

He raised his talon again, and the two Gunstians screamed and fell to their knees, their hands clutching the sides of their heads. The older man toppled over, his body writhing and convulsing as his flesh began to turn a sickly shade of green. His hair fell out, and then his teeth as he wept and howled. The younger man remained on his knees a little longer, until blackish blood started seeping from his eyes and ears, then he fell forwards onto the gravel. The two men each emitted one last cry of pain, then their heads seemed to decay, the flesh stripping off them until all that remained were two bare skulls, surrounded by a pool of noxious-smelling fluids.

'It is done,' said Malum. 'The Gunstian agents have paid for their crimes. Now, the rest of the Gunstian population must also accept their share of the blame. They harboured these criminals and spies, and it cannot be right that they are allowed to consume what food remains. No! It is far better that they are eliminated, so that the food they would have eaten can go to the loyal Zamatan population. This is my decree – all islanders of Gunstian stock are to die. My Bullan, you shall comb through the Serpent Isle, and ensure that none survive.'

'Yes, my lord,' said the lieutenant. 'Shall we start with the Gunstians from Chesson?'

Malum glanced up. 'There is no need. I shall take care of them in Lady Macsin's absence.'

The pale red dragon raised a talon, and the heads of every man, woman and child packed onto the loaded wagons exploded. A red cloud rose into the air, and the square fell into silence.

'Escort my beloved Takri back to Zamata Gataza,' Malum said to a squad of Bullan. 'I shall fly there now, and meet her later this evening.' He turned and glanced down at Leona, who was struggling to keep her face expressionless, her guts churning from what she had witnessed.

'This has been a good day, my fair Takri,' he said, 'and I couldn't have done it without you.'

CHAPTER 22
HEART OF THE EMPIRE

Great Gunst, Gunstian Empire – 18th Lexinch 1588

The rain swept down upon the Zamatan regiments as they trudged north along the wide, straight road. The lands around them were flat, and the high walls of Great Gunst loomed up ahead in the distance. In the ditches to the left and right of the road lay damaged wagons and carts, abandoned in the mud by the Dominion army as they pressed forward to lay siege to the capital of the Gunstian Empire. Despite being among the first to leave Toraq, the Zamatans were the last soldiers of the invasion force to reach Great Gunst. For days they had lingered in a makeshift camp, watching as the more professional elements of the Dominion army moved north past them. No explanation had been given to the Zamatans, but the reasons were clear – the dragons knew that their lack of training and expertise would make them almost useless in a formal siege.

Fifty yards to the left of the road lay a great wide river. It was curving round from the north-west, and the city of Great Gunst lay in the loop it created as it cut through the countryside. The river was deep enough for large ships to navigate it as far as the city, and several Dominion frigates had taken up position by the two huge stone bridges that spanned the waterway on the city's western flank. On the landward side, the Aucterian divisions had begun digging defensive earthen ramparts to encircle the city, cutting off the paved roads that ran out from Great Gunst like the spokes of a wheel. Lahnos glanced through the rain at the hundreds of mud-spattered Aucterians shovelling earth. Behind them lay the tents of the officers and commanders of the army, and a few grounded dragons were visible through the gloom, sitting with their wings folded in as they watched the soldiers at work.

'The walls go on forever,' muttered Karl, as the Zamatans marched forward. 'A lad from Kaugatz told me the other night that Great Gunst takes up more space than the whole of Zamata. Can you believe that?'

'They are about the same size,' said Efizel, his eyes on the squad as they moved through a gap in the ramparts. 'The biggest difference is the population. The Serpent Isle has... what? Eighty thousand people on it? Fewer now, I suppose, with all of the men over here. Great Gunst has over a million inhabitants, and that only includes those who live within its walls. Many more dwell in the unwalled suburbs to the north of the river.'

They passed a vast assembly yard, where eight tall siege engines were being constructed from parts that had been hauled all the way from the harbour of Toraq. Two dragons were standing guard over the wooden structures as carpenters and artificers toiled in the rain.

'Why are they building them on the wrong side of the ramparts?' said Jancke.

'There are more ramparts to the north,' said Efizel. 'We just crossed the southern edge of the Dominion camp.' The Bullan peered into the distance. 'If the Dominion are building defences on all sides, then a Gunstian field army might be close by, ready to attack our supply lines as soon as the siege begins in earnest.'

The Zamatan regiments came to a halt, and the men stood in the rain. Lahnos squinted ahead of them, but he couldn't see the front of the Zamatan column.

'The Aucterians will be deciding where to put us,' he said.

Efizel nodded. 'Yes. If we are lucky, the Zamatans will be ordered to protect the camp.'

'Will we get tents, sergeant?' said Karl.

The Bullan shrugged.

'The Dominion has given us nothing so far,' said Lahnos. 'Every crossbow, every shield and scrap of armour, and every pair of boots – we've had to scavenge them ourselves. Why would they now decide to give us tents?' He glanced up at the dark clouds overhead. 'And I thought it was summer.'

'It is summer,' said Efizel. 'If it were not, this rain would be freezing us where we stood.'

Lahnos stared at the city walls in the distance. They reminded him a little of the battlements that enclosed the monastery of Tsallon Anura, but on a much larger scale. There were towers and turrets every fifty yards or so, and fortresses at every point where the walls changed direction. The road they were standing on continued in a straight line right up to the walls, before it was swallowed up by a gatehouse larger than the fortress of Atzoun.

Lahnos found his thoughts drifting towards Reyn, as they often did during the long periods of inactivity since they had left the island. He had been wildly jealous of Bauchlie for a few days after the Demon Witch had told him that Reyn was with the rebel commander, his imagination running riot; but his thoughts had calmed since. It made sense that they would have met each other after the Bullan had raided Uncle Friel's mansion, and Lahnos was glad that Reyn had someone to watch her back. He pictured the way her tail swished when she was annoyed, and it made him smile. Would he ever see her again? With every day that passed, that prospect seemed to dim a little, but his longing for her only increased. Reyn was his first serious girlfriend, and he knew that he was her first serious boyfriend. Most marriages were arranged on Zamata, the details worked out between the two families, although couples were seldom forced into unhappy relationships. Among the part-Bullan, however, with no family structure to support them, the only thing that mattered was how you felt about the other person.

He glanced at his brother. 'Are you engaged yet?'

'Eh?' said Karl. 'This is a strange time to be asking that.'

'Well, are you?'

Karl looked away, as if embarrassed. 'No.'

'Why not?'

'Granny Jola was supposed to be sorting it out,' he said. 'After she died, Aunty Fenna promised that she would ask around the villages, but I don't think she ever got round to it.'

'If we ever get back,' Jancke said, 'then we'll have the pick of the girls. Hundreds of Zamatan men have died so far in this stupid invasion. All we have to do is survive, and then we can have any girl we want.'

Karl narrowed his eyes. 'You make it sound as though that's a good thing. Do you want all of the men to be slaughtered apart from you, just so you can get laid? With no men, Zamata has no future.'

'Zamata has no future whichever way you look at it,' said Lahnos. 'If the invasion succeeds, then do you think the Dominion will allow us to go home? We're soldiers in their damn army, and they'll send us wherever they choose. And if the invasion fails, then we won't be leaving Gunst. You lot will be enslaved until you kneel before their god, and the part-Bullan and Bullan will be annihilated.'

'If I believed that,' said Karl, 'then I would give up right now. The thought of seeing Fidalaimos again is the only thing that's keeping me going.'

The rain stopped, and the squad glanced up at the overcast sky.

'Do you really think we'll never get home, Lahnos?' said Jancke.

Lahnos stared at the city walls. 'I don't know. To be honest, I don't think I care about seeing Zamata again. I miss Reyn, but I don't miss the island. I'd like to see Aucteran and Inopei one day, and maybe even the land of the Bullan.'

Efizel smiled. 'Do you think those horns will protect you from my kinsfolk, young Laimos? My people tolerate no humans in their homeland.'

'So I'm a human to them, and a freak to the Zamatans, eh?'

'No one said life was fair.'

'It could have been me,' said Karl. 'I think about that a lot. It's just luck that I have no horns.'

Lahnos smiled. 'Yes, bad luck. There's still hope for our little sisters, though. Raba is only thirteen; she might start growing horns in a year or two.'

Karl shuddered.

'If she does,' Lahnos went on, 'will you throw her out of the village, too?'

Karl shrugged. 'Not if she files them off.'

Lahnos clenched his fists.

'That is enough,' said Efizel. 'Look; we are starting to move again. Keep your eyes open and your mouths closed.'

The long regimental column began stepping off the raised road and veering towards the right. Lahnos and the squad followed them, climbing down into the ditch and then back up the other side, where soldiers were starting to construct another earthen rampart. The column marched to the right of the new defensive line, their boots sinking into the soft, churned-up mud. They passed a large detachment of Aucterians sitting by their tents. Their uniforms were new, and fitted them well, while the Zamatan soldiers possessed the appearance of vagabond peasants.

They marched on for a further two miles, until they reached a long gap in the Dominion lines. The entire column came to a halt, and then a few Aucterian officers began to make their way down by the Zamatan soldiers, issuing orders as they walked.

'They are telling us to dig in here,' said Efizel. 'They want us to defend this section of the siege camp.'

'Dig?' said Jancke. 'With what, sergeant?'

'The ditch in front of you must be continuous,' an Aucterian captain was saying, 'with no breaks. It must be at least three yards deep and four wide. Pile up the earth on the near side, and ensure that sentries are posted on the rampart.'

'You heard the officer,' said Efizel, as the Aucterians passed them.

'You never answered my question,' said Jancke. 'What are we supposed to dig with?'

'Those things at the end of your arms are called hands,' said the Bullan sergeant. 'Get to work.'

The squad toiled throughout the rest of the day, using their three shields and four helmets to gather soil and move it onto the new earthen rampart that they were building. The rain came down for an hour, and their shallow ditch quickly filled with water, but Efizel drove them on until each man was covered in a thick layer of mud.

The bombardment began as night fell over the Gunstian plains. The Dominion artillery had been re-assembled, and the monstrous catapults and trebuchets loosed upon the city in the distance. The first few boulders fell short of the towering walls, but after a few adjustments had been made, the missiles began striking the battlements. Unable to continue work in the darkness, the squad rested alongside the others from their regiment, and they watched as the hailstorm of rocks flew over their heads. Several artillery pieces were aiming towards a massive gatehouse ahead and a little to the left of the squad's position, where tiny figures could be seen watching the besieging army from the parapets.

'At this rate,' said Smithy, as a boulder bounced off the massive walls, 'we'll have broken into the city by this time next year.'

'And then it'll be like Toraq again,' said Karl.

'It will be over sooner than you think, lads,' said Efizel; 'one way or another.'

'Why?' said Lahnos.

'Simple logistics,' said the Bullan. 'The Dominion does not control the countryside, so we cannot live off the land; therefore we are dependent upon supplies reaching us from Toraq. To get to Toraq, our supply fleets will have to sail past the Gunstian navy, which is waiting for them in the Great Bay. In other words, we do not have the luxury of time. We need to take Great Gunst soon, or we will never take it.'

'Then we should send out troops to take control of the countryside,' said Karl.

'And who would do that?' said Efizel. 'We have no cavalry, while the Gunstians do. The dragons can burn farms and fields, but they cannot occupy the ground needed to feed an army of this size.' He watched as a stone obliterated a small turret on the high walls. 'I think we shall attack tonight.'

'Then why did we waste our time digging that damn ditch?' said Lahnos.

'To catch the Gunstians off-guard,' he said; 'to make them think we are settling in for a long siege.'

'Is that good news or bad news for the Zamatan regiments?'

'It is too early to tell,' said Efizel. 'The harsh truth is that the Zamatans would be useless operating the siege engines, or doing anything that requires discipline and training; but, on the other hand, we might be thrown in to divert defenders from the main assault.'

'We'll be used as fodder again, you mean?' muttered Smithy.

'We should try to rest.'

'In this mud?' said Karl. 'What hope do we have of getting any sleep out here?'

'At least it isn't raining,' said Lahnos. He lay down on the slope of the earthen embankment and closed his eyes.

Lahnos felt a hand shake his shoulder. He opened his eyes and saw several dark shapes soaring overhead, their forms passing below the stars in the night sky.

'It is about to begin,' said Efizel.

Lahnos sat up. The rest of the squad were where he had last seen them, their gazes on the walls as more boulders pounded them. Eight huge siege engines had been moved forward from the camp, their wheels passing through a gap in the lines of ditches and ramparts. They were sitting idle in a long line that stretched away into the darkness, while companies of Aucterian soldiers were standing ready next to them.

Karl glanced at Lahnos. 'I don't know how you can sleep like that, brother. I wish I could do it.'

'Did I miss anything?' Lahnos said.

'Just more of the same,' said Smithy. 'That damn wall is tough.'

'I can hardly see a thing.'

'The dragons are gathering above us,' said Efizel. 'In a few moments, I imagine that things will brighten up.'

The words had barely left the Bullan's mouth when the first flames blasted out over the walls in front of them. Lahnos blinked in the light as fire poured down from the skies, scouring the battlements and incinerating the wooden structures on top of the gatehouse. More dragons soared forwards, and other parts of the curtain wall were enveloped in flames; then, over to the left, the enormous siege engines began to move again, pushed along through the mud by hundreds of soldiers. Other groups with ladders also started to move forwards, but the Zamatan regiments remained where they were, lined up or sitting on the long rampart they had built during the day. Whistles and horns sounded all over the camp behind them, and thousands of Dominion soldiers raced forward, the Aucterians on the flanks, and the Bullan regiments in the centre. A wave of dragons swooped and dived over the walls, burning everything in their path. One fell, struck down by multiple ballista bolts, and it crashed into the muddy land in front of the walls, ploughing through the soft earth until it came to a halt. The other dragons persisted in the attack, and two went for the tall doors sealing off the gatehouse. One landed close by, while the other cleared the battlements above with flames. The dragon on the ground used its forelimbs to tear down the doors, but as soon as they fell, a battery of ballistae positioned behind the gates loosed, and the dragon screamed as a dozen bolts struck him. Another dragon plummeted from the sky, seemingly untouched by any ballista bolt. It smashed into the thick mud by the base of the walls and howled in agony, its wings and tail thrashing around.

'The Gift of Pain,' muttered Efizel, as the squad stared at the tormented dragon.

A fourth dragon fell, but the others continued to attack as thousands of Dominion soldiers crossed the distance to the foot of the walls. The Bullan charged for the ruined gates with their shields up, their voices rising above the cacophony. Detachments of Aucterian soldiers raised dozens of long ladders and set them against the walls to either side of the gatehouse, while others shepherded the wooden siege engines into position by the base of the curtain wall. More flames came from the direction of the river, and a thick pall of smoke rose above the vast city, its towers, domes and spires silhouetted in the flames.

Efizel flinched as dozens of his kinfolk were shot down by the ruined gates, but their comrades kept up the charge, and the Bullan stormed into the gatehouse, racing past the fallen dragon and entering the city. On either side, the Aucterians were making little headway. Ladders were being flung down by Gunstian solders almost as soon as they had been set against the side of the wall, and archers were loosing at will into the huddled groups of Dominion soldiers attempting to access the parapets from the tops of the siege engines. Two of the great engines burst into flames, and Aucterians fell screaming into the sea of mud that lay at the feet of the wooden structures. Two dragons swept along the top of the walls, their claws raking through the Gunstians, and the hail of arrows ceased. The first Aucterians managed to scale the curtain wall, then more and more made their way up, as the dragons cleared the battlements of Gunstians.

'We're going to do it,' cried Jancke; 'on the first attack!'

A Dominion flag appeared on top of the gatehouse, then thousands of Bullan began pouring into the city, creating an enormous press of soldiers shoving their way through the open gates. With the battlements cleared, the Aucterians started crossing over to the parapets from the tops of the six surviving siege engines, while hundreds more were climbing the ladders, following the Bullan into Great Gunst.

The form of a great dragon soared overhead, his bronze scales glimmering in the light of the fires.

'The King,' muttered Smithy.

Naghad dived towards an untouched section of the curtain wall, then he banked, and hundreds of Gunstians up on the battlements cried out in agony and fell. The King extended his great talons, and began to rip out huge chunks of masonry from the walls, sending blocks of stone crashing to the ground. Several other dragons joined him, and together they ripped another breach in the curtain wall, while others continued to spray flames into the city beyond. At this, another division of Dominion soldiers moved forwards, leaving the camp behind and rushing towards the new breach in the walls.

'Everyone's getting involved except the Zamatans,' said Jancke.

'I am fine with that,' said Efizel. 'Remember that the walls surrounding Great Gunst are sixteen miles long, and we are concentrating our attack upon one small section.'

'Are you saying that you'd rather be out here?' said Karl.

Efizel frowned. 'In truth, I would prefer to be fighting alongside my kinsfolk. They were the first to break into the city, and if this is indeed a victory, then they will have won great honour by their actions.'

The press of soldiers at the two breaches began to lessen as more and more Bullan and Aucterians entered Great Gunst. The Dominion artillery ceased loosing, and several cheers rose up from the camp behind the Zamatans. King Naghad soared back from the city, and descended into the heart of the camp, and more cheers broke out. A final division of Aucterian soldiers was sent forwards, and they queued up in a long column to file through the breach in the occupied gatehouse.

'Is that it?' said Jancke. 'Have we won?'

'It seemed... too easy,' said Efizel. He glanced at a passing Dominion officer and stood. 'Sir? What are our orders? Are the Zamatans to advance?'

'You lot are to stay put for the moment,' said the officer. 'Remain here to protect the camp and baggage while the real soldiers capture the city.'

Efizel frowned. 'Yes, sir.' He sat back down and glared at the walls of the city. 'Guard the baggage?' he muttered. 'My family would disown me if they knew how low I had fallen.'

'You told us we'd be lucky to guard the camp, sergeant,' said Jancke.

'I did,' said Efizel; 'but what is fortunate for the Zamatans brings only dishonour to my name.'

The dragons attacking Great Gunst were flying further over the huge city, leaving the walls behind as they sent flames down into the streets beyond. They targeted a Temple of Chadura, its three tall spires shimmering with gold and silver leaf. The dragons soared past it in several waves, each one enveloping more of the temple in flames until the spires cracked and fell, their masonry tumbling down into the city below. Another dragon was struck by something, and its body disappeared from view as it crashed into a row of buildings.

The hours passed, and the squad sat in silence as they watched the assault on the city from the top of the earthen rampart. The sky to the east began to brighten behind the thick banks of grey clouds, revealing the vast area of mud that lay between the camp and the walls. More Dominion flags were fluttering from the battlements along the small section that had been taken, and Bullan soldiers could be seen high up on the parapets of the occupied gatehouse. No more Aucterian soldiers were entering the city, the Dominion camp having been almost emptied of its reserves, but a slow trickle was starting to emerge from the open gates – the wounded. A line of flat-bedded carts was pulled along, each with injured soldiers lying on the back, and they made their way towards the camp. Lahnos got up, and hurried down the slope of the rampart to get a better look.

'What's going on in there?' he shouted at the convoy of wagons. 'Is the city ours?'

A few wounded Aucterians glanced in his direction, but none spoke. Efizel joined Lahnos, and they strode towards a column of walking wounded. Efizel hailed an injured Bullan, his right arm in a sling. The soldier stopped, and they spoke for a few moments in their own language as Lahnos gazed at the wounded men. Some had been burned, their skin red and blistered, while others had wounds from crossbow bolts. The injured Bullan carried on towards the camp, and Efizel glanced at Lahnos.

'Great Gunst has not fallen,' he said. 'The Gunstians have constructed lines of barricades and walls to block the main roads, and are fighting for every street and building. The Dominion army is being contained within a relatively small part of the city. This makes no sense. It is almost as though the Gunstians were luring us into Great Gunst, and now they are waiting for something, but what? I don't understand their tactics.'

Karl joined them. 'Sergeant! Something's happening behind us, in the camp.' He paused, as a low rumble began to echo up from the ground, and the earth shook beneath their boots, sending Lahnos and Karl down into the mud. Lahnos pulled himself to his knees, and watched as the land rippled like a wave on the ocean. The wave moved away from the earthen ramparts and struck the captured section of the city with a grinding of stone. The gatehouse and its towers collapsed, along with the captured portion of the curtain wall, bringing down thousands of tons of masonry, and blocking the two breaches. The column of wounded was hit by flying rocks, and several wagons disappeared under the rubble. A great cloud of dust drifted through the air as the ground settled, then smoke and flames rose up from the area of the city where the Dominion forces had broken through.

Horns sounded from the camp, and a few dragons ascended into the air. Three soared towards the collapsed gatehouse, while others banked in the sky and headed south.

'The Gunstian army is behind us!' someone cried. 'Get your weapons and form up!'

The Zamatans pulled their gazes from the destruction of the walls and glanced back towards the camp. More flames were rising from that direction, while the horns were blasting out. Lahnos, Karl and Efizel ran back to their squad.

'The city, sergeant,' Jancke yelled. 'The Dominion army is trapped inside!'

'Forget about the city for now,' Efizel said. 'The Gunstian field army has swung round behind us, and has cut off our retreat to Toraq. Get ready to fight.'

The soldiers lifted their crossbows from the mud and laced up their tattered boots. The rain started again, heavier this time, and the squad prepared themselves amid the torrential downpour. An Aucterian officer ran along the line.

'Zamatans – about turn!' he cried. 'The enemy is approaching from the south. Protect the camp! Protect the wounded dragons!'

A dense hail of arrow and ballista bolts filled the skies to the south, and then rained down into the centre of the camp, two hundred yards from the rampart where the squad was loading their crossbows. Three injured dragons cried out and fell beneath the onslaught, while dozens of soldiers and camp servants were cut down next to them.

'Move, you useless Zamatan bastards!' the officer shouted. 'Repel the attackers.'

The Zamatans began to surge down from the rampart, as more bolts and arrows sliced through the air.

'Keep your heads down and stick together,' Efizel shouted, as they charged across the mud towards the centre of the camp. Ahead of them, Lahnos saw the first Gunstians begin to tear through the baggage wagons, setting them alight and slaughtering the horses and wounded. A dragon soared down, its flames consuming a dozen soldiers, then it screamed and fell from the sky as a Gifted in long dark robes pointed a finger at it.

Lahnos threw his crossbow to the ground as he ran through the rain, then he pulled his axe from his belt. The mud got worse as thousands of men converged around the centre of the camp, and he could barely tell Gunstian from Zamatan amid the carnage that was unfolding before his eyes.

The ground vibrated again as the roar of a dragon echoed across the camp. A huge form took to the skies amid the torrential rain, his bronze scales dulled in the gloom. The mighty dragon opened his jaws, and flames tore through the ranks of Gunstians soldiers attacking the camp, incinerating them where they stood. He lifted a talon, and the heads of several dozen exploded.

'I am King Naghad!' the dragon called out. 'Surrender or…'

The King's voice tailed away, then he bellowed in agony as the Gifted among the Gunstians in the camp raised their hands in his direction. Naghad's eyes rolled up into his head as he screamed. He seemed to hover for a moment, then his wings drooped and he fell, his enormous bulk crashing into the centre of the camp, obliterating wagons and soldiers as he ploughed through the thick mud.

'To the King!' Efizel cried, then Lahnos lost sight of the sergeant as the Zamatans collided with the soldiers from the Gunstian army.

Lahnos swung his axe, and the steel edge lodged into the breastplate of a Gunstian soldier. Lahnos tried to pull it out, and the Gunstian battered him on the chin with the boss of his shield. Lahnos went down into the mud, sinking deeper, as a boot cracked against his skull. Another body fell on top of him, squeezing the breath from his chest, and he lost consciousness.

CHAPTER 23
EAVESDROPPING

Western Lowlands, Serpent Isle – 18th Lexinch 1588

The fields of withered and blackened wheat stalks stretched out for miles, from the beaches that skirted the waters of the Hansarta, all the way to the hills that lined the western edge of the island. A network of irrigation channels ran between the streams that flowed down from the hills, but each was covered in a thick layer of dark green scum that stank. The streams, too, had been polluted, the rotten vegetation causing blooms of algae to flourish across their waters. Dead fish were floating by the steep banks, their flesh adding to the odour of decay that permeated the countryside.

'The autumn rains will lift the level of the rivers and wash all this away,' an old Zamatan farmer was telling the assembled group of Dominion officers, a mixture of army, Dragon Corps and Bullan among them. 'But, until then, there is little we can do.'

'And when will the autumn rains commence?' asked an army officer.

'That will be around the end of Luddinch,' said the farmer. 'Two months from now; one month after the harvest was supposed to take place.'

'How far does the devastation spread?' said another officer.

'It starts in the vineyards on the slopes south-west of Mount

Medamuna and extends all the way to the river that flows through Neeton,' said the farmer. 'I would reckon that four out of every five acres of wheat on Zamata has been destroyed. The vineyards are less affected. Most of the vines on the island are grown out by Belton and Chesson; and none of the olive or citrus groves were touched.'

'The livestock survived, yes?'

'Yes,' said the farmer, 'but the cattle will go hungry soon. We reckon we'll have to slaughter them all before autumn starts.'

'But the goats will be fine?' the officer went on. 'There will still be milk and cheese?'

The farmer nodded. 'The goats can graze among the rough hills north of Belton. They're hardy beasts; they'll survive.'

'Thank you,' said a major. 'That will be all.'

The farmer tilted his head slightly, then strode away along a track towards a low-lying set of farm buildings.

'The army can provide assistance with the cattle,' the major said to the group of officers. 'We will also take over the stockpiling of what food remains on the island, and impose a strict rationing system upon the native population. Fish, fruit and olives will remain free of any restrictions, but meat, milk and bread will be tightly controlled from now on. Priority will be given to children, young mothers and all those tending the surviving farms.'

'Might I ask about the second supply fleet, sir?' said a younger officer. 'It is due to reach the Serpent Isle a few weeks from now; could some of the stocks on board be diverted to refill the island's granaries?'

'Absolutely not,' said the major. 'Every ounce of food on those ships is to be sent onwards to feed the invasion forces in Gunst. The dragons were very clear about that.' He glanced at the Bullan officers. 'Ensure that your men guard the ships when they arrive. They are to take on water, but nothing shall be permitted to be removed from the vessels. I want them sailing west within a day of their arrival.'

'Yes, sir,' said the Bullan.

Cisca cleared her throat. 'Do we have an estimate of how many Zamatans will starve, Major?'

'Any estimate would be pure speculation,' said the major. 'The villages will have their own stores of food hidden away, and that might tide them over the worst months; but, unfortunately, this island has become overly dependent upon bread in recent decades, and the loss of the harvest will no doubt cause serious suffering. Moreover, we can expect trouble in Kaugatz once the rationing regime has been implemented. The spring harvest is nine months away; we should prepare ourselves for a long hard winter.'

A shadow flickered overhead, and the officers glanced up into the blue sky. Lord Rylan was flying above them, circling over the acres of devastation. He banked over the waters of the Hansarta, his shadow flitting across the surface, then he descended, landing a few yards from where the officers' carriages were waiting.

'Good day,' said the grey and yellow dragon, as the officers bowed their heads. 'My heart breaks for the dreadful suffering that is certain to follow this terrible act of sabotage. If only there was something we could do to remedy the situation, but the Serpent Isle is too remote for any aid to reach us.'

'My lord,' said the army major, 'we are grateful that the blessed dragons acted so swiftly to bring justice to the agents responsible.'

Lord Rylan tilted his head. Leona had told Cisca all about the carnage that had taken place in Kaugatz two days previously, and it was clear that Lord Rylan had played no part in the deaths of the Gunstians.

'It could have been much worse, my lord,' said another officer. 'Had the olive and citrus groves also been laid waste, then our prospects would be dire.'

'Indeed,' said the dragon. 'Has a system of rationing been drawn up?'

'It has, my lord,' said the major. 'We are due to implement it in the coming days.'

'And does this system allocate resources equally among all those living on the island, Major?' said Rylan.

The officers said nothing for a moment. The major hadn't explicitly mentioned any such discrimination when he had spoken earlier, but

Cisca had assumed that the Aucterians would be treated more favourably than the natives.

'I will ensure that the stocks are distributed equitably, my lord,' said the major, bowing low. 'However, I intend to see that the children of the island are not allowed to starve.'

'That pleases me,' said Lord Rylan. 'For my part, I shall speak with Lord Malum and Lady Macsin, to ascertain if there are any cuts to our food allowance that can be made to help with the situation.'

The officers bowed again, but none looked convinced by the suggestion, and Cisca wondered if Rylan would have the courage to do as he had pledged.

'We will now return to Zamata Gataza, my lord,' said the major. 'As soon as the rationing regime is ready, we shall send out soldiers to supervise its operation.'

'Then I shall see you all in the monastery,' the dragon said. He extended his grey and yellow wings and took to the skies, then he soared off towards the south-west.

The major frowned. 'I may have to make a few revisions to our plan.'

'Perhaps, sir,' said another officer, 'we should wait to see what Lord Malum says? The Governor has the final word on the allocation of resources.'

Cisca's anger flared. 'Why don't you just say what you're thinking, Lieutenant?' she said. 'Do you believe that the lives of the Aucterian settlers are worth more than those of the native Zamatans?'

The officers quietened.

'It is not a case of what I believe, ma'am,' said the lieutenant; 'I am simply looking to the future. In the long run, without any men of fighting age, the Zamatan population will shrink of its own accord. It could be seen as wasteful to provide them with too many resources, if it results in suffering among the Aucterians.'

'I agree,' said another army officer. 'In fact, it might be prudent to initiate a selective cull among the older members of the native population, to remove those who contribute nothing to the economy of the

Serpent Isle. If resources must be given to the sub-created Zamatans, then it should be targeted at those who remain productive. Something along the lines of what happened to the Gunstians could be organised. If, say, five thousand idle mouths could be removed from the island, then famine could be averted.'

Cisca remained silent, her ire growing with every word that came from the officer's mouth. She glanced away before she could say something that might lead the others to believe that her sympathies lay with the native Zamatans, but she noticed a few of them look in her direction.

'That is an interesting proposal,' said the major. 'I shall ponder it. In the meantime, orders shall be issued to Kaugatz. Any natives trying to circumvent the restrictions shall have their ration card removed. Take your carriages back to the monastery, and I will summon you all in the morning to discuss the way forward. Dismissed.'

The group of officers dispersed, and began to make their way to the line of carriages that sat by the coastal road. The long beaches were deserted, but several fishing vessels were out in the Hansarta. Cisca glanced at the small boats, wondering how many fish would be needed to feed everyone. With the men gone, most of the fishing fleet had been tied up in the harbours, but a few older men had been heading out each morning, and some of the younger women had been joining them, helping to bring in what they could. It was the same all over the island. Where once the women of Zamata had remained in their homes while the men went out to work, many had begun to labour on the farms and groves, toiling under the harsh summer sun to provide for their families.

Cisca climbed up into a carriage and sat down next to three junior army officers, who ceased talking as soon as they saw her. Cisca gazed out of the window as the line of carriages began to move off. The horses that pulled them along the road were well-fed and healthy, but if there was little to feed them then Cisca imagined that, like the cattle, they would also have to be slaughtered. Cisca turned back to look at the three army officers sharing the carriage, but each averted their eyes. Her paranoia grew. Did they suspect that she was helping the rebels, or was their discomfort due to what she had said about the allocation of resources? She told herself to calm down, then she closed her eyes and tried to get some rest.

When Cisca arrived back at her quarters in the ancient monastery, she found a note pinned to her front door.

Come to my rooms – immediately, it said, and was signed – *Takri*.

Cisca ripped the note from the door and crushed it in the palm of her hand, as a sense of foreboding settled in the pit of her stomach. She glanced along the empty corridor then turned for the stairs, her footsteps the only sound she could hear. She went to the level where Leona lived, and strode up to the two Bullan sentries on duty.

'Lady Takri is expecting me,' she said.

The soldiers nodded, then one rapped on the door. It opened an inch, and Leona's eyes peered out. She caught sight of Cisca and allowed her to squeeze past into the main living area. The balcony doors were wide open, and the room was full of fresh air and light.

'You wanted to see me, ma'am?' Cisca said.

Leona smiled. 'Not particularly.' She gestured towards the balcony. 'Someone else asked me to summon you.'

Cisca stepped out onto the wide balcony, and saw a man in an Aucterian officer's uniform. He was seated, and was gazing out at the view of the island. He stood when he saw her.

'Cisca,' he said.

She narrowed her eyes. 'Bauchlie.'

'Would either of you like a drink?' said Leona from the balcony door.

'Just water for me,' said Bauchlie.

'Me, too. Thank you,' said Cisca.

Leona walked back into the apartment, and Bauchlie gestured to a chair. He and Cisca sat, and she looked down at the island.

'I came here again to speak to Leona,' he said, 'but I also wanted to see you. You have been in my thoughts, Cisca.'

'Why?' she said.

He turned to her. 'I often think about what happened in the Dragon Palace. Did Lord Kheran get back to Aucteran in one piece?'

'Yes,' she said, 'though the new King was displeased by the tidings he bore across the ocean. He should have remained on Zamata.'

'Would that have prevented King Naghad's invasion of Gunst, and the removal of the menfolk from this island?'

'I don't know,' she said.

He looked into her eyes. 'I mistreated you.'

'Yes. You did.'

'I am sorry.'

'Colonel Friel Laimos passed on your apology when we met in Igatz.'

'I meant it. I was blinded by the cause.'

'You still are, by all appearances,' she said.

Leona emerged from the apartment with a tray, which she set down onto a little table.

She sat next to them, her eyes going from Bauchlie to Cisca amid an awkward silence.

'I visited the ruined fields today,' Cisca said.

'I know,' said Leona. 'Lord Malum told me that a delegation of officers had gone to view the damage. I assume that rationing will soon be introduced?'

'Yes – for meat, bread and milk. The army officers were discussing the potential culling of five thousand elderly Zamatans to alleviate any possible famine.'

Bauchlie's eyes darkened.

'I hope you didn't say anything to oppose these suggestions, Captain,' said Leona.

'I managed to remain silent when that was suggested,' Cisca said, 'but I spoke up against a proposal to give the Aucterian settlers a larger amount of rations than the Zamatans. I couldn't hold my tongue.'

Leona glared at her, her anger clear. 'If you have given those officers any reason to suspect your loyalty, Cisca, things could turn very ugly for us.'

'I know,' she said.

'Be more understanding, Leona,' said Bauchlie. 'Cisca is new to this, and she is under a lot of strain.'

'We are all under a lot of strain,' said Leona.

'You might be surprised by Lord Rylan,' said Cisca. 'He wanted to know if the Zamatans will be given the same rations as the Aucterians; and he seemed genuinely upset at the thought of the islanders suffering.'

'Lord Rylan may speak differently from the other dragons on the isle,' said Leona, 'but his heart is just as rotten. I find that he says whatever he thinks will please his present audience, but he is untrustworthy and duplicitous. There is a reason he was absent from the slaughter of the Gunstians; Malum and Macsin hold him in contempt, and they believe that he would have baulked at the task.'

Bauchlie eyed her. 'You seemed to cope without any difficulty.'

'If you think that, Bauchlie,' Leona said, 'then you don't know me at all. That was one of the worst days of my life. When this is all over, I will look back at my role in what happened, and I will know that it will have forever tainted my soul. It is worse than anything the colonel would have done.'

'But you are not him,' said Bauchlie.

Cisca frowned. 'Might I ask what you intend to do with Colonel Laimos? He is still isolated within his chambers, and has not been permitted to leave or talk to anyone since we got here.'

'We don't intend to do anything with him,' said Leona. 'His usefulness has diminished, as far as the rebellion goes; but that is not to say that I wish any harm to come to him. I remain very fond of Friel Laimos. However, it is the Demon Witch that I want to talk about. Have you managed to discover anything useful about the dragon's plans?'

Cisca shook her head.

'That remains our priority, Cisca. You must try harder. Bauchlie –

tell her.'

Bauchlie glanced at Cisca. 'I know it is difficult, but if the dragons capture or kill the Demon Witch, then this island will be crushed. I am not just talking about the cause of freedom – I am talking about Zamata's survival. Whether you believe in the cause or not, you must see that the future of every Zamatan is hanging in the balance. Without the Demon Witch, I fear that we shall be wiped out to make way for Aucterian settlers, just as the Dominion did to the original inhabitants of Inopei and Aucteran. Will you try?'

'Yes,' she said, returning his gaze. 'I will try.'

'Thank you, Cisca,' he said.

'You should go before the dragons start to wonder where you are,' said Leona. 'I will no doubt see you later.'

Cisca got to her feet, her eyes still on Bauchlie.

'Until the next time,' he said.

Cisca turned and walked through the main living area of Leona's apartment. She cursed her weakness. Why did Bauchlie make her feel that way? She had found it hard not to stare at him, and when he had asked her to help, she had almost cracked under his gaze. She went over every word he had spoken to her as she left the apartment and walked down the stairs to the cavernous basement. He had said that he had meant his apology, and she believed him; and he had spoken up for her when Leona had almost lost her temper. What did it mean?

She walked into the huge cavern, and bowed before Lady Macsin and Lord Rylan. Lord Malum was absent, but Cisca had already guessed that he wouldn't be there, as that would explain Leona having free time to sit in her apartment. The two dragons ignored her as she began to check the fresh water and food stocks.

'I think it is a pointless suggestion,' said Rylan.

'I thought you would,' said Macsin; 'but you are not thinking logically. Why should decent Aucterians starve while thousands of useless old Zamatans are given full rations? It makes no sense.'

'Aren't the Zamatans also citizens of the Dominion?'

Macsin snorted. 'Of course not! The Zamatans are sub-humans –

you know this. The blood of the Aucterians comes all the way from the world where our glorious father dwelt before coming to Athumia.'

'These old legends are immaterial to me,' Rylan said. 'A human is a human. To my eye, there is no difference between an Aucterian and a Zamatan.'

Lady Macsin stared at the younger dragon, then she glanced at Cisca, as if noticing her presence for the first time.

Cisca bowed. 'Is there anything I can do for you, my lady, my lord?'

'Yes,' said Macsin. 'I want you to forget the ridiculous nonsense that just came out of my half-brother's mouth; I wish I could.'

Cisca kept her gaze lowered, unsure how to respond.

'I was being facetious, girl,' said Macsin. 'Carry on with your tasks.'

'Yes, my lady,' she said. She walked over to the heaps of furs and blankets, and took a mental note of their cleanliness as she began inspecting them.

'Your foolishness astounds me at times,' Macsin went on, addressing Rylan again. 'I hope you do not harbour similar notions regarding the Demon Witch. You do understand the importance of capturing her, yes?'

'She murdered our father,' said Rylan. 'That is reason enough to hunt her down and kill her. I also miss poor Lenta. She did not deserve what the Demon Witch did to her. Might I ask – when will you and Lord Malum provide me with more details of our plan?'

'When you are ready,' said Macsin.

'And what were you discussing with Lord Malum when I walked in on you both yesterday? It was something about Lady Takri, was it not?'

'Again, you will be given appropriate information when Lord Malum and I deem it necessary. Do not concern yourself with Lady Takri.'

'Do you trust her now? I have not heard you utter a single word against her since you spoke with Lord Malum.'

'My ire against her has... cooled.'

'Why?' said Rylan. 'If you do not tell me, then I must assume that you trust her more than you trust me.'

'My mistrust of you is beside the point,' said Macsin. 'Lord Malum has forbidden me to discuss Lady Takri with you. However, perhaps this is the time to let you know a little more about my brother's scheme to ensnare the Demon Witch.' She paused. 'But first…' She turned to Cisca. 'Leave us, human. What I have to say is not for your ears.'

Cisca bowed. 'Of course, my lady.'

She walked to the entrance of the cavern and passed through the archway. As soon as she was out of sight, she turned and snuck into a shadowy alcove, her heart racing. She kept still, listening.

'You were saying?' said Rylan.

'My brother recalled some fragments of our father's words to us,' Macsin said, 'spoken a long time ago, when the children of Gahad's first mate were still young – around your age. I had forgotten most of it, but Lord Malum's recollections stirred some of my own memories. As you know, our father's consciousness did not always inhabit the form of a dragon. Before that, he walked on two legs as an immortal human. It was the great King Nathaniel who transferred his mind to a dragon. He learned how to do that from another mighty god by the name of Simon, but that is by the by. Anyway…'

Macsin fell silent.

As Cisca crouched in the dim light of the alcove, wondering why Macsin had stopped talking, a huge, scaled forelimb drove through the archway towards her. The clawed limb closed around Cisca's body, and pulled her back into the cavern.

'You filthy little sneak!' Macsin roared, as she squeezed Cisca. 'You were listening to our private conversation; don't try to deny it. I should rip your head off.'

'Wait,' said Rylan.

Macsin glared at the younger dragon. 'You had better not be about to make excuses for this worm's behaviour.'

'I wasn't,' Rylan said; 'but before you kill her, don't you think it would be a good idea to find out why she was listening?'

'You make a fair point, half-brother,' Macsin said. She released Cisca, who dropped three feet and landed in a heap on the rough cavern floor. 'Well? Why were you lingering in the shadows? Why did you want to find out about the Demon Witch?'

Cisca trembled as the two dragons stood over her. 'I... I was curious, that's all. I'm sorry.'

'Curious?' said Macsin. 'Do you think I am a fool, Captain Cisca?' She stared into her eyes, and Cisca felt a pain in the back of her mind. It increased, and Cisca clutched the sides of her head in agony, her thoughts trampled by the dragon's powers.

'Have you cast the truth spell?' said Rylan.

'I have,' said Macsin. 'Let us hear what this worm has to say. Cisca – why were you listening?'

Cisca felt as though she were no longer in control of her body. She wanted to scream, and her mouth opened.

'I wanted to find out how you were planning to trap the Demon Witch,' she said.

'That is quite obvious,' said Macsin; 'but why? What were you going to do with this information?'

'I was going to tell Leona,' Cisca said, her hopes crumbling as she sobbed.

'Leona?' said Rylan. 'Wasn't she a rebel? I forget what happened to her.'

'Leona is Takri, you fool,' said Macsin. 'Cisca – why does Takri want to know?'

'Because...'

'Yes?'

'Because she is an ally of the Demon Witch. She wants to stop the dragons from capturing her.'

Macsin's eyes blinked, and the cavern fell into silence. Cisca groaned on the ground, her head pulsing and burning with pain.

'Were you with Takri today?' said Macsin.

'I was,' Cisca gasped.

'When?'

'Just before I came here.'

'And what did you discuss?'

Cisca sobbed aloud. 'We were talking to Bauchlie about the rebellion.'

'Bauchlie is in the monastery?' roared Macsin. 'Rylan, summon the Bullan, and wake Lord Malum from his slumber. Be quick – as quick as you can.'

The younger dragon strode away, his low voice calling out for the Bullan. Several soldiers responded within seconds. They raced into the chamber, took one look at the situation, and aimed their crossbows at Cisca.

'This traitor is under arrest,' said Macsin.

'What should we do with her, my lady?' said a sergeant.

'Leave her where she is for now. I want Lord Malum to hear her speak.'

An angry dragon cry came from Malum's private cavern, then he and Rylan appeared in the main chamber.

'This had better be worth me being awoken, sister,' Malum said, his green eyes burning.

'Captain Cisca,' said Macsin, 'answer me this – is Takri a rebel and a traitor?'

'What is the meaning of this?' Malum cried. 'I shall...'

'Yes,' gasped Cisca. 'Leona is a traitor. She has never given up on the rebellion.'

Malum's gaze fell, and his talons scraped out great furrows in the stone floor, as more Bullan hurried into the cavern.

'Is Takri working with Bauchlie, Cisca?' Macsin went on.

'Yes,' she sobbed.

'And is Bauchlie in Takri's rooms right now? Answer me, Cisca.'

'He was there fifteen minutes ago.'

Macsin glanced up at her brother. 'Is that enough? Should we press her for more information?'

'I cannot bear to hear any more,' said Malum, as sparks flew across his jaws. 'Bullan, shackle this treacherous creature, and then arrest Lady Takri and anyone else you find in her apartment.' He stared down at Cisca with venom in his eyes. 'And then bring them to me.'

CHAPTER 24
RAGE OF MALUM

Zamata Gataza, Serpent Isle – 18th Lexinch 1588

Leona watched as Cisca walked out of the apartment, then she turned back to Bauchlie.

'I wish you had left her out of this,' he said. 'What you are doing to Cisca isn't fair.'

'Says the man who chained her up,' said Leona. 'You know, if it hadn't been for her feelings towards you, I wouldn't have had an opportunity to blackmail her.'

Bauchlie said nothing.

'And you?' she went on. 'Are you as interested in her as she is in you?'

Bauchlie stared at the view, his mouth closed.

Leona laughed.

'I should go,' he said. 'We have discussed everything that we needed to cover.'

'All apart from your blossoming relationship with a Dragon Corps officer.'

'There is no relationship,' he said. He got to his feet. 'She saved my life, and I'm grateful; and I regret the way I treated her, but...'

'But what?'

He shook his head. 'Nothing.'

'You don't want to say it? Is that because you know I will catch you lying?'

'You can be quite difficult at times, Leona. I preferred you when you were the colonel's shy, quiet assistant.'

Leona's head tingled, and she smiled. 'You probably shouldn't come here again. Twice is enough. Any more visits and the Bullan will start asking questions.'

Bauchlie nodded, then he turned and strode from the balcony. Leona picked up Cisca's untouched glass of water, waited for the sound of her front door to open and close, then took a sip. Her smile faded, and her heart darkened with all that she had done, and all that was left to do. She was usually comfortable and self-sufficient in her own company, but she was beginning to dread being alone, with no one to distract her from the memories of what she had seen in the public square in Kaugatz two days before. The dragons were evil. Perhaps not all dragons, but Malum and Macsin fitted that description perfectly, and Rylan wasn't much better. Was it any wonder that the Gunstians called them demons? The colonel had often told her that a negotiated peace would depend upon an agreement being reached between the Zamatans and the dragons, but Leona doubted that any such peace could be achieved if dragons like Malum were in charge.

Her gaze drifted over the island. The land was shimmering and the waters of the Cyasarta and Hansarta inlets were sparkling in the summer sunshine. The baked hillsides on the north coast had turned brown from the lack of rain, and Leona missed the bright colours of spring, when flowers and grass flourished over the wild spaces of the island.

Several minutes had elapsed before she became aware of shouts coming from the corridor outside her apartment. Leona got to her feet and glanced into the living room, then her front door burst open and battered off the inside wall. Bullan soldiers surged into the room, their crossbows loaded.

One pointed at her. 'There she is! Get on your knees, woman!'

At once, Leona could guess what had happened. Without hesitating, she lunged for the balcony railings and began to scramble up. She would jump. The fall would be terrifying, but her death on the rocks below would be quick. She reached the top of the railing and stepped off, but a Bullan soldier dived across the balcony and grabbed hold of her right wrist. Leona swung through the air, her arm twisting as she slammed against the outside of the monastery, her legs dangling. Another Bullan reached over the balcony and helped his comrade, and they pulled Leona back up. She struggled in their grasp, then one struck her across the face with the back of his hand. She was rolled onto her stomach, and her wrists were pulled back and bound together, as a knee pressed against her shoulders.

'Good work, sergeant,' said an officer, as he walked out on to the balcony. 'I thought we had lost her for a moment.'

'Thank you, sir,' said the soldier who had caught her.

Another soldier came out onto the balcony. 'We've searched the apartment, sir. There's no one else here.'

'Tear the place to pieces,' said the officer. 'Look for any signs that Bauchlie has been here.' He knelt by Leona as the soldier saluted and went back inside. 'Where is he, girl?'

'Kiss my ass, you Bullan bastard,' she muttered.

'We know that Bauchlie was here,' the officer went on, his features expressionless. 'How is he planning to leave the monastery?'

Leona closed her mouth and said nothing.

'Lift her up,' said the officer, standing. He gestured to the sergeant. 'Take her to Lord Malum. I shall organise a search of Zamata Gataza to hunt for the fugitive rebel leader. If he is still here, we will find him.'

Leona was hauled to her feet, but she refused to put any weight on them, and the two soldiers had to drag her into the apartment. Other soldiers were turning the place upside down, emptying the contents of her desk onto the floor and rifling through her clothes. Leona tasted blood on her lips from the blow to her face, but the pain was insignificant next to the dawning realisation that she had been discovered. Cisca – it had to be. Bauchlie had been right; Cisca had not been ready for the tasks Leona had set her, and now it was time to pay.

Defiance, she said to herself – it was all she had left to give.

The soldiers dragged her out of the apartment and down the corridor. They took the main stairs to the basement and descended quickly, an entire squad clustered round her to prevent her from escaping. At the bottom of the stairs, she was pulled into the enormous dragon cavern and thrown to the ground in front of Lord Malum, whose rage was palpable. He stared down at her, his dark green eyes burning, as sparks leapt across his open jaws. On his right was Lady Macsin, and to his left stood Lord Rylan.

'There was no sign of Bauchlie in her apartment, my lords and lady,' said a Bullan. 'A search is now being conducted of the entire monastery.'

None of the dragons acknowledged the words of the soldier, their full attention on Leona.

'My betrayer,' Malum said, his words barely comprehensible through his anger.

'Your conspiracy has been uncovered, traitor,' said Lady Macsin. 'Tell us everything, and you may receive a quick death.'

'Do not promise her that,' said Malum. 'This creature has defiled my heart. She made me trust her, and I grew fond of her, while all along she was laughing at me. Nothing will save her from an agonising end.' He glanced at a Bullan. 'Strangle her, slowly. I want to watch her life slip away as she weeps and begs for mercy.'

One of the Bullan soldiers bowed his head, then he stepped forward and crouched down by Leona, his arms extended. He reached out, grasped her throat in his hands, and began to squeeze. Leona choked, her arms under her back as she lay on the cold stone floor.

'Wait,' said Lord Rylan. 'What if she has more to tell us? I understand your rage, Lord Malum, but Captain Cisca said that she was an ally of the Demon Witch. She may have vital information.'

The Bullan soldier glanced up, the pressure on Leona's throat lessening a little. She gasped in a breath of air, as panic shoved out every other thought from her mind. Jumping from the balcony would have been over in an instant, but she did not want to die on the floor of the cavern.

'There is no use in questioning her,' Malum said. 'She can resist the truth spell.'

'Impossible,' said Macsin. 'None can resist our power.'

Malum glared at his sister. 'Then I grant you permission to try.'

'Stand back,' Macsin said to the soldier. The Bullan released Leona's throat, stood and took a pace backwards.

Macsin stared into Leona's eyes. 'I command you to tell us everything you know about the Demon Witch.'

'She is going to kill you all,' said Leona, 'just like she killed your father.'

Macsin blinked, her eyes widening.

'Do you now understand, sister?' said Malum. 'We will get nothing of any use out of her. The only satisfaction left to derive from Lady Takri is to watch her death.'

'But, brother,' said Macsin, 'she may still be of use to us.'

Rage swept across Malum's features. 'How?'

'Might I be permitted to tell Lord Rylan the secret we share concerning this traitor?'

'Is this relevant?'

'I think it is, brother,' Macsin said. 'Your anger is fully justified, but it may be blinding you to an obvious solution.'

Malum calmed a little. 'Proceed.'

'Lord Rylan,' said Macsin, 'Leona of Kaugatz is Gifted. She possesses the Gift of Truth, and this is why she was permitted to offer us counsel. She used her Gift to assist us in rooting out the Gunstian agents.'

Lord Rylan's eyes widened. 'The Gift of Truth? You mean she can sense whenever anyone is lying?'

'Indeed.'

'I still fail to see the relevance of this,' said Malum.

'But, brother, think of our plan to ensnare the Demon Witch,' said Macsin. 'You know that it will require great reserves of power, and that we might have to drain the energy from several humans to ensure its success. A Gifted human would have more power than an ordinary one, no? We should keep Leona alive for now, so that we can use her inner reserves when the time comes.'

Malum said nothing for a long, still moment, then he lowered his gaze. 'Thank you, sister. In my haste for vengeance I had not considered that. That would indeed be a fitting end to this little traitor. Let us also include Captain Cisca in this plan. Those who tried to harm us shall instead help us defeat the Witch.'

Leona glanced through the forest of legs around her and noticed Cisca on the floor of the cavern a few yards away. Her wrists had also been bound, and a Bullan soldier had placed a boot onto her back to pin her down.

'Our plan will involve the death of humans?' said Lord Rylan.

'It will,' said Macsin. 'Does that prospect offend you?'

'Not if the humans are criminals,' said Rylan. 'Should we also use the other two prisoners we are holding in the monastery? We still have Major Lyla and Colonel Laimos in custody.'

Macsin's eyes narrowed. 'I had forgotten about Laimos. It stands to reason that, if Leona worked as the colonel's assistant, and that the Demon Witch was her ally, then Colonel Friel Laimos might know more than he has been revealing to us. Brother, have you ever asked him directly about the Demon Witch?'

'Of course not,' said Malum. 'Why would I have done so? Prior to the unfortunate incident with Lenta, we had no idea that the Demon Witch was involved with this island.'

Macsin turned to a Bullan officer. 'Have Colonel Laimos brought here immediately.'

'Yes, my lady,' said the officer. He gestured to a squad, and they followed him out of the chamber.

'While we are waiting,' said Macsin, 'let us see if Cisca has anything left to tell us. Captain, you said that the Demon Witch and Leona of Kaugatz were allies. What did this alliance entail?'

Cisca howled in pain. 'I don't know!' she cried. 'All Leona told me was that the Demon Witch had helped with the rebellion. She said that everyone thought that Colonel Laimos was a genius, but it was the Demon Witch's assistance that ensured the success of the uprising.'

'That would make sense,' said Lord Rylan. 'I recall the debate in Nom Karta about how it could have been possible for a motley band of rebels to have defeated the garrison of the Serpent Isle. This would explain it.'

'Tell me, Cisca,' Macsin went on, 'were you also assisting the rebellion?'

'No,' Cisca sobbed. 'I was loyal to Lord Kheran and the Dominion.'

'Then why did you decide to betray us?'

'Leona blackmailed me.'

'Over what?'

The tears flooded down Cisca's cheeks as she writhed in pain. 'She knew I had feelings for Bauchlie, and she threatened to tell you.'

Macsin roared out in laughter, and Malum cast an angry glance at his sister.

'This is not amusing,' Malum said. 'The deception runs deeper than we thought.'

The squad who had left to collect the colonel returned, leading Friel into the chamber. The colonel's one eye gazed impassively at the dragons, then his mouth opened when he saw Leona and Cisca lying on the ground.

'Colonel Laimos,' said Malum, 'once again, it is time for you to speak the truth to us.'

Friel grunted in pain. He almost fell, but two Bullan soldiers gripped his arms and kept him on his feet.

'Did the Demon Witch help you in the rebellion?'

Friel shuddered. 'Yes.'

'How?'

'In many ways.'

'Be more precise.'

'She would supply us with information,' gasped the colonel; 'the location of the enemy forces, and the attacks being planned against us.'

'Did the Demon Witch speak to you directly?' said Macsin.

'No.'

'Did she speak to Leona?'

Friel shook his head. 'No.'

'Then to whom did she speak, Colonel?' said Malum.

'She was in communication with my nephew Lahnos Laimos,' Friel gasped.

'And where is this Lahnos Laimos?'

'I think he is with the Dominion army in Gunst,' the colonel said. 'He might be dead.'

Leona lay still on the floor as she watched Friel's face grimace with pain. Her thoughts, however, were on the words spoken by Macsin earlier about the plan to trap the Demon Witch. If she could do one thing before she died, it would be to warn the Demon Witch to stay away, to tell her that dragons were plotting her destruction.

'Let us try another tack,' said Macsin. 'You were hiding the truth about Leona, so you might know others in the rebellion with Gifts. Is that true?'

'I have known several Zamatans with Gifts,' said Friel.

'Let me rephrase the question – Colonel, do you know of any active rebels with Gifts who are alive and currently on the island?'

'Yes,' he grunted.

'Who?' said Malum.

Friel's body convulsed in the grip of the two Bullan. 'Me.'

'You?' cried Malum. 'You are Gifted, Colonel Laimos? What Gift do you possess?'

'The Gift of Kenning,' he gasped.

'And what power does this Gift bestow?'

'It gives me the ability to sense the Gifts of others.' He looked down at Leona.

'I see,' said Malum. 'Is that how you perceived the Gift of Truth possessed by this vile girl?'

'Yes,' said Friel. 'Leona was an asset to me, nothing more. Are you going to kill her?'

'We are,' said Malum. 'Would that pain you, Colonel?'

Friel closed his good eye. 'It would be her just reward for betraying me and for betraying the cause of Zamata.'

'You think she betrayed your foolish cause?' said Malum. 'You are wrong, Colonel. Leona has been conspiring against me from the moment she entered my service.'

'What?' said Friel. 'But...'

'Now we have two Gifted to aid our plan,' said Lord Rylan. 'What is the next stage? What preparations do we need to make to ensnare the Witch?'

'We can do nothing until the Demon Witch reveals her power to us again,' said Malum. 'We must be alert and ready to act.'

'What shall we do with our prisoners until then?' Rylan said.

'We should confine them all together,' said Macsin, 'so that we can fetch them quickly when the time comes. Do you agree, brother?'

Malum turned back to Leona, his eyes dark. 'I want to see you suffer and die, Takri. I want that more than anything I have ever wanted in my life. Never before has a weak human so utterly deceived me the way that you did. My shame will last a hundred years. Was it all truly an act?'

'Of course it was an act, you stupid lizard bastard,' Leona cried.

Malum extended his claws and raised them over Leona's body.

'She is trying to provoke you into killing her, brother,' said Macsin. She glanced at the Bullan. 'Confine these three prisoners with Major Lyla, before my brother does something that he will come to regret.'

'Yes, my lady,' said the officer. He signalled to his men, and soldiers pulled Cisca and Leona to their feet. The two women were dragged out of the cavern, while Friel Laimos was shoved along next to them. They climbed the steps from the basement, then followed a twisting set of lamplit passageways to a guarded entrance, where two soldiers saluted.

'Open the door,' said the officer. 'These three will be joining the major.'

A soldier withdrew a key, and the door was unlocked and swung open. Leona peered into the gloom, then she was pushed inside the small chamber. She fell to the stone floor, then Cisca landed next to her. Friel walked in on his own two feet, then the door was closed and locked.

'Some company, at long last,' said a voice from the dark shadows in the corner of the chamber. There was a long narrow slit high up in the wall that was allowing in a shaft of sunlight, but the rest of the room sat in a thick gloom.

'Is that you, Major?' said Cisca, getting up onto her knees.

'Cisca?' said Lyla. 'The last time we spoke, you told me that if I behaved myself then I might be released; and now you have been arrested?'

'Unfortunately,' said Friel, 'I don't think any of us are going to be released. Are your hands free, Major Lyla?'

'They are.'

'Then could you please remove the bonds tying our wrists?'

'Why would I want to do that? You are Colonel Laimos, are you not? You and Leona are rebels – you might murder me if I untied your wrists. Cisca, you may approach.'

Cisca managed to get to her feet, then she staggered forwards and turned her back to Major Lyla.

'These knots are tight,' said Lyla. 'I am not sure I will be able to loosen them.'

'There is a knife in my boot,' said Friel. He glanced at Leona. 'Aren't you glad I didn't use it?'

Leona said nothing, then she sat up with her back against the cell wall. At the same time, Lyla stood up and emerged from the shadows. Her features were drawn and tired, but she seemed unharmed. She glanced down at Leona, then stepped towards Friel.

'Which boot?' she said.

He smiled. 'My left.'

Lyla eyed him, then crouched down. She reached into Friel's left boot and slid out the slim blade that Leona had given to him when they had first arrived in the monastery. She got back to her feet, then turned and cut the cords binding Cisca's hands. The Dragon Corps captain gasped in relief. She rubbed her wrists, then sat down on the edge of the stone bench that ran along the walls. Lyla turned back to face the colonel, the blade clutched in her hand.

'What else shall I do with this knife, Laimos?' she said. 'Standing before me is a notorious criminal and traitor; an enemy of the Dominion. Perhaps I should do Athumia a favour and end your life?'

Friel turned round to face the wall. 'If you are going to kill me, then make it quick. I would hate to lie on the floor bleeding all over your lovely cell for hours.'

Lyla smiled, then she cut the bonds around Friel's hands. He flexed his fingers and turned.

'Thank you,' he said.

'I'm keeping the knife,' Lyla said.

'Think of it as a gift.'

Lyla turned her gaze to Leona. 'I notice that you have not asked me to cut your bonds,' she said. 'Would you prefer to remain bound?'

Leona struggled up to her knees, then Lyla leaned over and sliced through the ropes. Leona rubbed her hands together, and got to her feet.

'I am sorry I doubted you,' said Friel.

'My act needed to be good if it was going to fool the dragons,' Leona said. She glanced at Cisca. 'What happened?'

'I made a mess of everything,' Cisca said. 'This is all my fault. Lady Macsin asked me to leave the cavern, but I hid close by so that I could listen to what they were saying, and she caught me.'

Lyla narrowed her eyes. 'I seem to be missing something here. Captain Cisca, are you working for the rebels? Is that why you were arrested?'

Cisca nodded.

'I forced her into it,' said Leona.

Friel sat down. 'That was your mistake,' he said. 'You should never have involved an amateur. I trained you for years to operate undercover, and yet you expected a Dragon Corps officer to be able to master it in no time at all.'

Leona glanced down. 'Bauchlie said something similar.'

'Have you two been in contact?' said Friel.

'The monastery is being searched for him as we speak, but they won't find him. He knows a back way out of the building.'

Friel laughed. 'He was here? That lad has courage. Wait; if you know about his secret way out, then why didn't the dragons force it out of you? I assume they used the truth spell on you?'

'They tried,' said Cisca. 'The dragons tried, but it didn't work.'

'That sounds a little unlikely,' said Lyla.

'I know, but it's true,' said Cisca. 'I saw it happen with my own eyes.'

Leona glanced at the two Aucterian women. 'I told the dragons that it was a consequence of possessing the Gift of Truth.'

'You have the Gift of Truth?' cried Lyla. 'I have been sitting alone in this cell for weeks, craving for something to alleviate the boredom, but this... this seems like a bad dream. What am I doing in the same cell as a Gifted rebel?'

'We'll come to that soon,' said Friel, 'but first I need to ask Leona for the truth, because I know for a fact that her Gift does not make her immune to the power of the dragons.'

'It was the Demon Witch,' said Leona. 'She was in my mind, and she made me resistant to the truth spell.'

Lyla sat down on the stone bench, her eyes wild. 'The Demon Witch?' she said in a high voice. 'Slap me, Cisca. I am clearly having a nightmare.'

Leona sat down next to her. 'I wish it was a dream,' she said, 'but it's true. The Demon Witch is our friend.'

'She's not my bloody friend!' Lyla cried. 'She killed King Gahad; and she is responsible for all of the troubles that have afflicted us since that terrible day. I happened to be in Inopei when the Demon Witch slew our sovereign; so was Cisca. She can tell you all about it. That damned Witch is the greatest enemy ever faced by the Dominion.'

'That leads me on to your question about why we are all sharing the same cell, Major Lyla,' said Friel. 'It appears that the dragons have a plan to eliminate the Demon Witch; but to do so, they will have to kill a few humans first. Can you guess the identities of the four lucky humans they have chosen?'

'But... but I am not a traitor,' said Lyla.

'Isn't that why you were arrested?' said Leona. 'You called King Naghad a stupid lizard, or words to that effect. What the colonel said is true. We are all going to die. The dragons are going to draw our lives from our bodies to give them more power. Lord Malum has that ability.'

'But we have no idea when it will happen,' said Friel. 'It could be today, or it might be weeks away. Until then, we'll all be living together in this tiny room.'

'Shit,' Lyla muttered, then she started to cry.

Leona glanced at Cisca and Friel, but both were keeping their gazes lowered as Lyla sobbed. She turned her eyes upwards to the narrow window slat. Outside, it was still daylight, and she wondered if she would ever see the sun again.

It was night when the voice appeared in her head, awakening her.

Leona.

Demon Witch? Are you here to help us? The dragons have a plan to catch you. You must...

I only have a few seconds, the Demon Witch said. *Lord Malum's senses are already stirring at the use of my powers to contact you, and I don't want to get you into more trouble. I am here to tell you that I cannot save you just yet. Lahnos is in danger, and he needs me. I'm sorry, Leona, but you will be safe here for a little longer. Be strong, and I shall return when I can.*

The voice vanished before Leona could say anything else. She cursed, and rolled on to her back, her eyes seeing nothing in the darkness.

'Are you awake?' whispered Friel from the floor next to her.

'Yes.'

'Did something happen?'

'No,' said Leona. 'Go back to sleep. Nothing happened; nothing at all.'

CHAPTER 25
TORMENT

Outside Great Gunst, Gunstian Empire – 19th Lexinch 1588

Get up.

Lahnos stirred. His eyes opened, but he could see nothing but darkness, then he felt a great weight on top of him, pressing him down. He tried to move his head, and one of his horns struck something. He managed to bring his right hand up to his face, then he realised that he was lying in thick mud. A low roar met his ears – were people cheering? And rain; yes – it was raining. He felt by his head and touched the object he had struck. It was a boot. The weight keeping him held to the ground was made up of bodies – dead bodies. He shivered from the damp and cold, and lay his head back down onto the soft mud.

He was going to die.

No. You are strong and determined.

'Leave me alone,' he gasped.

No, Lahnos. I will not. Be strong and brave, resolute and bloody-minded. When I first saw you, you were the most confident young man I had ever met. Be that confident again.

Lahnos felt something surge through his body, yet his mind tried to resist.

Thousands of Zamatans have been taken prisoner.

'Then why don't you free them?' he said.

Not unless I free you first. Believe in yourself.

'Is the battle over?'

The battle has been over for hours.

'And we lost? I mean the Dominion lost?'

They did. But you are still alive, and so are most of the Zamatans. Take them home.

The voice vanished and Lahnos felt himself jolted fully awake, his senses clearing. He peered ahead at the thick jumble of legs, arms and torsos. Most were wearing Dominion uniforms, and the face of a young Aucterian soldier stared vacantly at him just next to his left shoulder. Lahnos started to crawl, his boots digging into the thick mud, and his horns snagging on a dead soldier's belt. He shoved a body out of his way, and the heap shifted. More soldiers fell onto him, but he persisted, beginning again. He freed his left arm, then used both hands to paw and wriggle his way towards the edge of the mound of slain. His fingers went deep into something soft, and he saw a gaping sword wound right in front of him. He threw up, his chest heaving, but only bile and a thin dribble of saliva came from his lips. He crawled over the body with the sword wound and pressed on, until, exhausted, he broke through and tumbled out and down the side of the heap, rolling to a stop in the mud below. He lay on his back with his mouth open, and the rain pelted against his face. Drops hit his parched tongue, and he savoured each one.

Well done. Get on your feet and walk.

I have horns, you stupid witch, he said in his mind. *The Gunstians will see them.*

They won't if I make you invisible.

You can do that?

Yes. What I shall do tonight will require all of my powers, and there is much that you will have to accomplish in a short time.

I will do it, but this doesn't mean that I like or forgive you.

I know, but what else am I to do? I cannot abandon you here to die, Lahnos.

He got to his feet. His limbs and back were aching, and his hands were red from touching the bodies on the mound. He looked down. His ragged uniform was coated in a thick layer of wet mud, which was reflecting a dull red glow. Fires, he thought. He raised his head. A section of the great city was burning, and smoke and flames were funnelling upwards into the overcast sky. He knew which part of Great Gunst was aflame – it was the same area that the Dominion army had been occupying before the curtain wall had collapsed, blocking the ways in and out.

The Dominion forces are being annihilated, said the Demon Witch. *The Aucterians, the Bullan, and even the dragons. The Gifted of Gunst have surrounded them, and are using their powers to destroy them utterly.*

'The dragons cannot all be dead,' he said. 'Where is the King?'

Naghad lives, but he is a prisoner, along with several of his kin. The Gunstians are torturing and executing them.

'Where?'

Turn around.

He did as the Demon Witch suggested. He was in the middle of the Dominion baggage camp, not far from where he and his squad had been building their section of the earthen rampart. Looted wagons and equipment were lying close to several great mounds of the dead, while Gunstians soldiers were cheering and singing. In the distance, the forms of several dragons became visible, their scales gleaming in the torchlight. Some lay dead, their long necks severed, while those still alive were writhing in agony. Around them, protected by lines of soldiers, robed men and women were standing with their hands raised, their gazes locked on the chained and tormented dragons. One of the shackled dragons was larger than the others, and his bronze scales were marked with dozens of small wounds. His wings were also chained, and a giant muzzle was enveloping his jaws. Above the muzzle were two red eye sockets, which were bleeding freely.

The King of the Dominion was blind.

A noise came from behind Lahnos and four Gunstians soldiers strode past him, seemingly oblivious to his presence. They walked onwards, then stopped to gaze at the captive dragons. As they were speaking to each other in low voices, Lahnos felt the Demon Witch's presence in his mind throb and pulse.

What are you doing to me? he said.

Something I should have done a long time ago, she said. *You understand the Gunstian language, and I am drawing it from your mind, so that I can understand their words and thoughts.*

In the centre of the large crowds of jubilant Gunstians, an old woman wearing black robes was helped up onto the back of a wagon, and the soldiers fell silent.

'Soldiers of Gunst,' she cried, her voice ringing out over the camp; 'holy warriors of the mighty Chadura – witness the downfall of the arrogant demon lizards and their hordes from the East! See how the blessed Chadura deals with those who dare to trespass upon the soil of Her faithful people. The Gifts of Pain, Stone, Immolation, and every other Gift we used to defeat the enemy were bestowed upon us by our loving and merciful god; praise be Her name!' She raised an arm and pointed towards the high walls of the city, from where smoke and flames were still rising. 'Behold the destruction of the proud army that sailed from Aucteran!' She turned her arm to point at the shackled King Naghad. 'And behold their fallen King! For centuries, the demons have cast their eyes towards Gunst, looking with envy at the last free nation upon Athumia. The Gunstian Empire has never invaded their lands – no! Not once have we sailed across the ocean with ships full of soldiers to burn their homes and slaughter their people; for Gunst is a peaceful nation, united in our devotion to the one true faith, which counsels forgiveness and love, not aggression and war. What have we ever done to provoke the anger of the Dominion? The demons occupy Elso and their soldiers trample over the people of Irlan, our brothers and sisters of the West; and yet all we wish to do is defend ourselves. Three times the demons have attacked Gunst, and three times, with the help of the blessed Chadura, we have crushed their imperialist forces. Today is a day of great victory!'

The soldiers cheered, but the woman cut them off.

'But we should not celebrate,' she said. The crowds quietened again, and the woman's eyes darkened. 'Thousands of our people have been slain, and tens of thousands have been rendered homeless and destitute by the unprovoked aggression of our arrogant neighbours across the ocean. Farms have been destroyed, and the city of Toraq is in ruins. We even had to sacrifice a portion of our great capital city to ensure the annihilation of the enemy army. We would be fools to think that the Dominion will not come again. The lizard demons will weep and wail when they learn of this catastrophe, but then they will begin to make their plans anew, plotting our conquest; for they will not rest until the entire world is under their control. There is only one way to stop them. No, we are not advocating an invasion of the Dominion homelands – for that would be pure folly. Instead, the government of the Gunstian Empire has this night decreed that our sole target shall be the island of Zamata. It is a mere speck in the wide ocean but, without it, the Dominion will be unable to stage any more attacks upon our shores. And, was this island not once a part of the West, and not the East? Are the native islanders not our distant cousins, rather than the strangers who hail from Aucteran and Inopei? Therefore I say to you – rejoice in our victory, but do not rest, for there shall be no rest until Zamata falls back into our hands. Our army and navy shall be marshalled in the coming days, and then we shall strike while the Dominion is still reeling from its defeat.' She raised her hands into the air. 'All praise to Chadura! All thanks to Chadura! We bow before Her wisdom and mercy, and beg Her to help us in our noble cause. We are humble and weak before Her almighty divinity, but with Her assistance, we cannot fail!'

The crowd of Gunstians roared and cheered, their weapons held aloft in the flickering light of the dozens of torches and camp fires. Drinks were passed around, but Lahnos noticed that it was only water that was being offered to the soldiers.

King Naghad let out a howl of anguish as a robed man pointed at him. The bronze dragon tried to move his forelimbs, but the chains had been attached to thick iron posts in the ground, and his efforts were in vain.

I feel your sympathy for the King of the Dragon Dominion, Lahnos, but you cannot linger, said the Demon Witch. *Walk through the crowd, and you will come to a great enclosure where the Zamatan prisoners are being guarded.*

How am I supposed to free them? Even if I am invisible, the Gunstians will see thousands of Zamatans if they try to leave the camp.

Trust me. Now go. My powers are at their limit, and I do not have much time.

Lahnos set off, his heart racing as he approached the great crowds of Gunstians. Hundreds of them were watching the torment of the captured dragons, while others were cleaning up the detritus left behind by the battle for the baggage camp. Lahnos walked among them, but none glanced in his direction. He carried on until the crowd began to thin again. Ahead of him, across a patch of darkness, a long line of torches was illuminating the edges of a large field. Lahnos walked closer. In the midst of the field, thousands of men were huddled together, crouching on the muddy ground, their weapons gone. Gunstian soldiers had been posted along the perimeter, and were watching the prisoners, their crossbows loaded and ready. On the northern side of the field ran a ditch and a gate, where more soldiers were gathered. Lahnos scrambled down the bank of the ditch, splashed through the water at the bottom, then climbed up the tall embankment on the far side. The Zamatans turned. Behind Lahnos were the fires of the camp, and his horns and mud-covered appearance were causing the Zamatan prisoners to stare at him as though he were a vision. Several got to their feet, and while many hung back, a few approached.

'Who are you?' said one. 'You're not Bullan.'

'I am Zamatan, just like you,' he said.

'And you just walked into captivity?' said a sergeant. 'Are you insane? You should be running, boy.'

'We're leaving,' Lahnos said; 'all of us.' He jumped down from the earthen embankment, and approached the Zamatans. 'We have the

Demon Witch on our side, lads,' he said. 'Follow me, and I will lead you to safety.'

The sergeant's eyes went hazy for a second, then he blinked. 'Do as he says,' he cried. 'Follow the part-Bullan.'

More Zamatans were getting to their feet to see what was happening, but no sound came from the soldiers guarding the perimeter. The eyes of every sergeant in the vicinity glazed over, then each began to rally their men.

'Follow the part-Bullan,' said another sergeant. 'Stay quiet and get into line.'

'This is madness,' said an older soldier. 'The Gunstians will cut us down if we try to escape.'

'Do as you're told,' said a sergeant. 'Follow the part-Bullan.'

Lahnos watched as the Zamatans began to assemble in the muddy field. His eyes went over the ragged crowds, searching for his brother.

He took hold of a sergeant's arm. 'Have you seen the squad from Fidalaimos?'

The sergeant shook his head, then he nodded to a couple of his men. 'Find the lads from Fidalaimos; the part-Bullan wants to see them.'

The two soldiers raced off into the mass of Zamatans, then a great cry rose up from the main part of the camp behind them. Lahnos turned and raced back up the embankment, and several Zamatan sergeants followed him. In the distance, one of the captured dragons had gone berserk. He had broken free of his shackles and was charging back and forth through the crowds of Gunstians. Reinforcements hurried to contain the rogue dragon, and he blasted flames at them.

Quickly, Lahnos, said the Demon Witch. *This distraction will not last long. Take the Zamatans out of the northern gate, then turn west for the river. Once you are past the perimeter of the camp, no one will see you, and your absence will not be noticed for some time.*

Lahnos pulled his eyes away from the frenzied dragon.

'We must hurry!' he cried. 'Come on.'

Lahnos ran back down the slope. More sergeants had been

persuaded by the Demon Witch to obey him, and they began shoving and cajoling the Zamatans, until everyone was on their feet and moving towards the gate. A small group barged through the crowd, and Lahnos saw Karl among them. He ran forward and, before Karl had even seen him, Lahnos threw his arms around his brother.

'You're alive,' Lahnos said.

Karl stared at him, his expression fraught with a mixture of relief and anxiety. 'So are you, brother.'

'Did the rest of the squad...?'

Karl gestured to his left, and Lahnos saw the other Zamatans from Fidalaimos gathered next to them.

'They're here,' Karl said. 'You and the Bullan sergeant were the only ones missing.'

'Is the Bullan not here with you?'

Karl shook his head. 'He was taken away by the Gunstians when we were captured. I thought you...'

'I know. I thought the same. Come on; we're getting out of the camp. Follow the others to the gate.'

'But...'

'Trust me, brother,' said Lahnos. 'We're not going to die here.'

The entrance to the field was closed when they reached it, but no Gunstians were in sight. Two sergeants ran forwards. They unbarred the iron gate and pulled it to the side, and then the other sergeants began to lead the Zamatans through.

'Stay close to the others,' Lahnos said to the men from Fidalaimos, then he ran through the mud to the front of the crowd. He gestured towards the large ditch they had dug the previous day, and the Zamatans crossed it as the rain grew heavier. Thunder rumbled overhead, then the downpour became torrential. Lahnos glanced over his shoulder, but the edge of the camp was barely visible in the mist and rain.

He gathered a group of sergeants as the Zamatans gathered on the northern flank of the ditch.

'Take everyone to the river,' he said. 'You will know what to do when you get there.'

The sergeants saluted, then Lahnos turned away from them and began walking towards the camp, as the Zamatans rushed through the rainstorm towards the west.

What are you doing, Lahnos? said the Demon Witch. *Why are you turning back?*

I cannot leave without looking for Efizel.

We don't have time for this, she said. *The mad dragon has already been killed, and the soldiers are beginning to return to their posts.*

I don't care. If you needed to rescue me, then I need to rescue Efizel. Where is he?

I don't know.

Why not?

I cannot understand the language of the Bullan, which means I cannot read their thoughts. And, I admit that I cannot tell the difference between one Bullan and any other. The vast majority of them are lying dead within the walls of the city.

Efizel wasn't in the city. Karl said he was taken away by Gunstian soldiers. Can you see any Bullan in the camp?

Yes, I can see some.

Are they being held prisoner?

No, Lahnos, they are being executed.

Show me.

An image formed in Lahnos's mind of an area to the rear of the captured dragons. It was a field that the Dominion had been using as a paddock, but the horses were gone, and in their place were a few dozen Bullan soldiers. The paddock was surrounded by Gunstians with shields and crossbows, and a robed man was standing in front of the unarmed Bullan prisoners, flanked by more soldiers. Gunstians were pulling Bullan out from the small crowd and dragging them one at a time towards the robed figure. When they reached the front, the robed man would touch the prisoner with a hand to their face, and the Bullan would cry out and die. To the left was a growing pile of corpses, and

Gunstian soldiers were digging through the mound, removing horns and tails from the dead Bullan as souvenirs.

Lahnos set off at a run, racing back through the rain towards the centre of the camp. The crowds thickened as he approached the place where King Naghad was being tormented, and Lahnos ran into a soldier in his haste, his boots slipping on the wet ground. The Gunstian turned, his eyes wide, but his gaze passed right through where Lahnos stood.

'It is time!' cried a voice. 'Gather round and watch.'

Lahnos glanced up. The old robed woman was still standing on the back of the wagon, her arms raised as the rain fell from the dark sky. More Gunstians piled into the centre of the camp, and they quietened.

'Never before,' the old woman said, 'has the King of the Dominion dared to come in person to our shores, and for that I salute Naghad's courage, if not his wisdom. Some among the government argued that we should hold him as a hostage, so that we could negotiate a long-term peace treaty with our great enemy, but the majority understood that the lizard demons cannot be trusted – their oaths are worthless. Therefore, it has been decreed that Naghad shall pay the ultimate price for his crimes of aggression against the Gunstian Empire.'

The huge crowd stilled in the falling rain. Every soldier in the camp was watching, or so it seemed to Lahnos as he squeezed his way through. Behind the wagon, a tall, well-built Gunstian soldier appeared with a long axe in his hands. The soldiers in his way parted, and the man strode towards Naghad. The bronze dragon writhed and struggled, but his shackles were too strong, and he raised his blinded head in anger and fear. His jaws strained against the muzzle, and a few sparks leapt out, but no fire took hold. His wings had been shredded to ribbons of leathery flesh during his torment, and he wailed and howled as the massed soldiers watched in silence.

Lahnos reached the edge of the thick crowd, but rather than run towards the Bullan paddock, he stopped, and turned his gaze towards Naghad.

How could it be possible? King Naghad was not as strong or as powerful as Gahad his father had been, but he was still a mighty dragon. How could he have been reduced to a whimpering, blinded mass of wounds and chains? The man with the axe came to a halt next to Naghad's long bronze neck, and raised the weapon above his head. He glanced at the old woman on the wagon.

'Slay the demon-king!' she cried. 'Finish him!'

The man brought the axe down with a powerful swing. The blade drove into the bronze scales of Naghad's neck, shearing off a chunk of flesh. The King of the Dominion screamed, and the man raised the axe again. He took a step back, steadied himself, then delivered another great blow. The axe penetrated deeper, cleaving through sinew and bone, and Naghad's head drooped as he gasped and choked. The man struck for a third time, and the dragon's neck was sliced through. Blood poured out from the severed flesh by Naghad's shoulders, spilling onto the muddy ground and splashing over the man's boots.

The crowd stared in stunned silence, the rain pelting off their faces.

'You may take your mementoes of this historic occasion, my soldiers!' the old woman cried, and the crowd surged forwards. Gunstians began scrambling over the head and body of the slain King, their knives gleaming in the torchlight as they prised off scales and pulled out the dragon's teeth. Lahnos turned away, sickened by the frenzy of desecration. The soldiers were laughing and slapping each other on the back, while others were fighting over their scavenged souvenirs. Amid the tumult and cheers, Lahnos stole away. He started running again, so that he could be far away from the scene of Naghad's final humiliation.

He raced over the empty fields, then reached the paddock. Many of the soldiers he had seen on guard had gone to witness the death of the King, but the robed figure was still dealing death to the small number of Bullan survivors.

Help me, Lahnos cried.

I shall, said the Demon Witch, *but my powers are almost exhausted. After I have done this, I will not be able to help you again this night, Lahnos. Good luck.*

Lahnos edged closer to the paddock, then he halted as the

remaining Gunstian soldiers on guard duty fell to the ground in a clatter of shields and crossbows, their eyes closing as sleep overtook their senses. The Gifted man in robes turned, his eyes wide as he stared at the unconscious Gunstians on either side, then the Bullan who had been next in line to be executed sprang at him, launching himself upwards from the blood-soaked, muddy ground. The Bullan's hands went to the robed man's throat, as the dozen or so survivors jumped into life. One ran forwards and stamped his boot onto the robed man's head, splitting the back of his skull open. Another picked up a crossbow and shot the Gifted Gunstian through the eye at point blank range.

'Follow me,' said Lahnos.

The surviving Bullan turned. Rage and grief was evident on each of their faces, and two aimed stolen crossbows at him.

'No!' cried one. 'He has saved us!'

'He has horns,' said another.

'He is my friend,' said Efizel, as he ran between Lahnos and the other Bullan, his hands raised.

Lahnos and Efizel looked at each other for a moment, then the two men embraced amid the rain and mud.

'Let us seek vengeance,' said another Bullan, as the rest of the dozen survivors armed themselves from the unconscious Gunstians.

Lahnos released Efizel.

'No,' he said. 'I did not rescue you so that you could throw your lives away. Come with me, and live.'

'We can trust him,' said Efizel. 'This is not the first time that Lahnos Laimos has saved the lives of Bullan soldiers from the Gunstians. What is your plan, my friend?'

'The river,' he said. 'Follow me.'

Lahnos turned, and began running through the rain towards the west. He sensed Efizel by his side, then he heard the boots of the other Bullan as they raced after him. They reached the ditch on the southern edge of the baggage camp, and followed it for a few minutes, leaving the sound of the victorious Gunstians to fade into the distance behind them.

Thunder rumbled again, and a flash of lightning crackled overhead. Lahnos and the Bullan reached the sodden ground by the banks of the river, and they came to a halt by the wide waterway. A Dominion frigate had been sunk close to the opposite bank, and its masts were poking up through the surface of the river.

'What now?' cried a Bullan. 'Are we to swim?'

Lahnos narrowed his eyes as he stared at the raindrops hitting the river. A thick mist was rising up, shrouding the waterway from the rest of the camp.

'Look!' said another Bullan. 'Barges.'

They turned, and saw a long line of flat-bottomed supply vessels being punted downstream. They began to pass the grassy bank where Lahnos and the others stood, their dark forms moving silently towards the south.

'Are those Zamatans on board?' said Efizel.

The Bullan soldiers began shouting for attention, and one of the barges was steered towards the bank. Its hull beached a few yards from the shore, and a Zamatan sergeant jumped down from the deck, the water coming up to his thighs.

'Is that you, Lahnos?' the sergeant cried through the rain. 'We thought we had lost you. The barges were waiting for us by the banks of the river – how did you know?'

Lahnos stepped into the river and waded out towards the barge, as the other vessels continued moving past. The Bullan followed him, and they pushed the barge back into deeper water, then clambered on board, each being pulled on to the flat deck by the Zamatans packing the vessel. Lahnos was the last to leave the river, and he fell forward onto the deck, as exhaustion sapped his strength.

'You did it,' said Efizel, crouching by his side. Tears were streaming down the Bullan soldier's cheeks as he held Lahnos's hand. 'You came back for us.'

'I would never leave you,' Lahnos said.

'Thank you,' said another soldier, as Bullan and Zamatans surrounded Lahnos on the deck.

The mist grew thicker, and the vessel joined the others being punted downstream towards Toraq and the south. The banks of the river disappeared in the fog, and thunder rumbled again as the rain fell from the dark sky.

'What about the King?' said a Bullan. 'Does anyone know what happened to the King? Should we go back?'

'There is no going back,' said Lahnos. 'The King is dead.'

CHAPTER 26
CORPOREAL

Zamata Gataza, Serpent Isle – 20th Lexinch 1588

Cisca stood on the stone bench, her face at the narrow opening. For about fifteen minutes each morning, the sun shone through the window into the cell, and Cisca closed her eyes for a moment as its rays warmed her skin. The cell was cold at night, and Cisca had barely slept, her mind oscillating between fear and resignation. The benches were too narrow to sleep on safely, leaving all four prisoners to lie next to each other on the stone floor. Colonel Laimos and Major Lyla seemed to have had a good night's rest, but they had both been imprisoned for weeks, and were used to sleeping in an uncomfortable cell.

'You look terrible, Leona,' said Lyla. Tiny particles of dust were shining in the narrow strip of sunlight above her head as she knelt on the stone floor, folding up the thin blankets in the gloom.

'I feel terrible,' said Leona.

'Shush,' said Friel, who was standing by the cell door, his ear cupped in his hand.

Lyla raised an eyebrow. 'Are you pretending that you understand the language of the Bullan again, Colonel Laimos?'

'I am not pretending,' he whispered; 'I do understand it; well, I understand a little. However, I can hear nothing while you lot are chattering.'

'And what have you gleaned?'

'Not much,' he said. He moved a finger up to his face and scratched the scarred area under his eye patch. 'The two soldiers outside don't have a lot to say to each other.'

Lyla grimaced. 'I wish you wouldn't do that.'

'Do what?'

'Scratch your wound,' she said. 'It turns my stomach.'

'I can't help it,' he said. 'It gets itchy. Perhaps you could clean it for me? I struggle to do it on my own, and our kind jailors have neglected to have supplied us with a mirror.'

'I would rather die,' said Lyla.

Cisca turned back to the view out from the narrow window. On the left was nothing but the rocky slopes of Mount Hodzulat, but she could just make out the Hansarta on the other side, its waters reflecting the rays of the sunrise.

'I am so tired,' said Leona.

'You have only been in this cell for two days,' said Lyla. 'You get used to the cold and discomfort. Don't despair just yet.'

'I am not despairing,' said Leona. 'I will never give up while the Demon Witch is still on our side.'

Lyla raised an eyebrow. 'There you go again, talking about some ghostly apparition. Tell me – do you have any actual proof that the Demon Witch exists? Have you ever seen her?'

'No, but I thought you believed in her existence,' said Leona. 'You told us you were on Inopei when King Gahad was slain.'

'That is true,' said Lyla; 'but I was only there for a few days and, besides, rumours are not the same as hard evidence. As far as I am concerned, this Witch could be a figment of your fevered imagination, or a ruse to instil false confidence within the supporters of your doomed rebellion. "Never fear, my Zamatan patriots, for the Demon Witch shall come to our rescue!" If she is so wonderful, then why didn't she stop the dragons from re-conquering this blasted island? If she could slay King Gahad, then why hasn't she brought Malum low? If she killed that arrogant lizard, then I might start to believe you; in fact, I would cheer her on.'

Cisca turned to the major. 'Are you being serious, ma'am? Are you on the side of the rebellion now?'

Lyla stacked the folded blankets under the stone bench and shrugged. 'Does it matter? I have been condemned for treason. I might as well act as a traitor should.'

'Do you think the Dominion should be overthrown?'

'Oh, I wouldn't go that far,' Lyla said, 'though I do happen to despise its current leadership. None of this would be happening if Lord Tegru had won the contest to become King.'

Friel turned his good eye to the major. 'What would be happening?'

'It is difficult to say with exactitude,' said Lyla, 'since Lord Kheran returned to Nom Karta after Lord Naghad had already been anointed King; hence Lord Tegru had fled by the time it became clear that the Serpent Isle had been taken by rebels. All the same, Lord Tegru's approach differed profoundly from that of his younger brother. Instead of outright aggression, I believe that Tegru would have negotiated a settlement with the island; that is why Naghad called him weak. That damned lizard was wrong, of course – a willingness to speak to one's enemies does not equal weakness. Unfortunately, many of the other dragons disagreed.'

'If only we could send a message to Lord Tegru,' said Friel. 'We could offer to assist him, in return for Zamata's freedom.'

'That ship has sailed, my deluded rebel,' said Lyla. 'Naghad left enough dragons behind to continue the hunt for Lord Tegru. They are probably chasing him all over Aucteran, while we fester in this cell.'

'A dragon civil war?' said Friel. He walked away from the door and sat down on the stone bench next to Leona. 'That sounds promising. Let us hope that Tegru remains at large.'

'I don't believe that any dragon would willingly grant Zamata its freedom,' said Leona. 'They couldn't take the risk that we would side with the Gunstians. I...' Leona's voice tailed off, and her eyes stared into the distance.

The other three cellmates glanced at her.

'Is she quite all right?' said Lyla.

Leona gasped, then her features flickered with a succession of emotions – hope, fear, relief. Lyla snapped her fingers under her nose, and Leona jumped.

'What are you doing?' said Lyla.

Leona stared at the major. 'The Demon Witch is in my head right now,' she said. 'She... she's exhausted. Naghad is dead, and the Zamatan men have fled from Great Gunst. She told me to tell you this. She...'

Friel grabbed her hand. 'Tell her she must leave,' he said. 'If Malum senses her...'

'Wait,' said Lyla. 'Naghad is dead? That awful lizard is dead? But how...?'

'Leona, listen to me,' said Friel. 'Tell the Demon Witch that she is in grave danger. She must leave your mind immediately.'

Leona turned to him. 'The Demon Witch is not afraid of the dragons. She...' Leona screamed, her cry piercing the small cell. She fell from the stone bench, as Friel kept a tight grip of her hand, and then she writhed on the floor, her eyes closed. She bit her own tongue, and blood trickled from the side of her mouth. Cisca jumped down from the bench and joined Lyla and Friel as they crouched by Leona's convulsing body. Friel slapped her across the face, then tried to hold down her shoulders.

'That isn't helping,' said Lyla. 'The girl is having a fit. Leave her be.'

Friel ignored her, his hands pushing Leona's shoulders down onto the stone floor. The writhing slowed, then ceased, and Leona lay still.

'Can you hear me?' said Friel. 'Leona?'

The cell door swung open, and Bullan soldiers piled into the chamber. Two pulled Friel off Leona, and dragged him from the cell, then more came in. Cisca's arms were pulled behind her back, and she was hauled to her feet. Lyla lashed out with a fist, and caught one of the Bullan on the nose. The soldier smothered a cry, then pulled her out of the cell by the arm. Cisca was shoved into the long corridor outside the cells. Ahead of her, Friel was being dragged along by the shoulders, his boots trailing on the stone slabs. Cisca glanced over her shoulder. Lyla was right behind her, struggling and screaming, while two soldiers were carrying Leona.

'Damn the lizards!' Lyla cried. 'And damn the Bullan!'

The four prisoners were dragged, shoved and carried down the corridor, and then they descended the stairs to the underground caverns beneath the ancient monastery. The three dragons were waiting for them, along with over a hundred more Bullan. Cisca was pushed to the floor of the cavern next to Friel and Lyla, while Leona was laid down next to them. The woman's eyes were still closed, her chin streaked with blood.

Cisca remained still on the ground, but raised her eyes. The three dragons seemed preoccupied, their features tight as though they were in the midst of a great struggle. Malum's claws were scoring lines in the stone floor, and his dark green eyes were burning. Next to him, Lord Rylan toppled over, falling to the ground unconscious.

'Quickly, my brother,' grunted Macsin; 'before the Witch can escape.'

'We must open Takri's eyes,' said Malum, 'in order to seal the Witch's spirit within her. Prepare yourself, sister. Bullan – open the girl's eyes.'

Two Bullan hurried forwards, then both crouched next to Leona's prostrate body. One gripped the sides of her head, then the other leaned over the body, and pinched open one of Leona's eyes. The young woman screamed again, a long sharp cry of pain, then she fell still.

'She has gone!' Macsin said. 'The Witch is fleeing.'

'She is weak,' said Malum. 'Bring forth all of your powers, my mighty sister, and drive her back into Takri's body. Draw upon the lives of the other prisoners.'

Cisca felt a powerful presence within her mind, and she groaned in pain. It was as though she was being subjected to the truth spell again, and she could feel Macsin's dragon strength inside her head, like boots trampling over a flowerbed. Next to her, Friel and Lyla were also moaning in agony, as Bullan soldiers stepped forward to hold them all down. Cisca's arms and legs were gripped, and she began to feel her energy being pulled from her body, draining her. An image of her parents in their home in Naeth appeared before her eyes, and she wished she could tell them how much she loved them. All their hopes and dreams had been transferred to their daughter's career as an officer in the Dragon Corps; they were so proud of what she had achieved. Now, they would be lucky to receive a terse letter from the government, informing them of her death.

'I'm sorry,' she gasped. The world around her dimmed, and she was barely aware of the others in the huge cavern as she began to succumb.

Then, at once, the presence in her mind vanished. A second later, the cavern echoed to the sound of another scream, but this time it wasn't coming from Leona. Cisca managed to open her eyes. Friel and Lyla were lying to her right, alive but also weakened. The scream rang out again, and the ground shook under Cisca. It was Macsin – the great dragon was on her side, her jaws open as she screamed her cries of agony. Her tail flashed out, bowling over three Bullan soldiers, and sending their bodies flying backwards through the air.

'Resist,' cried Malum. 'You must fight her, sister. You are a daughter of Gahad – you are stronger.'

Macsin's eyes opened, then she blasted fire at her brother, enveloping him in flames. The blistering heat washed over Cisca as Malum disappeared for a moment within the inferno. The Bullan moved back a few paces, unsure what to do, then Macsin turned her fiery gaze towards them, and raised her claws. She lunged forwards, and the talons raked through a line of Bullan, decapitating some and slicing through the torsos of others. The Bullan refused to fight back against the dragon, and she charged at them. Her jaws opened and she lifted a Bullan officer from where he was standing, then ground his body between the rows of teeth, spraying the cavern floor with blood. The other Bullan retreated, and Cisca pressed herself against the ground as Macsin approached the prisoners. Too weak to move, Cisca prepared to die, but no attack came. Instead, Macsin turned towards the still form of Lord Rylan by the rear of the cavern. She blasted more flames at Malum, then attacked the younger dragon, her claws extended. Rylan was oblivious, his eyes closed as he lay slumped on the ground, and Macsin's claws ripped through his wings in seconds, reducing them to tatters. She opened her jaws, and went for Rylan's neck.

Malum charged forwards, his pale red scales still smoking from the flames, and his great bulk struck Macsin before her jaws could close round Rylan's throat. The two dragons went down, their claws flashing out as each tried to gouge the other. They rolled together, and another group of Bullan was killed as the huge bodies of the dragons crushed them into the ground. Friel got to his knees, swayed, then crawled over to where Leona was lying unconscious. He pawed at her shoulders, but he seemed too weak to be able to move her.

'Leona, wake up,' he whispered. He turned to Cisca. 'Help me.'

Cisca tried to get up, but her elbows gave way and she fell back to the ground. The writhing mass of duelling dragons was thrashing around over the cavern floor, and a swinging tail missed the four prisoners by a few feet. Macsin bathed her brother in flames, and more Bullan were consumed as the fires scorched the side of the cavern. Malum rolled over, crushing Rylan's left forelimb. The younger dragon cried out, awakening from his stupor, then he shuddered in agony from his injuries. In terror, he tried to pull away from Macsin and Malum, but the pale red dragon's body was pinning his forelimb to the cavern floor.

Malum raked his claws down his sister's face, driving through her scales and ripping out her left eye.

'I am sorry, my beloved sister,' Malum grunted, 'for what I am about to do.'

The pale red dragon pressed his great forelimbs down against his sister's face, driving her head to the ground, then his eyes glowed an emerald green. Macsin screamed, a cry of such despair that Cisca trembled as the cavern shook. Friel was ignoring the dragons, his eyes on

Leona as he tried to drag her clear of the violence and destruction. Lyla got to her knees, and crawled over to Cisca's side.

A squad of Bullan pointed their crossbows at the prisoners.

'Do not move!' shouted one.

'Are you insane?' cried Lyla. 'The dragons have gone mad; they will kill us all!'

One of the Bullan clubbed Lyla on the back of the head, and she fell back down to the cavern floor. Friel and Cisca raised their arms as the Bullan eyed them.

The fight between Malum and Macsin began to settle. Malum had his sister under him, his forelimbs pressed against her face, as Macsin began to weaken. A few claw wounds on Malum's back and flanks seemed to heal of their own accord, the injuries closing up, then Macsin whimpered. The light in her eyes began to fade, and she seemed to almost shrink, as though her body was withering.

'May I be forgiven for this sacrilege, my sister!' Malum cried. 'I have no choice.'

Macsin's body went limp, but Malum did not move. The last of his wounds healed, as his sister's body shrunk into a dried-up husk.

'You killed her!' cried Rylan, as he crawled into the corner of the cavern, his wings in shreds, and his left forelimb broken and hanging limp. 'You drained her life to heal yourself!'

'Be quiet,' Malum said. 'You understand nothing. The Demon Witch's presence is trapped within my sister's body. As soon as she dies, the Demon Witch will die with her.'

'What you are saying is impossible,' said Rylan. 'No one will believe you. I will tell King Naghad that you slew your own sister.'

'Silence!' Malum roared, then he hesitated, as though pondering the younger dragon's words. 'Perhaps I do need proof,' he said, after a long pause. 'King Naghad has no knowledge of the Demon Witch's actions upon this island; there is a chance he will not believe me. However, it is too late for my beloved sister – she has suffered wounds that cannot be healed.' He turned back to Rylan. 'You will help me.'

'I am injured,' said Rylan. 'Look at my wings! I will not fly for months; and my limb...'

'Cease complaining,' said Malum. 'You have your life, which is more than you deserve. How I wish that the Demon Witch had entered your body instead of that of my sister; you are nothing compared to her. I command you to assist me with every last ounce of your strength. If you refuse, I will kill you.'

Rylan cowered in the corner of the cavern. 'What do you want me to do, my lord?'

'We shall find another suitable vessel in which to house the spirit of the Demon Witch,' said Malum.

'That makes no sense,' wailed Rylan. 'It cannot be done!'

'You fool! Did not the great Nathaniel place the spirit of Gahad into the form of a dragon?'

'Nathaniel is a god.'

'And so am I,' said Malum. 'Gahad's blood runs strong within me.' He turned to the four prisoners. Leona and Lyla were lying unconscious next to Cisca and Friel, who still had their empty hands raised in the air.

'We shall keep Takri alive,' Malum said, 'as I wish for King Naghad to question her. Cisca and Laimos also understand the truth about the Demon Witch – they will be required as witnesses, to prove that what I did to my sister was necessary.' He gazed at Lyla. 'That leaves this one. Rylan, you will allow me to drain your powers. I have taken the life force of my sister, but I shall require more for what I am about to do.'

Rylan said nothing, his eyes wild with disbelief and fear.

Malum glanced at the remaining soldiers. 'Break Major Lyla's neck.'

The surviving Bullan glanced at each other, then a sergeant ran forwards. He knelt by Lyla, his eyes on her unconscious form, then he reached down with strong hands and twisted her neck. There was a horrible cracking sound, and Cisca broke down in tears.

'Now, open her eyes,' said the pale red dragon.

The Bullan nodded, then used his fingers to prise open one of Lyla's eyelids.

Malum turned back to Macsin.

'Farewell, my sister,' he said, then his eyes glazed over.

The pale red dragon grunted, his features straining, then he cried out in anguish and exhaustion. Rylan also emitted a loud cry, then both dragons fell to the ground. Malum lifted his head a few inches, his gaze upon the body of Lyla.

'Awaken,' he said, his voice low and filled with pain.

Lyla's neck aligned itself with a crack and her chest began to rise and fall again.

Malum's eyes burned with power. 'Enjoy your new home, Demon Witch,' he gasped, 'for you shall never escape its mortal confines.'

The pale red dragon's eyes closed, and the cavern fell into silence.

'What are our orders?' said a Bullan soldier.

The sole surviving officer surveyed the scene. 'I think we are to keep the prisoners alive,' he said. 'Lord Malum mentioned that he wished for them to be interrogated by His Majesty King Naghad upon his return.'

A sergeant leaned over Lyla. 'She is breathing. I don't understand, sir; I broke her neck.'

'Lord Malum has power over life and death,' said the officer. 'You killed her, and he revived her.'

'But why, sir?'

'It is not our place to question the orders of the dragons,' said the officer. He gestured to some of his men. 'Check Lord Malum and Lord Rylan to see if they still live.'

Several Bullan ran forwards, then slowed as they approached the huge bodies of the three dragons. Lady Macsin was clearly dead, her scales dull and withered, and her eyes vacant. Two of the soldiers neared Rylan, and they turned.

'Lord Rylan is alive, sir,' one shouted, 'but he is in dire need of medical attention.'

Lord Malum opened his eyes, and the Bullan bowed.

'Praise the serpent gods that you live, my lord,' said the officer. 'What are our orders?'

'Does the prisoner live?' gasped the pale red dragon.

'All four prisoners are alive, my lord.'

'Then my struggles were not in vain. Awaken Major Lyla, but first ensure that she has a crossbow aimed at the back of her skull.'

'Yes, my lord.'

The Bullan surrounded the four prisoners. Cisca and Friel were dragged over to where Leona was still lying unconscious, then one of the soldiers placed the tip of his loaded crossbow to the back of Lyla's head, as another slapped her across the face.

Lyla choked, then threw up, vomiting down the front of her uniform. She tried to roll over, but a soldier was holding on to her legs. She groaned, and opened her eyes.

'Major Lyla is awake, my lord,' said the officer.

Lord Malum crawled forwards, using his claws to pull his weakened body over the floor of the cavern. He leaned down and sniffed Lyla, then stared into her eyes.

'You have lost, Demon Witch,' he said, 'and I have won, although my victory has come at a terrible cost. Your powers are useless within your new prison; I can sense you trying to use them, but your efforts are in vain. What do you have to say, now that you are my prisoner?'

Lyla stared at him blankly, her mouth open.

'Answer me, Witch!' Malum roared.

Lyla did not respond.

'I don't think she can understand what you are saying, my lord,' said the officer. 'Is it possible that Major Lyla remained dead for too long? It is difficult to judge, but I would estimate that several minutes passed between her death and her resuscitation. Perhaps her brain has been damaged beyond repair.'

Malum said nothing.

'Should I summon the monks, my lord?' said the officer. 'Lord Rylan's wounds require urgent attention; as do yours.'

'Yes,' said Malum. 'Bring the monks. Before you do so, however, take these prisoners away and secure them within their cell. Except for Major Lyla – imprison her alone, and have her shackled and hooded. I must rest now; yes, I must rest. Never before have I felt so weakened and drained.'

The officer snapped his fingers, and the Bullan began to pick up the prisoners. Cisca's legs would not support her, and she was dragged out of the cavern by two soldiers, while Friel, Leona and Lyla were carried out behind her. They ascended the stairs, then soldiers took Lyla's body by a different route. Cisca glanced at her old superior officer as she was carried away, unable to believe Malum's version of what had occurred. It was hard enough to comprehend that she had been brought back from the dead, but the idea that the Demon Witch's spirit was now encased within Lyla's flesh seemed too unreal to accept.

The other three prisoners were taken back to Lyla's old cell, and were thrown in. Cisca landed on the hard ground and lay still, her body shuddering with exhaustion. Friel crawled over to Leona and took her hand.

'What have they done to you, Leona?' sobbed Friel. 'My girl, my poor girl.'

He wept over her unconscious body, and Cisca turned away, curling up into a tight ball on the rough stone floor. Her entire body was trembling, and she longed for a sip of water to soothe her parched and aching throat. Images of Macsin's death flashed before her eyes, then she relived the moment when Lyla's neck had been snapped by a Bullan soldier. She began to cry, then she slipped into unconsciousness.

CHAPTER 27
DYING FOR THE CAUSE

Zamata Gataza, Serpent Isle – 21st Lexinch 1588

No dreams occupied Leona's mind as she lay in oblivion, and she could not remember where she was when she opened her eyes. The chamber she was in was shrouded in darkness, apart from a narrow slit of greyish light high up on the wall. She tried to recall what had happened to her, but her head was throbbing. As she lay in the gloom, she became aware of the sound of breathing close to her. She almost panicked. Who was there? She let out a cry, then forced her mouth closed, lest she stir whoever was next to her.

The breathing quietened.

'Leona?' whispered a man's voice. 'Are you awake?'

She felt a hand touch her own and she pulled it away.

'Leona, it's me; it's Friel. Can you hear me?'

'Friel?' she said.

The colonel moved in the darkness. 'Yes. You are awake, at last. I wasn't sure if you would ever open your eyes again.' She heard him crouch by her side. 'Are you in pain?'

'Water,' she gasped.

'Cisca – wake up,' Friel said. 'Cisca.'

Another figure in the room groaned.

'Pass me the water skin,' Friel said.

'What?' Cisca groaned.

'The water skin,' Friel repeated. 'Leona is awake.'

There were more sounds, then Leona felt something touch her lips. A hand went round to the back of her head and raised it a little, then cool water flowed into her mouth. Leona spluttered and coughed, then drank. She panted as she pushed the water skin away, then rested her head into Friel's arm.

'Where are we?' she said.

'We are back in Major Lyla's cell,' said Friel. 'You have been unconscious for a whole day and most of the night.'

Some of Leona's memories began to return.

'The Zamatan men are alive,' she gasped, 'and Naghad is dead.' She frowned. 'Did I dream that?'

'No,' said Friel, his voice full of warmth. 'That really happened. The Demon Witch was in your mind, but the dragons sensed her, and... and...'

'And what? I don't remember anything after that.'

Friel fell into silence. Next to him, the shadowy figure of Cisca was also silent. Leona squinted into the gloom, but could see no one else.

'If we are in Lyla's cell,' she said, 'then where is she? Did the dragons kill her?'

'Yes,' said Friel; 'and... no. To be honest, I am not sure how to answer that question. The dragons performed some kind of arcane ritual. It nearly destroyed them. Macsin is dead, and Malum and Rylan were grievously wounded.'

'Help me sit up,' said Leona.

She winced as Friel lifted her by the shoulders. He pulled her along the floor until her back was leaning against the stone bench. Leona raised the water skin to her lips again and drank.

'I have some bad news,' said Friel. 'The ritual had one purpose – to imprison the spirit of the Demon Witch within mortal flesh. You were supposed to be the vessel, Leona, but the Demon Witch put up a fight.'

Leona's hands shook. 'Is the Demon Witch dead?'

'No,' said Friel. 'Or, well, I don't think so. According to Malum, the Demon Witch is now occupying Major Lyla's body.'

'It's not true,' said Cisca from the shadows. 'It can't be true.'

'I am only repeating what Malum told us,' said Friel. 'Perhaps Captain Cisca is correct. Such power seems beyond anything I can comprehend. But, didn't Malum tell Rylan that the same power has been used before – to place Gahad's spirit into the body of a dragon? Even if it is false, I think Malum believes it to be true.'

'He has to believe it,' said Cisca; 'otherwise, he killed his own sister for nothing.'

'Malum killed Macsin?' said Leona.

'Yes,' said Cisca. 'The Demon Witch entered Macsin's body after escaping yours, and Malum had to fight her. He won, and then he drained her life energy from her body. He murdered her.'

'But not before transferring the Demon Witch to the body of Lyla,' said Friel. 'At least, that's what he said. Could it be true, Leona? You have studied these matters more than I.'

Leona said nothing for a moment, her thoughts trying to catch up with all that she had been told.

'Did he kill Lyla after that?' she said.

'No,' said Friel. 'She's being held somewhere else, but his stated intention was for her to live long enough for King Naghad to return to the island to interrogate her. Of course, that will no longer be possible. Malum has no inkling yet of the death of the King.'

'A Bullan soldier broke Lyla's neck,' said Cisca, 'and then Lord Malum revived her, but she seemed... damaged. Her eyes were open, but I don't think she could understand what Lord Malum was saying to her. If I had to guess, then I would say that the Demon Witch remains on the loose. I think Lord Malum knows this to be true, but he cannot admit it to himself.'

'He might be telling the truth,' said Leona. 'King Gahad had powers that we barely knew about, and Malum is one of his eldest children. Gunstian histories that I have read mention the art of reviving someone after their death. The dragons would breathe new life into the dead, and force them to fight on their behalf, like animated puppets. I found those passages to be far-fetched, but if you two saw it happen with your own eyes, then I must have been mistaken. Cisca, I hope that you are right, for if Malum succeeded in placing the Demon Witch into Lyla's reanimated body, then I fear that she will never be sentient again.'

Friel rubbed his face with a hand. 'Did the Demon Witch tell you anything else about what is happening in Gunst?'

Leona nodded. 'The Dominion army has been annihilated. A dozen days, that's all it took. A dozen days from landing by the city of Toraq to being utterly destroyed in Great Gunst. The invasion force no longer exists.'

Cisca put her head in her hands.

'The Zamatan men are among the only survivors,' Leona went on. 'Lahnos is leading them down the river back to Toraq.'

'Lahnos?' said Friel. 'My horned nephew is leading them?'

'Just as he did during the siege of the Dragon Palace,' said Leona. 'The Demon Witch helped him, but I don't know what is supposed to happen when they reach Toraq.'

'Perhaps the Demon Witch was going to lend them her assistance again?' said Friel.

'Yes. But, if she is trapped within Lyla's body...'

'Do neither of you care about Lyla?' said Cisca, her voice filled with anguish. 'She was my friend, and that Bullan broke her neck as if she were nothing. Did she deserve that?'

'No, Cisca,' said Leona; 'she didn't.'

'She was in prison because she said a few silly things under the truth spell,' Cisca went on. 'I hate the dragons; how could they treat an officer like Lyla as though she were dirt? I weep for all of the dead soldiers of the Dominion, but I am glad Naghad is dead, and I am glad Macsin is also dead. Curse them all.'

'Spoken like a true rebel,' said Friel.

'Shut up,' said Cisca. 'You are just as bad as the dragons. You put your stupid cause above the lives of those you are supposedly trying to help. How many Zamatans have died because of your pointless rebellion? And you, Leona, are worse than Colonel Friel. You stood by and watched as thousands of innocent Gunstian civilians were butchered in Kaugatz.'

'Hold on,' said Friel. 'What happened to the Gunstians?'

'Macsin and Malum slaughtered them,' cried Cisca, 'while your so-called assistant was pretending to be Lady Takri.'

'How many died?'

'All of them. Every last Gunstian on the Serpent Isle was hunted down and killed.'

'It's true,' said Leona, 'and I bear some of the blame. I helped the dragons find the agents responsible for destroying the crops with the Gift of Famine, but I did nothing to stop Malum when he decided that every Gunstian needed to die.'

Friel fell into silence, his head bowed.

'Look where your cause has brought us,' said Cisca. 'I wish I had died in the cavern. I wish it had been my neck that was broken.'

In the silence that followed, Leona thought she heard a shout coming from outside the cell window. She suppressed the guilt and shame that Cisca's words had triggered in her and listened. She had done what she had needed to do, and she refused to give up. If the Demon Witch was free, then the weakened and injured dragons were vulnerable. And if the worst had happened, and the Demon Witch's spirit had been imprisoned within Lyla, then the struggle remained. She got to her feet, ignoring the pain in her head and her aching limbs, and clambered up onto the stone bench, the cold night air brushing against her face.

Again, a shout. The Bullan were on the move, somewhere to the east of the monastery, where the road snaked up from the lowlands below. She caught a glimpse of steel reflecting the light of the waning moon in the undergrowth below the monastery walls.

'I wonder when Malum will discover the truth about the King,' said Friel. 'If...'

'Quiet,' hissed Leona. 'Something's happening outside.'

Friel stepped up next to her, while Cisca remained sobbing on the floor of the cell. Leona shifted a little to the left to allow Friel to see out, and their eyes scanned the undergrowth.

'I see it,' he whispered. 'Figures are moving towards the monastery entrance; but who?'

'I saw a weapon a moment ago,' Leona said, 'or maybe armour.'

Another shout rang out, louder, followed by a howl of pain, then flames erupted by one of the monastery outbuildings. The structure was out of sight of the narrow window, but the rising smoke and flames were visible as they lit up the night sky. Whistles sounded, and Bullan soldiers started appearing in the undergrowth, their uniforms easy to see in the light of the raging fire. There was a low thrum, and two Bullan soldiers fell into the thick bushes, crossbow bolts embedded into their chests.

'It's a rebel attack,' Friel whispered, his eyes alive with nervous excitement. He pointed. 'Look – I can see fighters by the road.'

More Bullan came into view as they advanced towards the gated monastery entrance, and the noise increased. Swords were drawn, and a running skirmish developed in the thick undergrowth below the cell window. A young rebel fighter in leather armour ran past, wielding a crossbow in her hands. She knelt, loosed, then raced out of sight. Friel's eyes widened.

'A woman?' he said.

'Who else is there?' said Leona. 'Do you think the men are the only ones who care about this island?'

There was a whoosh, and another fire exploded through the outbuildings by the entrance to the monastery. The Bullan charged down the hill, and two rebel fighters fell, their leather breastplates pierced by the soldiers' swords.

'They're dying,' said Friel. 'They cannot win this fight. The Bullan are too strong; even a trained army would be unable to break through the front gates. Why are they throwing their lives away?'

Another woman fighter fell, a crossbow bolt striking her eye, and Friel stepped down from the stone bench.

'I cannot watch this,' he said. 'My heart is breaking.'

A key sounded in the lock, and the cell door swung open. Leona turned, and saw three figures in the shadows outside the cell. The tallest one gestured to them.

'Out; now,' he said. 'Move.'

'Bauchlie?' said Friel.

The tall, scarred fighter gestured to his two comrades. 'Drag them out if you have to; we only have a few moments to spare.' He stepped forward and lifted Cisca up by her shoulders, setting her on her feet as the other two fighters ran into the cell. Both were women, and one of them had a set of blunt horns on her head.

'Reyn?' said Leona.

'Shut up and move,' said Bauchlie.

He led Cisca out of the cell, his arm round her shoulder, then Reyn and the other fighter shoved Friel and Leona out after them. Lying in the corridor were two dead Bullan soldiers, their throats cut.

'The attack outside,' said Friel; 'that's...'

'A diversion,' said Bauchlie. 'My contacts in the monastery told me that Macsin was dead, and that the other two dragons were injured. Forty rebels are outside, drawing off the Bullan long enough to get you three out of here.'

Friel came to halt and his eyes darkened. 'You sent Zamatan women to die?'

'I asked Zamatan rebels to fight,' said Bauchlie. 'Are they not fighting, father? Are they not dying, so that you, Leona and Cisca can be free? If you squander their sacrifice I shall place you back into your cell.'

Cisca stared at him. 'Colonel Laimos is your father?'

He stared back at her. 'Yes. Let's go. Bullan reinforcements will have been summoned by now.'

'Wait,' said Cisca. 'What about Lyla? We can't leave her here.'

'Who?' said Bauchlie.

'She's my friend,' said Cisca. 'Please, Bauchlie; we can't abandon her.'

Bauchlie narrowed his eyes as he gazed at Cisca. 'And that's all – just

Lyla; there's no one else?'

'Yes,' said Cisca.

'I agree,' said Leona. 'We have to rescue Major Lyla; it's imperative that we don't leave her here.'

'*Major* Lyla?' said Bauchlie. 'Another damn Aucterian officer?'

'We have to go,' said Reyn. 'Even if we are collecting this Lyla on the way, we can't stay here, Commander.'

'Shit,' muttered Bauchlie. 'Where is she?'

'She's in another cell,' said Cisca, 'but I don't know which one.'

'There are more dungeons on the level below us,' said Bauchlie, 'but that will take us close to the dragon caverns. All right; follow me.'

Bauchlie set off, and the others hurried after him, Reyn at the rear with her crossbow ready. They passed another pair of dead Bullan soldiers, and then descended a flight of stairs, the wall lamps illuminating their steps. They reached the next floor down, and Bauchlie paused as he peered along the corridor that led to the dragon caverns.

'Wait here,' he said. 'I have another dozen rebels close by, watching to see if the dragons come. I will fetch them, and then we shall find Major Lyla.'

A great roar of anger reverberated through the underground tunnel, and dust fell from the ceiling.

Bauchlie cursed. 'That was Malum,' he said. 'Reyn, take Cisca, Friel and Leona to find Lyla. I will gather the rebels here and we will hold off the dragons until you return. Be quick.'

'What?' said Cisca. 'No, Bauchlie. Malum will kill you.'

He looked at her, then he disappeared into the shadows by the cavern entrance. Reyn shoved Cisca along the passageway in the other direction, and they raced towards a door set into a wall. Reyn opened it a few inches, and peered through.

'Two Bullan,' she whispered, her blunt horns silhouetted above her face.

She knelt by the door, and the other rebel stood over her, both aiming their crossbows through the gap.

'Call to the soldiers in their own language,' Leona said to Friel.

'This isn't right,' the colonel said. 'Women should not be...'

'Shut up and do as I say,' snapped Leona.

Friel stared at her, then shouted something unintelligible to Leona's ears. The sound of footsteps approached, and the two rebel fighters loosed. A cry rang out, then the fighters reloaded their bows. The door was kicked open, and a Bullan appeared, a bolt embedded into his left thigh. He rammed his sword into the standing rebel's chest, then Reyn aimed up and loosed into his face. The bow juddered in her hands, and the Bullan staggered, then fell to the ground. Reyn and the others gazed at the body of the dead rebel, then Cisca picked up the spare crossbow, and they carried on.

They passed the body of the other Bullan they had shot and came to a cell door. Leona rifled through the Bullan's pockets, found a set of keys, and placed the largest one into the lock. She turned it, and Reyn pushed the door open. Inside, shackled and hooded, was the figure of a woman lying on the floor of the cell. Leona ran in, then she and Friel pulled the hood from Lyla's head, while Cisca and Reyn stood guard by the door.

Leona gazed down at Lyla. Her eyes were closed and she seemed to be sleeping.

'Lyla,' said Leona. 'Get up.'

'I don't think she can hear you,' said Friel.

Leona took the keys again, and unfastened the padlocks holding the chains to Lyla's body. She and Friel pulled them loose, but Lyla remained unresponsive.

'What's wrong with her?' said Reyn.

'That,' said Friel, 'is a long story.'

Cisca glanced down the passageway. 'I think I can hear someone coming.'

Leona took one of Lyla's arms. Friel took the other then, together, they lifted her up. Lyla's head lolled from side to side, and she put no weight onto her legs.

'She's heavier than I expected,' said Leona.

'I will carry her across my back,' said Friel. 'Hold her steady for a moment.'

He leaned down then dug his left shoulder into Lyla's midriff, grabbed on to her legs, and picked her up, her head and arms dangling down his back as he stood. He swayed for a moment, then nodded to Leona.

'Shit,' muttered Reyn; 'Bullan.'

She and Cisca took cover by the doorway as two soldiers bounded towards them. The Bullan glanced down at the bodies of the rebel and their fallen comrades, then hoisted their crossbows into position. They loosed, and the bolts flew past the entrance to the cell, one striking the open door with a thud.

'Come out with your hands in the air,' cried one of the Bullan, as they reloaded.

Friel took a step forwards, Lyla still over his shoulder. He glanced at Leona, then at Cisca and Reyn, who were sheltering by the doorway, their bows in their hands.

'I'm coming out,' he said. 'I am unarmed. Don't shoot.' He winked at Reyn. 'You can shoot, by all means,' he whispered. 'Let me distract them first, then do what you have to do.'

Friel walked from the cell, his right hand raised, while his left was holding on to Lyla's legs.

'Step forward, Laimos,' said one of the Bullan, as both soldiers took aim.

'Certainly,' Friel said, as he took a step towards them. 'I am surrendering, as you can see.'

'Place the prisoner onto the ground,' said the Bullan.

Friel crouched to his right as if he were about to lower Lyla down, then he shouted something in a language Leona didn't understand. The two Bullan gasped, and looked over their shoulders in alarm.

Cisca and Reyn loosed at the same time. Reyn's bolt struck the first Bullan under his left ear as his head was turning, and he fell to the floor; while Cisca's bolt ripped through the flesh of the second Bullan's right shoulder. The second Bullan grunted in pain, then loosed his own bow. The bolt spat out, and hit Friel in the waist. The colonel let out a cry, dropping Lyla to the ground. The Bullan drew his sword with his left hand and charged. He lunged at Friel, stabbing the blade into the colonel's stomach, just inches from where the bolt had hit him moments before. Friel fell, then Reyn stepped out from the doorway and shot the Bullan in the back of the head. The Bullan sunk to his knees, then collapsed onto the floor, leaving the sword protruding from Friel's stomach. Leona ran out into the corridor and crouched by him. Her fingers went to the hilt of the sword, but he pushed her hand away.

'I am finished,' Friel gasped. 'You need to go, but first you must listen to me. Come closer – these words are only for you to hear.' He coughed, and blood came from his lips. 'Lahnos,' he went on, his voice a low whisper; 'he has other Gifts – Gifts that he is completely unaware that he possesses...'

Leona felt no tingle in her mind. 'Which ones?'

'I recognised one of them,' said Friel, 'but the other is new to me - I have never sensed it from anyone else. I think... I think it might be the Thirteenth Gift. If he comes back, be careful.' He reached out and touched her face. 'Bauchlie was right about you. I die knowing that the island is in safe hands, my beautiful Leona.' He coughed again, and his eyes tightened. 'Tell my son that I love him.' A faint smile touched his lips. 'Did you hear me shouting at the Bullan?'

Leona clutched his hand. 'I did.'

'I told them that Bauchlie was right behind them,' he said. 'Did you see how scared they looked? That boy, that damned boy...'

His eye closed.

Leona stared at him, unable to pull her gaze away.

Reyn walked over and touched her shoulder. 'I'm sorry, Leona, but we have to go.'

'It's my fault,' said Cisca. 'If my bolt had been better aimed, then...'

'No,' said Reyn. 'These things happen; they're not anyone's fault. Colonel Laimos gave his life so that we could escape. Cisca, help Leona carry Lyla, and we'll go.'

Cisca shouldered her bow, then she crouched by Leona and

removed her hand from Friel. Leona felt tears come to her eyes, but she knew Reyn was right. Cisca helped her up, then she took Lyla's arms while Leona grasped hold of her legs, and they carried Lyla down the passageway as Reyn led the way.

They reached the hallway that led into the dragons' cavern. At the end of the corridor, three rebel fighters were lying dead, their clothes and flesh smouldering and smoking. Beyond them, the door to the cavern was lying open.

'Did you think me weakened, rebel cowards?' boomed a voice from within the cavern, and Leona's heart sank.

It was too much. Friel's death had yet to sink in, and Malum's voice almost drove Leona into utter despair.

'Where are the others?' Malum's voice went on. 'The one who tells me shall earn a quick death.'

Reyn stole forwards without a word, and Cisca went after her, pulling Leona along as they carried Lyla. Reyn raised a hand as she reached the entrance to the cavern, and they peered inside. Malum looked gaunt and exhausted, but his dark green eyes had a fierce gleam to them as he stared down at Bauchlie and a handful of rebel fighters. They were kneeling before Malum, while, next to them, the bodies of another four rebels lay dead, their bodies ripped to pieces by the dragon's claws. Behind them lay an assortment of abandoned weapons – crossbows, swords, and a long spear.

'What others?' said Bauchlie, his head held high. 'I don't know what you are talking about.'

'You came here to kill me, didn't you?' said the dragon. 'You heard that I was in pain, and you wished to take advantage of my suffering. You were wrong! I possess the power over life and death, and I am still strong enough to kill you all at a glance.'

He stared down at one of the four rebels by Bauchlie's side, and her head exploded in a crescendo of noise and blood.

By the entranceway, Lyla's eyes opened, and she screamed. In fright, both Cisca and Leona let go of the woman, and she fell to the ground convulsing, her scream piercing the air. Malum looked over, and his eyes widened.

'I will kill you all for this outrage!' the dragon boomed. He glanced at Bauchlie, but nothing happened. 'My powers,' the dragon gasped. 'Where are my powers?' He opened his jaws, but no sparks flew, and, for a brief moment, there was fear in his eyes. Lyla was still screaming, and he glanced back at her.

'Witch?' he said. He lunged forwards, his forelimbs out-stretched as he reached for Lyla.

Bauchlie gripped the long spear that was lying by the other weapons. He leapt into the path of the charging dragon, braced the iron butt into the stone floor, then held the point out as Malum lunged over him. Bauchlie disappeared under Malum's forelimbs, then the dragon's head arched back, and he howled in agony as the tip of the spear was driven deep into his chest. The other three rebel fighters picked up crossbows, and they joined Reyn as Malum's head lowered, his eyes consumed with pain.

'Kill him!' shouted Reyn, and the four women loosed into the dragon's face.

Malum screamed as blood poured from his pierced eyes. Leona picked up a sword as the rebels reloaded. She ran up to the dragon and rammed the blade through his blinded left eye, using both hands to drive it deep into Malum's brain. The four rebels pointed their crossbows and loosed again into Malum's face.

'Take his head!' Leona cried, her hands still gripping the hilt of the blade that had penetrated Malum's brain.

The four rebels dropped their crossbows and took swords from the pile of weapons. They ran to Malum's long neck and began swinging their arms, the four blades hacking through scales, muscles and sinew. Blood streamed from the wound, covering Leona as she held the sword driven through Malum's left eye. Reyn brought her blade down two-handed, and the steel edge severed the dragon's spinal column. The pale red dragon let out a choking gasp, then his head crashed to the floor of the cavern.

Cisca ran forward as if a spell had been broken. She dug under the scales by Malum's left forelimb, and began pulling.

'Help me!' she cried.

The others joined her, and they heaved at Bauchlie's legs, and hauled him out from under the forelimb. The broken butt of the spear was still grasped in his hands, which were covered in Malum's blood.

Cisca cradled his head. 'Bauchlie! You shall not die; I forbid it!'

Bauchlie opened his eyes and coughed. 'Did we get him?' he gasped.

'Yes,' said Leona; 'we got him.'

Bauchlie looked up at Cisca, then he turned his head to gaze at the body of the dragon. 'Something stopped his powers from working,' he said; 'otherwise...'

'It was Lyla, I think,' said Leona, then she noticed that the screaming had stopped. She got up, and ran back to the entranceway. Lyla was splayed out on the ground. Her eyes were closed again, but her chest was rising and falling.

'That doesn't make sense,' said Reyn. 'How could a Dominion officer stop the powers of a dragon?'

'I have a theory about that, but it will have to wait,' said Leona. 'Help me carry her.'

One of the three surviving rebel fighters hurried over and helped Leona lift Lyla up from the ground. Cisca, Reyn and the two other rebel women assisted Bauchlie to get to his feet, and they gazed around at the carnage for a few moments in silence.

'Your father is dead,' said Cisca. 'I'm sorry, Bauchlie. He was brave. He saved us.'

Bauchlie said nothing. He glanced down at the blood on the cavern floor.

'Can you walk?' said Leona.

He nodded. 'With a little help, yes.' He glanced at Reyn. 'Lead us to the boat.'

. . .

An hour later, the escaped prisoners and the surviving rebels were huddled together on the deck of a small fishing vessel as it sailed through the darkness along the west coast of Zamata. High cliffs to their right were blocking the first signs of dawn, and the moon had set, leaving only the stars above them. The men and women crewing the boat were all rebels who lived with Bauchlie in the ruins of the monastery of Medamuna Gatzoun, and they had given their passengers food, water and wine as they had pulled away from the coast. Leona stared up at the cliffs, her last moments with the colonel imprinted into her mind. She knew that thousands of Zamatans would mourn his death, but none of them, not even Bauchlie, had known him as well as she had.

She remembered what he had said about Lahnos – that he was in possession of two more Gifts. From the old Gunstian book she had read, she knew the names and attributes of twelve out of the thirteen Gifts of Theodora. The colonel had read the same book; it was one that he had often thumbed through, and if he suspected that Lahnos had the obscure and semi-mythical Thirteenth Gift, then she had no reason to doubt him. Leona also recalled what the colonel had said about her – that the island was safe in her hands. Was it true? She felt the weight of responsibility push down on her shoulders. It had to be true, she told herself. She would make it true.

'We lost twenty fighters this night,' Bauchlie said, as he sat clutching his bruised and bandaged chest, 'and my father is dead. I wish I had been kinder to him. I wish I could have had the chance to say goodbye.'

'He loved you,' said Leona. 'His last words were about you. Not the cause, or the island – you, Bauchlie.'

The tall man glanced at the dark water. 'Thank you, Leona. For his sake, and for all of the other fighters who fell, I am glad we killed Lord Malum. Perhaps we should have also killed Lord Rylan.'

'We were right not to,' said Cisca. 'Lord Rylan is more reasonable than Malum or Macsin. Things will be different on the Serpent Isle with him in charge.'

Bauchlie eyed her. 'Your faith in the dragons astounds me, Cisca. After all they have done, you would still trust Rylan?'

'I'm not sure if trust is the right word,' she said, 'but Rylan seems rational, rather than driven by anger and hatred.'

'He will still act in the interests of the Dominion,' said Leona.

'That is true,' said Cisca.

Bauchlie glanced over his shoulder at the unconscious woman lying on the deck behind them. 'Tell me about Lyla.'

'I will,' said Leona, 'but I want to speak to Reyn first.'

The part-Bullan was standing by the vessel's starboard railings, and she turned. 'Speak to me about what?'

Leona got to her feet on the deck. Should she tell Reyn about Lahnos's hidden Gifts? No, she thought; not yet, not before she understood what it could mean. 'Thank you for coming to Zamata Gataza,' she said. 'You always said you wanted to fight, and you meant it. Lahnos would be proud.'

Reyn cast her gaze back out towards the dark cliffs. 'Lahnos is probably dead,' she said; 'all of the men are. Gunst is their grave.'

'No,' said Leona. 'Lahnos is alive, and he is leading the men of Zamata out of danger. They are not safe yet, but they were the only ones to escape destruction in the battle for Great Gunst.'

Reyn came closer, her eyes tight. 'Lahnos is alive? How do you know this?'

'The Demon Witch told me,' said Leona. 'After she and Lahnos fell out, she started speaking to me. She last spoke to me yesterday, and that was when she told me about Lahnos.'

Reyn put a hand to her face.

'And where is the Demon Witch now?' said Bauchlie. 'Can we expect any more help from her?'

Leona glanced at Lyla. The woman had her eyes closed, but she looked to be at peace as she lay unconscious.

'Let me tell you a story about Major Lyla,' she said. 'Cisca was there, but she doesn't believe it.'

'I don't know if that is true any more,' said Cisca. 'I doubted it, yes; but after what happened in the cavern, I... I don't know.'

Bauchlie narrowed his eyes. 'Who is this Lyla?'

Leona said nothing for a moment as she gazed at the unconscious body of the major. Would they believe her? She glanced at Bauchlie.

'She is the Demon Witch.'

CHAPTER 28
MURDER

Toraq, Gunstian Empire – 22nd Lexinch 1588

After three days, the rains had stopped. The ruins of Toraq were wet and glimmering in the light of the sun as a westerly wind broke up the clouds in the sky overhead. Steam was rising from the heaps of ash that blocked many of the roads, and the Zamatans began to emerge from the basements where they had been sheltering from the storms. Lahnos and Efizel climbed onto the torso of an enormous statue of a man that had been knocked over in the Dominion's attack on the city. The head had fallen into the river, and only the long, pointed beard was sticking up through the waters as they flowed towards the harbour. Lahnos sat by the carved buckle of a belt, and gazed south. Half a mile away in the distance, what remained of the Dominion fleet was berthed along the ruined and half-collapsed quaysides and jetties – empty troop transports, a handful of destroyers and frigates, and six huge dragon carriers, five of which were anchored out in the harbour basin. When the Zamatan men had arrived in the city two days before, the thousands of Bullan and Aucterian soldiers guarding the port had barred them from boarding the ships. They had called them deserters, and had refused to believe that the great invasion force had been obliterated. To avoid bloodshed, Lahnos had pulled the Zamatans back. They had looted some meagre scraps of food from the last of the supply barges that littered the side of the river, and then they had waited, hungry and exhausted.

'Where is she, Lahnos?' said Efizel.

'Stop asking me that,' he said. 'If the Demon Witch appears in my head, I promise that you will be the first to know.'

'What was her plan?' the Bullan went on. 'Did she give you any indication of what was to transpire after we arrived?'

'No. The last I heard from her was just before I freed the Bullan from the Gifted. She sent the soldiers to sleep and then... nothing. I think she was exhausted.'

'Too exhausted to come back after three days?'

'I don't know,' Lahnos said, his irritation growing.

Efizel glanced up at the clearing sky. 'Do you realise what this weather means? The Gunstians will be moving south to destroy us. Including the Zamatans, there must be nearly sixteen or seventeen thousand Dominion soldiers and sailors in Toraq. When they get here, they will annihilate us.'

'What do you suggest?' said Lahnos. 'Do you want us to launch an attack on the harbour?'

'That would be imprudent, to say the least,' said Efizel. 'The one Bullan regiment stationed in the harbour would be enough to defeat seven thousand untrained Zamatans, Lahnos. On top of that, there are another three thousand Aucterian soldiers. It would be carnage.'

'So we stay here, only to be crushed between the Gunstians from the north, and the Dominion forces occupying the harbour?' Lahnos shook his head. 'Shit. The Zamatans would have been better off kneeling before Chadura.' He glanced up. 'And where are the other dragons? There must be a few who escaped the slaughter outside Great Gunst. I was hoping the good weather would bring them out into the open.'

'I know of one dragon in the harbour,' Efizel said. He pointed at the dragon carrier berthed by the long quay. 'Lord Sigum Mon Sigil is on that ship, but he won't be flying any time soon. He was sent back here days ago, after getting injured while the army was marching north towards Great Gunst. One of his wings was broken when he was brought down by a Gifted.'

'And the others?'

Efizel frowned. 'If there are others,' he said, 'then I expect that they will have fled Gunst by now, if they are aware of the King's death.'

'Where could they flee?'

'To the Serpent Isle.'

Lahnos frowned at him. 'What?'

'A strong and healthy dragon can travel over four hundred miles in a single flight; did you not know this?'

'No.'

'That is because you are used to seeing dragons arriving on the Serpent Isle aboard carriers, Lahnos. The great ocean spans two thousand miles – too far for even the strongest dragon to cross. The Serpent Isle, on the other hand, is only two hundred and fifty miles off the eastern coast of Gunst. Any fleeing dragon would have to avoid the Gunstian cities and armed forces along the way, but if they are cautious, and clever, they could reach the Serpent Isle in around seven or eight days.'

'They would abandon the soldiers and sailors in Toraq?'

'They would, Lahnos.'

He shook his head. 'Bastards.'

'Maybe so,' said Efizel, 'but you must remember that they share a different set of morals from us mere humans and Klediomira Haga. Their lives are measured in centuries, not decades, and the Children of Gahad are immortal. Well, at least none have ever died of natural causes; I do not know if they are truly immortal. Perhaps only King Gahad knew.'

'None of this is helping,' said Lahnos. 'I had hoped that a few dragons would be here, and that they would be willing to fight the Gunstians when they arrive. Without them, the Gifted will tear us to pieces.'

'Unless the Demon Witch returns.'

Lahnos said nothing. His eyes roamed over the grey, ruined stumps of the apartment blocks that lined the clogged streets. The sun was starting to warm his skin, and he willed the clouds to come back, but the wind was scattering them to the east. Below the torso of the huge statue, a young Zamatan shouted up, trying to hail them. Efizel nudged Lahnos, and he glanced down.

'Gunstian scouts have been seen, Lahnos,' the Zamatan cried up to them. 'They are moving down the main roads from the north, on both sides of the river.'

'I'll be down in a moment,' Lahnos shouted back, then he rubbed his face.

'They must have been waiting for the rain to stop,' said Efizel. 'What now?'

'We will pull every Zamatan south, and move them as close to the harbour as the Dominion forces will allow us to get; and then... then we shall see.'

Efizel nodded, then he began to clamber down from the statue. Lahnos remained where he was for a moment.

'Where are you, Witch?' he muttered. 'We need you.'

The next few hours passed painfully slowly, as Lahnos and the rescued Bullan coaxed and urged the tired and hungry Zamatans away from the routes being taken by the approaching Gunstian army. Some had lost all hope, and refused to move, while others were limping along without boots, their bare feet blistered and cut from walking over the ruins. Lahnos led them south towards the harbour, then halted just out of range of the Bullan defending the large roadblock that led to the quays. With a white sheet raised in his left hand, Lahnos, Efizel and the handful of Bullan he had saved from Great Gunst walked the last few yards towards the barricade.

'Come no further, or we shall loose upon you!' cried a voice from the roadblock.

'The Gunstians are coming,' Lahnos yelled back. 'They are moving down the roads towards the harbour.'

'We know,' said the Bullan officer. 'We have scouts, too, horned boy; only ours are a damn sight more discreet than your lot.'

'If you don't let us into the harbour, the Gunstians will slaughter us,' said Lahnos.

'We have our orders,' said the officer.

'Do you believe us now?' said Lahnos. 'Do you accept that the Dominion army was defeated at Great Gunst? We didn't desert; we escaped from captivity.'

The officer chewed his lip, saying nothing.

'We are on the same damn side,' Lahnos yelled. 'What are you going to do when the Gunstians get here – are you going to watch them kill us all? And then what? If you stay in Toraq, you will all die.'

'We were told to defend this harbour until further orders,' said the officer; 'and no new orders have arrived.'

'That's because there is no one left to give them,' said Lahnos. 'King Naghad is dead. Have your scouts confirmed it yet?'

The officer glanced at his men defending the roadblock, then he nodded. 'They have; yes.'

'What about Lord Sigum Mon Sigil?' said Efizel. 'If no other dragons are present in Toraq, then Lord Sigum should now be in overall command of the invasion forces.'

The officer shouted something back in the language of the Klediomira Haga, and Efizel and the other Bullan standing next to him bristled with anger.

'How dare you say that to us?' said one. 'We, who have survived the catastrophe of Great Gunst? Have you no honour?'

The officer looked away. A few of the soldiers manning the roadblock also looked aggrieved at whatever the officer had said, and a few were staring at him.

'You know your duty,' said Efizel. 'You must confer with Lord Sigum Mon Sigil, and ask him for fresh orders, once he has been apprised of the situation.'

The officer turned and strode away, heading towards the harbour.

'What did he say to you?' said Lahnos.

'He called us cowards for allowing a part-Bullan deserter to speak for us,' said Efizel.

'He shamed only himself with his words,' said another Bullan. 'We who know you are grateful for what you did, Lahnos Laimos.'

'We can only hope that he will do his duty,' said Efizel.

'He will,' said another. 'He saw the way his own men were looking at him.'

Lahnos glanced over his shoulder. The streets behind him were crowded with Zamatans. Only a few were armed, and fewer looked as though they were in any condition to fight.

Efizel nudged him, and he turned back to the barricade. A junior Aucterian officer was walking out from the roadblock towards them, his hands raised.

'Can we help you?' said Lahnos.

'Are you the delegation from the Zamatan regiments?' the officer said.

'We are.'

'A group of officers from the navy, the Bullan and from the Aucterian battalions are assembling,' the officer said. 'We intend to speak to Lord Sigum Mon Sigil, and some of us believe that you should come along, so that the Zamatans have a voice at the meeting.'

Lahnos frowned. 'Is this a trick? Are you going to arrest us if we cross the roadblock?'

'It is no trick,' said the officer. He lowered his hands. 'You are not the only ones who think we should withdraw from Toraq before the Gunstians arrive. Will you join us?'

'We will,' said Lahnos. He glanced at the Bullan standing next to him. 'I will go, and I will take Efizel. The rest of you will stay here with the others, in case we don't come back.'

The Bullan nodded, though their eyes remained mistrusting. Lahnos and Efizel stepped forward, and walked towards the roadblock. The officer fell in by their side and they passed the Bullan soldiers guarding the barricade. There was no wall surrounding the harbour, but hundreds of soldiers were occupying every road junction and building along its landward flank, and the officer led them past another heavily-guarded position, where ballistae had been set up facing the street to the north.

'The Bullan in charge of that roadblock doesn't speak for all of us,' the officer said, as they passed the ballista battery. 'When you first arrived here, we were suspicious, but news of the King's death has changed everything. Some of the Bullan want to stay and fight it out to the death, but the rest of us... we just want to go home.'

They came to the end of a street and emerged on to a long quayside. The buildings running down its flank were all damaged, and many of the wooden piers had been destroyed. Lahnos looked for the pier where they had landed in Gunst when the invasion had begun, but he couldn't recognise it amid the ruined debris and heaps of rubble. The harbour basin was littered with sunken vessels, their masts poking up from the surface of the water. Most were troopships, but the carcass of a gigantic dragon carrier was lying on its side close to a long jetty. Four intact destroyers were tied up by the quay next to Lord Sigum's dragon carrier, while the other five carriers were anchored a hundred yards from the shoreline.

The officer led Lahnos and Efizel along the quay to the foot of a gangway leading to an open hatch in the side of the dragon carrier. Armed sailors were standing at the bottom, along with a collection of army officers. The Bullan from the roadblock eyed Lahnos, and his nostrils flared.

'What is this deserter doing here?' he cried.

'The Zamatans deserve to be heard,' said the Aucterian officer.

The Bullan jabbed a finger into the young officer's chest. 'I expressly forbade them from coming to this meeting. They fled the field of battle and left our King to die.'

'You weren't there,' said Lahnos. 'You didn't see what happened.'

The Bullan turned to him. 'How else can you explain your escape? The Zamatans are the only units to return from Great Gunst.'

'We were the only regiments not to enter the city,' said Lahnos. 'We were ordered to remain outside the walls to guard the baggage; that is how we survived. If we had gone into Great Gunst, then we would be dead like the others.'

'And then you fled.'

Lahnos clenched his fists. 'Yes. The Gunstians were celebrating their victory, and we escaped down the river in a rainstorm. Should we have died for a few wagons?'

'You should have died to save the King!'

'Silence!' roared a great voice.

Lahnos and the officers looked up from the quayside. The silvery-green head of a dragon was visible, his dark blue eyes staring down at them from the flight deck of the carrier. The officers bowed their heads.

'My lord,' said an Aucterian officer, 'we have come to request new orders. The Dominion forces that attacked Great Gunst have been destroyed and King Naghad is dead. If we linger here, then the Gunstians will drive us into the sea. What should we do?'

The silvery-green dragon said nothing.

'We were ordered to defend this harbour,' said the Bullan officer; 'and we shall, to the death. Fleeing would be dishonourable, my lord.'

'I disagree,' said another Aucterian officer. 'We should save as many soldiers and sailors as we can, my lord, before every one of us is slaughtered. The invasion has failed.'

The dragon raised his head and gazed out over the harbour. 'The Imperial Gunstian Fleet lies somewhere between us and the Serpent Isle,' he said. 'If we leave Toraq, they shall find us. The Zamatan regiments can enter the harbour, but only to add to its defence. We are going nowhere. That is my command.'

The Bullan officer bowed low. 'As you will, my lord.'

The dragon pulled his head back, and the officers glanced at each other.

'You heard his lordship,' said the Bullan. 'We stay; we fight.' He glared at Lahnos. 'Bring your rabble into the harbour; there is nowhere else to run.'

. . .

The sound of the approaching Gunstian army grew as the sun lowered into the western sky. No sign of them could be seen from within the confines of the harbour, but the Gunstian soldiers were singing and chanting as they reoccupied the ruins of Toraq, and their voices could be heard by every Dominion sailor and soldier packed along the crowded quayside. The Zamatans had been told to defend the southern section of the harbour, but there were no spare weapons to give them, and most remained unarmed. Lahnos tried to rest for a while with Karl and the others from the Fidalaimos squad, but he was summoned back to the quayside. He took Efizel and the dozen loyal Bullan with him and strode away from the Zamatan positions. When they reached the quay, a large crowd had gathered by a long jetty, their eyes on the sea. Entering the harbour were nine vessels, each flying the standard of the Dominion.

'Who are they?' said Lahnos.

'It's what remains of the first supply convoy,' said an Aucterian sailor. 'They set off from Naeth a month ago with over forty ships.'

'Supply vessels?' said Lahnos. 'You mean each is full of food?'

The sailor nodded.

The first supply vessel docked along the jetty and the crowd moved to greet its arrival. A gangway was set down, but before the crew could disembark, a mob of hungry soldiers ran up onto the deck, and began ransacking the supplies. Army and navy officers tried to restore order, but hunger and desperation had eroded the discipline of the men, and the jetty descended into chaos. Fights broke out between the sailors and the starving soldiers, while, in the background, the low drone of the Gunstians' voices grew louder. Seeing what was happening on the jetty, the other eight supply vessels had come to a halt, and were lowering their sails as they anchored in the harbour basin.

Lahnos and the dozen Bullan stood back, watching the violence. Crates that had been carried off the ship were being broken up on the jetty, and groups of soldiers were eating what they could. A struggle erupted on the deck of the supply vessel as a prisoner wearing the uniform of a Gunstian naval officer was brought up from the hold. Armed sailors gathered round him, protecting him from the fury of the starving Dominion soldiers. The crowd surged across the deck, and the sailors bundled the captive down the gangway.

'Stay back!' cried an Aucterian naval officer. 'This prisoner knows the location of the Imperial Gunstian Fleet. We didn't bring him here so that you bastards could kill him. Where are the dragons? We need the dragons to use the truth spell on this man.'

'The sailors don't know what happened to the invasion force,' muttered Efizel.

'Does Lord Sigum have the power to use the truth spell?' said Lahnos.

Efizel shook his head. 'Lord Sigum is not related to the family of King Gahad. He is a mortal dragon.'

'Come with me,' said Lahnos. 'I am about to do something stupid, and I need you to protect me.'

'What are you going to do, Lahnos?' said Efizel.

'Save us all,' he said.

Lahnos began to push his way through the crowd, and the dozen Bullan followed him. The Gunstian prisoner was being surrounded by armed sailors as they tried to make their way along the jetty. Most of the soldiers ignored them as they passed, their full attention on the looting of the supply ship. Lahnos got closer to the ring of sailors, and his hand went to the knife by his belt.

Lahnos waited until the captive was only a few yards away, then he sprang forward, shoving his way between two sailors. He lunged at the Gunstian officer, as the Bullan formed a ring to shield him from the sailors. The Gunstian officer cried out in alarm, then Lahnos barged into him, knocking him to the ground. Lahnos lifted the knife, and the officer stared at him, fear consuming his features.

'I am sorry,' Lahnos said in Gunstian, then he drove the knife into the officer's heart.

Bedlam broke out around him as the dozen Bullan fought off the sailors. Lahnos twisted the knife, and watched as the Gunstian under him took his last breath. Lahnos placed his left hand onto the man's forehead.

Fear and panic surged over him as his vision clouded, but Lahnos knew it was the Gunstian's emotions he was feeling. He controlled his Gift, and swept the officer's last moments aside, plunging deeper into the dead Gunstian's memories. He saw the dank, cramped cabin where he had been held on board the supply vessel, then an image appeared of his capture. His warship had floundered in a storm halfway along the Gunstian Straits, and the survivors had been plucked from the sea by the sailors from the Dominion supply vessel. As the only officer among them, the Gunstian had been interrogated and then placed in the ship's brig. Lahnos went in further. The officer had been on board the Gunstian flagship before being transferred to his own vessel. He had been present in the admiral's cabin when the plan to destroy the remnants of the Dominion navy was being planned. Lahnos saw an oak-lined room with silver lamps, and heard the voice of the admiral. The Gunstian fleet would lie in wait, the admiral was saying, ready to ambush any Dominion vessels that tried to leave Toraq. He saw the charts laid out on a long table. Around the table stood dozens of Gunstian naval officers, watching as the admiral pointed at a chart with a finger. 'Here,' said the admiral. 'The fleet shall wait here.'

Lahnos lifted his hand from the dead officer's forehead. He stood. His dozen Bullan were surrounding him, keeping the sailors and soldiers back.

Lahnos raised his arms. 'I know where the Gunstian fleet is,' he cried. 'I am a death-reader.'

The crowd hushed. A few soldiers were still bringing crates down the gangway from the vessel, but everyone who had heard his words turned to stare at him.

'We must take Lahnos to the dragon,' said Efizel. 'Stay close to him, and stop for nothing.'

The Bullan closed ranks and charged through the crowd, shoving past anyone who got in their way, while Lahnos was bundled along in their midst. They left the crowded jetty and ran along the quayside. The sailors next to the huge dragon carrier stared at them as they approached, then they raised their crossbows.

'You are not permitted on board,' shouted one. 'Stop, or we shall loose.'

Lahnos came to a halt. He looked up, but saw no sign of the silvery-green dragon.

'Lord Sigum,' he cried. 'I know where the Gunstian fleet is hiding.'

A scaled head appeared, and the dragon glanced down at the quayside.

'And how did you come by this information, part-Bullan?' said Lord Sigum.

'I am a death-reader,' said Lahnos. 'I read the memories of a Gunstian officer.'

'You claim to be Gifted, boy? Who are you?'

'I am Lahnos Laimos.'

'The leader of the Zamatans? I have heard of you, and I saw you here earlier today. I thought you would be older.'

'If you order the Dominion forces onto the remaining ships, we can sail around the Gunstians. We could be halfway to the Serpent Isle before they realise we have gone.'

'And you just happened to find a recently-dead Gunstian with the knowledge we required?'

'He was a prisoner on a supply vessel,' said Lahnos. 'I killed him.'

'You slew an unarmed prisoner?'

'I did.'

The dragon said nothing for a moment, then he turned his gaze to the sailors guarding the gangway.

'Allow him to board my ship,' he said, 'but he must come alone.'

'Make sure the Zamatans are by the quayside, ready to board any vessel that will carry them,' Lahnos said to Efizel.

'This could be a ruse to subdue and arrest you,' said Efizel.

'I have to trust the dragon,' he said. 'Do you hear the Gunstians?

They are close. By sunset, the harbour will be overrun. This is our only chance.'

He embraced Efizel, then strode to the gangway. The sailors parted to let him pass, and he walked up to the hatch in the side of the carrier. Sailors stared at his horns and his tattered uniform as he ascended to the flight deck, where the dragon was waiting for him. Lord Sigum's left wing was broken, and it had been braced and bandaged; but other than that he seemed fit and healthy as he sat upon the wide deck. Behind him, the sun was close to the horizon, while the voices of the chanting Gunstians were echoing off the ruined buildings lining the harbour.

'Why should I believe you, part-Bullan boy?' said the dragon.

'Because I am placing my life into your hands,' said Lahnos.

'You murdered a prisoner.'

'The shame and responsibility for that lie upon my shoulders; but if you use the information that I took from his mind, then you will have saved the lives of thousands of Dominion soldiers and sailors.'

'And seven thousand Zamatans,' said the dragon.

'Yes,' said Lahnos. 'The Dominion took over ten thousand men from my island; should not seven thousand be allowed to see their homes and families again? We fought for you, and we died for you; but it is over. We lost.'

The silvery-green dragon gazed over the ruins of Toraq. 'I, too, wish to see my home again, but I cannot bear to be shamed among my kin. My father will think me a coward for fleeing.'

'Have not other dragons already fled?'

'They have,' said Sigum, his eyes darkening. 'I know of at least five who flew to the east some days ago, as soon as they had learned of the King's death.'

'Then you will not be shamed – they will. For you will have led the survivors home, rather than abandoning them here to die.'

'My wing...' said the dragon. 'I could not have flown away with the others, even if I had wanted to.'

'I do not believe that you would have fled,' said Lahnos. 'You have honour, and you are responsible for every sailor and soldier still here.'

Sigum kept his gaze on the ruins for a long moment, then he turned to a senior naval officer who was standing close by.

'Bring the charts,' said the dragon, 'and then order the evacuation. We are going home.'

The Gunstian army broke through the roadblocks and barricades in several places, their forces charging through the ruined harbour buildings towards the long quayside. When they got there, it was empty. On the flight deck of a mighty dragon carrier, Lahnos stood next to Efizel, as hundreds of Zamatans sat on the deck, every eye on the harbour of Toraq as it retreated into the distance. Sailing alongside Lord Sigum's vessel were five other dragon carriers, seven destroyers, two frigates, and the nine supply vessels, each crammed with Zamatan and Dominion soldiers and sailors. The flotilla reached the enormous breakwaters where so many had died in the opening moments of the invasion, and then they passed through, sailing out into the vast open waters of the Great Bay.

The ships turned for the south-west, their sails filling as the last light of the sun began to fade, casting long shadows over the coastline of Gunst, and the grey ruins of Toraq.

Lord Sigum stood on the flight deck, his silvery-green scales gleaming in the sunset. 'We failed,' he said. 'The King is dead and the mighty Dominion has been humbled.'

'You have not failed us, Lord Sigum,' said Lahnos. 'Seven thousand Zamatans will be able to see their homes again because of you.'

'And because of you, death-reader,' said the dragon. 'But before your men can see their families again, we must first brave the straits. Knowing the location of the Gunstian fleet will allow us to slip past them undetected, but we may encounter other enemy vessels before we are safe.'

'If that happens,' said Lahnos, 'then we shall have a dragon to defend us.'

'A dragon who cannot fly.'

'I would rather have a dragon who cannot fly on our side than ten dragons who care nothing for the lives of the men under their command. The Zamatans will not forget this.'

'And I doubt that they will forget you, either, Lahnos Laimos. They would follow you anywhere, I think.'

Lahnos glanced up at the dragon. 'There is only one place I want to go.'

Lord Sigum tilted his head. 'Admiral, take us to the Serpent Isle.'

AUTHOR'S NOTES

JULY 2023

Thank you for reading Demon Witch! I started writing this book as soon as I had moved into my new garden office, as the paint was still drying... In some ways, writing the middle book of a trilogy can be challenging – the author is no longer setting the scene, nor are they tying up the loose ends – but I found Demon Witch a joy to write, especially every chapter that contained Leona. I hope you enjoyed it.

Next comes Death Seer – the last book of the Serpent Isle Trilogy, and book three of six of the Dominion series.

RECEIVE A FREE MAGELANDS DOMINION SHORT STORY

Building a relationship with my readers is very important to me.

Join my newsletter for information on new books and deals and you will also receive a Magelands Dominion short story that is currently EXCLUSIVE to my Readers' Group for FREE.

www.ChristopherMitchellBooks.com/dominion

ABOUT THE AUTHOR

Christopher Mitchell is the author of the Magelands epic fantasy series.

For more information:
www.christophermitchellbooks.com
info@christophermitchellbooks.com

Printed in Great Britain
by Amazon

35785033R00233